Inn Civility

INN CIVILITY

Urban Taverns and Early American Civil Society

VAUGHN SCRIBNER

New York University Press

NEW YORK

NEW YORK UNIVERSITY PRESS
New York
www.nyupress.org

Portions of chapters 1 and 2 previously appeared as "Cosmopolitan Colonists: Gentlemen's Pursuit of Cosmopolitanism and Hierarchy in Colonial American Taverns," *Atlantic Studies: Global Currents* 10.4 (December 2013): 467–496. Portions of chapters 3 and 4 previously appeared as "'Quite a genteel and extreamly commodious House': Southern Taverns, Anxious Elites, and the British American Quest for Social Differentiation," *Journal of Early American History* 5:1 (April 2015): 30–67.

References to Internet websites (URLs) were accurate at the time of writing. Neither the author nor New York University Press is responsible for URLs that may have expired or changed since the manuscript was prepared.

Library of Congress Cataloging-in-Publication Data

Names: Scribner, Vaughn, author.
Title: Inn civility : urban taverns and early American civil society / Vaughn
    Scribner.
Description: New York : New York University Press, [2019] | Includes
    bibliographical references and index.
Identifiers: LCCN 2018042633 | ISBN 9781479864928 (cl : alk. paper)
Subjects: LCSH: Taverns (Inns)—United States—History. | United
    States—Social life and customs—18th century.
Classification: LCC GT3803 .S45 2019 | DDC 394.1/20973—dc23
LC record available at https://lccn.loc.gov/2018042633

New York University Press books are printed on acid-free paper, and their binding materials are chosen for strength and durability. We strive to use environmentally responsible suppliers and materials to the greatest extent possible in publishing our books.

Manufactured in the United States of America

10 9 8 7 6 5 4 3 2 1

Also available as an ebook

For my parents,
Craig and Susan Scribner

CONTENTS

Acknowledgments

Although writing a book can be an isolating pursuit, it is, ultimately, a collaborative effort. As such, this work has benefited from the considerable efforts of a large pool of people and institutions over the past ten years. Any strengths are owed to them, and any mistakes are entirely my own.

At the University of Kansas, Paul Kelton was an ideal academic guide, colleague, and friend. J. C. D. Clark, Steven Epstein, Adrian Finucane, Megan Greene, Sheyda Jahanbani, Jeff Moran, Ted Wilson, Nathan Wood, and Don Worster also contributed vital assistance. At Kansas State University, Louise Breen and Donald Mrozek were instrumental in my development as a writer and thinker.

I have appreciated the contributions of various colleagues and friends who read and commented on early versions of the manuscript. Paul Kelton read the full manuscript more than once, and his affinity for clear prose and detailed argument greatly aided me. Benjamin Carp, Emma Hart, and Wendy Lucas also read drafts of the manuscript, and proved vital in developing its final form. Ben's organizational suggestions were critical, and Emma's and Wendy's nuanced understanding of the early modern British Empire pushed me to rethink many of my previous assumptions. Craig Scribner contributed his eye for eloquence, helping my prose to flow, and Neil Oatsvall proved key in my final editing. Robert Blankenship, J. C. D. Clark, Winchell Delano, Adrian Finucane, Richard Follett, Joshua Nygren, Neil Oatsvall, Joshua Piker, L. H. Roper, Joe Ryan, Adam Sundberg, and David Welky each commented on portions of the manuscript at different stages. Conference participants at the British Group in Early American History, the North American Conference for British Studies, and the Kinder Institute on Constitutional Democracy also offered invaluable advice, and various colleagues in the University of Central Arkansas history department helped me along in this process through support and conversations. I could not have asked for a better history department to land in.

Financial support has been imperative to the completion of this book. While at the University of Kansas, the Hall Center for the Humanities' Jim Martin Travel Award, the Donald R. McCoy Research Award, and the Department of History Outstanding Doctoral Dissertation Award provided valuable research funds. Since then, the University of Central Arkansas history department, College of Liberal Arts, and University Research Council awarded me funds for travel, research, and conferences.

I have accumulated several debts in my research. Special thanks to the staffs of the University of Kansas Library, the University of Central Arkansas Library, the Library of Congress, the New York Historical Society, the Beinecke Rare Book and Manuscript Library, the Massachusetts Historical Society, the Library Company of Philadelphia, the Early Gregg Swem Library, and the Virginia Historical Society. They made my research experience pleasant and productive. I would also be remiss not to thank Google Books, Archive.org, and HathiTrust Digital Library for their staggering number of fully accessible volumes, without which my travel expenses would have been far larger and my source material much sparser. Thanks also to my editor at New York University Press, Clara Platter, who believed in my ideas throughout the process, and the production staff (especially copy editor, Sheila Berg), as well as the anonymous readers for the press.

Travel and research, of course, are contingent on those who support you in your frenzied peregrinations. I cannot thank Art Allen enough for offering his apartment whenever I visit New York City; he has been a stalwart supporter and friend and never ceases to amaze me with his vast connections and keen insight. Pamela Osowski, also of New York City, deserves mention for her friendship during my visits. In Washington, DC, Jon and Jeni Freed have welcomed me to stay with their delightful family more than once, while Nick Barnes of Boston has also provided invaluable aid. Keith Floyd helped me to remain mindful throughout my journey. My amazing cohort of fellow University of Kansas graduate students made graduate school so much more fun than I thought it could be.

In closing, I also want to thank my parents, Craig and Susan Scribner, to whom this book is devoted. Without their selfless support over the past thirty-two years, this volume would not have existed. They taught me how to think and how to remain accountable for my actions. My siblings are also continuing sources of motivation, while my grandmother Mildred Kallenbach's (1920–2011) passion for genealogy helped to inspire my own love for the past. Last, but certainly not least, is my immeasurable gratitude to my wife, Kristen. She is my rock, and always helps me find my way.

INN CIVILITY

Introduction

In 1747, Dr. Alexander Hamilton met with fifteen members of his Tuesday Club at an Annapolis, Maryland, tavern. After enjoying some wine and rum punch, the genteel group set off on their "first grand anniversary procession" through Annapolis's streets. Resplendent in "badges and Ribbons" to distinguish themselves "from the common Rascallion herd of men," Dr. Hamilton and his club members found that "persons of all Ranks and degrees" crowded to watch their well-planned pageantry. This was exactly what Dr. Hamilton wanted. Having grown up in Scotland, received his education throughout the British Isles and Europe, and recently traveled North America's eastern seaboard, Dr. Hamilton (not to be confused with the first U.S. secretary of the treasury) believed that because "the number of the wise is but small, and that of the foolish and Simple very great, so there is an absolute necessity for the use of these magnificent trappings and Embellishments . . . to keep the great Leviathan of Civil Society under proper discipline and order." Though Dr. Hamilton realized that a "perfectly well regulated Society" was beyond reason, he—like so many other elitist British American colonists—relied on self-dictated notions of "Civil Society" to maintain "proper discipline and order" in their ongoing quest to "regulate [British America's] motions in such a manner, as that the frantic animal may not destroy itself."[1]

If only it were this simple. While Dr. Hamilton's Tuesday Club did in fact exist in Annapolis, Maryland, at midcentury, their parade probably never happened. *The History of the Tuesday Club*, in which Dr. Hamilton recorded the account of their parade was a fictional narrative of the club's proceedings in which Dr. Hamilton satirized the vices and disorders that constantly plagued his whimsical club, as well as society at large. At one point, the men's fondness of luxury almost threw them into "Civil Combustions" so drastic as to destroy the club's very foundations, and in another instance the tavern club purchased so many "expensive Liquors" that their funds grew light. Though most likely fictitious, the Tuesday Club's 1747 parade reveals colonial gentlemen's deep-seated anxieties about the proper maintenance—and realization—of British American civil society. If elitist men could plot such societal order on the page, many wondered, why not in the developing arena of colonial cities?[2]

Inn Civility uses the urban tavern—the most numerous, popular, and accessible of all British American public spaces—to investigate North Americans' struggles to cultivate a civil society from the early eighteenth century to the end of the American Revolution.[3] Such an analysis, this book argues, demonstrates the messy, often contradictory nature of British American society building and how colonists' efforts to emulate their British homeland ultimately impelled the creation of an American republic. In so striving to realize a monarchical society based on mercurial tenets of civility, order, and liberty, colonists inadvertently created a political society that the founders would rely on for their visions of a republican America. This is not to argue that independence was inevitable; rather, a fuller understanding of America's (unexpected) independence demands a deep analysis of midcentury colonists' societal dreams and, importantly, anxieties.

Societal fantasies, confusions, and disappointments were hardly unique to the Revolutionary Era. In fact, conflicts over social order and imperial control originated in a time that many colonists (and historians since) liked to think of as a "golden age" of colonial American stability, success, and hope.[4] The birth of republican American civil society, in short, was as much wedded to its monarchical past as the dreams of a republican future. Most of America's founders, after all, had spent their lives striving to comprehend, if not create, a British-style civil society in North America. These same men were forced to repackage many of their midcentury societal goals to fit American notions of republicanism, which were not as different from colonial American ideals of civil society as many colonists would have liked to think. Just as they had during North America's monarchical period, republican leaders remained wedded to fantasies of a civil society where they maintained order over the masses and continued to be disappointed when such fantasies proved empty and contradictory. Old habits die hard.[5]

As key microcosms of eighteenth-century life, urban taverns especially allow us to follow North Americans' struggles at creating a civil society. In one sense, the diverse array of licensed urban taverns served as pedestrian parts of white colonists' everyday lives by providing routine services like food, drink, camaraderie, and lodging for a vast swath of society. Urban taverns thus acted as important societal filters: as the main customers, white men represented the bulk of those deemed worthy of civil society. They expected supposed inferiors like unfree whites, enslaved blacks, Native Americans, and women, meanwhile, to remain in either servile roles or simply stay out of the tavern altogether, thus maintaining a sense of societal harmony and order.[6] Yet white men's efforts at physical and symbolic demarcation in the tavern space proved fragile. Not only had "uncivil" peoples long fostered a thriving network of unlicensed drinking spaces, but most tavern keepers sought to serve as many customers as possible, thereby upholding a diverse—and socially confusing—public sector. The fallout of the American Revolution only heightened such disorder, as urban taverns descended into war-torn dissipation and their rural counterparts emerged as bastions of republican militancy. As revolutionaries relied on altered ideologies of civility, order, and liberty to support their nascent ideas of republicanism, taverns became sounding boards for the past, present, and future of North American civil society. Taverns, then, represent ideal locations in which to study the artificial boundaries and liminal spaces between civil and uncivil society.

The Shallow Roots of American Civil Society

Although certain colonials attempted to replicate their European brethren's notions of civil society as closely as possible, the reality of life in North America—particularly its distance from the mother country, lack of landed gentry, larger number of unfree and non-British peoples, agricultural identity, and smaller cities—necessitated local variances. Where European thinkers generally leaned on historical precedent and law in their philosophies of civil society, colonists harnessed the commercial success and growing public sector of their cities to build their own social capital and, in turn, curb what they considered a disintegrating social order.[7] Yet the confusing reality of urban society often outstripped gentlemen's civil pipe dreams. Though elitist colonists liked to represent themselves as powerful leaders of an ever-improving society, their day-to-day interactions with each other and their social inferiors demonstrated that the British Empire was not neatly split into civil and uncivil peoples, nor were gentlemen above the "rude" behavior that they so often associated with ordinary colonists. The American Revolutionary Period only compounded elitist colonists' flawed perceptions of European-style civil society as nascent ideologies of republicanism clashed and overlapped with midcentury notions of civility.[8]

British American colonists linked their understandings of civil society with their ardent assertions of a "civilizing process." From the moment Englishmen invaded North America, they contended that they brought with them measures of improvement. "Savage" Native American customs were destined to be replaced by "civilized" European traditions of urban growth, agricultural development, and global trade. Englishmen also asserted their mastery over the surrounding "wilderness" through massive, slave-driven cash cropping and military measures. Although the seventeenth century brought a surge of famine, death, and warfare to British settlers, by the mid-eighteenth century colonists believed that they had finally gained a foothold in North America. Their cities multiplied by the decade, farms stretched into the backcountry, enslaved African laborers piled off boats by the scores, and competing empires trickled away. While civil society might have been only a dream for their seventeenth-century forebears, a growing number of eighteenth-century colonists trusted that their recent success would bring a new level of civilization and order to North America.[9]

This expansion had noticeable effects on the commercial importance of colonial North America and, in turn, the living conditions of ordinary and wealthy colonists alike. The economist Alice Hanson Jones argued that British American colonists enjoyed a standard of living during the mid-eighteenth century that was "probably the highest achieved for the great bulk of the population in any country up to that time." The historians John McCusker and Russell Menard echoed Jones's sentiments, contending that midcentury colonists "were better off not only than their predecessors in the colonies or than most of their contemporaries elsewhere in the world but also than their descendants were to be again for some time to come." Although the Caribbean colonies outstripped British North America in economic importance for the British Empire, mainland colonists considered themselves leaders in contentment and reputation.[10] The colonist Thomas Jones referred to the midcentury period as "the *Golden Age* of New York," and another urbanite exclaimed in 1764, "We think ourselves at present the happiest people . . . of any people under the sun, and really are so."[11]

Such assertions of a "golden age" of colonial America and the happiness of its peoples were firmly intertwined with British Americans' zealous devotion to mercurial notions of British liberty. Broadly defined according to equally vague ideals of an English constitution that limited the power of the monarchy in addition to promising the rule of law, self-representation, and access to private property, liberty remained central in British Americans' understanding of the British Empire and where they fit into this globalizing entity. British liberty also afforded colonists a sense of superiority over their imperial rivals such as France and Spain, which they considered lesser because of their absolute monarchs. Notions of British liberty necessarily impelled colonists' quest for a British American civil society, and vice versa. It is no coincidence that colonists lauded New Jersey governor Francis Bernard for his "accurate Knowledge . . . of the Constitution, just Sense of Liberty, and the common Rights of Mankind" when he arrived in North America in 1758. By midcentury, many colonists liked to think of themselves in a "golden age" of civil society with all the liberties that this hopeful vision offered.[12]

Reflections on this alleged golden age, notably, in terms of political, economic, and demographic development, extended beyond British North America. Philosophers across western Europe also grappled with how best to order their societies in the face of recent expansion. An ideal of societal progress based on tenets of urbanity and law that stretched back to ancient Greece and Rome, civil society struck the English philosophers Thomas Hobbes and John Locke as especially useful in bringing order to the disorder engendered by rampant commercialism, urbanization, exploration, and revolution. Ideas of order and disorder had long retained a central place in English society. Medieval Englishmen based their society on strict notions of hierarchy, as did the first Englishmen who attempted to colonize North America. Eighteenth-century English thinkers cultivated such maxims for their own purposes, insisting that a true civil society would exist independent from church and state, therefore completing, in Locke's words, the "perfect freedom" and the "rights and privileges [enjoyed by men under] the law of nature." Eighteenth-century Scottish philosophers, including Adam Ferguson, Adam Smith, and Francis Hutcheson, fleshed out their English colleagues' contentions by asserting that civil society was, in essence, a successful commercial society internally constituted of strict notions of order, interdependence, and a thriving public sphere.[13]

Continental philosophers also adapted ideologies of civil society to their locales. In Germany, Immanuel Kant struggled over the connection between the emergence of a civil society as detached from the state and how a free thinker might exist and thrive in this society while also respecting mankind's inherent rights.[14] French thinkers joined Kant— Du Marsais argued that French philosophes considered the "order and rules [of] civil society . . . a divinity on earth," while Jaucourt used notions of civility and order to distinguish natural and absolute equality. Although all men were born naturally equal, Jaucourt asserted, they did "not know how to remain so," for "different ranks, grades, honors, distinctions, prerogatives, subordinations . . . must prevail in all governments." Diderot and Rousseau also championed the importance of difference and order for a successful civil society. Diderot believed the "maintenance of society [demanded] that men establish among themselves an order of subordination," and Rousseau asserted that only by adopting a "social contract" where everyone was willing to forgo their personal gain for the betterment of the larger community could a true civil society ever thrive.[15] The Italian Borghese family, finally, warned those who entered their seventeenth-century pleasure garden, "If anyone willfully and deliberately, with evil intentions, breaks the golden rules of civility, let him beware, lest the rather irate estate manager break the token of friendship on him." Ultimately, while thinkers throughout Europe had different conceptions of how to achieve a civil society, they agreed that it would be one based on notions of difference, order, and control.[16]

Certain would-be gentlemen struggled to adapt British and European paradigms to their colonial locality. Although some especially wealthy and powerful men also pursued a British American civil society, most colonial gentlemen were not elite in the European sense: as men who worked with their hands and did not come from money, they were more akin to the "middling sorts" or "middle classes" of western European society.[17] "Continuously remaking themselves" and working within different social, economic, and political spheres, these self-employed landholders, skilled artisans, manufacturers, physicians, preachers, and teachers would not have equaled European elites in terms of prestige or title.[18] What they did share, however, was an insecurity regarding notions of civility and order, which they buttressed with dreams of achieving "polite" identities and, in turn, helping to realize a North American civil society. Such men were thus elitist more than elite: they viewed themselves as gentlemen leaders destined to direct America into a bright future, even if their European counterparts looked down on them as little more than colonial upstarts who had to work with their hands for a living.[19]

For example, Dr. Alexander Hamilton, introduced earlier, was a Scottish-born physician whose scant opportunities in Edinburgh forced him to emigrate to Annapolis, Maryland, to pursue his trade. Hamilton's laborious occupation would not have provided him much prestige in a metropolis like London, or even in smaller British cities like Edinburgh or Bristol. Yet Dr. Hamilton, along with other aspiring gentlemen in North America, utilized voluntary societies, public institutions, material goods, and sociable opportunities available in the colonial city to obtain "social capital" and assert themselves as masculine leaders of a distinctly British American civil society. In many ways, elitist colonists were bigger fish in a much smaller pond than they probably could have ever been in European cities.[20]

Self-professions of gentility and social superiority were key to American gentlemen's civil crusade. According to Samuel Johnson's 1755 *Dictionary of the English Language*, a civil identity necessitated the ability to demonstrate one's "politeness, complaisance[,] . . . elegance of behaviour," and "freedom from barbarity." Rather than simply rely on conspicuous consumption of expensive goods and services, elitist colonists like Dr. Hamilton worked hard to obtain social capital beyond material wealth—specifically, by cultivating an identity based on societal power, advanced education and sociability, and the capacity to contain one's own primal urges, which they believed created boundaries between themselves and their more vulgar urban compatriots. For self-professed leaders, the accumulation of social capital was imperative to the stability and success of a British American civil society. This minority populace of North America sought to control the majority of economic, political, religious, and social operations.[21]

Despite gentlemen's attempts to denigrate those they considered their social inferiors, ordinary colonists are imperative for understanding the formation of a British American civil society, both because of their concrete utility in supporting colonial America's day-to-day operations and because of the anxieties that they caused elitist men. The social hierarchy of North America's white population seemed to blur by the day, becoming more horizontally than vertically oriented. This social reorganization opened new opportunities for many ordinary white men. Broadly termed the "lower sorts," "lower classes," "plebeians," or "laboring people" by historians and contemporaries alike, these mariners, journeymen, lesser artisans, servants, and wage laborers utilized many of the same consumer, social, and labor networks as their supposed superiors to carve out their own future in British America. Accounting for most of the white population in British North America, ordinary men and women did not own as much land or property per capita as their social superiors, but their influence nevertheless increased through sheer numbers, in addition to their necessity for the colonies' economic expansion.[22]

Such social confusion worried many self-professed gentlemen. Elitist colonists were especially concerned by the lower classes' alarming disregard for Old World traditions of deference. Acts of defiance ranged from the mundane to the extreme: disapproving preachers experienced disdain from their social inferiors; constables struggled to maintain power over colonists who thought laws "good for nothing," and roving gentlemen like Dr. Hamilton found that they had to "submit to the discipline" of their "inferiors" in taverns. Thus while scholars continue to argue over the role of deference in colonial American society, colonists like Dr. Hamilton had made up their minds on the subject: deference existed, but it did not yet endure to the degree they wished.[23] Many colonial leaders believed that the controversial rhetoric of midcentury transatlantic religious revivals only further inspired such behavior, since celebrity preachers such as George Whitefield and Johnathan Edwards urged colonial American Protestants to think beyond the staid traditions of the Anglican Church. One citizen damned Whitefield and his followers' "monstrous" message as "strongly tinctured with impertinence and disrespect toward their superiors in that they are perpetually endeavoring to level all ranks and do away with all distinctions."[24]

Even long-reliable methods of criminal punishment seemed to grow stale. Having caught a man named Watt counterfeiting money in 1733, Philadelphia magistrates ordered that he be "whipt, pilloried and cropt" in the city's public market. Leaders also encouraged onlookers to throw debris and snowballs at Watt, which they hoped would further humiliate the villain while also creating a common bond of hatred against anti-deferential acts like counterfeiting. Unfortunately, Watt "behaved so as to touch the Compassion of the Mob, and they did not fling at him (as was expected) neither Snow-balls nor any Thing else." Elitist colonists grew more anxious every time ordinary colonists thumbed their noses at leaders' expectations of deference.[25]

As the historian David Shields has contended, colonists' notions of civility enabled otherwise disparate peoples to "bridge distinctions . . .

[and] make common cause with them." In theory, Shields was right, as gentlemen repeatedly asserted the need for harmony and order among the diverse peoples of North America in their professions of civil society. Yet such an ideal was much easier to debate in small communities of "belles lettres" than to realize on the hardscrabble streets of the city or at the raucous table of a tavern. Philosophies of British American civil society did not develop from a preexisting harmony of accord but rather out of an intense anxiety among a growing sector of the urban populace. These self-styled leaders worried that if they rose as the "Representative[s]" for their local populace, they might be "guilty of the highest public crime that can be thought of in civil society": allowing the uncivil masses to steer the fate of North America.[26]

Benjamin Franklin used the example of an urban fire to expound on Old World tenets of social stability and deference.[27] Franklin contended that during a 1733 Philadelphia inferno he witnessed "active Men of different Ages, Professions and Titles; who, as of one Mind and Rank, apply themselves with Vigilance and Resolution, according to their Abilities," to conquer the conflagration. Housekeepers, local leaders, and itinerants alike threw themselves into the "flaming Shingles" to save the home and its occupants: "They do it not for the Sake of Reward or Money or Fame. . . . But they have a Reward in themselves, and they love one another." Franklin could only conclude, "Here are brave Men, Men of Spirit and Humanity, good Citizens, or Neighbours, capable and worthy of civil Society." Here, then, was gentlemen's dream of a British American civil society. Men would come together "as of one Mind and Rank" but would still divide themselves "according to their Abilities." Those "chiefest in Authority" would maintain their social superiority in their ability to "direct" their inferiors, who with "Courage, Industry, and Goodness" demonstrated their worthiness. Harmony and order coexisted in extreme efficiency. Everyone knew their place, and they embraced it.[28]

Similar aspirations resonated throughout colonial American cities. Franklin—a man who, like Dr. Hamilton, worked with his hands and clawed his way up the social ladder through genteel sociability—continued his reflections on civil society in 1735, asserting that a British American civil society "has no other Master here besides the Consent of the Plurality, or the Will of one or more whom the Plurality has appointed to act for the Good of the whole body." An anonymous writer to the *Boston Evening Post* in 1760 similarly contended, "It is a truth acknowledged by all who have examined into the constitution of civil society, that the strength and vigour of the whole, depends on the union and harmony of the particular constituent parts." For these men, the heart of a British American civil society was contingent on "union and harmony." They believed that a small group of men should "act for the Good of the whole body." Such assertions mirrored Dr. Hamilton's assertion of the need to maintain "proper discipline and order" over the masses just as they recalled Franklin's 1733 claim that the "chiefest in Authority" should "direct" the operations of the fire crew. Ultimately, these contentions revealed growing anxiety among self-styled leaders of colonial society. Elitist men worried that if not properly regulated, the increasing number of ordinary and unfree peoples—the "great Leviathan of Civil Society"— would destroy America's civil society before it could truly blossom. Even more than their counterparts in Europe and Britain, who did not have to contend with vast tracts of "wilderness," large numbers of "savage" Indians, and a lack of cities, British American gentlemen came to believe that their civil society needed equal measures of harmony and control. Harmony would reign as the "Plurality" accepted their station "according to their Abilities," which would in turn allow certain men to organize and direct civil society to a successful end.[29]

Such professions of a civil society ruled pseudo-democratically by those deemed most "fit" would not have seemed at all foreign to revolutionary Patriots, or America's founders for that matter. In fact, as *Inn Civility* contends, revolutionary American notions of republicanism, liberty, and civility were in many ways midcentury ideals of British American civil society simply remodeled to fit rebels' dreams of a New World order. The American Republicanism that Patriots championed, in short, was largely reliant on midcentury elitist colonists' failed attempts at a British-style civil society. Whether Patriots liked to admit it, the two ideologies remained firmly intertwined.

Asserting one's vision for civil order in the local newspaper was easy; achieving that vision in the untidy chaos of the real world proved something else entirely. Just as anxiety and discontent distinguished British Americans' efforts to craft a civil society during the first two-thirds of the eighteenth century, so too did insecurity continue to shape the evolution of American civil society during the tumultuous period of violence and revolution (1765–83). The Stamp Act Crisis of 1765–66 was more than a crisis of commercial policy; for many colonial leaders, it also felt like a crisis of civil society, as tavern goers and publicans from Boston to Charleston joined to formulate riots beyond the control of magistrates, burning leaders' effigies and threatening their lives and property. Although Parliament repealed the Stamp Act in 1766, the ensuing years only brought further difficulties for elitist men, as masses of ordinary colonists grew in power and one new tax after another arrived on their shores. The elusive hierarchical and ideological lines that certain middling- and upper-class gentlemen struggled to realize over the past sixty-five years steadily transformed in the face of imperial rupture.

By the time the American Revolution began in 1775, many colonists had recast notions of a British American civil society into what they believed was a more equal and virtuous governing ideology: American republicanism. Yet, like the mercurial ideals of civil society that impelled colonists' midcentury societal goals, republicanism proved hard to pin down. In fact, American republicanism was not all that different from colonial American civil society. Rebels simply repackaged midcentury ideas of liberty, civility, and order to fit their emerging—and equally mercurial—ideas of democracy, antimonarchism, and militancy. "Unbecoming British" and "becoming America" overlapped more than diverged, and perhaps nowhere was this complicated, contradictory, and fitful process more apparent than the tavern.[30]

Imperial Pubs and the British American City

The amplification of British American urban centers was imperative for elitist colonists' efforts to create a civil society. North America's population expanded at an unprecedented rate in the eighteenth century, growing from just over 250,000 people in 1700 to more than one million souls by 1750. Besides natural population growth, this boom coincided with an influx of immigrants and enslaved laborers on America's shores. English, Scottish, Irish, German, Dutch, French, Spanish, and African peoples carried with them myriad traditions and worldviews to North America, which affected the continent's cultural landscape. As mainland cities including Philadelphia, New York City, Boston, Newport, Charleston, Williamsburg, and Annapolis finally caught up to their peers, England's "country towns," in sociable amenities, population growth, commercial prosperity, and civic development, urban colonists perceived themselves as especially valuable members of the British Empire.[31]

British American colonists constantly weighed themselves against competing empires, religions, and supposed "others" in their hopes of "another Great Britain rising in America." In 1757, one colonist described fellow patriots as those "who have always distinguished ourselves by a Jealousy of our Rights; by our Loyalty; and our Zeal for the common Interest of His Majesty's Dominions on the Continent." Seven years earlier, Benjamin Franklin had sold the fifth edition of *Britain's Remembrancer* at his Philadelphia print shop. Basically a how-to guide for becoming a good Briton, *Britain's Remembrancer* provided readers with cultural and political insights. Politically, it offered "Some Hints, shewing what is in the Power of the several Ranks of People, and of every BRITON, to do toward securing the State from all its Enemies." The volume also took a cultural approach to acting the Briton, investigating "the Character of this Age and Nation," in addition to a "brief view of the Effects of the Vices which now prevail in the British Dominions." Franklin assured his colonial customers that the book was "acceptable . . . to the Publick," as their comrades in England had already purchased over four thousand copies. Eighteenth-century urban colonists now more than ever before could assert their British allegiance through a diverse array of cultural and social actions.[32]

Although only about 5 percent of colonists lived in North American cities by the mid-eighteenth century, these urban centers were far more influential than their size or proportion of the population suggests. As the historian Gary B. Nash has argued, colonial American cities developed at an astounding rate and represented the "cutting edge" of social change in British North America.[33] For a growing number of British and European thinkers, the city represented the unbridled potential as well as pitfalls of civil society. One midcentury New Yorker, for instance, sent his son to study in New York City "in Hopes of his increasing there in human Urbanity, and genteel Civility," while the New York City gentleman Cadwallader Colden reveled in "all the publick Intertainments" that the city offered. Such "publick Intertainments," of course, might offer as many opportunities of vulgarity to a gentleman as they did civilizing experiences. Although prostitution, debauchery, violence, and drunkenness were no doubt widely available in the surrounding agricultural hinterlands, the city crowded these vices into closer proximity than anywhere else in the colonies. The city thus reflected elitist colonists' coinciding notions of hope and fear: one might embrace such urban opportunities for incivility as much as civility.[34] Colonists' perceived struggles for civil society became especially apparent within the urban tavern.

Colonial American taverns have received much attention over the past quarter century. Historians generally approach North American taverns as sites where we can follow transformations that ultimately helped spur the American Revolution or as spaces where lines of difference were heightened during the eighteenth century. David Conroy, for instance, used the taverns of colonial Massachusetts to reveal how New Englanders opposed the authority of their leaders, while Peter Thompson delved into Philadelphia's eighteenth-century tavern culture to understand how the "interplay of community and society" in the Quaker city unfolded during the Revolution. Benjamin Carp, finally, investigated how New York City's taverns allowed colonists to combine "drunken disorder as well as orderly mobilization" in the years immediately preceding the American Revolution.[35] Other scholars, including Sharon Salinger and David Shields, took a broader approach—regionally and methodologically—to integrate colonial tavern going into larger social constructions. Salinger surveyed rural and urban taverns in the thirteen colonies to reveal those peoples excluded from tavern going and, in turn, public life, while Shields delved into eighteenth-century gentlemen's attempts to cultivate an air of exclusivity by interacting with "belles lettres" in urban taverns and coffeehouses in Boston, Philadelphia, and Charleston. Ultimately, then, scholars have primarily relied on taverns for their utility in analyzing the lead-up to the American Revolution or as spaces that reveal the inequalities of colonial American society.[36]

Inn Civility builds on these works—temporally and geographically—by utilizing urban taverns as critical spaces through which to investigate the inherent contradictions and conflicts of British American societal negotiation from midcentury to the end of the American Revolution. More specifically, this book demonstrates that midcentury tavern goers inadvertently fostered a society that eventually played into American revolutionaries' emerging notions of republicanism, liberty, and civility. In many ways, eighteenth-century urban taverns—the most numerous and popular public spaces in colonial America—emerged as ideal breeding grounds for early American republicanism, even if many colonists would not have understood them as such. Taverns' popularity and ubiquity make them the perfect places to track Americans' evolving sense of self, place, and time.

Urban taverns were dynamic spaces that matched the philosopher Henri Lefebvre's conception of "an image of a complex of mobilities, a nexus of in and out conduits."[37] This is not to argue that other "public spheres" should retreat to the fringes of urban society: the booming of sociability that characterized midcentury colonial cities fostered an important web of public spaces, ranging from newly steepled churches to crowded markets and street fairs to genteel academies, libraries, and hospitals. The urban tavern must be comprehended as wholly encompassed by larger networks of urbanization, commercialism, and sociability.[38] Such a framework reveals that societal contestation was not limited to

Conroy's New England or Thompson's Philadelphia taverns. Colonists' efforts to create (or, in some colonists' minds, destroy) a civil society bled into every facet of their public lives, and the tavern remained a central component of public life for white, urban-dwelling men.

As colonial cities thrived at midcentury, taverns evolved into their most numerous public spaces. One Bostonian reckoned in 1750 that "an Eighth Part of our Houses are either Dram Shops or Taverns." He was not far off. By the mid-eighteenth century, Philadelphia boasted approximately 120 licensed taverns, New York City about 220, and Boston around 150. To put such a figure in perspective, New York City had one tavern for every 115 people.[39] Farther south, Charleston maintained around 100 licensed taverns for its 4,000 residents. While Williamsburg boasted only 15 taverns by the mid-eighteenth century, this number falls in line with the proportion of licenses to total population in larger cities: one tavern for every 100 to 130 residents. No official record exists for Annapolis's tavern numbers at midcentury, but it is likely that Annapolis, with just about 1,000 residents by 1750, maintained roughly 8 taverns. At least three new taverns were constructed in Annapolis between 1735 and 1750, indicating a growing demand for these popular spaces as the city's population and economic power spiked. Of course, such statistics take only licensed taverns into account. Unlicensed taverns proliferated throughout British North America as well, vaulting taverns' public frequency to dizzying heights.[40]

Beyond numbers, urban taverns' assorted amenities made them ideal gathering spots for a diverse set of white men. Following their compatriots in England, colonial tavern keepers offered patrons a staggering array of imported goods, ranging from Asian tea and West Indian rum to East Indian spices. Tavern services also broadened, as colonial tavern goers could book passage on ships traversing the Atlantic Ocean or watch as an itinerant English acting troupe performed in a tavern's main hall. Imperial celebrations such as the king's birthday, the arrival of a visiting governor, or the anniversary of a British holiday regularly occurred in taverns. Sermons from transatlantic preachers, African slave auctions, cock fights, and public debates over war and taxation echoed between taverns' walls, and tickets for traveling exhibits and horse races cluttered their bars.[41]

Urban taverns also served as key societal filters. Although one need not be wealthy, well connected, or pious to step into most colonial American taverns, one did need to be a white man to enjoy the full benefits of the urban tavern. Reflecting white males' repeated efforts to direct

British American society, mainstream urban taverns emerged as masculine spaces where women and "others" were, at least in theory, relegated to the fringes of public society. Despite leaders' efforts to bar blacks, Native Americans, servants, and women from public life, many still found their way into their own tavern spaces. These supposed societal inferiors opened their own unlicensed taverns where they could interact with whomever they wanted and purchase (often stolen or black market) goods deemed above their station. Although unofficially restricted from the public world of taverns, many women used the tavern trade to extend their roles into imperial and patriarchal networks. Other female tavern workers, however, became further entrenched in the world of domestic servitude as male tavern goers often sexually and verbally accosted them. Diversity hardly bred equality.[42]

Urban taverns emerged as central components—both symbolically and physically—of colonial America's developing metropolitanism. In a more figurative sense, Britons and foreigners came to associate urban centers with a flowering tavern culture. As the Englishman Thomas Walduck jested in the early eighteenth century, "Upon all the new settlements the Spaniards make, the first thing they do is build a church, the first thing ye Dutch do upon a new colony is to build them a fort, but the first thing ye English do, be it in the most remote part of ye world, or amongst the most barbarous Indians, is to set up a tavern or drinking house." Visitors to the colonies noticed the preponderance of tavern going in British American public life. Upon touring British America in the 1760s, one Frenchman remarked that because "Tavern Keeping is the best business that is Caryed on" in large and small towns alike, "they are well stocked with taverns." With such a variety of services and customers, urban taverns—arguably more than other public spaces like squares, churches, or markets—forced colonists to reconstitute their sense of an urban or public "center." Yet the centrality of taverns extended beyond symbolism, for they also served as tangible fulcrums of commerce, trade, and sociability. When John Goodsell of New York announced the sale of his land and homestead in 1759, he hoped that an innkeeper might purchase his holdings because taverns were, in Goodsell's reckoning, "here much needed."[43]

Not every urban tavern was the same; in fact, diversity remained one of their biggest selling points and a major goal for business-oriented owners. As other historians have posited, different taverns attracted specific facets of society—for example, taverns directed at local dockworkers or ethnic groups and coffeehouses catering to businessmen.[44]

They gained reputations for their service and amenities, as well as the character of their owners and workers. Several eighteenth-century tavern keepers designed their businesses to reflect the most up-to-date architectural trends, adding extra stories to their structures with new rooms intended for specific purposes. In certain rooms, exotic mahogany furniture replaced grooved pine, alluring art hung from walls, and books, pamphlets, and newspapers covered tables. Those patrons who considered themselves socially elite and did not wish to rub elbows with their uncivil social inferiors could escape to such rooms, and, eventually, whole taverns, that looked and felt much like their own fine parlors.

Other licensed tavern keepers served a humbler clientele. Their spaces crowded around a pipe-littered great room with basic decoration, services, food, and amenities. The various unlicensed taverns existed in a separate sphere—improvised spaces in back alleys, basements, and backrooms. Some taverns stood as grand edifices on the corner of a bustling market street, while others were hidden in a motley array of businesses and private homes. Others, finally, existed in a more liminal sphere, emerging to serve certain clandestine exchanges just as fast as they receded into relative anonymity. Taverns were wholly engrained in the diverse web of urban public life.

Even appreciating the inherent diversity of urban taverns, these central public spaces provide a unifying lens of analysis. Though factors such as geography (the northern colonies versus the southern colonies, for example), population numbers (larger vs. smaller cities), inhabitants (a slave society vs. a society with slaves), and personal preference had noticeable effects on the way colonists in different areas lived, urban taverns retained consistent purposes, as white men required the same basic things from a tavern: food, drink, lodging, and camaraderie.[45] Accordingly, a licensed tavern in a smaller southern city like Williamsburg, Virginia, would have operated similarly to one in Boston, Massachusetts. Such relative uniformity allows us to concentrate on patterns, networks, and developments that transcended local environments.

The following six chapters analyze urban tavern goers' complicated struggles to realize a civil society in early America and ultimately reveal how midcentury conceptions of civility drove republican dreams of an independent America. The first two chapters take a double-pronged approach to understanding elitist colonists' aspirations for how a British American civil society might look and operate. Chapter 1 investigates gentlemen's attempts to transplant Old World notions of spatial exclusivity, consumer power, and social capital into city taverns and coffeehouses at midcentury. In their minds, such spaces would allow them to rise above the muck of ordinary colonists and direct British American society into a more civil future.

Chapter 2 follows this line of thought into elitist tavern goers' cosmopolitan ambitions. Having established a variety of polite drinking spaces, gentlemen hoped to cultivate erudite identities of cosmopolitanism, which they believed would only further their civilizing efforts. Yet, as was so often the case with colonists' civil aspirations, their cosmopolitan endeavors revealed the inherent contradictions of civil society more than its unbridled potential. Specifically, tavern goers' allegedly cosmopolitan interactions entrenched their sense of ethnocentrism, hierarchy, and nationalism rather than broadening their worldview.

As chapters 3 and 4 demonstrate, elitist tavern goers' failures at cosmopolitanism hint at a much broader trend of contradiction and confusion in midcentury British American cities. Gentlemen's pipe dreams of a well-ordered, well-defined civil society steadily disintegrated in the face of reality. Chapter 3 reveals that while elitist colonists managed to carve out a small niche of exclusive coffeehouses and city taverns in British American cities, most urban taverns opened their doors to anyone with a pocketbook. Their owners, after all, needed to bring as many men into their businesses as they could if they were to stay afloat in such a competitive market. Accordingly, most taverns operated nothing like the exclusive, polite, and regimented coffeehouses of elitist colonists' dreams. On the contrary, urban taverns—like British American society at large—were generally jumbled environments of social confusion in which men of differing classes and creeds struggled to establish their position in a world defined by indecision.

Yet, as chapter 4 uncovers, mixed-class taverns were only the beginning of the story, for ordinary and unfree peoples also cultivated a healthy network of unlicensed taverns, or "disorderly" houses. And though in theory elitist colonists would never lower themselves to visiting such hives of vice and debauchery, in reality gentlemen were some of the most visible customers of these "uncivil" spaces. In an ongoing balancing act of contradiction and power, supposedly civil men often donned the guise of the rake to frolic in unlicensed taverns and, in turn, assert their influence over their social inferiors while thumbing their noses at genteel modes of behavior. Just as elitist men repeatedly attempted to dictate the parameters of civility through cosmopolitan endeavors like club meetings, literary debates, and consumerism, so too did they violate and reconstruct these civil constraints with little to no repercussions.

Chapters 5 and 6 follow the contradictions and confusions of British American civility into the "revolutionary period"—1765 to 1783—of North America and demonstrate how Patriots relied on such mercurial ideologies to build their own society in North America. Chapter 5 investigates the pitfalls of such societal dissonance through the lens of the Stamp Act Crisis of 1765–66, demonstrating how the growing power of the lower sorts further fractured previous ideals of civility and order. Disorder defined British America's cities from August 1765 to April 1766, as diverse tavern goers sought to overturn taxes they considered inimical to civil society. As chapter 5 demonstrates, colonists' interactions in taverns during the Stamp Act Crisis brought the contradictions of civil society into sharp and devastating focus. Tavern keepers, well aware of their spaces' communal and economic centrality, steadily transformed them to match the tumultuous political atmosphere of British American urban centers after 1765, which further aided in the transformation of midcentury societal aspirations. Thus, while many tavern-going colonists liked to believe that their success in repealing the Stamp Act through a combination of violence and coercion marked a high point of societal order and imperial allegiance, the following ten years forced colonists loyal and rebellious to alter their previous notions of civil society.

Chapter 6 investigates how between 1766 and 1783 colonists commandeered taverns according to their unpredictable visions of civility and liberty, which ultimately helped to restructure midcentury notions of civil society to fit Patriots' nascent notions of republicanism.[46] Before the Revolutionary War officially broke out in 1775, colonists divided themselves among urban taverns: tavern committees looked to the Stamp Act Crisis as a model for resistance efforts, stalwart Loyalists remained wedded to previous notions of British civility and order, and many in between attempted to navigate the murky parameters of British American societal flux. Although the series of riots, misbehavior, and resistance measures that marked the thirteen colonies between 1765 and 1775 might be termed "relatively minor provincial uprisings" in the context of "a general crisis of imperial rule" that erupted throughout the Atlantic world beginning in 1765, these "tremors" nevertheless proved vital in transforming colonial American society.[47] By 1775, burgeoning notions of republicanism, combined with the disorders of war, had begun to render midcentury British American civil society (at least in name) unpopular. Once bastions of societal experimentation, colonial cities descended into occupied hell holes, and their taverns served as escapes from society more than spaces through which to shape it. Although rural taverns had been common facets of North American society since the seventeenth century, their fringe location became a benefit rather than a hindrance during the American Revolution, as these rural spaces arose as republicans' testing grounds for their vision of an American civil society. Amidst such disorder, ordinary colonists established themselves as some of the most violent and influential men in North America. This divide would define America for years to come.

By the close of the American Revolution, the deference that midcentury elitist men so struggled to attain had been set aside, at least temporarily, as the radical rhetoric of revolution forced leaders to repackage many of their core ideologies to fit this nascent form of republican rule. The revolutionary societal environment had allowed radical American Whigs to direct societal development, often through violence and coercion. Such militancy had created hitherto unimaginable levels of partisanship and mistrust in the early republic, as Americans divided themselves along notions of civility and political allegiance. Understanding party politics as a destructive and selfish pursuit that would only destroy the United States of America before it ever truly emerged, those elites who met in Philadelphia to craft the Constitution in 1787 believed that midcentury ideologies of civil society—specifically, order and hierarchy—would help to unify their fractured collection of nascent states.[48] They simply had to adjust these ideas to fit the new brand of American republicanism that had taken aggressive hold in America. This decision would change western society forever.

1 / Coffeehouse Coteries: Civil Dreams of Exclusivity and Consumer Power

On June 2, 1768, the Philadelphian Josiah F. Davenport advertised his "genteel House of Entertainment," the Bunch of Grapes City Tavern, by appealing to elitist colonists' civil aspirations. Realizing a growing demand for exclusivity within the messy bustle of British America's urban centers, Davenport guaranteed prospective customers that his tavern would offer the "civilest treatment" with luxurious private lodgings, fine stables for their steeds and carriages, and the availability of "an elegant and spacious room" for a private ball (or meetings like those of the St. Andrew's Society whose genteel members chose Davenport's City Tavern as their gathering place). The shrewd Philadelphia publican also, importantly, played to elitist colonists' need for commercial prowess. Located on "one of the grandest avenues in this city [Third Street] . . . in the neighborhood of many principal merchants and capital stores," the City Tavern's prime real estate automatically plugged its customers into a booming world of global consumerism. Taking such commercial expectations into account, Davenport "furnished his house with the best liquors" for gentlemen whose taste buds had grown fond of the cloying heaviness of Madeira wine and the burning smoothness of French brandy. He also assured prospective customers that "every other requisite suitable to [their] design" had been taken care of, from mahogany chests filled with fine china to well-furnished public rooms stocked with the latest newspapers and pamphlets. Davenport was hardly alone in his rush to satisfy a more genteel customer through a canny combination of exclusivity and commercialism. In fact, he joined a multidecade movement, as city taverns and coffeehouses like Phila-delphia's Bunch of Grapes sprouted up in every British American urban center at midcentury.[1]

British American gentlemen struggled to transplant their visions of civil society from the page to the pavement. Believing that they needed their own spaces through which to cultivate dreams of British Ameri-can civility, elitist colonists followed in the footsteps of their London brethren by demanding (and sometimes opening) their own exclusive city taverns and coffeehouses. Anchored by Old World notions of spatial exclusivity, consumer power, and social capital, coffeehouses and city taverns emerged as concrete representations of certain colonists' ulti-mate vision for civil society in which a small group of men might order the masses.[2] Yet, like their efforts in realizing a civil society, middling-and upper-class colonial urbanites' creations of their own coffeehouses and city taverns were not only inextricably linked to processes, goods, and ideas from across the Atlantic Ocean, but were also firmly tethered to North American environmental and social factors.[3] Realities on the ground, once again, necessitated that British American men adjust these British and Continental traditions to the North American environment.

Specifically, colonial urbanites understood themselves as constantly bombarded by the supposed savagery of their New World environment and thus believed that their genteel drinking spaces needed to be more exclusive than those of their European counterparts. In many colonists' minds, excessive interaction with uncivil factions of society like Native Americans, blacks, and poor whites would not only tarnish their civil sheen, but might also denigrate their minds and bodies. As the historian Jennifer Van Horn has demonstrated in the context of colonists' "civil" consumer actions, "fear of the other was really Anglo-Americans' fear of the savagery barely contained within themselves and provoked by the presence of Indians or African Americans."[4] Elitist colonials felt espe-cially impelled to construct spaces of protection from the uncivil facets of society that supposedly lurked around every corner. In doing so, self-professed gentlemen were not simply attempting to bury their heads in the sand. Rather, these men also hoped to impose their ideals of civility, order, and genteel consumption on their urban localities.

Beyond transforming coffeehouses and city taverns into multifaceted spaces of polite exclusivity, British American gentlemen also hoped to use these spaces to fulfill expectations of consumerism. If colonists could achieve any tenet of civil society, many urbanites believed, it would be commerce and industry. British North America's rampant population growth, agricultural production, urban development, and disposable wealth made it the ideal place in which to test such a commercial civilization. The Reverend John Barnard reflected on the development of Marblehead, Massachusetts, from a backwater village into a globally connected entrepôt in 1766. Where in 1714 the isolated town had "not so much as one proper carpenter, nor mason, nor tailor, nor butcher . . . nor any thing of a market worth naming," and was filled with "rude, swearing . . . poor" people, the city's steady inclusion in larger trading networks had a civilizing effect on its inhabitants. Barnard exclaimed that by midcentury Marblehead had "between thirty and forty ships . . . engaged in foreign trade" and was filled with "many gentleman-like and polite families." Marblehead's newfound commercial prowess apparently affected even lowly fishermen's demeanor, as they "generally scorn[ed] the rudeness of the former generation." Here, in Barnard's opinion, was the importance of commercial success for a thriving civil society, and vice versa: "The manners of the people [were] greatly cultivated."[5]

Such development resounded throughout British American cities by the mid-eighteenth century, helping to solidify the colonies' commercial importance in the empire. Upon visiting Philadelphia in 1751, the Englishman James Birket argued that if built "according to the Plan," Philadelphia would "be large enough for the Head of an Empire." He especially attributed Philadelphia's grandeur to its commercial viability, calling the city "the largest and best market in America." The New York City resident William Smith Jr., meanwhile, asserted that *his* city was "the Metropolis and grand Mart of the Province." "Through our Intercourse with the *Europeans*," Smith continued, "we follow the *London* fashions. . . . Our affluence [has] introduced a Degree of Luxury in Tables, Dress, and Furniture, with which we were before unacquainted." Residents of southern cities, finally, gained a commercial reputation of their own. As South Carolina's slave trade steadily increased after 1700 and rice production boomed, for instance, Charleston emerged as the commercial center of the southern colonies. Charleston's expanding population demanded more imported consumables than ever, and local merchants and tradesmen were happy to answer their pleas. In one resident's opinion, "The way of living in Charlestown, [was] much after the English manner." From Williamsburg to Boston, colonial urban centers thrived largely as a result of their integration in international consumer networks.[6]

Elitist colonists had arrived at a crossroads of consumerism. On the one hand, they were determined to consume as many foreign goods as possible, as "material objects offered colonial subjects a mechanism to mold their social identities as they associated to become members of the civil society that they formed on the margins of the British Empire."[7] Yet, if consumed "improperly," without the guidance of gentlemen, leaders believed that these same goods and the spaces associated with them could represent the disintegration of civil society and, in turn, their own tenuous influence on the masses. For these self-styled leaders, consumerism, fashion, and gentility symbolized the possibilities—and pitfalls—of civil society. They proceeded with caution.

Coffeehouses and city taverns emerged as clear symbols of gentlemen's hopes and anxieties surrounding the future of British American civil society. In struggling to adjust these Old World edifices to their emerging society, elitist colonists especially latched onto the exclusivity and consumer power they believed city taverns and coffeehouses promised. Not only did gentlemen desire social capital and distinction, but they also anticipated that their nascent cities might serve as more fertile nurseries for civil impulses like hierarchy and commercialism than the aged metropolises of Great Britain and the Continent. As Benjamin Franklin so famously opined in his "Observations Concerning the Increase of Mankind" (1751), where "Europe is generally full settled with Husbandmen, Manufacturers, &c. and therefore cannot now much increase in People," North America had only just begun its period of commercial and population growth and would soon outstrip England in total Englishmen. "What an Accession of Power to the British Empire by Sea as well as Land," Franklin continued, "What Increase of Trade and Navigation!"[8] Gentlemen colonials like Franklin hoped to transform Old World institutions of civil society to fit—and ultimately shape—British North America into the purest realization of British power abroad. For many, this mammoth task began in individual spaces like coffeehouses and city taverns.

Global Beans, British American Sprouts

The popularity of coffee and coffeehouses throughout the British Empire was a product of early seventeenth-century British imperial penetration into the Ottoman Empire. As coffee made its way through the Ottoman Empire, moving up from Yemen through Arabia to Egypt, next to Aleppo, Anatolia, Smyrna, and finally Constantinople, globetrotting Englishmen sipped this caffeinated beverage while also familiarizing themselves with the ancient customs associated with coffee drinking. The

English adventurer George Sandys remarked in 1610 that although Constantinople was "destitute of Taverns," the city harbored "Coffa-houses, which something resemble [English taverns]." Sandys continued to note that in coffeehouses Turks conversed while imbibing "a drinke called Coffa . . . in little *China* dishes, as hot as they can suffer it: and black as soote, not tasting much unlike it." Like the taverns of Sandys's England, Turkish coffeehouses encouraged male sociability, drink, music, and conversation. Because Sandys's Muslim associates did not generally consume alcohol, moreover, coffeehouses enjoyed unprecedented success throughout the Ottoman Empire. Coffee's caffeine-induced buzz hooked English merchants, who found that "this *All-healing-Berry*" made them "at once . . . both *Sober* and *Merry*." Combined with Ottoman coffeehouses' hospitable nature, this addicting bean was practically unstoppable.⁹

Coffee's consumer traditions made their way west when an English merchant sponsored his Greek Orthodox servant, Pasqua Rosée, in setting up the Western Europe's first coffeehouse in London in 1652. London became "the pre-eminent city of coffeehouses" over the next hundred years as addicted gentlemen flocked to these spaces to sip coffee, read the news, and escape the bustle of the city. Coffeehouse owners often ground the beans at a customer's table, allowing eager onlookers to "consume" the Mediterranean traditions of coffee drinking and coffeehouses.¹⁰ The Englishman Alexander Pope described one such experience in his early eighteenth-century poem, *The Rape of the Lock: Canto 3*:

> For lo! the board with cups and spoons is crown'd,
> The berries crackle, and the mill turns round.
> On shining altars of Japan they raise
> The silver lamp; the fiery spirits blaze.
> From silver spouts the grateful liquors glide,
> While China's earth receives the smoking tide.
> At once they gratify their scent and taste,
> And frequent cups prolong the rich repast.¹¹

One can imagine the flood of excitement to an Englishman's senses as the strange coffee mill crushed the fragrant berries, emitting their pungent scent throughout the room. "Shining alters" of Asian porcelain transferred these "grateful liquors" into the eager consumers' mouths. Coffee and coffeehouses were consumables and spaces wholly devoted to making Englishmen feel connected to the world beyond their walls. They thrived on the "exoticness" of "scent and taste" that coffee represented.

Though English coffeehouses remained relatively exclusive during the second half of the seventeenth century, inclusiveness and social diversity defined these spaces by the beginning of the eighteenth century. It seemed that every Englishman had his own coffeehouse. Regional affiliations lured men to certain venues, while business and political allegiances called different men to others. So many coffeehouses lined London's streets by midcentury that one Englishman disgustedly exclaimed that these once-proud establishments had "degenerated" into "mere alehouses." Another worried, "Pre-eminence of place, none [at the coffeehouse] should mind. . . But take the next fit seat that he can find." One English elite damned these supposedly egalitarian institutions for being "free to all Comers, so they have Humane shape." "Here," this angry author declared, "there is no respect of persons."[12] Another Englishman denounced coffeehouses' inferior company, arguing, "As you have a hodge-podge of Drinks, such too is your Company, for each man seems a Leveller, and ranks and files himself as he lifts, without regard to degrees or order." Whether elites liked it or not, English coffeehouses evolved into key spaces of commercial urban society where a diverse set of people could meet and commiserate.[13] British American colonists were taking notes.

Many British American men had experienced English coffeehouses firsthand by the mid-eighteenth century. The Virginia gentleman William Byrd II visited Will's Coffeehouse almost daily while living in London from 1717 to 1720. He also spent much time at Ozinda's and Garraway's Coffeehouses. Dr. Alexander Hamilton so missed the drinking culture of his native Scotland that shortly after moving to Annapolis in 1738 he asked his brother (who lived in Edinburgh) to "be so good as Remember me to all the members of the whin-bush Club. . . . Inform them that every Friday, I fancy myself with them. . . . I Long to see those merry days again." Ever the aspiring gentleman, Benjamin Franklin also frequented London's many coffeehouses while residing in the lively metropolis in 1725. He remembered meeting the famous English physician, Henry Pemberton, at Batson's Coffee House: "[He] promis'd to give me an opportunity, sometime or other, of seeing Sir Isaac Newton, of which I was extreamly desirous."[14] English coffeehouses, in brief, would hardly have been foreign to the colonial gentlemen who most desired these spaces.

By midcentury, British America's urban centers boasted numerous coffeehouses. New York City had the Exchange Coffee House, the Merchant

Coffee House, the Whitehall Coffee House, and the Burns Coffee House. Philadelphia's postmaster, Henry Flower, ran "the old Coffee House" in 1735; other genteel establishments such as Roberts' Coffee House, the West Indian Coffee House, and the James Coffee House followed. Thirsty Bostonians could gather in the Crown Coffee House. Though not harboring as many souls as northern cities, Charleston, Annapolis, and Williamsburg each boasted at least one coffeehouse by midcentury as well.[15] And while not *officially* restrictive like many of the fee-charging "penny universities" of seventeenth-century London, midcentury colonial American coffeehouses nevertheless operated according to a variety of exclusionary measures.[16]

British American newspaper advertisements were especially effective in conveying an air of civility surrounding coffeehouses. The Philadelphia publican Margaret Ingram, for example, gave "Notice to all Gentlemen" in 1748 that she "opened the West Indian Coffee House, where they may depend upon being genteely entertained" by virtually every material amenity that the empire offered. The owner of New York City's Exchange Coffee House similarly advertised its grand opening in December 1749, assuring "all Gentlemen" that they "may depend upon the Best Entertainment from their humble servant."[17] Farther south, Mary Bedon, owner of the Charleston Coffee House in 1740, assured "all Gentlemen . . . so kind as to be her Customers" that they would "meet with the best Reception and Entertainment in her Power," while Annapolis's Coffee House played host to elitist clubs such as the Homony Club. Many shrewd midcentury tavern keepers also played to gentlemen's need for civility, promising prospective customers that they could "depend on civil Treatment . . . for themselves, Servants, and Horses."[18]

Yet not every genteel colonial American drinking place fell under the umbrella of the coffeehouse. Some tavern keepers opened equally exclusive and genteel city taverns—or simply adjusted existing taverns—to cater specifically to elitist colonists' needs. As early as 1743, Edward Jenkins of Charleston distinguished his tavern as a place where "Gentlemen may be handsomely entertain'd, and depend on the best Usage in every Respect." Echoing Jenkins, in 1759, Thomas Mackreth (also of Charleston) announced the grand opening of his "genteel Tavern," where he proposed "to give all possible Satisfaction to Gentlemen who shall think proper to their Custom, who may depend upon being served with the best of LIQUOR & Attendance." Such genteel taverns were, of course, not limited to Charleston. In 1751, Benjamin Pain of New York City overtly sought out a genteel customer base by naming his new establishment

the Gentlemen's Coffee House and Tavern. Annapolis's Mary Fonne-
reau promised "good entertainment" for gentlemen, "their servants, or
horses" at her city tavern in 1755.[19]

It is also important to note that while leaders expected ordinary tavern keepers to cater solely to men, genteel city taverns and coffeehouses
occasionally hosted balls, exhibits, and dinners that welcomed elitist
women in otherwise masculine spaces. One would not find a woman
sidling up next to a gentleman during the day-to-day commotion of a
coffeehouse's operation, but for special events women were welcomed to
lend a further air of delicacy and propriety. The Boston gentleman merchant John Rowe recounted dining with companies of men and women
at a local city tavern on several occasions in the 1760s. Upon visiting Boston in 1750, the elitist New Yorker Francis Goelet recalled convening in
a city tavern for "turtle frolics" and balls alike with "gentlemen & ladies
of the best fashion in Boston." According to long-held notions of civility,
femininity, and masculinity, interaction with women in otherwise male-
controlled spaces might foster a different sort of civil conversation than
was the norm—in John Adams's words, "a civil sort of Impertinence,
Remarks made with excellent Judgment upon the Fashions." Though
self-professed gentlemen like Adams found certain polishing factors in
public interactions with their female counterparts, they were also sure
to stress the alleged dangers of such association (particularly gossip,
luxury, and, ultimately, emasculation), and thus believed that gender-
mixing public events such as balls, dinners, and exhibits should only be
held sporadically.[20]

Although publicans tirelessly advertised their spaces' gentility and
grandiosity, most colonial coffeehouses and city taverns were little more
than urban taverns with a new name and, perhaps, slightly nicer equipages and services. Coffeehouse owners knew their customers' preference
for all things British and hoped to use this "branding" to attract well-
heeled colonists with little extra effort. Many wealthy colonists attended
coffeehouses during their visits to London and the Continent and still
harbored fond memories of these experiences. Others like Dr. Hamilton
had just recently moved to North America and were pining for the public
sociability of Old World coffeehouses. Yet these coffeehouses and city
taverns only partially satisfied many of these men's demands, since most
were operated by men and women who ultimately sought profit more
than gentility and exclusivity. If middling- and upper-class urbanites
were to truly realize their ambitions of a civil society where they held
ultimate sway over the uncivil masses, they needed their *own* spaces that

FIGURE 1. William L. Breton, *London Coffee House* (Philadelphia: Kennedy and Lucas, 1830). Used with Permission of the Library Company of Philadelphia, Philadelphia, PA. Print Department. BW-Hotels, Inns, Taverns [9245.Q.20].

they both constructed and controlled. In 1754, William Bradford and Philadelphia's gentlemen tavern goers made this dream a reality.

With the opening of Philadelphia's London Coffee House in 1754 (Figure 1), William Bradford and his elitist subscribers triggered the emergence of a new sort of colonial American drinking space built specifically around civil notions of hierarchy and consumerism. While Peter Thompson pointed to the opening of Bradford's London Coffee House as a moment that highlighted certain Philadelphians' "dissatisfaction with mixed tavern assemblages" and Sharon Salinger noted that such elitist taverns increasingly insulated themselves in the center of cities, neither fully integrated the London Coffee House's genesis into larger processes of civil exclusivity and anxiety—both geographically and ideologically—that coursed through the colonies' urban centers at midcentury. Bradford's London Coffee House did mark a new moment for public drinking spaces in British North America, but it must be understood in its larger context, as it was hardly the first space of its kind.[21]

Rather than privately control the London Coffee House (like the aforementioned establishments), Bradford followed in the footsteps of Philadelphia's library and academy by forming a committee of elitist subscribers to manage the coffeehouse's construction, development, and regulation. By midcentury, a growing number of gentlemen decided that the only walls that might truly satisfy their ideals of civility, order, and imperial allegiance would have to be new, exclusive ones. These spaces would still exist in the public but would be owned, funded, and controlled by elitist thinkers. Only those deemed worthy of civil society would enter these spaces' doors. Urban spaces like libraries and secular universities emerged as elitists' ideal spaces. Allegedly devoid of uncivil chaos, these monuments of order would fulfill gentlemen's needs for exclusivity and polite conversation.[22]

Elitist colonists tirelessly erected structures to reflect their prosperity, gentility, and worldliness. Rising above the mass of small, frame, one-story houses and a smattering of seventeenth-century estates, colonists' Georgian mansions projected their power onto the landscape. These fine estates sported brick and painted clapboards, ornamented doorways and window openings, large sash windows distributed symmetrically across the facade, broad open staircases, and decorated chimneybreasts. Middling- and upper-class gentlemen decorated their interiors with art, sculptures, and antiquities and often hosted balls, lectures, and dances in their great halls and barbecues on their manicured grounds. Moreover, the grandeur of these estates often extended into carefully cultivated surrounding gardens.[23] For all their splendor, however, mansions' inherent privacy afforded elitist colonists limited control over public spaces. Gentlemen's reconstruction of urban public spaces consequently mirrored their own haunts in form and function but somewhat diverged from their private "resorts of gentility" in purpose. To demonstrate their order and civility, gentlemen decided to create their own bastions of power.

As one of the colonies' most preeminent figures, Benjamin Franklin led the charge in this endeavor as he constructed a variety of civil institutions at a staggering pace. Having spent a year in London as a young man, Franklin returned to the colonies with plans to transform Philadelphia into a place that might "Benefit . . . Mankind in general."[24] Philadelphia's Library Company proved the genesis of his public efforts. Originally established in 1731 by Franklin and other aspiring leaders to instill "Learning Virtue and Politeness in the city's inhabitants," the Library Company was public in that "so many Persons of different Sects,

Parties and Ways of thinking" gained access to its volumes. The Library, however, was also a private endeavor; fifty gentlemen formed the company through donation and nominated ten "Directors or Managers" to manage the Library. By 1741, around seventy Philadelphians paid for membership.[25]

While the company often labeled their project a "Publick Library," access remained restricted. To become a member of the Library Company, one had to earn a nomination from a director and pay for a share in the company (the founders pledged an initial donation of fifty shillings and promised to pay ten shillings every year thereafter, which was a cost beyond most colonists' limited budget and only grew in expense with book accumulation and building development). Nonmembers could borrow a book in exchange for "a Sum of Money proportion'd to the Value of the Book borrow'd," but since most colonists could not afford a bound book, this fee excluded the majority of the lower classes.[26] Moreover, although literacy had spiked by the mid-eighteenth century, reading for pleasure was still a primarily middling- and upper-class pursuit (who else had the time and resources?).[27] Philadelphia's leaders had extended the gentleman's library into the public sphere while still maintaining and even extending its private, polite, and exclusive peculiarities. And because "the Mother of all the North American subscription libraries" provided such "a Source of Instruction to Individuals and conducive of Reputation to that Public," gentlemen from New York City to Boston followed Philadelphia's lead by constructing subscription libraries of their own. These were spaces from which elitist men could simultaneously project their power over and shield themselves from the masses.[28]

By 1749, Franklin and his genteel colleagues decided that an even more enlightened space was necessary to fulfill his and others' ideals of civil society: the Academy (or College) of Philadelphia. Besides advocating a more secular education than existing colonial colleges (e.g., Harvard, William and Mary, and Yale), Franklin's college focused on a more scholastic goal than its predecessors which, in the vein of Oxford and Cambridge Universities, served as resorts of gentlemanly revelry. Franklin contended that British North America's secular colleges should focus on a "polite and learned education." Leaders hoped these colleges would extend their ideals of gentility and hierarchy to a hitherto unobtainable degree.[29]

In the same vein as the Library Company, a group of elitist trustees organized, funded, and controlled Philadelphia's Academy. Their primary goal remained the transformation of Philadelphia's youth into budding leaders, which would in turn aid future efforts to develop the colonies, their cities, and their citizens. As Franklin explained:

> Nothing can more effectually contribute to the Cultivation and Improvement of a Country, the Wisdom, Riches, and Strength, Virtue and Piety, the Welfare and Happiness of a People, than a proper Education of Youth, by forming their Manners, imbuing their tender Minds with Principles of Rectitude and Morality, instructing them in the dead and living Languages, particularly their Mother-Tongue, and all useful Branches of liberal Arts and Science.[30]

Philadelphia's College (now the University of Pennsylvania) catered primarily to gentlemen since trustees required a considerable sum for attendance. "When the fund is sufficient to bear the charge," Franklin noted, "poor Children shall be admitted and taught gratis, what shall be thought suitable to their Capacities and Circumstances." Similar to the Library Company, then, poor colonists gained restrained access to the Academy but only at the trustees' discretion. Even more, per Franklin's design, instructors taught "poor Children" what they deemed "suitable to their Capacities and Circumstances." Within each class, students were seated and treated according to their social rank, while younger students were expected to defer to upperclassmen. Leaders deemed hierarchy crucial to the education of future gentlemen. It was the hallmark of order.[31]

Though the movement to create colonial colleges largely arose from churches vying with each other to found seminaries, by midcentury, certain American colleges also came to represent gentlemen's need for their own enlightened spaces among the disorder of their cities' public spaces. In New York City, William Livingston led the charge to establish an elitist-controlled, secular university in 1753. Using his popular periodical, the *Independent Reflector*, as a sounding board, Livingston argued that a college would be "a Blessing . . . to the Community," and "Every Man who loves Liberty and the Province" should support the endeavor.[32] Livingston was not alone in his professions of the importance of colleges for the future of British America. Upon succeeding to the English throne in 1760, King George III contended that American colleges would prepare young British Americans for the "just use of rational Liberty." Such colonial "college enthusiasm" resulted in the creation of nine institutions of higher learning in colonial America by 1770. Within these spaces dedicated to rendering British American "Youth better Members of [civil] Society," gentlemen hoped that their young charges might shape the colonies into reflections of their forebears' desires.[33]

Bradford's London Coffee House was thus a product of larger urban developments and anxieties. Gentlemen from Philadelphia to New York City to Charleston had already begun to imagine similar spaces in every sphere of public life, as exclusive academies and libraries steadily emerged in urban environments. Within such spaces, current and future gentlemen could hone their skills at politeness, business, and the belles lettres among a hand-chosen company of their genteel peers. With Bradford's London Coffee House, subscribers simply extended these same attributes to their favorite of all public spaces, the tavern.

Bradford's coffeehouse reflected other exclusive institutions in its diverse purposes. The first floor served as a polite tavern where private associations like "the Sea Captains Club" met; the second floor was intended as a genteel coffeehouse and business "exchange" where more business-oriented customers could escape the enervating temptations of the bottle. William Bradford's other profession only spurred such pursuits. Bradford owned a printing shop attached to the coffeehouse where, besides publishing the *Pennsylvania Journal*, he printed a wide variety of other popular pamphlets, books, and broadsides. As the historian Phyllis Whitman Hunter contended, "Prompted by a constant need for up-to-date information from around the world to govern business decisions, overseas traders fostered a growing demand for public print." Bradford provided his customers just that: a gentleman could spend the whole day in the confines of Bradford's London Coffee House, sipping coffee and wine, poring over books, debating international business, and conversing with traveling strangers. In Adam Smith's opinion, when combined with public discourse, "the art of printing" would allow a "man of letters . . . [to] communicate to other people the curious and useful knowledge which he had acquired himself." Within such a well-controlled environment, gentlemen could close the door on incivility and shape themselves into polite managers of a British American civil society.[34]

If the promise of exclusivity brought elitist colonists into city taverns and coffeehouses, the pull of global consumerism helped to keep them there. The gentlemen merchants, planters, and businessmen who frequented these spaces harbored a keener understanding of global networks of commerce than perhaps any other colonists. Thus while ordinary colonists gained access to a broader array of goods than ever before, elitist men hoped to combine their knowledge of the world with their purchasing power to cultivate their identities as civil leaders. Nestled within the safe confines of their coffeehouses and city taverns, gentlemen strained to retain their power over their local market and, in turn, the British American colonies.

British American coffeehouses' and city taverns' interior decoration, furniture, and myriad consumer services reflected elitist colonists' urge for exclusive consumption within the expanding midcentury marketplace. In contrast to William Phillip's and George Emlen's late seventeenth-century Boston and Philadelphia taverns, which were sparsely decorated with rustic furniture, sturdy trimmings, and simple beverages, Boston's Crown Coffeehouse boasted its Coffee Room, an elegant, exclusive space decorated with ten painted panels, sixteen prints, and a "timepiece." Similarly, Mrs. Macgregor of Charleston advertised in 1748 that she had cultivated orange gardens around her "Genteel Coffee-House." When the New York City tavern keeper Samuel Fraunces sold his city tavern in 1768, he informed all that the "noted tavern" had twelve fireplaces, two large "dancing rooms," and "eight other good rooms, with every conveniency for the reception of company." These were spaces in which a gentleman would have felt equally comfortable after leaving the tobacco smoke and brandy of his private library.[35]

Besides having grander architectural markers and decorations than other drinking spaces, coffeehouses and city taverns marked their civility through a broad array of expensive alcoholic beverages. Boston's eighteenth-century Crown Coffee House sold far more brandy, rum, and wine than coffee. At the time of his death, the owner of the Crown Coffee House held 5,000 gallons of foreign wine (Madeira, Canary, Fayall, Vidonia, and Port), in addition to 691 gallons of rum, 210 gallons of brandy, and 112 gallons more of his "best" brandy. Alexander Smith similarly promised prospective customers to his New York City Coffee House "the certainty of being served with neat Wines, Punch, Beer, and all other Best Liquors . . . in the most genteel manner." Thus, only after establishing a variety of available alcoholic beverages did this coffeehouse owner note that he also served coffee "at any hour of the day." Here colonists followed in the footsteps of eighteenth-century London coffeehouses. When the Prince of Wales's Coffee House opened in London in 1749, its owner publicized the abundance of "the best Liquors of all Sorts . . . for those Gentlemen who will be pleased to use the said House," in addition to a billiards table. Nowhere in the advertisement did the coffeehouse owner mention coffee; although gaining in popularity as public beverages, coffee, tea, and chocolate remained secondary to alcohol for gentlemen tavern goers.[36]

The consumption of intoxicants and information went hand-in-hand by the eighteenth century: as one early modern European thinker opined,

"When I drink I think; and when I think, I drink."[37] Well aware that many colonists considered foreign news, or as one Englishman called it, "the MANNA of the day[,] . . . the true and genuine food of the mind," proprietors of city taverns and coffeehouses also stocked their genteel rooms with locally and globally sourced newspapers, tracts, broadsides, and magazines.[38] When two Philadelphians opened the Whitehall Coffee House in 1762, they assured prospective gentlemen that "a correspondence is settled in London & Bristol to remit every opportunity all the public prints & pamphlets as soon as published; & there will be a weekly supply of New York, Boston & other American newspapers." George Burns, owner of Philadelphia's Burns Coffee House/City Tavern, similarly advertised in 1750 that he "constantly [took] in the Boston, Philadelphia, and New-York *Newspapers*."[39] Such stocks of newspapers, however, were not restricted to Philadelphia's city taverns and coffeehouses. Any eighteenth-century colonial tavern keeper worth his salt kept regular collections of newspapers for discerning patrons. Dr. Hamilton often visited taverns to catch up on local and international events. The *Pennsylvania Gazette* further confirmed Hamilton's experiences, exclaiming in a broadside, "As to the Heart, flows Blood from every Vein, *To Taverns, Inns, and Coffee-Houses* . . . the rambling News runs crowding in."[40] City tavern and coffeehouse owners knew that their demanding patrons would get their news one way or another. They thus promoted their spaces as the most accessible news outlets in colonial America.

Various other publications detailing global news, fashion, and literature littered coffeehouse tables alongside piles of newspapers. Intended for the aspiring gentleman, popular periodicals such as the *Spectator, Tatler,* and *Gentleman's Magazine* sought to bring "Philosophy out of Closets and Libraries, Schools and Colleges, to dwell . . . in Coffee-Houses." These publications not only taught a British subject how to be "in his Element" among diverse company, but also how to observe the world around him with a civil air of erudition and detachment. Combined with tracts published throughout the British Empire on topics ranging from foreign travel to natural history and classic literature (sometimes in several languages), the litany of pamphlets accessible to colonial tavern goers during the eighteenth century exploited urban gentlemen's considerable interest in defining and understanding their position in the larger world. They provided yet another course that colonists could consume in their ongoing quest to negotiate a British American civil society.[41]

Eighteenth-century British American city taverns and coffeehouses also served as unofficial postal centers.[42] When the Swedish naturalist

Peter Kalm arrived in Philadelphia in the second half of the eighteenth century, colonists rushed his ship inquiring for letters. The ship's captain ordered "those [letters] which remained . . . to be carried on shore and to be brought into a coffee-house, where everybody could make inquiry for them, and by this means he was rid of the trouble of delivering them himself." At Todd's City Tavern in New York City, Dr. Hamilton received a letter from his French friend La Moinerie (whom he had met in the Boston tavern), who sent it "by a medical doctor from Barbados who [was] going to Rhode Island." Benjamin Franklin, postmaster general of the colonies, hoped in 1763 that the owners of "all Coffee Houses where Bags are put up" might "bring such Bags of Letters to the Post Office before they are sent away." Franklin was even willing to sweeten the pot, suggesting that "the Coffee House [be allowed] a half penny per letter, for their Trouble in Collecting them." Coffeehouses were the perfect spaces for mail collection and delivery, as those gentlemen and merchants who most often utilized the transatlantic "republic of letters" were also coffeehouses' primary customers. Although such "polite" company did not entirely prevent the opening and theft of letters, coffeehouses and city taverns nevertheless served as some of the most trusted public spaces for information consumption before the widespread existence of official post offices.[43]

Sometimes a gentleman wanted to ship more than a letter. City taverns and coffeehouses frequently emerged as sites where colonists could sign up to board or send freight with a departing ship. In the years between 1754 and 1763, Philadelphia's London Coffee House offered colonists "Freight or Passage" on ships traveling throughout the British Atlantic empire, including Antigua, Nevis, St. Christopher's, the West Indies, London, and Leith, Scotland. A Philadelphian who wanted to travel to Madeira in 1749 could contact "George Bascum, merchant, at his lodgings at the Widow Evans's, at the sign of the Crown, in Market street." He could also enjoy "freight or passage" to Jamaica by signing up at "Roberts's Coffee house," or to Antigua by meeting with the ship's master at the Tun Tavern. Finally, any of New York's "Gentlemen Adventurers . . . inclinable to go to the Cruize" had only to "repair to the House of Mr. Benjamin Pain, at the Jamaica Arms [Tavern]."[44] These ships' freight and passage services helped colonial gentlemen ship valuable goods—and themselves—around the world.

Owners of coffeehouses and city taverns also regularly reserved their taverns as auction houses where they either served as the auctioneer or the auction's impresario. Williamsburg's "Norfolk coffee-house" advertised the sale of "An Assortment of European and East India GOODS, RUM, SUGARS, &c." in the mid-eighteenth century, and Philadelphia's London Coffee House sold "Four Chests of small Spanish Silver, each chest containing 2000 Ounces," on November 23, 1758. Besides other random loot like "good Muscovado Sugar in Barrels," Madeira wine, indigo, sweet oil, crocus, and linens, interested gentlemen could peruse book sales.[45] Thomas Blythe, for instance, advertised the sale of "a choice collection of Books, neatly bound in calf and letter'd" at his Charleston, South Carolina, tavern in June 1749. A curious patron could thumb through a series of catalogs before making his purchase. The Philadelphia publican William Bradford released a broadside in 1755 listing over 190 books available at his bookstore (attached to his coffeehouse). Finally, a colonist could often buy a ship, its outfitting, "Appurtences," or cargo in portside drinking spaces. A coffeehouse in Philadelphia, for example, promoted the sale of a captured vessel, "the Cape Fear Hawke, mounting 16 Carriage Guns, 4 Pounders, and 22 Swivels, together with her Tackle, Furniture and Apparel, and a large Quantity of warlike stores" in 1759. Like their brethren in London, elitist colonists used coffeehouse auctions to demonstrate their genteel consumerism and, in some cases, consume the narrative of a deceased person's life through the purchase of their estate.[46]

Yet inanimate trade goods were not the only consumer choices available at city tavern and coffeehouse auctions. These genteel spaces also offered patrons the opportunity to purchase human beings within their parlors. One British visitor to Williamsburg, Virginia, in the late eighteenth century remarked that "more business has been transacted" at the Raleigh Tavern "than on the Exchange of London or Amsterdam." Reflecting the truth of the Briton's observation, an unidentified party advertised in the March 28, 1745, edition of the *Virginia Gazette* that "a young Negro Wench perfectly well qualified for all sorts of House-work" and "a young Negro Fellow who understands driving a Chariot" would "be Sold at publick Sale" at Jane Vobe's Williamsburg city tavern.[47] And tavern slave auctions were hardly limited to the southern colonies. Philadelphia's London Coffee House (predating Bradford's establishment with the same name) advertised the sale of "a very likely breeding Negroe Woman . . . fit for any Business either in Town or Country" in 1736 and in 1763 similarly offered for sale "a likely healthy Negroe Wench, about 24 Years of Age." A potential buyer would not have to worry about the second woman's untimely death since she had already survived the measles and smallpox. Her knowledge of business affairs only heightened her desirability.[48] As a thriving institution of British expansion in the eighteenth century, the African slave trade offered gentlemen a chance not only to extend their local power but also to connect indirectly with larger networks of imperialism and consumption. Elitist colonists viewed the purchase of an African slave at their local tavern much as they did the purchase of other consumption goods—as a means of positioning themselves as powerful members of the British Empire. Colonial tavern goers commoditized people into things that could enhance their own status and satisfy their various consumer fantasies.[49]

African slaves, however, were hardly the only international "curiosity" available for viewing and purchase in British American city taverns and coffee houses. The owner of Philadelphia's Indian King Tavern, for example, provided inquisitive gentlemen the chance in 1740 to gaze at a camel, an exotic animal they could not have possibly seen roaming North America's wilds. By purchasing a ticket at the city tavern's front door, Philadelphians with "ingenious Curiosity" could view the camel "brought with great Difficulty from the Deserts of Arabia in that Quarter of the World which is called Asia, to New-England" and finally to Philadelphia. But the Indian King Tavern did not end its bizarre exhibits with this camel. In 1744, the same tavern keeper advertised "A Beautiful Creature, but surprizingly fierce, called a Leopard; his Extraction half a Lion and half a Pardeal; his native Place of Abode is in Africa, and Arabia."[50] This tavern keeper thus took advantage of colonists' cravings for knowledge of foreign lands, creatures, and people to attract more business. He was not alone.

Eye-catching exhibits intended to broaden colonists' worldview filled genteel taverns and coffeehouses by the mid-eighteenth century. Williamsburg's Raleigh Tavern sold tickets in October 1755 for "that elaborate and celebrated Piece of Mechanism, call'd the Microcosm, or, the World in Miniature." Although most simply a clock, the Microcosm was a far more detailed work of art devoted to onlookers' dreams of a grander world order. Constructed in England in 1733 by the architect Henry Bridges, the contraption stood over ten feet high and six feet wide and was composed of over 1,200 moving wheels and pinions. Externally, it boasted "a number of levels [that] displayed representations of the nine Muses on Parnassus, Orpheus charming the wild beasts in the forest, a grove with birds flying and singing, a clock with both the Ptolemaic and Copernican celestial systems and a landscape with a prospect of the Ocean and ships sailing." A teeming city scene played out in the foreground of the machine, as coaches, carts, people, birds, and dogs moved in tandem in front of a carpenter's yard. Music from an organ, harpsichord, spinet, flute, and whistle also tickled spectators' senses. Those gentlemen or ladies who wished to play their own music could do so with the organ's keys. Onlookers would have been absolutely dazzled by the sights and sounds that played out before them. Any customers inclined to a more exclusive experience could purchase a private showing of the Microcosm.[51]

Wax effigies of famous figures were especially popular tavern attractions. In 1749, for instance, the Sign of the Dolphin Privateer in New York City advertised "The Effigies of the Royal Family of England, In a Composition of Wax . . . as big as LIFE." Recently arrived from London, these wax effigies included the Prince of Wales, the Queen of Hungary and Bohemia, and even a famous English actress. Charlestonians with enough money for a £20 ticket could view "three elaborate Figures in Wax-work" at John Gordon's tavern in 1753, while by 1768 William Holliday of Charleston offered tavern goers the opportunity to see "a complete Set of Artificial Figures, representing diverse Masquerade Characters." Holliday extended his showmanship to new heights with water fountains and fireworks.[52] Although ordinary colonists surely also found these effigies interesting for their novelty, aspiring gentlemen displayed a distinctive social capital in their ability to recognize and converse upon famous individuals they had only ever seen represented in two dimensions. Not surprisingly, colonists paid money to see wax re-creations of foreign rather than domestic figures.

When mechanical contraptions or wax figures were not available, sugar sufficed. Upon paying one shilling, visitors to one Philadelphia tavern in 1765 could look upon "a very fine and elaborate Piece of SUGAR WORK . . . done by a German Confectioner." "Being such as never before was exhibited in this Part of the World," the "gigantic" sugar temple boasted architecture and symbolism from throughout the globe. While the king and queen of Britain's names were inscribed on a laurel wreath at the structure's peak, the king of Prussia and the goddess Pallas stood inside the temple's walls. Trumpeters and drummers on horseback, meanwhile, invited "the four Quarters of the Globe" to the front of the castle. These international visitors arrived "in triumphal Cars, drawn by Lions, Elephants, Camels and Horses." "Having for many Years served the Imperial, the Royal Prussian, and other princely Tables," the German confectioner who constructed this piece knew his customers well. He realized that his creations must play to colonists' global interests if he wished to garner the most business possible. He did just that, using an impressive amount of West Indian sugar to build a glittering monument to empire and civility.[53]

Perhaps the most generally lauded of all tavern exhibits, however, was the New Yorker John Bonnin's "Philosophical Optical Machine." As Bonnin toured New York City and Philadelphia from 1748 through 1749, he amazed curious tavern goers with "Perspective Views of most of the famous Palaces and Gardens in *England, France*, and *Italy*[,] . . . the siege of *Barcelona*, and the cities of *Rome, Naples*, and *Venice*." Imported from London, Bonnin's Philosophical Optical Machine was a mirrored mechanism that projected three-dimensional images of famous scenes onto a small screen. When gazing into Bonnin's machine, colonists felt as if they were "walk[ing] to *Kensington, Hampton-Court, Vaux Hall, Ranelagh House*, and other grand Palaces and Gardens in and about *London*." New York's aspiring elites found that "there's no Body can set up the least Face for Politeness and Conversation, without having been to Mr. *Bonnin*." While foreign travelers could once impress New York City residents with tales of their global travels, colonists who had looked through Bonnin's machine felt that they could now "detect [foreigners'] false pretended Description" of palaces, gardens, and monuments. Bonnin's Philosophical Optical Machine permitted British American gentlemen to travel and "see the world" without leaving their home cities. By simply entering the tavern space, these urbanites were whisked away to countless exotic places.[54]

Ultimately, the various consumer and entertainment opportunities available in British American city taverns and coffeehouses contributed to gentlemen's quest for civility. Private coffeehouses and city taverns emerged at midcentury as a reaction to certain colonists' demands for more selective public spaces. Like libraries and academies, these spaces touted their ability to offer condescending gentlemen an opportunity of refinement and exclusivity available nowhere else. They also tied themselves to larger commercial developments. Within these refined spaces, genteel colonists could sip beverages sourced from around the globe, peruse a dizzying variety of imported goods, rub elbows with foreign travelers, catch up on international news, send a letter to the farthest reaches of the empire, lounge among exotic woods and porcelain, sample fine cloths, peruse classic literature, book passage on a transatlantic privateer ship, or hand pick an African slave. And they could do so, importantly, without having to worry about supposedly disrespectful ordinary tavern goers. Ultimately, then, the evolution of exclusive coffeehouses and city taverns was a natural outgrowth of gentlemen's ongoing anxieties surrounding the future of civil society.

The intertwined nature of gentlemen's aspirations for the future of civil society and their reliance on coffeehouses and city taverns coalesced around the creation of "The Free Debating Society." Held at Philadelphia's Indian Queen Tavern (where Thomas Jefferson would draft the Declaration of Independence in 1776), this society only accepted "young Gentlemen" under the age of twenty-one. The author of the announcement, who dubbed himself "Philomath" (i.e., a lover of learning), consciously anchored his society to long-held notions of civility, order, and improvement. In one instance, Philomath assured future members that "assuming Dictators" would not be allowed within the tavern society. Rather, "a Liberty of Expression and Language [would be] granted" to each member (once, of course, they had agreed upon "Regulations . . . necessary for [the society's] good Government"). Hearkening back to "Rules of Good breeding and Decency," Philomath stressed that the "only Aim of this Institution is Improvement" and that, through such civilizing interaction, the society would help to form "a Race of Orators, Patriots, Philosophers, and shining Members of Society."[55] Ultimately, then, the Free Debating Society was a polishing stone for future gentlemen. Here they could meet in an exclusive city tavern to cultivate social capital and, in turn, effect real change in their locales. And, as demonstrated in the next chapter, these young Philadelphians were hardly alone in their reliance on the blossoming network of exclusive coffeehouses and city taverns for personal and societal improvement.

2 / "Citizens of the World?": Coming to Terms with Cosmopolitanism

Writing to the *New-York Weekly Journal* in 1749, an author who identified himself as "Per Se" excitedly described the cosmopolitan merits of New York City gentlemen who "formed themselves into a Club, and meet every Week, to Discant upon learned Subjects, in a private [tavern] apartment." Consisting of a dozen "Men of the Finest Parts, true Taste, solid Judgments, deep Erudition, and a Talent to display it . . . The American Royal Society . . . IMPROVED, upon the Plan of the other *Royal Society* at London" by relieving the mind of "Ignorance and Prejudice." In contrast to so many other men who supposedly existed "in a total Ignorance, of every thing Genteel and Manly," members of the American Royal Society declared themselves "Enemies to *Nonsense* and *Vice*" who resolved "to improve the *Taste*, and *Knowledge*, to *Reform*, and *Correct*, the manners of the Inhabitants of [New York City]." By assembling such a variety of "Skill, Art and Erudition"—musicians to educate members on the intricacies of sound; physicians, the human body; and mechanics, the myriad philosophical, mechanical, optical, and astronomical instruments—the Royal Society provided its elitist associates with various cosmopolitan impulses and, in turn, helped them to extend an air of civility over New York City's public arena. Crafting themselves into "citizens of the world," and their city taverns and coffeehouses into spaces specifically catering to their ideals of cosmopolitanism, these gentlemen believed they would help to finally realize a British American civil society.[1]

As the British Empire became an increasingly global power at midcentury, Britons such as those members of the American Royal Society adjusted their worldviews to fit—and perhaps transcend—the boundaries of empire. These tavern-going gentlemen hoped to emulate their cosmopolitan peers in London by creating their own Royal Society in New York City. They foresaw a future where civility would reign supreme and those not literate in the language of gentility, masculinity, and worldliness would retreat to inferior spheres of interaction. Yet the American Royal Society's vision of civil cosmopolitanism promised more than simple emulation of the British metropolis. After all, the American Royal Society sought to improve on the London Royal Society by concentrating, above all else, on the philosophy of humanity. At its core, the creation of the American Royal Society reveals certain urban colonists' attempts to come to terms with their own British American conceptions of cosmopolitan civility. The Society offered these New Yorkers the opportunity to reflect on their current positions in the British Empire and to define how they wanted to proceed into a bright future.[2]

The pathway to civility was not as simple as building coffeehouses, sipping expensive beverages, retreating to exclusive rooms, or espousing one's superior social capital. As demonstrated by elitist tavern goers' efforts to nurture their cosmopolitan identities, the reality of civil society lay in gentlemen's anxieties surrounding the social repercussions of imperial development as much as—if not more than—their desire for wider humanism. Gentlemen tavern goers' supposedly cosmopolitan experiences actually entrenched their sense of ethnocentrism, hierarchy, and nationalism. Such exclusive attempts at cosmopolitan civility led many urban tavern goers to scorn far more than celebrate, and thus helped to structure civil society around notions of prejudice far more than equality. British American civil society was predicated on anxiety as much as aspiration as urbanites transformed Enlightenment ideals to fit their realities on the ground.[3]

British American colonists took a three-pronged approach to cosmopolitanism. The path to becoming a citizen of the world lay within one's self. First and foremost, urban men had to fashion themselves into cosmopolitan leaders through a variety of civil actions. Yet aspiring cosmopolitans required specific environments to reach their full potential. As demonstrated in chapter 1, British American tavern goers cultivated exclusive spaces devoted to gentility: coffeehouses and city taverns. Aligning with similar efforts surrounding academies and libraries, self-conscious gentlemen used these arenas of civility to barricade themselves from their supposed inferiors. They could sip beverages sourced from around the world among carefully arranged mahogany and gilded furniture, convene in invitation-only clubs and, most important, assert themselves as important, reflective members of civil society. Having adequately fashioned themselves and their public environments according to prevailing notions of cosmopolitan civility, elitist urbanites assumed that they could then extend their sphere of influence throughout the rest of the colonies and, they hoped, the British Empire. Developing along prescribed lines of hierarchy, nationalism, and order, British American civil society would become more successful by the day.

With roots in ancient history, cosmopolitanism has long been an ideal of international humanity. Enlightenment thinkers took much of their understanding of cosmopolitanism from Roman Stoic philosophers, who embraced four common themes: first, humans are part of a larger community and share responsibility as well as a similar moral and political fate; second, humans have a common capacity for reason and communication, which forms the basis of their community; third, there is a universal natural law and teleological purpose to humanity; and fourth, human reason should be in harmony with nature and universal law.[4] To the Roman Stoics, cosmopolitanism was a philosophy devoted to altruism and acceptance—a lofty but in their minds achievable goal for the future of a civil society.

Although the Roman definition of cosmopolitanism as a unifying goal of universal human equality remained relatively intact into the eighteenth century, Britons steadily adjusted the philanthropic theory to fit their personal and imperial agendas. A "citizen of the world" as an eighteenth-century Briton understood the term was "subject to no master, obeying no law, regardless of the opinions of his own times, and looking only for the esteem of the wise and the suffrage of posterity."[5] Sir Francis Bacon similarly described a cosmopolitan man as one who was "gracious and courteous to strangers" and whose heart was not "an island cut off from other lands, but a continent that joins to them."[6] The self-proclaimed citizen of the world John Knox declared that to become a cosmopolite, one must "be of no nation, no partial plan of politics," and "consider, in every point of view, the pretensions, the just claims, and the rights of one country as well as those of the other."[7] According to his 1763 eulogy, a Mr. Kennedy who possessed Boston's various cosmopolitan attributes—a "Thirst for knowledge," wide travels, self-improvement, familiarity with a variety of languages, and "openness of mind"—had defined him as a true citizen of the world.[8] The Earl of Chesterfield contended in 1759, "To sacrifice one's own self love to other peoples is a short, but I believe, a true definition of civility."[9] Here Chesterfield, like so many other Britons throughout the empire, combined ideals of civility and cosmopolitanism into a workable ideology.[10]

The journey to becoming a citizen of the world was complicated, for those middling- and upper-class gentlemen who claimed to distance themselves from irrational local and national bias were often the same men expected to support the British Empire without question. As the historian Roy Porter noted, "The eighteenth century brought conflicts of allegiances for intellectuals, torn between cosmopolitan leanings and local loyalties."[11] With the fear of being labeled unpatriotic, or even worse, traitorous, British American cosmopolites attempted to discern between rational and irrational patriotism. One anonymous writer in the December 11, 1752, edition of the *New-York Mercury* contended that a "ridiculous and absurd" patriotism was one marred by irrational, unbending cultural and social myopia. In contrast, rational, benevolent, and enlightened worldliness defined the sober, sensible cosmopolitan patriot. He would "deliberate[,] . . . resolve," and "rise into Action with a Heart undismayed, and a Courage invincible," the contributor to the *Mercury* added. Moreover, beyond simply loving his country, a true cosmopolitan patriot would also become "a *Lover of Mankind*," which was "far more noble and God-like."[12] In order to resolve the seemingly inherent contradictions between excess patriotism and moderate cosmopolitanism, gentlemen touted sensible cosmopolitanism as the most noble, rational, and enlightened path to a modern patriotism.[13] Cosmopolitan hopefuls realized their fates were firmly intertwined with the British Empire and thus adjusted their ideological goals to bolster this all-encompassing, global entity.[14]

Midcentury elitist colonists such as Benjamin Franklin and Dr. Alexander Hamilton tied themselves to global networks to foster their cosmopolitan identities. Franklin, for instance, described himself as "a man of the world" and required members of his Junto Club, itself an organization intent on fostering enlightened cosmopolitanism, to declare that they "love[d] mankind in general; of what profession or religion soever." Dr. Hamilton similarly professed his aspirations to achieve cosmopolitanism by dissociating himself from certain New York City tavern-going "fops" with "narrow notions, ignorance of the world, and low extraction" who "commonly held their heads higher than the rest of mankind and imagined few or none were their equals."[15]

Though Franklin is often touted as a classic embodiment of British American civil cosmopolitanism, Hamilton exemplified colonial cosmopolites' proclivity for criticism of their fellow colonists in his description of the New York City "fops." In Dr. Hamilton's opinion, the problem with these "aggrandized upstarts in these infant countrys of America" stemmed from their inattention to the world around them, which in turn denied them the capacity to "observe the different ranks of men in polite nations or to know what it is that really constitutes that difference or degrees."[16] Not only were these "fops" narrow-minded in Dr. Hamilton's view, but their inability to understand the necessity of hierarchy also made them dangerous to civil society. These were not idle concerns. Civil and uncivil facets of urban society struggled to find balance in the milieu of the colonial city.

City taverns and coffeehouses largely fulfilled cosmopolites' material and ideological needs, as they afforded gentlemen unmatched opportunities for sociability with genteel men from near and far. Important nodes where patrons could meet "for the purpose of rational conversation, and to learn news," these exclusive spaces helped cosmopolites such as William Black to extend their worldviews beyond "the Length of [their] Nose."[17] As one globetrotting British tavern goer poetically explained, "Mountains could not, but men who go and see the world can, meet each other."[18] Following the Englishman William Hutton's contention that "the intercourse of one with another, like two blocks of marble in friction, reduces the rough prominences of behaviour, and gives a polish to the manners," colonists such as Dr. Hamilton sought out tavern conversations with men from around the world. Communicating with diverse peoples, gentlemen like Hutton argued, would "render men sociable" and consequently provide them with yet another set of civil attributes.[19]

Dr. Hamilton's North American peregrinations provide a keen opportunity to peer into aspiring cosmopolites' city tavern and coffeehouse interactions with various foreigners. Upon arriving in Philadelphia in 1744, Dr. Hamilton found refuge in a city tavern, where he shared a table with a "mixed company" of "Scots, English, Dutch, Germans, and Irish[,] . . . Roman Catholicks, Church men, Presbyterians, Quakers, Newlightmen, Methodists, Seventh day men, Moravians, Anabaptists, and one Jew." As the men's bellies were full and their spirits light, they drifted into conversations on politics and the possibility of war with the French. Dr. Hamilton eavesdropped on a group of Quakers discussing transatlantic flour prices and religious change while a gentleman next to him inquired about news regarding Maryland. Later in his Philadelphia stay, Dr. Hamilton discussed the merits of the Freemasons with "a Barbadian gentleman" and shared a quick lunch with "a trader from Jamaica" in two separate Philadelphia taverns. One "gentleman . . . from Coracao [Curaçao]" confided in Hamilton the devastating death toll of his home island while they lounged in a New York City tavern.[20] Dr. Hamilton could hardly help but rub elbows with gentlemen from beyond North America's shores in his urban tavern visits.

Dr. Hamilton was not the only colonist who recognized the opportunities for interaction with men from around the world in urban taverns and coffeehouses. James Birket, for example, noted in 1751 that taverns in the city of Portsmouth, New Hampshire (with a population of around 4,500 at midcentury), were "little frequented by any but Strangers."[21] William Byrd II—who described himself as one who "knows the World perfectly well, and thinks himself a citizen of it without the . . . distinctions of kindred sect or Country"—delighted at dining with "a Frenchman of great learning" at a Williamsburg tavern. And Nicholas Cresswell confirmed Byrd's mention of French company later in the eighteenth century when he remarked on the "Great numbers of French men" in Williamsburg's taverns. The Dutch Labadist, Jasper Danckaerts, noted that he met one tavern goer in New York City "who had formerly lived in Brazil, and whose heart was still full of it." Benjamin Franklin remembered conversing with a fellow in a tavern outside of Philadelphia who he supposed had been "an itinerant Doctor, for there was no Town in England, or Country in Europe, of which he could not give a very particular Account."[22] As perhaps the most multifaceted public spaces in British American cities, taverns and coffeehouses brimmed with guests from around the world. Aspiring cosmopolites had only to seek them out.

Like the British American gentlemen who frequented common social spaces to enhance their own knowledge and sociability, travelers from abroad utilized British American city taverns and coffeehouses to interact with locals. While visiting New York City in the first half of the eighteenth century, the Irish Huguenot John Fontaine entered genteel taverns to enmesh himself in civil society. Once included, he participated in French and Irish clubs and gossiped and dined with all sorts of locals, ranging from lawyers to landladies.[23] The Londoner Alexander Mackraby also frequented taverns and coffeehouses during his mid-eighteenth-century tour of North America. Mackraby noted that in his tavern interactions he "made about three times as many acquaintance" as his local friend acquired "in so many years. . . . I dine with governors, colonels, and the Lord knows who." Mackraby later "danced, sung, and romped and eat and drank, and kicked away care from morning till night" in a genteel tavern with twenty-nine Philadelphians.[24] Though generally incredulous in his opinion on British America's various drinking spaces, Mackraby could not deny their social and cultural importance. While global travelers utilized urban taverns and coffeehouses as places of lodging, drink, information, gossip, and ties to home, they also afforded British American cosmopolites unrivaled international connections. There were few other chances for a Dutch Labadist and a down-on-his-luck English gentleman to confide in each other.[25] Consequently, colonists and travelers alike sought out taverns and coffeehouses for connections they could gain in no other colonial public space.

As consumer goods, flashy exhibits, and random tavern conversations provided colonial gentlemen with the international interactions they craved, well-organized, male-dominated tavern clubs became one of cosmopolites' most dominant pursuits. Britons established as many as twenty-five thousand clubs and societies throughout the empire during the eighteenth century. A number of these clubs emerged in North America's bustling urban centers.[26] One colonist explained, "Our little Clubs or Societies are the last Things we take our Leave of. . . . They must have them in Coffee-Houses, Taverns, or private Assemblies: And few are able to live without 'em."[27] As spaces "where Taste is refin'd, and a Relish giv'n to Men's Possessions, by a polite Skill in gratifying their Passions and Appetites," city taverns and coffeehouses became central to the transatlantic craze for gentlemen's private tavern clubs.[28]

A prime public arena for cosmopolitans-in-the-making was the male-dominated, exclusive, tavern club, and Dr. Alexander Hamilton is one of the most famous cosmopolitan clubbers in British American history. Born into the Scottish gentry in Edinburgh in 1712, Dr. Hamilton received a genteel education that spanned Scotland, England, and Holland before heading to Maryland in the winter of 1738 to pursue his profession as a physician.[29] The Scottish immigrant shortly thereafter, in 1739, joined the Ugly Club—a group of men who met mainly "to argue and debate upon various Subjects, and to discuss points of a knotty and abstruse nature"—but this club did not satisfy his cosmopolitan yearnings, nor did his lifelong position as Annapolis's common councilman.[30] Somewhat ironically, Dr. Hamilton's bout with tuberculosis spurred him to delve into British America's intellectual, cosmopolitan public scene as he traveled North America's northeastern seaboard in 1744 to escape Maryland's muggy summer.

He visited a variety of urban societies during his journey, including the Hungarian Club (a group of New York City gentlemen who, for some reason, pretended they were Hungarian), the "Physicall Club" (a medical society formed by Boston's gentlemen), the Scots' Quarterly Society (a group of Bostonians who touted their connections to Scotland), the Music Club (a coterie of Philadelphians who loved music), the Governor's Club (an assembly of the New York governor's choosing), and numerous other unnamed groups. While clubs became popular forms of tavern-going culture in the mid-eighteenth century, one of their primary connecting fibers remained the larger goal of cosmopolitan civility. Aspiring gentlemen like Dr. Hamilton liked to publicly avoid clubs dominated by drinking, whoring, gluttony, and carousing, instead opting for more polite, erudite clubs that, as "Per Se" of the "American Royal Society," wrote, sought "to improve the *Taste*, and *Knowledge*, to *Reform*, and *Correct*, the manners" of their members.[31] Dr. Hamilton especially enjoyed the Governor's Club in New York City, which he described as "a society [of] gentlemen that meet at a tavern every night and converse on various subjects." With "entertaining" conversation ranging from international trade and politics to "English poets and foreign writers," a mixed company of strangers and important locals (including the governor), and plenty of good food and drink, the Governor's Club met most of the condescending physician's cosmopolitan expectations.[32] Within this collectively and self-consciously genteel space, Dr. Hamilton could interact with men from his own station while also indirectly contributing to a larger, enlightened conversation.[33]

Yet not every club experience satisfied Dr. Hamilton's cosmopolitan cravings. One evening, Hamilton fell in with a group of "two or three toapers" (colonists often referred to fellow, loquacious drinkers as "topers") in New York City's Hungarian Club who "seemed to be of opinion that a man could not have a more sociable quality . . . than to be able to pour down seas of liquor and remain unconquered while others sunk under the table."[34] Falling to their challenge that night, Dr. Hamilton left drunk from alcohol rather than enlightened from cosmopolitan debate. Another evening in Newport, Dr. Hamilton was a bit disappointed to realize that the Philosophical Club's members did not deliberate on erudite matters but rather prated on about "privateering and building of vessels[,] . . . disputes and controversys of the fanaticks of these parts, their declarations, recantations, letters, advices, remonstrances, and other such damnd stuff of so little consequence to the benefit of mankind or the publick." Considering his time spent with the Philosophical Club "thrown away," Dr. Hamilton went elsewhere for a more cosmopolitan variety of company.[35]

As a principal facet of club interaction, improving conversation became a "pragmatic arena for 'politeness'" in the British Empire.[36] Early modern gentlemen published countless works in newspapers, periodicals, and broadsides detailing proper and improper conversation etiquette. In a November 15, 1750, issue of the *Pennsylvania Gazette*, for example, an author warned how "a Man of Wit and Learning may nevertheless make himself a disagreeable Companion." Self-professed gentlemen viewed excessive boasting and drinking as especially inconsiderate and unbecoming of a "man who loves company" and is "formed for [civil] society." A polite conversation "in company" thus required constant pragmatism, self-awareness, and discretion. One had to be careful to distinguish himself as civil and clever while not becoming too witty or loquacious: a man could make conversation enjoyable and improving or utterly destructive.[37]

Beyond the balancing act of gentility and wit, discretion "in company" was a maxim of supposedly cosmopolitan conversation. As one New York City gentleman exclaimed in the *New-York Weekly Journal* on January 9, 1748, "the bad faculty of *Tattling*" was "not only base and unworthy of a Gentleman, but destructive to the very end of Private Societies." In this gentleman's opinion, "Relating Matters" of a discreet conversation to the general public only "promotes Dissentions, raises Quarrels, and is the Source of unspeakable Confusion and Disorder." "Tattling," quite simply, fractured civil society. Just as these cosmopolites sought privacy and genteel conversation in the tavern space, they also expected members to uphold such exclusivity by keeping topics of conversations to themselves. A loose tongue could only destroy the respectability, honor, and sanctity of a cosmopolitan club setting.

Even if gathering within their own city tavern or coffeehouse, elitist colonists organized their clubs according to strict notions of internal exclusivity. The tendency of cosmopolite clubbers to assemble in a separate, isolated room was in line with their feelings of selective company. While attending a club at Withered's Tavern in Boston, Hamilton embarrassed himself twice by sitting with the wrong club after leaving his own assembly to talk with the tavern keeper. The first time Hamilton stepped into the wrong room he mustered an apology, but on his second "slip" he was so confused and "saw them so inclinable to laugh that [he] ran out at the door precipitately without saying any thing" and hurried to "the right company."[38] These were not men who welcomed a stranger into their exclusive space, ranks, and conversation. Rather, one had to be invited to a club by its members and prove himself worthy of such an audience through correct conversation and conduct.

Cosmopolitan clubbers also shunned fellows who displayed poor conversational abilities. John Adams lamented that the Boston lawyer James Otis would "spoil the Clubb" because he "talkes so much and takes up so much of our Time, and fills it with Trash, Obsceneness, Profaneness, Nonsense and Distraction, that We have no [time] left for rational Amusements or Enquiries." Wealth did not always equal cosmopolitanism or civility. Thus while Adams and his fellow cosmopolites initially welcomed Otis into their ranks because of his social and hierarchical standing, Otis's weaknesses in conversation, conduct, and civility unsettled his standing in their exclusive club.[39]

Dr. Hamilton reflected on the core principles and quality of discussion in his numerous club experiences. He fondly remembered the "agreeable and instructing" conversation available among "a company of philosophers and men of sense" at the Governor's Club in Philadelphia and lamented the company of "One Mr. Clackenbridge" who used a club at Withered's genteel Boston tavern to constantly "argue against all the company . . . like a confused logician." For all these positive and negative conversations, however, Dr. Hamilton's disdain for one fellow New York City tavern clubber named Dr. McGraa outshone any other conversationalist in his travels. Although McGraa came across as a modest man, "when the liquor began to heat [McGraa] a little, he talked at the rate of three words in a minute." Dr. Hamilton remarked that he "never met a man so wrapt up in himself," nor did he "ever see a face where there was so much effronterie under a pretended mask of modesty." In Dr. Hamilton's opinion, McGraa was just the sort of man who tarnished the delicate sheen of civil society.[40]

A subsequent heated tavern dispute between Dr. Hamilton and McGraa reflected the intricacies of polite conversation and the ongoing quest for civil cosmopolitanism. Although Dr. Hamilton regretted the harsh exchange of "hard physicall terms" during a discussion of the effect of the moon on liquids, and therefore tried to discontinue the debate, "it being dissonant to good manners before company, and what none but rank pedants will be guilty of," McGraa kept "teizing" him. Dr. Hamilton found himself embroiled in a quarrel of words with McGraa, "one of those learned bullys who, by loud talking and an affected sneer, seem to outshine all other men in parts of literature where the company are by no means proper judges." The Annapolis doctor found McGraa to be the sort of man knowledgeable enough to masquerade as a gentleman among lesser company but not polite enough to actually serve as one. When McGraa declared that he was "troubled with open piles" and "pulled out a linnen handkercheff all stained with blood and showed it to the company," Dr. Hamilton lashed out at McGraa by comparing his bloody condition to that of a woman's menstruation cycle. Dr. Hamilton claimed he "only intended to play upon" McGraa, but the doctor took Hamilton's quip as an affront and challenged him to a battle of the wits. After McGraa proclaimed his knowledge of "attraction, condensation, gravitation, rarification," and mathematical and astronomical theories, he also professed his supposed cosmopolitanism by pretending "to have traveled most countrys in Europe, to have shared favour and acquaintance of some foreign princes and grandees and to have been at their tables, to be master of several languages." Dr. Hamilton gave McGraa up "as an unintelligent, unintelligible, and consequently inflexible disputant" who could not speak good French and "merely murdered Latin" and thus retired from this unfortunate tavern conversation.[41]

McGraa was, for a knowledgeable gentleman like Dr. Hamilton, the epitome of a fool impersonating a gentleman. Besides requiring over-indulgence of alcohol to hold a conversation, McGraa "spoke in a very arbitrary tone as if his opinion was to pass for an ipse dixit (the truth)," bullied lesser men into listening to him, and committed an act that "exceeded everything [Hamilton] had seen for nastiness, impudence, and rusticity" when he displayed his bloodstained handkerchief at the food-laden club table. When Dr. Hamilton chided McGraa with what he perceived as a playful, scientific reprimand, the drunken McGraa once again overstepped the bounds of civility by bluntly professing his own learned attributes (which Dr. Hamilton passed off as unintelligible and false). Although this exchange was quite different from so many other "agreeable and instructing" conversations that Dr. Hamilton sought out in clubs, it nonetheless revealed the conflicts, contradictions, and intricacies of cosmopolitan conversation.[42] Those who did not follow the rules were ousted from a cosmopolitan coterie.

The Contradictions of Cosmopolitanism

Having established their own city taverns and coffeehouses where they could mix with the men, ideas, and consumer goods of their choice, British American cosmopolites felt that they could truly craft themselves and their society into civil manifestations of imperial might. Yet what emerged was not a civil society defined by acceptance and worldliness.

Rather, in their numerous attempts to become cosmopolitan and, in turn, shape a British American civil society, colonial cosmopolites actually reinforced and exposed their own ethnocentrism and internal contradictions. Struggling with a bruising inferiority complex, colonial American gentlemen arguably fostered more heightened ideologies of ethnocentrism and social difference than their English, metropolitan compatriots, who believed with little doubt that they resided in the most civil, forward-thinking society in the world. Of course, civil cosmopolitanism was just as much of a pipe dream in England as it was in North America, but Englishmen retained stronger *confidence* in their own societal progress.[43] Colonists, meanwhile, understood that they lived in a land three thousand miles from London, with a lack of Old World cities, larger numbers of unfree and "savage" peoples, and expansive tracts of unimproved "wilderness." They had their work cut out for them.

British American gentlemen's shared notions of British Protestant superiority—which they adopted from English and Scottish Enlightenment thinkers—compounded their underlying nationalistic and hierarchical biases and anxieties. As Governor Thomas Pownall of Massachusetts asserted in his inauguration speech in 1757, "Where the spirit of Virtue and Knowledge is, there is Civil and Religious Liberty; I shall therefore always support the one, as I mean conscientiously to maintain the other." For Pownall and so many other colonists, being a Briton meant being a Protestant, and vice versa: British American civil society should be based on "Civil [i.e. British] and Religious [i.e., Protestant] Liberty." Imperial success was thus firmly tied to the Christian mission.[44]

Just as Britons jealously guarded their Protestant civilizing mission, so too did they often understand difference—whether in creed, nationality, or social status—to signify inferiority. Catholics and their Native American allies endured opinions ranging from suspicion to outright hate, while French, Dutch, and Spanish visitors to the colonies were met with condescension and derision. During the throes of the French and Indian War (1754–63), Virginia's governor contended that the colonies' most important mission was to preserve "the most invaluable, and by all Mankind esteemed, the most dear and most desirable of all human Treasures, Religious and Civil [British] Liberty" from the savagery of the French and their Indian allies. In many colonists' minds, "the true Spirit of Patriotism" and "Duty to the King and Love for your Duty to the King and Love for your Country" was an ultimate signifier of British identity. Civil cosmopolites set an example of myopic prejudice, not worldly tolerance.[45]

Although aspiring cosmopolitans often touted city taverns and coffeehouses as the perfect places in which to meet foreigners, they often lauded these same establishments for the exclusive Anglocentric societies that congregated within their walls.[46] The Freemasons often convened in genteel coffeehouses and city taverns. In Philadelphia, they met at the "Tun Tavern" where "a very Elegant Entertainment was provided" and "several . . . Persons of Distinction" often "honour'd the Society with their Presence."[47] Along with many other British American clubs and societies, the Freemasons allegedly urged members of the Society "not only [to] refrain from Prejudices, but cheerfully condescend to equal Terms," but contradictorily they upheld notions of hierarchy and deference.[48] Although the historian Margaret Jacobsen suggested that the Freemasons became "a social nexus that bridged profound class differences," on closer investigation the British American Masonic Society concurred in its club practices with the elitist colonists' desire for intense social stratification.[49] At their rule-bound, secretive tavern meetings, patrician men donned aprons and jewels and studied the tradition of the magical arts in search of a universal wisdom. Furthermore, while the oft-ridiculed Freemasons professed openness to members of all social backgrounds, elitist Masonic rulers like Benjamin Franklin excluded the majority by privileging "brothers of talent and orators of merit." Talent and merit remained entirely subjective, and those men deemed acceptable in such skills (especially in public speaking) mostly came from wealthy or cosmopolitan backgrounds. A cooper's apprentice hardly had the time or resources to study Demosthenes and fine-tune his balance of wit. The Freemasons, in other words, pursued a cosmopolitanism that thrived on exclusivity.[50]

While the Freemasons are among the most studied and controversial of all colonial American fraternal organizations, numerous other Anglocentric societies found their way to British America's taverns and coffeehouses. Ethnic societies were especially popular in British America. Boston supported a Scots Society after 1658; New York harbored an Irish club in 1716 and its own Scots Society in 1744; and Philadelphia boasted the Society of Ancient Britons after 1729, an informal St. George's Society from the 1730s, and a well-ordered St. Andrew's Society after 1747.[51] Established in London in 1715 to demonstrate Welsh loyalty to the Crown (in the face of Jacobinism), the Society of Ancient Britons often advertised their meetings in the *Pennsylvania Gazette* after instituting themselves in Philadelphia.[52] The Society frequently held feasts "in Honour of Her Majesty Queen CAROLINE'S Birth Day, and the Principality

of WALES" on St. David's Day at "the Indian King in Market Street."
With tickets priced at five shillings, however, these feasts were reserved
for the city's "Hon. Proprietor, Governor, and principle Gentlemen."[53]
Other ethnic societies like the Scottish-centric St. Andrew's Society also
utilized the *Pennsylvania Gazette* to announce meetings and functions
at the Tun Tavern until they established their own lodge in 1759.[54]

Besides serving the somewhat cosmopolitan purpose of connecting members throughout the empire, British American ethnic societies such as the Society of Ancient Britons and St. Andrew's bolstered
potent nationalistic feelings. As the Scottish Bostonian Benjamin Colman noted in the early eighteenth century, "Strangers from Great Britain
love one another's company and draw one another off." Having recently
immigrated to Philadelphia from Edinburgh, Andrew Elliot similarly
remarked in 1750 that "even Country borne [colonists] call Britain . . .
home."[55] Colonial gentlemen might live in North America, but the
majority found their true identity in Britannia's shores. Hence their
ongoing efforts to cultivate a British-style civil society and exclude those
they deemed unworthy of that society.

British colonists went to great lengths in their tavern interactions to
seek out their "countrymen." While traveling through the colonies, Scottish-born Dr. Hamilton conversed with any Scottish natives he encoun-
tered "about affairs at home." Hamilton bought his "countrywoman Mrs.
Blackater" (his Boston tavern keeper) a pound of chocolate, met with
"Mr. Grant, a Scotch gentleman," in a Newport coffeehouse, and noted
that his Albany "landlady, happening to be a Scotswoman, was very civil
and obliging to me for country's sake." While staying in Boston, Hamilton was sure to visit the Scots' Quarterly Society, "which met att the
Sun Taveren." After contributing "3 pounds New England currency" for
the relief of Scotland's poor, Hamilton stayed to chat with the Society's
president about (presumably Scottish) "news and politicks."[56] The Irish
Huguenot John Fontaine similarly spent at least two evenings "with the
Irish Club" while staying in New York in 1716.[57] Finally, the "bored" and
homesick Scottish gentleman living in South Carolina, Alexander Gordon, joined the Charleston branch of the St. Andrew's Society in order
to connect with his home country as well as gain a stronger foothold
among the most powerful men in the province, including the Reverend Henry Heywood, a Baptist preacher "esteemed one of the greatest
scholars in *America*."[58] Although such actions might be written off as
homesickness, the fact that Hamilton, Fontaine, and Gordon sought
out certain taverns with the express purpose of conversing with fellow

countrymen also speaks to tavern goers' entrenched nationalism. Ethnic societies were hardly cosmopolitanism in the literal sense of the term but were in perfect line with colonial gentlemen's sense of self. They were exclusive spaces for like-minded men from similar backgrounds to meet, converse, and distinguish themselves from their uncivil, not to mention foreign, compatriots.

In their numerous attempts to become cosmopolitan, then, gentlemen reinforced and exposed their ethnocentrism. Traveling through the North American colonies in the second half of the eighteenth century, Nicholas Cresswell engaged himself in countless cosmopolitan pursuits. The aspiring gentleman attended balls where "Punch, Wines, Coffee and Chocolate" were served, enjoyed the company of "sensible, polite" men in various taverns, helped to found "the Black-eyed Club" in one Virginia tavern, constantly sought out global news, sipped coffee in public and private venues, complimented one fellow because he had "seen a great deal of the World," dined with a group of Frenchmen in Hampton, Virginia, and befriended a group of Scotsmen.[59] Cresswell's friendship with his "good friends," the Scotsmen "Mr. Bailey, Captn. B. Knox and Mr. Wallace," especially displayed his cosmopolitan hopes. These gentlemen had cared for Cresswell when he was deathly ill after arriving in the colonies. Upon leaving his Scottish friends, Cresswell remembered how he had once disliked their nation. "Owing to the prejudice of [his British] education," Cresswell "was taught to look upon [the Scots] as a set of men divested of common humanity, ungenerous and unprincipled." Yet after enjoying the company and largess of the Scots, Cresswell openly exclaimed:

> I have always found them the reverse of all this, and I most heartily condemn this pernicious system of education by which are taught to look upon the inhabitants of a different nation, language or complexion, as a set of being far inferior to our own. This is a most illiberal and confined sentiment, for human nature is invariably the same throughout the whole human species, from the sooty Africans down to the fair European, allowance being made for their different customs, manners and education.

Recognizing the error of his learned bias, Cresswell touted a cosmopolitan worldview in which "human nature is invariably the same throughout the whole human species." He made allowances for the "different customs, manners, and education" of the Earth's various peoples and seemingly accepted them as equals.[60]

Yet in line with cosmopolites throughout the British Empire, Cresswell's cosmopolitan acceptance was more imagined than real and more based on strict social stratification and national bias than tolerance. Less than two months after his supposed revelation about the Scottish character and universal acceptance, Cresswell confirmed his complicated sense of cosmopolitanism, hierarchy, and nationalism during a visit to Long Island, New York. While walking home from a tavern, Cresswell and his friend, Mr. Furneval, came across a young woman in distress. Finding the lone woman in labor, Cresswell and Furneval carried her to the nearest building, owned by an "Irish rogue of a sadler." Cresswell watched as an "old drunken woman" delivered the young woman's child. Although the birth gladdened Furneval (he swore he would "stand God-father to the child"), Cresswell's coldness emerged in his belief that the bastard child would be "dead before morning." After the young woman recounted "a long story about her virtue and sufferings," Cresswell indifferently concluded that he did not believe her "since she [was] an Irish woman."[61] Here Cresswell—the man who less than two months earlier had self-consciously declared that he accepted everyone—not only pronounced a young woman's story moot because of her perceived Irish heritage but also deemed her newborn child good-as-dead. No amount of tavern clubs, genteel traditions, international goods, or worldly literature could destroy the entrenched national and hierarchical biases of cosmopolites like Cresswell.

Cresswell was not alone in his intolerant behavior. Although historians have lauded Dr. Hamilton for his general tolerance, his interactions with foreigners and strangers demonstrated the tension between his cosmopolitan urges and his deeply entrenched notions of superiority.[62] Like so many other supposed cosmopolites, Dr. Hamilton could not shed the cloak of chauvinism and hierarchy in favor of a universally tolerant one: he simply adjusted cosmopolitanism to fit his ideals of civil society.[63]

A not uncommon tendency among eighteenth-century Britons was to generalize all other nations' behavior and characteristics.[64] Throughout his British American travels, Dr. Hamilton constantly remarked on "general" features of the French, especially their supposed loquaciousness. Dr. Hamilton noted that his French tavern keeper in Boston "had much of the humour of that nation [France], a deal of talk, and a deal of action." While dining at a Boston exchange, Dr. Hamilton (a speaker of French) described a group of French prisoners as "very loquacious, after the manner of their nation." The next day, the Annapolis physician breakfasted with his French tavern keeper and her daughter. He noted that the young Frenchwoman was "a passable handsom girl" and displayed "nothing of the French spirit in her but rather too grave and sedate." After speaking with "a very handsome . . . and well behaved" Spanish prisoner, Dr. Hamilton remarked that the Spaniard engendered "none of that stiffness and solemnity about him commonly ascribed to their nation but [was] perfectly free and easy in his behaviour, rather bordering upon the French vivacity."[65]

Eighteenth-century Anglo-French relations were marked by tension and occasional rancor. Since France posed the biggest challenge to Britain's imperial goals, subjects of the British Crown constantly sought to prove the inferiority of their French rivals. Yet Britain's relationship with France was more complicated than sheer hatred. For many British gentlemen, demonstrating one's knowledge of French culture symbolized one's gentility and cosmopolitanism. French and British cosmopolites, after all, traveled the same lands, consumed the same goods, read the same books, enjoyed similar public amusements, and followed similar aristocratic customs. Lower-class Britons, however, generally detested Francophone ways. A group of common Dorset citizens jeered at the French traveler Macky as he walked through their streets, screaming "Frenchie" at him, and the German composer Leopold Mozart complained during his stay in London, "Whenever the street urchins see anyone decked out and dressed in a vaguely French way, they immediately call out: Bugger French! French bugger!"[66] Although upper-class Britons overtly flaunted their English pride while visiting France, they often spoke French, dressed in the French fashion, read French literature, and generally "acted French" on returning home. Yet, as illustrated by Mozart's experience, displaying one's French leanings was a dangerous game, as too much French dress or custom could cause a gentleman to be labeled a "frenchified coxcomb," or worse, traitorous. Gentlemen throughout the empire thus stressed Francophilia as yet another defining factor of becoming a citizen of the world but did so carefully.[67]

But just because British cosmopolites touted their French acceptance did not mean that they fully embraced Francophone ways. In fact, even if certain Britons did believe themselves to be especially cosmopolitan, they often still harbored deep-set, complicated, and contradictory prejudices toward France, in addition to ascribing demeaning characteristics, including loquaciousness and bad hygiene, to the French. Professing one's inclusive worldview remained a rather superficial attempt to associate one's self with larger ideas of cosmopolitan civility. Actually *practicing* such cosmopolitan professions was something else entirely.[68]

Dr. Hamilton's extended stay at a Boston tavern provides a window into the complications inherent in British views of the French and in turn the prejudiced view of a self-professed cosmopolite. Although this experience afforded Hamilton an unrivaled opportunity to objectively observe one Frenchman, it reinforced his bias and xenophobia. When Hamilton first met Monsieur de la Moinerie at a tavern in Boston, he described the Frenchman as "chatter[ing] like a magpie in his own language," and further acquaintance with his "fellow lodger" only bolstered his British presumptions. Dr. Hamilton noted that La Moinerie "was the strangest mortal for eating I ever knew" after noticing that the Frenchman ate all his meals on a trunk in his disorderly room: "here a bason with relicts of some soup, there a fragment of bread, here a paper of salt, there a bundle of garlick, here a spoon with some pepper in it, and upon a chair a saucer of butter." To Hamilton's surprise, La Moinerie also employed the same basin to eat soup, clean cabbage, shave, and bathe. Compared to the hypersensitive sensibilities of a self-professed British gentleman like Hamilton, this supposedly polite Frenchman's seemingly uncivil behavior was nothing short of shocking. Never mind that, as an early modern Briton, Dr. Hamilton would have rarely bathed, nor would his eating habits have satisfied twenty-first-century standards.[69]

Despite the Annapolis doctor's condescension, after weeks of "comicall chat" with La Moinerie, he realized that he was going to miss the loquacious Frenchman. Hamilton lamented on departing Boston:

> Nothing I regretted so much as parting with La Moinerie, the most lively and merry companion ever I had met with, always gay and chearfull, now dancing and then singing tho every day in danger of being made a prisoner. This is the peculiar humour of the French in prosperity and adversity. Their temper is always alike, far different from the English who, upon the least misfortune, are for the most part cloggd and overclouded with melancholy and vapours and, giving way to hard fortune, shun all gaiety and mirth.[70]

Although Hamilton fostered a more amiable attitude toward the French than most Britons—especially considering that King George's War between France and England (1744–48) raged when he met La Moinerie—he was still not able to divorce himself from ingrained prejudice, noting even after his close friendship with La Moinerie that the French "temper is always alike."[71] Consuming international goods as well as reading and discussing works on international topics might have made men like Hamilton more familiar with the world around them, but it did not dispel their deeply entrenched ethnocentricity, nor did it erase chauvinism toward their most significant imperial opponents. In fact, such enhanced acquaintance with the larger world might have done as much to bolster Britons' sense of superiority as it did to dispel any such notions.

The French and Indian War (1754–63) only fanned the flames of an already raging fire of anti-French, anti-Catholic sentiment in the British Empire in America. One Philadelphian who called himself "Philanthropos" warned "the Inhabitants of Pennsylvania" in 1754 that because the "French have long meditated our Ruin" and schemed "for universal Empire in North America," the colonists had no choice but to band together against "those inhuman Butchers . . . of that anti-Christian Church." Philanthropos' detestations resounded throughout colonial taverns after 1754. Albany's leaders toasted to the "total Extinction" of Catholic France's "Fortresses in America" in 1756, while a group of New York City gentlemen assembled in 1759 to express their "Gratitude and Joy" about British success in "the Reduction of that long dreaded Sink of French Perfidy and Cruelty, Quebec." A "Society of Gentlemen," finally, convened in Philadelphia's recently opened "British Punch-House" in 1759 to form the "Antigallican Society." Originally established in England around 1745 to oppose French goods in and French influence on English society, the Anti-Gallican Society of Philadelphia sought out "all such Gentlemen, who have a hearty Zeal for the Honour and Prosperity of their Country."[72] Such colonial denunciations of the French were one among many from 1754 to 1763 and were not the words of men who hoped to understand or connect with their French brethren. Rather, they were indicative of British—and British American—negative sentiment toward the French empire.

Aspiring cosmopolites helped to shape a British American social world based far more on prejudice and ethnocentrism than acceptance. As French colonists like the Huguenots in South Carolina and French Canadians in New England made up a growing number of the colonial American populace, popular opinion of the French deteriorated around midcentury. Writing under a Quaker persona in his *Pennsylvania Gazette* in 1733/34, Benjamin Franklin declared that the French were "composed of the scum, the most profligate, wicked, and abandoned of the Nation . . . [who would] ravish our Wives and Daughters."[73] Such distaste trickled down to the masses. While the aforementioned New York City gentlemen convened in a tavern to celebrate the downfall of Quebec in 1759, commoners gathered outside around a raging bonfire and fireworks.[74] A Frenchman traveling in North America in 1765 worried about walking Boston's streets, as the city's "ranck Bigoted presbiterians" would not treat him well. The French Catholic man could only conclude, "Of these sort of people preserve me o Lord." Upon arriving in New York City and relying on its public spaces for sociability and sustenance, the same French journalist exclaimed, "All religions are permitted here except the roman Catholique."[75] By midcentury, anti-French sentiment raged more than ever in British America's various public spaces as the British Empire in America found itself either ramping up for, engaging in, or emerging from war with France and its Native American allies. Whether sipping a glass of Madeira in a genteel coffeehouse or pushing through a crowded tavern, colonists of every stripe increasingly defined their notions of urban civility and British pride as contrary to "others" such as the French and Native Americans.

Yet the French were not the only nation that Britons regularly opposed. Like others who espoused deep-seated prejudice toward the French, Dr. Hamilton joined a long trend of British distrust of the Dutch. Mirroring previous British generalizations of the Dutch as ungrateful, cruel, and treacherous moneygrubbers who wished only for universal monarchy and a monopoly on all trade, the supposedly cosmopolitan Hamilton exclaimed that Albany's Dutch "live in their houses . . . as if it were in prisons, all their doors and windows being perpetually shut. But the reason of this may be the little desire they have for conversation and society, their whole thoughts being turned upon profit and gain which necessarily makes them live retired and frugall. Att least this is the common character of the Dutch everywhere." In Hamilton's estimation, the Dutch cared little for cultivating or participating in civil society; the weight of their pocketbooks outstripped any proclivities to sociability and gentility. The Swedish naturalist Peter Kalm, described as "a man of broad sympathies and of cosmopolitan understanding" by the historian Oscar Handlin, similarly remarked that "the avarice, selfishness, and immeasurable love of money of the inhabitants of [largely Dutch] Albany are very well-known throughout all North America." British cosmopolites deemed the Dutch insufficiently conversational (and thus lacking in cosmopolitan virtues) because of their allegedly greedy and isolated nature. Britons accepted the supposedly loquacious but effeminate French, on the other hand, as lesser but still legitimate cosmopolitans.[76]

Benjamin Franklin, whose polite and scientific endeavors caused contemporaries to label him "a provincial cosmopolitan," also harbored intense biases against the German and Dutch nations.[77] By 1750, as more

German and Dutch immigrants flooded into Philadelphia, Franklin lamented that Pennsylvania "will in a few Years become a German Colony: Instead of [German and Dutch colonists] Learning our Language, we must learn theirs, or live as in a foreign Country." British colonists, "uneasy by the Disagreeableness" of Germans' "dissonant Manners," fled neighborhoods where German families settled. Even worse, since the Dutch immigrants "under-live[d]" (i.e., did not live up to what Franklin expected in a productive, civil citizen) and were "thereby enabled to under-work and under-sell the English," colonists became "extreamly incommoded, and consequently disgusted" by their Dutch neighbors. Franklin, who declared himself "a man of the world" and required members of his Junto Club to declare that they "love[d] mankind in general; of what profession or religion soever," had little confidence in the quality of the Dutch and Germans as British American subjects. In Franklin's words, Britons had always, through "an ardent Spirit of Liberty, so gloriously distinguished [themselves] from all the Rest of Mankind." Against this measure, non-British migrants failed all the tests.[78]

Although some colonial gentlemen utilized British American taverns as spheres of cosmopolitan interaction, they simply could not become true "citizens of the world" in the literal sense of the term. Rather, elitist colonists adjusted cosmopolitanism to fit their own hierarchically determined ideals of civility. These "Men formed for society" did everything they could to assert their authority as polite cosmopolitans in their tavern interactions, yet through and perhaps because of these efforts, anxious gentlemen did more to protect their upper-class status and reinforce their own class and national prejudices than to become "citizens of the world."[79] Though cosmopolites proclaimed to view the world as "a great school, wherein Men are first to learn, and then to practice," they could not help but constantly attempt to uphold a world where they retained control, confidence, and power.[80]

Certain colonial gentlemen thus favored cosmopolitanism not because of its solid footings in classical thought but rather because they could easily transform this mercurial ideology to support their ever-changing comprehensions of civility, order, and imperial allegiance. City taverns and coffeehouses were the perfect spaces through which to tout one's cosmopolitan identity, as they offered seemingly endless opportunities for sociability, consumerism, and—somewhat paradoxically—exclusive privacy. British American gentlemen eagerly sought to demonstrate their cosmopolitan leanings but only in the context of the hierarchy and nationalism that they held dear. Ultimately, however, anxiety and fear of societal disintegration spurred these pursuits. No matter how much sway leaders believed that they held within the walls of genteel coffeehouses or city taverns, the reality of everyday life in colonial American cities bustled just beyond their private doors. And in reality, self-professed gentlemen's power over the masses proved tenuous at best. The mass majority of colonists did not share elitist men's obsession with crafting a civil society in North America. Even if they did, they would have had a hard time coming to terms with the glaring contradictions inherent in this ideology. As would become so clear in the years leading up to the imperial rupture of 1765, the messy reality of civil society far outstripped leaders' tidy pipe dreams.

3 / "We that entertain travellers must strive to oblige every body": Urban Taverns and the Messy Reality of Civil Society

Upon arriving at a Baltimore, Maryland, tavern in 1744, Dr. Alexander Hamilton came across a "drunken club . . . of Bacchanalians" riding away "helter skelter as if the devil had possessed them, every man sitting his horse in a see-saw manner like a bunch of rags tyed upon the saddle." An elitist physician traveling up and down North America's eastern coast, Dr. Hamilton was not keen to mix with such disorderly company. "Uneasy until they were gone," Dr. Hamilton looked to the tavern keeper, who explained "that he did not care to have such disorderly fellows come about his house; he was always noted far and near for keeping a quiet house and entertaining only gentlemen or such like, but these were . . . his neighbors, and it was not prudent to disoblige them upon slight occasions." Finding Dr. Hamilton unconvinced by his apology, the contrite landlord exclaimed, "Alas, sir . . . we that entertain travellers must strive to oblige every body, for it is our dayly bread." Whether Dr. Hamilton liked it or not, most urban publicans were only concerned with keeping "the great Leviathan of Civil Society under proper discipline and order" so much as it might keep their businesses afloat in a competitive market. The reality of urban life extended well beyond gentlemen's pursuits of genteel distinction and cosmopolitanism in their private coffeehouses and city taverns, as ordinary urban taverns became symbolic spaces of the contradiction and confusion inherent in the milieu of British American urban life.[1]

As the most common drinking spaces in British America, urban taverns forced anxious gentlemen to extend themselves beyond their comfort zones and come face-to-face with the realities rather than their fantasies of British American civil society. Finding themselves in such proximity to ordinary colonists, elitist colonists *perceived* a lack of deference from their social inferiors more sharply in their mixed-class tavern interactions than perhaps anywhere else. Not only did these important public spaces harbor a diverse set of colonists in a relatively "open" space, but copious amounts of alcohol tended to disintegrate norms of interaction. Such a jumbled environment bred social confusion, which impelled colonists of every stripe to rethink notions of order and difference.

Always looking to demonstrate their power over their social inferiors, colonial gentlemen approached urban taverns with equal measures of criticism and caution. In one sense, taverns rested at the nexus of urban social interaction and were thus the perfect places to demonstrate one's superior social capital. Yet urban taverns also extended beyond staid traditions of strict order. Peter Thompson argued that eighteenth-century Philadelphia taverns permitted a "socially and culturally heterogeneous" crowd to "abandon the constraints that governed interaction in most public situations" in order to "drink alongside one another." David Conroy contended that New England tavern goers used these "public stages" to test "the authority of their rulers and social superiors in the hierarchy of Massachusetts society." Benjamin Carp brought a similarly hierarchical slant to revolutionary New York City, arguing that the city's taverns "brought together a broad array of white men and made them feel equal to any army officer, merchant, or member of Parliament of the Assembly."[2] These social anxieties compelled self-conscious leaders to confront the uncomfortable truth that their visions of order and civility were hardly a universal maxim.

Colonial gentlemen believed that the success of a British American civil society relied on a clear distinction of ranks. One midcentury Newport, Rhode Island, resident reminded his fellow citizens, "It behoves every Member of Civil Society, at all Times, to pursue that Course of Behaviour which will most effectually subserve the Peace and good Order of the Community to which he belongs." A Bostonian expanded on the Newport citizen's professions in 1757, contending, "In large and populous Cities, especially in the Metropolis of a flourishing Kingdom, Artificers, Servants and Labourers compose the Bulk of the People, and keeping them in good Order is the Object [of leaders]." For this citizen, "Religion, Education, and good Breeding" provided "the superior Rank of Mankind" the unique ability to "prevent those Disturbances, Irregularities, and Injuries to our Fellow Creatures, that happen among the

illiterate and lower Order of the People." Mercurial notions of social capital ("Religion, Education, and good Breeding"), in short, distinguished
certain men as most fit to rule society.[3]

Thus, though gentlemen repeatedly professed the importance of ordinary colonists for the maintenance of civil society, the last thing many
of them wanted was to rub elbows with their supposedly uncivil peers.
The Anglican itinerant preacher Charles Woodmason lamented being
"exposed to the Rudeness of the Mobb" after lodging in a South Carolina
tavern. John Adams recalled in 1760 that "the Rabble filled the House"
at a New England tavern; he continued, "Every room, kitchen, Chamber
was crowded with people" who danced the night away.[4] In an even more
public announcement of civil hierarchy, one man who called himself
"R.D." published a poem in the October 22, 1750, edition of the *New-York
Weekly Journal* to express his dissatisfaction at being forced to mingle
with "coarse" company during a tavern stay:

Spue-scented rooms of noisy inns,
And Chamber maids that reel!—
What sorer punishment for sins
   Can *drowsy* mortals feel?
Footmen, and fidlers, rakes, buffoons!—
   (Such company but coarse is;)
Polite, bold blust'ring *blood* and o—n!—
   With plaguy modish curses
Such *dancing!—scraping!—whistling!—bawling!*
   Wild blades, that *rant* and *roar!*—
Drunkards, that all the night are *brawling*;
   And, in the morning, *snore!*
Confounded cur, in kennel *howling*;
   (Sweet comfort, past compare!)
And, in the yard, such *catterwouling!*—
   'Twou'd make a *parson* swear.
Rather, 'twou'd make him heav'n Invoke,
   When got into a nest
Of *hellish brutes*, and dev'lish folk,
   That thus disturb'd his rest.
O hideous sign of *hell brake lose!*
   What *cursing! Stinking! Smoaking!*
Of precious time, O vile abuse!
   Most monstrous!—most provoking!

Slaves to the tyranny of *sin*!
Lew'd, filthy, desp'rate crew!
Dire medley of *infernal* din!
Adieu! Adieu! Adieu![5]

Elitist disapproval of social mixing in urban taverns reverberated throughout the colonies in the eighteenth century. Dr. Hamilton echoed Woodmason's, Adams's, and R.D.'s complaints during his 1744 intercolonial tavern peregrinations. While in one Philadelphia tavern, he disgustedly "observed severall comicall, grotesque phizzes" who "talked there upon all subjects . . . most of them ignorantly." He came across a house full of "low, rascally company" in another tavern. "Not being over fond of quarelling with such trash," the Annapolis physician left the tavern when one "sawcy fellow" tried to handle his expensive pistols without permission. The German priest Henry Melchior Muhlenberg, finally, was relieved to note in 1751, "In the evening the Lord again provided us with a room to ourselves in the [Pennsylvania] inn so that we did not have to be among the vulgar mob, though we did have to listen to their clamor and horseplay."[6] These were not men who sought out taverns for their class-mixing opportunities. Despite a series of legal measures, eighteenth-century leaders could not keep everyone they deemed socially inferior out of the tavern, let alone control them in the larger urban scene.[7]

By the early eighteenth century, colonists celebrated the expansion of their cities as indicative of their success in civilizing the supposedly savage New World, and magistrates began to contemplate in earnest how such development would affect streets, sewage systems (or the lack thereof), and food supply chains. Civilized life was not without its growing pains. With few mechanisms for social differentiation, colonial urbanites existed in a close-knit, mixed-class environment: a wealthy merchant would have shared a street with a tailor and a beggar, and all resided within one or two blocks of primary churches, city buildings, and a variety of taverns and businesses (Figure 2). While many wealthy colonists built country homes on the fringe of cities, moreover, most of their economic and social opportunities still resided in the crowded city, where these men relied on most of the same public buildings and services as poor and unfree peoples. Private haunts like coffeehouses, city taverns, and academies afforded condescending elitists only limited privacy from and even less power over the populace.[8] Such necessary class mixing raised the hackles of many self-professed leaders. If certain men were

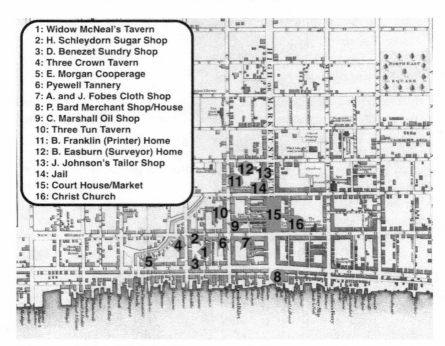

1: Widow McNeal's Tavern
2: H. Schleydorn Sugar Shop
3: D. Benezet Sundry Shop
4: Three Crown Tavern
5: E. Morgan Cooperage
6: Pyewell Tannery
7: A. and J. Fobes Cloth Shop
8: P. Bard Merchant Shop/House
9: C. Marshall Oil Shop
10: Three Tun Tavern
11: B. Franklin (Printer) Home
12: B. Easburn (Surveyor) Home
13: J. Johnson's Tailor Shop
14: Jail
15: Court House/Market
16: Christ Church

FIGURE 2. "Map of Philadelphia in 1747, with (Approximate) Locations of Businesses, Taverns, Homes, and City Structures (formulated from issues of the *Pennsylvania Gazette*, 1747)." Created by author from Benjamin Easburn, *A Plan of the City of Philadelphia, the Capital of Pennsylvania, from an Actual Survey* (London: Andrew Drury, 1776). Retrieved from the Library of Congress, Washington, DC, https://www.loc.gov/item/gm71002155/.

to direct a successful British American civil society, they believed, they needed to do so from a position of power, not while slogging through the muck of uncivil society and its denigrating pitfalls.

But certain gentlemen's disgust with class mixing had little effect on the day-to-day operations of most urban taverns. Eighteenth-century urban tavern keepers, after all, were shrewd business owners intent on serving as many customers as possible. Publicans accordingly adjusted their businesses to appease colonists of every class. They were happy to sell genteel goods to those customers who could afford them (despite how a condescending colonist might judge that person), just as they would not hesitate to expel a disorderly sot with force. Yet just because most eighteenth-century urban taverns were spaces where a "socially and culturally heterogeneous" crowd could gather together did not mean that disparate peoples melded into a homogeneous mass. On the contrary, such proximity incited more confusion than confidence and necessitated new attempts at distinction. Attempting to allay the relative commotion inherent in such class mixing while also satisfying as many customers as possible, urban tavern keepers constructed separate rooms intended for those of disparate social standing, offered goods and services of varying quality and expense, and encouraged customers to find spaces of distinction rather than inclusion. "Wealthy gentlemen and legislators" indeed attended the same taverns as "craftsmen and labourers," as certain scholars have argued, but they did not rub elbows unless absolutely necessary.[9]

The historical record contains few examples of gentlemen interacting with their supposed inferiors in urban taverns.[10] Such records, moreover, are almost exclusively from the perspective of elitist colonists, which presents an even more biased view of these interactions. The scarcity of documentation, however, can tell us much. For one thing, it might point to the simple fact that little (desired) cross-class mixing occurred in taverns. As shown by the previous anecdotes, elitist colonists did everything they could to avoid the "mob." Yet perhaps self-professed gentlemen were not alone in their urge to interact with their supposed equals. Ordinary colonists were also much more apt to drink with each other than among their social superiors. As the historian Jessica Kross contended, "Choice of drinking companions was a decision based on the human need for predictability and safety." Recent sociological research has only furthered Kross's analysis. Contending that social stratification is still "pervasive in [America's supposedly horizontally oriented] social life," in 2015 sociologists directly correlated bar patrons' inebriation with an increased preference for hierarchy and difference. Whether congregating in a British American tavern or a twenty-first-century college-town bar, patrons have long preferred to drink with those they perceive as their social equals.[11]

Despite (or perhaps because of) ordinary colonists' ubiquity in urban taverns, gentlemen patrons often perceived their social inferiors as harboring vindictive intentions. Elitist men especially feared that poor tavern goers would steal from them as they tippled among the "rabble." One Mr. Theophilus Elsworth, for instance, endured a troublesome evening in 1752 when he "had his Pocket-Book stole out of his Pocket" while supping with a mixed-class group of around twenty men in Mr. Richardson's New York City tavern, "the Sign, the Bear." Finding his pocketbook missing, Mr.

Elsworth searched everyone in the tavern but to no avail. One tavern goer, however, remembered a man "in a dirty White frock Coat with a Scar or black mark over his Eyes come into the Room whilst Elsworth was there, and leaning over Elsworth's Shoulder took up the Bowl of Punch from the Table and said here go and drank and went immediately out of the Room." Believing this tavern guest their culprit, Elsworth and a few friends took to the city's streets to find the mysterious figure in a dirty white frock coat but were once again unsuccessful. But justice ultimately prevailed. Later that same night, Kennedy, "a Servant to a Shoemaker," brought a portion of Elsworth's money back to Richardson's tavern and confessed that he had been in "bad company" with one "Journeyman Shoemaker named Roach" who had stolen the money and given Kennedy a portion to keep him quiet. While Roach was jailed for his crime and forced to return the pocketbook, he apparently managed to either spend or hide one-sixth of the wallet's original sum. For a crook like Roach, a busy, mixed-class space like Richardson's tavern was the perfect arena for crime. And poor Elsworth was not alone. Elitist colonists throughout mixed-class urban taverns reported regular thefts during the eighteenth century.[12]

Elitist patrons worried about more than theft in urban taverns. For one Bostonian who called himself "Atticus Police," the problem with class mixing in taverns came down to overt temptation. Asserting that "the Riches and Strength of [civil society]" relied on the common people "being usefully and constantly employed," this contributor to a 1757 issue of the Boston Evening-Post argued that mixed-class taverns proved too much of a "Temptation to Idleness" for ordinary colonists. Especially as ordinary colonists hobnobbed with their social superiors, the Bostonian contended, they would come into increased contact with the "Diversions . . . necessary to fill up those dismal Chasms of burdensome Time among People of Fortune" and therefore steadily fall into "all Temptations to Idleness," which would only "enervate Industry" among an already inferior set of colonists. For Atticus Police, the "mixed company" of certain urban taverns demanded an especially wary publican— a "Protestant . . . who has been bred to Trade," ideally, and who could keep those of lower standing in their rightful place, regulate their drinks, and refuse them the opportunity to participate in idle "diversions" like gaming, cards, and gambling. As in their efforts to demarcate and control society at large, gentlemen hoped to structure taverns according to the ideals of hierarchy and order.[13]

Underlying confusions and anxieties required that colonists develop a distinct language of difference—and distinction—in their tavern interactions. A Charleston tavern goer complained of being "hiss'd . . . out of Doors" in 1732 when he failed to meet the gambling expectations of his highly intoxicated, wealthy tavern "company" in their private room. An Englishman remembered meeting with fellow gentlemen at a tavern "in a Room one pair of Stairs, set apart for [an exclusive] purpose."[14] Always attempting to find "the right company" in their public interactions, these men cordoned off the tavern in any way possible to create internal division within an otherwise mixed space: they relied on walls to separate themselves from those of separate social standing, consumed the finest goods, and established their presence in mixed-class rooms by employing a medley of sociable (and exclusive) actions. Throughout each of these distinctive impulses, elitist tavern goers hoped to demonstrate the social capital that supposedly separated them from their inferiors and in turn distinguished them as powerful leaders of a British American civil society.

No matter elitist colonists' attempts at difference, the reality of urban tavern interactions revolved around social confusion more than clarification and mistrust more than camaraderie.[15] In one Connecticut tavern, Dr. Hamilton met a "rabble of clowns" who tried to speak on matters beyond their rank. While at Todd's New York City tavern, Dr. Hamilton was himself the object of curiosity when one of Governor Clinton's "court spies [who] made it his business to foist himself into all mixed companies to hear what was said and to enquire into the business and character of strangers" began to question the physician's true identity. Luckily, Dr. Hamilton's friend Todd (and the owner of the tavern) informed the spy of the doctor's true rank and intentions.[16]

Yet certain wealthy colonists did indeed use the anonymity of the tavern space to drink below their station. While lounging with a mixed group of men in a New York City tavern, Dr. Hamilton watched as a "grave parson-doctor" wearing a "mean attire" consisting of a weather-beaten wig, old greasy gloves, and "a pair of old leather spatter-dashes, clouted in twenty different places" left the house after the landlord "sung a bawdy song." When the "old grave don" had to return to the tavern to retrieve his greasy gloves, the publican informed Dr. Hamilton that the "grave parson-doctor . . . was a man worth 50,000 pounds sterling." As was so often the case in British American taverns—and colonial America in general—men were not always what they seemed. Such anonymity apparently made many local tavern goers suspicious of newcomers. Realizing colonists' general wariness of strangers, a young Benjamin Franklin joked that he entered new taverns by announcing to the company,

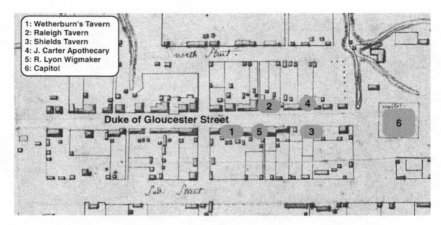

FIGURE 3. "Map of Eastern End of Duke of Gloucester Street, Williamsburg, 1755 (formulated from issues of the *Virginia Gazette*, 1755)." Created by author from the "Frenchman's Map of Williamsburg, Virginia (May 11, 1782)." Used with permission of the Special Collections Research Center, William and Mary Libraries, Williamsburg, VA.

"My name is Benjamin Franklin, I was born at Boston, am a printer by profession, am travelling to Philadelphia, shall return at such time, and have no news—Now what can you give me for dinner?"[17]

Architectural records like those from Williamsburg's mid-eighteenth-century Wetherburn's Tavern, along with probate inventories, provide further insight into how tavern keepers accommodated gentlemen's insatiable urge for exclusivity and control while also satisfying colonists of lower social rank.[18] Wetherburn's Tavern sat on Williamsburg's lively Duke of Gloucester Street—the city's social, consumer, and legal center and a space open to all—and shared the block with other popular establishments like the Raleigh Tavern and the Shields Tavern, not to mention various shops, homes, and the capitol (Figure 3).[19] Having operated the Raleigh Tavern since the 1720s, the widow Mary Bowcock was already a shrewd businesswoman by the time she married Henry Wetherburn in 1731. After helping Bowcock run the Raleigh Tavern for a few years, in 1738 Henry decided to open another tavern, Wetherburn's Tavern, across the street. By 1751, unfortunately, Bowcock had died. Realizing the need for joint ownership, Wetherburn married Anne Shields (widow of one tavern keeper and daughter of another), who helped him expand his business interests.[20] Wetherburn and Shields realized that they had to adjust to the times and define their establishment as accommodating to every need, common or genteel, even if it meant increased initial cost. They consequently added a "great room" (large communal hall) to the popular tavern in the early 1750s, echoing a building boom in Williamsburg and an increasing preference for diverse entertainment. By the mid-1750s, Wetherburn's Tavern became the most popular haunt for politicians when they came to Williamsburg to serve in Virginia's House of Burgesses.[21]

In some ways, Wetherburn's Tavern might seem an odd choice for an analysis of an eighteenth-century British American urban tavern. The tavern existed in Williamsburg, Virginia, after all, which harbored about fifteen taverns and around two thousand residents at midcentury. Only when court days brought a massive influx of visitors from the surrounding countryside did the urban center balloon into something resembling a northern city. Yet, even given its relative smallness, population flux, and distance from other colonial urban zones, Williamsburg maintained an impressive status of urban sociability: it hosted the British American colonies' first official playhouse, regularly welcomed visitors from around the world, supported the College of William and Mary, and cultivated a diverse array of genteel gardens and public grounds.[22] Thus Williamsburg represented colonists' shared devotion to urbane improvement. Whether residing in the landlocked city of Williamsburg or the port center of New York City, urbanites sought to define themselves—and their urban surroundings—as orderly and civil.[23]

Taverns like Wetherburn's symbolize the development of colonists' notions of social difference in their public interactions at midcentury. Middling- and upper-class gentlemen had long sought polite exclusivity in their public endeavors, which tavern keepers like Wetherburn and Shields were more than happy to accommodate. While urban tavern keepers realized elitist tavern goers' preference for exclusivity, they also had to serve as many customers as possible if they were to stay in business. These shrewd mid-century tavern keepers accordingly sought to craft their spaces around prevailing notions of hierarchy, which would hopefully bring in a wide swathe of their local community while also satisfying their demands for deference and order.

Willing to accept the enhanced cost of running a larger tavern, Wetherburn and Bowcock officially opened Wetherburn's Tavern in 1738. By the early 1750s, the two-story tavern contained twelve separate rooms (Figure 4). Besides stocking their tavern with fine furniture, accessories, decorations, consumer goods, and liquors, Wetherburn and Bowcock kept seventeen sheep, four cows, two horses, and four donkeys in their stables. To attend to their customers and livestock, the proprietors owned twelve African slaves, who were the tavern's most valuable (and costly) asset. While a tavern keeper, and perhaps his wife and children, could manage a small, simple business, a larger establishment such as Wetherburn's Tavern relied on servants to keep up with the day-to-day affairs of running such an accommodating business. Expansion was expensive, but as demand grew for taverns that could serve a more diverse populace during the eighteenth century (as did the opportunity for profit), tavern keepers like Wetherburn and Bowcock eagerly attempted to satisfy their genteel and common customers alike.[24]

Wetherburn's "Bullhead Room," on the ground level, exemplified dedication to accommodating customers who demanded equal measures of polite consumption goods and exclusivity. Containing various items associated with genteel culture, including one dozen mahogany chairs, a mahogany tea table, a desk and bookcase with glass door, "1 Eight Day clock," a mirror, a printed picture, and a pair of fine pistols, it was the most refined of the tavern's eleven rooms. A silky wood from the rainforests of Jamaica, mahogany was expensive and exotic in the mid-eighteenth century. Furniture made from this valuable material was scarce in more public rooms, as was a bookcase with a fragile glass door. A group of men residing in the Bullhead Room could glance at their reflections in a mirror to assure themselves of their own polite fashion, keep track of the time, scrutinize printed art, and admire a pair of fine pistols. And unlike those rooms in private coffeehouses and city taverns, importantly, the Bullhead Room could be purchased by any group of men willing to pay for its reservation fees. One did not have to own a genteel mansion to enjoy its superfluous comforts, nor did one have to meet elitist tavern goers' condescending standards of gentility. Whether certain gentlemen liked it or not, the blossoming of the British Empire in America had made the physical markers of civility open to more people than ever before.[25]

Urban tavern keepers throughout the colonies stocked similar rooms intended to sell gentility to all comers. When the Charleston publican Benjamin Backhouse died in 1767, the advertisement for the public sale of his tavern—"the best accustomed house on the Bay, and well adapted for a public house"—was sure to note its remaining stock of "carved . . . Mahogany bedsteads," "six mahogany tables of different sizes, looking glasses, china . . . glass ware of all kinds," and "a very good billiard table." A closer investigation of the accompanying

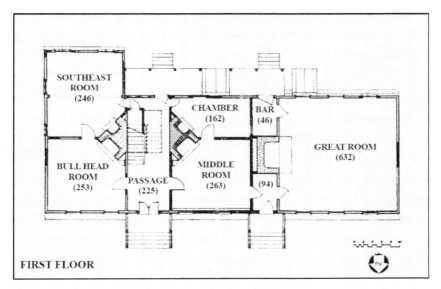

FIGURE 4. "First Floor of Henry Wetherburn's Tavern, Reconstructed According to Archaeological Records and His 1760 Estate Inventory." Adapted by the author from Cynthia D. Jaworski, "Wetherburn's Tavern Planned Preservation Project Completion Report, Block 09 C." Colonial Williamsburg Foundation, Williambsburg, VA, 2004.

probate inventory reveals that Backhouse kept other genteel goods, such as a gilt-decorated dressing table (with a mirror), a painted "Cordial Case," a fine dressing box, and numerous "looking glasses." Tavern keepers along the eastern seaboard followed suit. When the Boston tavern keeper Edward Bardin died in 1770, his executors advertised the auction of his tavern goods in the *Boston Post-Boy*. Besides three slaves (a "like Negro Man" suitable for housework, an eight-year-old "Molatto Boy," and a "Negro Woman . . . who is an excellent Cook"), the article listed genteel goods such as a "Mahogany Desk and Book Case, Bureau, Looking Glasses, a great Variety of Glass and China Ware . . . and a variety of Table Linnen." Whether a customer would have actually passed for a gentleman or not, he could enjoy the same sort of fineries in a private tavern room as elitist colonists enjoyed in their lavish homes. A cursory survey of the midcentury New York City gentleman John Beekman's probate inventory reveals a set of goods nearly identical to urban tavern keepers' holdings. Mahogany furniture decorated

Beekman's rooms, looking glasses hung on his walls, linen draped his tables, and African slaves met his every need.[26]

Tavern keepers also offered rooms that more closely resembled the respectable abodes of the middle classes. A second room on the ground level of Wetherburn's Tavern, the "Middle Room," for instance, was also intended for private use but did not have quite such luxurious trappings as the Bullhead Room and was also probably less expensive to reserve. Rather than mahogany furniture, the Middle Room contained walnut tables and chairs as well as an "Old Card Table." While the Bullhead Room was reserved for elitist customers, Wetherburn and Shields intended the Middle Room (considering its slightly inferior decorations and furnishings) to appease his customers whose pocketbooks were a bit lighter. Everyone won, for such rooms accommodated patrons' need for gentility within the melee of the tavern and did so with less cost to Wetherburn and Shields. Other tavern keepers, once again, offered parallel alternatives. When Daniel Lovell advertised that he was renting out his "large commodious house," the Crown Tavern (in Halifax, North Carolina), at midcentury, he mentioned that a second-story room "was made use of for a ball room, or mason's lodge." When New York City's popular tavern, the Sign of the Free-Mason's Arms, went up for sale, similarly, John Jones advertised that the house had "eight . . . good rooms, with every conveniency for the reception of company." Samuel Wethered, finally, held in the "front Lower Room" of his Boston tavern "Walnut Leather Bottom'd Chairs," a mahogany table, and a "Hand Bell" for elitist colonists to call for more drinks. Such spatial and material differentiation reveals just how much customer demand dictated taverns' ongoing development.[27]

Moreover, select examples of glassware and silverware in Wetherburn's Tavern denote a diverse clientele intent on every consumer finery that the empire promised. For instance, Wetherburn and Shields kept "5 Blue and White China Bowls," "2 Japan Mugs," a set of white flowered china, one teapot with stand, one sugar dish, multiple teacups, and six coffeepots in the tavern. While the lower sorts had begun to drink coffee and tea in limited quantities (mostly in private homes), both beverages still primarily represented civil consumption, especially in the tavern space. Wetherburn's Tavern also possessed a large number of silver utensils, including "19 Tea Spoons & Sugar tongs," "2 Punch Ladles," "1 Tea Kettle," "1 Tea Pot," "1 Coffee Pot," and "10 Silver Hand Knives and 11 Forks with a Case." Like the glassware, these silver utensils accompanied displays of politeness. Elitist tavern goers required fine tea, coffee, and punch utensils for their meetings and feasts. Moreover, the special "Silver Hand Knives" and "Forks with a Case" were set apart from Wetherburn's "Black handle" and "Buck Knives," which were probably intended for ordinary tavern goers.[28]

Urban publicans throughout the colonies rushed to stock their cabinets with genteel accessories. For instance, the Charleston, South Carolina, tavern keeper, Benjamin Backhouse, filled his tavern with expensive dishes such as "China Plates," China Sugar Dish[es]," "Wine & Cyder Glasses," "Large China Bowls," and "Tea Cannisters," while John Reynolds, a middling Annapolis tavern keeper, held genteel items like "China Bowls," "Looking Glasses," and sugar tongs at the time of his death in 1745. Farther north, Wethered kept a litany of fine consumption accessories in his Boston tavern, including "1 China Dish" and "1 3 Quart China Bowl." Such accessories defined their owners as willing and ready to provide the most demanding genteel customers with the most fashionable food and beverages. Wetherburn and Shields kept small reserves of genteel alcoholic beverages like Madeira wine and claret, as did Backhouse and Reynolds. These libations were more expensive than their more popular counterparts such as rum (Wetherburn owned over 4,300 gallons of rum at the time of his death) and thus became signs "of wealth and refinement" throughout the British Empire.[29]

But diversity transcended consumer beverages, as tavern keepers like Wetherburn and Shields rented out tavern rooms to select companies. Self-professed gentlemen often leapt at this opportunity for exclusivity.[30] Traditionally, elitist Anglican worshippers physically separated themselves from the lower classes by using private pews on the first floor of the church. One had to pay a "pew rent" in order to enjoy such a space, which only the middle and upper classes could generally afford. Although George Whitefield's midcentury tours of North America somewhat disrupted traditional notions of Anglican hierarchy in certain areas, most elitist colonists remained firmly tethered to these ideals of public separation.[31] While wealthy churchgoers sat as close to the preacher as possible, when they visited the theater they relied on raised boxes to separate themselves from their social inferiors, who were crammed into the "pit," which was on the ground floor, right in front of the stage. Wealthy theatergoers also often required iron spikes around the edges of their boxes to even further distance themselves from the uncivil masses, and sometimes even purchased seats on stage (also protected from the pit by iron spikes), the best seats in the house, which projected their social standing to the audience.[32]

Gentlemen extended these same notions into the tavern space by utilizing private taverns rooms like those in Wetherburn's Tavern for various exclusive purposes, including club and Masonic meetings, dances,
feasts, lectures, classes, and gambling. In 1747, Benjamin Franklin chose
a Philadelphia tavern as the site in which to present "the Better sort of the
People" with a tract detailing the dangers of a French attack.[33] Deceased
Anthony McKitrick's trustees rented a room in Williamsburg's Raleigh
Tavern where his creditors could meet "in Order to settle their Claims
and receive a Dividend," as did "The Members of the Mississippi Company" during the court days of 1752. After teaching fencing classes from
1741 to 1743, Richard Lyneall advertised in 1756 that he would continue
instructing "all gentlemen who desire to learn the right Method and
true Art of DEFENCE, and pursuit of the Small Sword in its greatest
perfection" at Philadelphia's Tun Tavern. Eighteenth-century gentlemen,
including Dr. Alexander Hamilton, William Black, William Byrd II,
John Adams, and William Smith Jr., finally, often mentioned select clubs
and meetings they attended in urban taverns' private rooms.[34]

Although midcentury urban tavern keepers like Wetherburn, Bowcock, and Shields strove to offer rooms of varying expense and gentility, their spaces still revolved around the most public, or "shallow,"
of all rooms—the "great room." Great rooms were traditionally large
spaces intended to foster close interaction. Wetherburn's great room,
for instance, measured roughly 625 square feet and occupied the totality
of the east wing, while rooms like the Bullhead Room and the Middle
Room occupied only about half that space. Tavern keepers consciously
crafted these spaces for mixed clientele of varying group sizes. Visitors
to Wetherburn's great room would have found a central "large . . . table"
intended for sizable groups, in addition to six "small square tables," one
"walnut table," and over a dozen chairs for those customers who desired
a more intimate drinking experience.[35] Customers in the great room
generally purchased cheaper drinks like ale and straight rum, in contrast
to the pricier and more exotic arrack punch and Madeira wine that elitist
colonists gulped just down the hall.[36]

Many elitist colonists understood the great room of a tavern in the
same vein as the pit of the theater or the balcony of the church: a space
where uncivil society garnered relative power and had more chances to
display a dangerous disregard for deference. But what if a group of civil
tavern goers could not reserve a tavern's private room? Since private
rooms were not always available—especially during periods of intense
population influx like fair, market, court, or celebration days—elitist

colonists were occasionally forced to mingle with their social inferiors in taverns' main, and most public, rooms. Although not exactly thrilled about making their way into the crowded, loud, and confusing great room, many gentlemen still found ways to construct physical and ideological dividers even in these more public, shallow spaces.[37]

Because a tavern goer sang opera tunes and whistled in "a full House . . . as if he were in an empty Room," one anonymous writer to the *Spectator* contended that Englishmen should "divide the Spaces of a Publick Room."[38] British American tavern groups did just this. Various eighteenth-century publicans, including Wetherburn and Shields, kept one or more "screens" in their great rooms.[39] Although these screens were most likely intended to protect tavern goers from the heat of the great room's blazing fireplace (a key attraction for many customers), groups of men desiring privacy could also use screens as physical dividers to create exclusivity within such public spaces. Thus a group of self-professed gentlemen forced to occupy a raucous great room could have used a screen to shield themselves from the rabble rather than the fire. Necessity was the mother of invention.[40]

Beyond the possibility of physical separation in a tavern's great room, elitist tavern goers could also utilize numerous forms of material and ideological separators to establish distinction from the lower sorts. Self-professed gentlemen literally wore their status on their sleeves in their attempts to keep up with the most recent European fashions. Although often behind the latest Old World fashion due to their distance from metropolitan centers like London and Paris, British American gentlemen nonetheless adhered strictly to the ebbs and flows of British style. Ever the example of elitist condescension, Dr. Hamilton often remarked on the attire of those he met and observed in taverns. At one country tavern, Hamilton distinguished himself from the "company of patch'd coats and tattered jackets," and in a New York City tavern, Hamilton found solace in meeting a well-traveled Scottish merchant who he described as "a little, dapper young fellow with a gaudy laced jacket."[41] Dr. Hamilton—who often donned a "dark colour'd silk coat," a "laced hat," a brace of pistols, and a sword—fully realized the importance of dress for denoting status.[42]

Clothing emerged as such an important marker of status in the eighteenth century that if one were to pass as civil he better well dress the part. Yet costume sometimes proved confusing. The famous colonial "imposter and confidence man" Tom Bell, for example, repeatedly used a shrewd variety of dress and deport to lie, cheat, and steal his way into

British American genteel society between 1738 and 1755. When Bell arrived in Charleston in February 1745, his infamy was such that the *South Carolina Gazette* warned citizens "the famous TOM BELL, alias *Burnett*, alias *Rowland*, alias *Fairfair*, alias *Wentworth*, alias *Livingston* alias *Rip Van Dam*, &c. &c. &c. is arrived among us." Apparently, Bell had arrived in Charleston the week before using the name Nathaniel Butler and carrying with him a letter of credit signed by one "*Y P Randolph*." Ever wary of such pretenders, the newspaper's editor warned fellow Charlestonians that Bell "is a slim fellow, thin visage, appears like a Gentleman, talks of all Persons of Note as if intimately acquainted with them, and changes his Name and Cloaths very often." Bell was a true imposter in civil society. Unlike one middling man who Dr. Hamilton had lambasted in 1744 for unsuccessfully trying "to look like a gentleman" with certain articles of clothing, Bell repeatedly tricked supposedly shrewd gentlemen (often during tavern encounters) into believing that he was their social equal. Though frequently discovered in his fraudulency, Bell nevertheless utilized an ever-changing array of costumes and characters to infiltrate genteel society. Such contrivances extended beyond Bell in the eighteenth century, as escaped slaves often donned stolen clothes and forged passes to act as freemen in port cities. One 1763 *Virginia Gazette* slave runaway advertisement warned of a mulatto servant "by name James Harn, alias Harringham," who "affects to be and speak above the common rank," while another alerted colonists of a gaming-fond house slave who "carried with him a Variety of Clothes."[43]

While the parameters of costume identity grew murkier by mid-century, the once-clear distinctions associated with consumption of "fine" goods became even messier. Fifty years earlier, simply drinking exotic beverages like coffee, tea, or Madeira from expensive equipages such as china and silver were more than enough to set would-be elites apart from rum- and beer-guzzling commoners in the great room.[44] But times had changed. As colonists' demand for imported goods increased by 120 percent from 1750 to 1773, tea became affordable enough for ordinary colonists to consume, and while coffee began to show up on more shelves, it remained costly until the end of the eighteenth century. No matter how much elitist colonists derided their social inferiors for their "foolish fondness of Foreign Commodities & Fashions . . . and a hunger for things above their station in life," British America's "empire of goods" catered to a wide swath of the colonial population and in turn made the balancing act of social distinction more difficult by the day.[45]

Thus *how* self-professed gentlemen consumed their drinks did as much to distinguish them from their social inferiors as what they consumed.[46] The ceremony and politeness surrounding genteel consumption goods and services especially served to differentiate gentlemen from ordinary colonists who were unfamiliar with such civil rituals. Drinking rituals like toasts, then, were primary ceremonies of inclusiveness *and* exclusivity. Though toasting "promoted a style of drinking that identified and built upon what a company had in common," what these toasters usually shared was social standing.[47] While drinking in a Boston tavern in 1750, for instance, Francis Goelet commented that he joined "a large company of gentlemen drinking toasts & singing songs." Josiah Quincy Jr., moreover, overheard a tale of two Charleston gentlemen who came to blows over toasting in a tavern.[48] Such spur-of-the-moment toasts were vital for genteel culture but did not "relax or eliminate . . . consciousness of rank."[49] Rather, by toasting—whether in the private tavern club or in a public great room—elitist tavern goers asserted their position as exclusive men of poise and order.

Besides informal tavern toasts, gentlemen often transformed toasting into grand performances of social power and imperial belonging. Having met in a Charleston tavern at midcentury to celebrate St. George's Day (April 23), the gentlemen of the St George's Club used toasting to proclaim their allegiance to the Crown as well as their influence over Charleston's future. The St. George's Club made sure to publish their myriad toasts in the *South Carolina Gazette*. According to the article, after inviting the governor of South Carolina, James Oglethorpe, "and several other gentlemen" into their tavern for an "elegant Supper," the powerful coterie drank to the health of "His Majesty, the Queen and Royal Family; his Excellency the Governor," and, finally, "Prosperity to the Province of *South-Carolina*." Such celebrations were rather common among genteel companies throughout the colonies: Williamsburg's gentlemen and ladies celebrated the anniversary of King George II's birthday "with a Ball, and an elegant Supper" in 1739, and Boston's "Troop of Guards" celebrated the fourth year of King George III's reign with an "elegant dinner" at the Greyhound Tavern in 1763, "to which Entertainment his Excellency the Governor and several principal Gentlemen were invited."[50] Genteel tavern goers used toasts and dinner to create yet another sphere of polite exclusivity. Everyone around such a group heard their loud toasts to power and empire, which the toasters hoped might remind their peers of their power.[51]

Leaders also utilized urban taverns to issue legal accords over their social inferiors.[52] When the New York City farrier Stanford Cornehill neglected to pay debts in 1755, the local constable entered his house around midnight "without leave" to serve a warrant. Cornehill complained to a New York City lawyer, John Tabor Kempe, that he had been "hurried like a Fellon! that Night Above Ten Miles & detain'd at a Publick Inn until day." The next day men stood guard over Cornehill as his plaintiffs attended the tavern to collect their dues.[53] The Virginia planter William Byrd II and his fellow magistrates extended their court proceedings from the courthouse to a variety of taverns (and often back again) during Williamsburg's midcentury court days. On June 11, 1740, for example, Byrd noted in his diary:

> I had several visitors and about 10 went to the capitol where we sat till 3, then dined with Wetherburn [at his tavern] and ate broiled chicken. After dinner I walked to the coffeehouse and read news, then received some money of Lidderdale.[54]

Philadelphia's county commissioners, similarly, held their meetings in Robert's Coffee House and Widow Jones's Sign of the Three Crowns from 1747 to 1748.[55]

Just as genteel tavern goers utilized a variety of measures to separate themselves from their social inferiors, so too did the lower sorts establish their own "knots of men rightly sorted" in taverns.[56] Ordinary tavern goers tended to seek the company of their social equals rather than attempt to shove themselves into elitist circles. The colonial gentleman William Keith attested to such tavern structure in the 1720s when he recalled a conversation with a "poor Labouring man" named Roger who assured Keith that he had "no fancy to be acquainted with great Folks, or to keep Company above the pitch of a plain . . . understanding." Though not seeking the camaraderie of gentlemen, ordinary colonists like Roger still expected a modicum of civility from their social superiors. Only when one "Great Man" displayed "such a *wounded conceit of his Own Person*, that he [could not] condescend to be *commonly Civil* to his Betters or Equals, and disdain[ed] to be at the trouble of shewing the least *Humanity* to those below him," for instance, did Roger display any sort of unhappiness regarding mixed-class taverns' social milieu. For colonists like Roger, while certain men were no doubt more fit to rule society, "the whole Business of all Civil Government" should ultimately reside in benefiting the most people possible and displaying a degree of paternal civility for their social inferiors. Few ordinary colonists, in brief, believed that they should sit at the same table as their social superiors. Yet they increasingly demanded a level of respect—particularly in terms of economic security and general benevolence—that many of their social superiors refused to accord them.[57]

Taking into account such expectations of paternal difference, ordinary tavern goers also developed a complex language of revelry—specifically, chaos-inducing drinking cultures—that distinguished them within the tavern space. While tippling with friends at Philadelphia's mixed-class, multistory Red Lion tavern, for example, the plasterer Thomas Apty bet his comrades that he could drink a gallon of cider in only an hour and a half. Much to his company's surprise, Apty did indeed guzzle the gallon of cider. Unfortunately, Apty followed this imbibing feat with a second act: he "fell down . . . and then expired."[58] As in gentlemen's exclusive interactions, ordinary colonists used drinking rituals to establish and confirm camaraderie in their ranks, and these feats sometimes ended badly. Such activities served to further distance ordinary tavern goers from condescending elitist customers, which was probably just fine with all companies involved.

Within a tavern's multifaceted great room, ordinary colonists also used elitist tavern goers' notions of social stratification to negotiate and establish their own drinking companies. Dancing, it appears, was one of ordinary colonists' favorite tavern pastimes. When John Adams arrived at a tavern just outside Boston in 1760, the condescending gentleman watched as "Zab Hayward, not finding admittance to the Chamber [a more exclusive room in the tavern where Adams sat], gathered a circle round him in the lower Room [the great room]." Adams somewhat disgustedly noted that he looked on as "a wild Rable of both sexes and of all Ages" partook in "Fiddling and dancing, in a Chamber . . . in the Lower Room, singing dancing, fiddling, drinking flip and Toddy, and drams." Denied access to a genteel tavern chamber, Hayward took to a more public room and helped define himself and, eventually, his fellow revelers as separate from their elitist peers. Hayward was hardly alone. When the Quaker leader Thomas Story arrived at a colonial tavern in the early eighteenth century, a group of "young people" who had been "singing, fiddling, and dancing" exited the tavern "as soon as they saw [Story and his pious compatriots]." Apparently these youngsters did not desire a religious sermon. While traveling through the Carolina backcountry at midcentury, finally, the Anglican itinerant Charles Woodmason similarly complained that ordinary colonists flocked to mixed-class taverns for "Shooting, Dancing, Revelling, [and] Drinking Matches" rather than worshipping in their local churches. Pastimes like dance and music thus unified ordinary tavern goers.[59]

Costume would have also allowed ordinary tavern goers to identify each other and gather in select companies. No matter certain colonists' attempts to emulate their social superiors through clothing, their attire was often secondhand, more threadbare, and made with lesser quality fabrics than the upper classes' fine garb. Dr. Hamilton referred to their "patch'd coats and tattered jackets," while others littered runaway advertisements with detailed descriptions of the lower class's "Cotton Pair of Breeches" or "Ordinary blue Cloaths, patched with Canvas." Contrast these descriptions with that of an unidentified gentleman found drowned in the Ashley Ferry River (South Carolina) in 1739: "he appeared pretty well dressed, having on a good brown Coat, white Waistcoat, Buck-skin Breeches, white Stockings a pair of new Shoes or Pumps, with Silver Buttons in his sleeves, and a pair of Spurs." Even though the consumer revolution had made once-exclusive goods and services more accessible to ordinary people than ever before, the lower "sorts" often donned clothes patched with mismatching, cheap fabrics that lacked the streamlined silhouette of tailored attire. Although such outward markers of status and wealth could be deceiving, dress was still a generally trustworthy identifier in the murky social environment of colonial America.[60]

Language and conversation patterns also distinguished the lower sorts. Dr. Hamilton mocked a tavern company of ordinary colonists for their conversation consisting of "'damne ye, Jack," and 'here's to you Tom,'" while another Philadelphian regretted that on entering many taverns in the city he immediately heard phrases like "*d—n* me, *Jack*, what detained you so long?" or "by *G-d*, I shall drink five bumpers." Though literacy levels were improving across the social hierarchy by the eighteenth century, many ordinary colonists still did not thumb through erudite texts like conduct books or histories that imparted a certain linguistic direction. Thus when the Virginia planter Thomas Dansie advertised that four of his white "Servant Men" had run away in 1751, he informed his colleagues that the fugitives spoke "very bad English." While these men might have been Irish or Scottish, more educated immigrants like Dr. Hamilton would never have been characterized as speaking "very bad English" because of their native accents. Such an inability to blend in to colonial speech patterns only further sullied an ordinary colonist in the haughty eyes of leaders.[61]

Smell also differentiated companies within the clustered milieu of the urban tavern space. It is no coincidence that the elitist author of the 1750 *New-York Weekly Journal* poem began his criticism of ordinary taverns with "*Spue* [spew]-*scented* rooms of noisy inns." By linking lower-class tavern rooms with the scent of "spew" (i.e., vomit), this writer associated ordinary tavern goers with smells that elitist men associated with drunkenness, debauchery, and incivility. Living in a society in which men and women rarely submerged themselves in water, most colonists would smell ripe to modern olfactory senses. However, body odor was common in colonial America. By the second half of the eighteenth century, elitist colonists like William Byrd II and John Adams had begun to experiment with bathing in controlled mineral springs and spas, but such activities were still occasional at best. After bathing in a New England spa in 1771, the elitist Philadelphian Elizabeth Drinker did not submerge herself in water again until 1798.[62] Averse to bathing, elitist colonists needed a different way to differentiate themselves from the masses.

Certain elitist tavern goers accordingly relied on cloying, expensive combinations of scented waters, essences, and perfumes to mask their bodily odors and thus project their wealth and gentility to anyone close enough to smell them. In this way, gentlemen created their own "artificial atmosphere" to distinguish themselves in close spaces. Lacking the funds for such perfumes and often working in trades that induced sweat or were associated with a variety of organic and inorganic scents, ordinary colonists did not necessarily smell worse than their supposed social superiors (masking body odor with perfume, after all, remains less than ideal); they just smelled different.[63] Chameleon con men like Tom Bell who could successfully emulate the sounds, appearance, and smells of their social superiors, in short, were the exception to the rule.

By the mid-eighteenth century, urban taverns reflected the messy reality of elitists' visions for a British American civil society. Hoping to keep the populace "in good Order" and "a Just and regular motion," elitist tavern goers did everything in their power to distinguish themselves from, and hopefully impose order on, "the Gross body of the Common people." They depended on mercurial notions of consumption and sociability to demonstrate their "fitness" for rule. Ordinary colonists, meanwhile, worried little about achieving the lofty goals of their supposedly civil compatriots. Realizing such hierarchical impulses, urban tavern keepers strove to uphold spaces where a "mixed company" could congregate. Yet publicans did not craft spaces that encouraged tavern goers to cross class boundaries. On the contrary, tavern keepers like Henry Wetherburn, Mary Bowcock, and Anne Shields of Williamsburg developed their businesses into divisionary public spheres where notions of civil and uncivil society were expressed in material and ideological forms. Steadily but fitfully, elitist colonists realized that if "the Great political machine [of Civil Society]" was to "move on undisturbed," they had to recognize the messy realities of societal development as necessary facets of civilization and order. Ordinary colonists were here to stay, and many gentlemen decided that their "uncivil" societal norms might be just the thing elitist men needed to maintain local power.[64]

4 / "Disorderly Houses": Rakish Revelries, Unlicensed Taverns, and Uncivil Contradictions

The New York City gentleman-merchant Francis Goelet spent the night of October 1, 1750, drinking his way through Boston. Having shared numerous alcoholic beverages with a group of about forty gentlemen in a private home, Goelet and his intoxicated company "went upon the rake," sallying forth into Boston's commons where they "surprised a company [of] young men & women with a violin at a tavern, danceing & makeing merry." Goelet proudly noted that "the women fled" on seeing such a raucous and libidinous crowd of gentlemen enter their lower-class tavern and take "possession of the room." After gathering a fiddler and a keg of sugared dram, Goelet and his rakish companions spent the rest of the night "very merry," chasing the remaining women through the house and guzzling copious amounts of alcohol.[1]

According to elitist colonists' self-promotion campaign, such behavior marked the "unruly" masses, not gentlemen like Francis Goelet and his powerful Bostonian friends. Dr. Hamilton and his Tuesday Club, after all, had sallied forth in a civil procession of order in 1747, not rushed through Annapolis in a blur of booze and violence; elitist Philadelphians had opened the London Coffee House to harbor exclusive gentility, not encourage rakish whoring and overconsumption. Yet theory often played out quite differently from reality in the messy negotiation of British American civil society. In reality, self-styled gentlemen fell prey to the same vices as their alleged inferiors, frolicking and whoring at the theater, inciting disorder at the market, and, of course, drinking to excess in the tavern. Urbane politeness, in short, "generated, rather than precluded, a fascination with *impolite* behavior." Nowhere were gentlemen's fascination with impolite behavior—and, consequently, their ongoing contradictory behavior—clearer than in elitist tavern goers' enchantment with acting as "rakes" or "libertines."[2]

By following gentlemen "libertines" as they left their civil coffeehouses and city taverns to go on the rake in lower-class taverns, this chapter further demonstrates the messy and confusing nature of British American civil society. Gentlemen's rakish interactions reveal the "shifting fictions" of masculinity and civility that scholars and contemporaries alike have often represented as "impenetrable to such impulses."[3] As numerous historians have investigated in the context of early modern England (particularly London), urbanites increasingly utilized the identity of the rake to assert their masculinity and power over social inferiors. By spilling into the city's various lower-class taverns and "bawdy" houses, these supposedly genteel citizens displayed conduct deemed below their station through excess in all, including violence, "wenching" (aggressively pursuing sex), drinking, rioting, and blaspheming. And they often did so, importantly, with limited legal repercussions, as early modern British American society generally understood such actions as an aristocratic man's "right." Yet, as the historian Anna Bryson recently asserted, Englishmen's rakish behavior cannot be understood in binary terms. Such "libertine codes of conduct" depended on the personification of certain uncivil modes of behavior just as much as the "open transgression of some of the forms of 'civil' nobility." Idealized notions of early modern masculinity ranged from drunken brutality to polite claret sipping. British American rakes and libertines somewhat contradictorily appropriated uncivil behavior in order to distinguish themselves in their urban locality.[4]

Thus, when Goelet and his friends "went on the rake" in Boston in 1750, they were not doing so to make friendly with the masses. By forcing themselves into a tavern filled with a surprised "company [of] young men and women," these rowdy gentlemen established their *distance* from their social inferiors. This is not to say, of course, that condescending gentlemen rakes and libertines did not enjoy all that uncivil society (particularly disorderly houses) had to offer. On the contrary, by midcentury colonial gentlemen had established a system of rakish behavior that upheld the very networks of disorderly taverns that many of those same colonists attempted to control. They often did so, importantly, through violent measures, thereby establishing their alleged power—both physical and legal—over ordinary and unfree peoples.

Disorderly houses and their supposedly uncivil attendants proved key to gentlemen's rakish behavior, for just as elitist men constructed their own city taverns and coffeehouses as exclusive sanctuaries where they hoped to craft themselves into civil cosmopolitans, so too did needy citizens maintain a network of licensed and unlicensed taverns intended to serve ordinary and unfree people. Although we have no way of knowing whether ordinary and unfree tavern goers attended these spaces with the express purpose of shirking notions of deference or asserting their own ideals of a British American civil society, we do know how self-professed gentlemen *perceived* them: disorderly, crude, and dangerous spaces that might hurt their efforts at urbane civility.[5]

Gentlemen represented ordinary and unfree peoples as their base opposites. An apparently civil man would have deemed public drunkenness as "Unfit for *Civil* Society" and wholly indicative of the constant lure of uncivil behavior in the sociable swell of British America's urban centers.[6] Yet the "progress vision of civilization" that so many early modern citizens (and, in turn, historians thereafter) attempted to identify was hardly linear. Although elitist men could well define uncivil behavior and those who most often embodied it, this did not occlude elitist men from assuming uncivil characteristics themselves, nor did it halt uncivil society's steady progress. Certain elitist men, in fact, considered uncivil behavior a mutable series of actions that could be used to strengthen boundaries between themselves and their social inferiors. Here, then, was the ultimate contradiction of civility: elitist colonists believed they (and only they) should be allowed to break the very societal rules they so ardently sought to impress on their social inferiors. British American civil society was not so much a hardline set of statutes as it was a vague, nebulous ideal of civilization in which a small set of men made up the rules as they went.[7]

Such internal chaos did not obstruct gentlemen in their efforts to control the world around them. Living in a developing urban world, elitist urbanites adjusted ideals of civil society to fit their local environment, specifically, North America's large proportion of unfree or inferior peoples. Colonial urban centers harbored a much larger number of slaves than their European and British counterparts. By midcentury, one-fifth of New York City's population were slaves. This put New York City behind only Charleston, which boasted a slave population accounting for half of its total population. Charleston's black population was so considerable that, on arriving in the city in 1772, a visitor wondered whether "my Guide, instead of showing me the Way to this Town, had conducted me to Africa." Portsmouth contained one-third of the slaves in New Hampshire, and Boston, finally, funneled almost half of Massachusetts's slaves into its jumbled streets. Though weakened by years of conflict, disease, and coercion, moreover, Native Americans remained common facets of colonial cities as they passed through for treaties and trade. These larger groups of "others" not only necessitated different sorts of legal measures from anxious leaders; they also increasingly cultivated their own spheres of public interaction within the tangled web of urban life. British American civil society was, once again, defined by local realities as much as static laws or conflict.[8]

Though relegated to the fringe of the historical record because of their limited presence (especially in a positive light) in the world of print culture, uncivil taverns were no less important for British American civil society than their genteel counterparts. In fact, taverns operated by lower-class and unfree people rested at the nexus of urban uncivil society—a world where pickpockets and thieves lurked, black market goods exchanged hands beneath tables, women and men sold their bodies for profit, drunks fought each other to the death, greasy politicians mustered support by the punch bowl, and harsh words erupted among numerous parties. Although leaders did everything in their power to institute legal and controlling measures in such spaces, their efforts had little effect, as lower-class and unfree tavern goers increasingly cultivated a "rival geography" of urban spaces where they might realize alternate methods of societal development and belonging.[9] Uncivil society had taken hold in colonial cities by the eighteenth century, and perhaps nowhere were the implications of this "rude" sector of society more apparent than the tavern.

Many leaders perceived lower-class taverns as the most concentrated examples of the decline of deference and order and thus constantly struggled to control them. A writer who called himself "A.B." complained to the *Virginia Gazette* in April 1751 that his city's taverns had "become the common Receptacle, and Rendezvous of the very Dreggs of the People." A.B. went even farther, contending that such lower-class taverns had descended into "Schools" that would train colonists to become a "Part of Satan's Service."[10] Not only did these spaces seem to develop beyond elitist statutes by the mid-eighteenth century, but, according to many distraught officials, lower-class taverns also bred laziness, drunkenness, and devolution. One midcentury writer to the *Boston Evening Post* worried about "the poorer sort of People" who were too "often swilling in the Tavern while their poor Families are suffering for want of Bread at

Home."[11] Such enervating developments could have only one outcome in many leaders' opinion: a less successful civil society.

For a growing number of gentlemen, the alleged problem began with overconsumption of alcohol. But alcoholic consumption was a complicated endeavor, for just as elitist colonists utilized the transatlantic liquor trade to bolster their wealth (and also drank to excess), so too did they equate drunkenness and certain types of strong liquor with the debauchery of the lower classes and attendant societal ruin. One mid-century Georgia colonist described a drunkard as "the trouble of civility[,] ... his own shame, a *walking-swill-tub*, the picture of a beast, and the monster of a man," while the aspiring elite Nicholas Cresswell lamented that overconsumption might not only "destroy his constitution" but also cause him to "sink ... below the level of a brute." While gentlemen liked to represent themselves as above gross intoxication, their actions hardly backed this up. Nevertheless, elitist colonists engaged in an ongoing smear campaign against their social inferiors.[12]

Widely available, highly alcoholic, and relatively inexpensive, rum gained a reputation among colonial gentlemen like William Byrd II as a destructive poison that "breaks the constitutions, vitiates the morals, and ruins the industry of most of the poor people of this country." The founder of Georgia, James Ogelthorpe, similarly did "not allow [his Georgia laborers] Rum, but in lieu, [gave] them *English Beer*" as they constructed urban public works. Elitist colonists directly correlated rum consumption with plebeian self-destruction. Upon arriving in one southern town, for example, Byrd exclaimed, "There is a rum ordinary for persons of a more vulgar taste."[13] New England rum generally cost about one-third as much per gallon as Jamaican rum, while French brandy sold for almost twice as much as Jamaica rum.[14] Liquor, in short, was stratified along levels of cost, status, and taste. In Byrd's eyes, this tavern primarily sold cheap rum and was thus intended for lesser company with inferior decision-making skills.

Whether conflated or not, colonial newspapers regularly printed accounts of lower-class colonists' death at the hands of rum, or "kill-devil" as many disgusted onlookers termed the alcoholic liquor.[15] The *Pennsylvania Gazette* ran a story in 1753 detailing a "labouring Man" who "being at work in a House in Town, got to a Bottle of Rum [at a tavern], of which he drank so freely, that he died soon after."[16] The *Virginia Gazette* published the tale of "a most dreadful Instance of the Effects of Drunkenness happening [in Williamsburg] lately . . . as a Warning to others." The article centered on the unhappy end of William Hunt, a Williamsburg tailor prone to leaving his wife and children to "take a Frolick, and get drunk 3 or 4 Days together." Coming off a three-day tavern drinking binge, Hunt staggered to his neighbor's house for aid. The kindly neighbor let Hunt sleep in a locked upstairs room, but on waking up and finding that he was not in his own home, the still intoxicated Hunt rashly jumped out of the second-story window. The fall shattered his leg to such an extent that "the Violence of the Pain, and Heat of the Liquor" threw him into a fever. When his leg began to "mortify" soon thereafter, the surgeon contended that Hunt was too weak for surgery, and Hunt "died in a most lamentable Condition."[17]

The "problem" of lower-class taverns extended beyond over intoxication. Leaders worried about myriad other vices that emanated from certain taverns. Gaming, for example, came under fire in the eighteenth century as a tavern activity that would only bring poorer colonists to absolute destruction. Although gambling had long enchanted gentlemen in their tavern experiences, they strove to keep these same pastimes away from the lower sorts. One Bostonian worried that, as time was "the Labourer's Stock in Trade," such tavern distractions as "Cards, Dice, Draughts, Shuffle Boards, Mississippi Tables, Billiards, and covered Skettle Grounds" were "the Thieves that rob the Journeymen and Labourers of their precious Time, their Little Property, and their less Morals."[18]

Cautious magistrates issued acts to prevent gaming in ordinary taverns. Lamenting that tavern gaming caused youngsters to "frequently fall in company with lewd, idle, and dissolute persons," resulting in "the ruin of the health and the corruption of the youth of this colony," Virginia's leaders enacted a 1740 law forbidding "gaming at ordinaries." New York officials similarly passed "An Act to Restrain Disorderly and Unlawful Gaming-Houses" in 1741, citing that gaming in taverns had, "by Fatal Experience, been found to be attended with many evil Consequences, not only by corrupting and vitiating the Manners of the People [and] . . . encouraging them to Idleness, Deceit, and many other Immoralities; but hath moreover a manifest Tendency to the Ruin of many." Issued from North Carolina to Georgia to New England in the mid-eighteenth century, such laws sought to stop men from becoming "wicked" gamesters who ruined themselves, their families, and civil society. Punishments for those who continued to gamble (as well as those who allowed them to) ranged from fines to jail time. New York magistrates, interestingly, would reinvest half of the fines in "the Poor of the City, Town, County, or Precinct" in which the offense occurred. Just as they hoped to keep ordinary colonists away from drunkenness and gaming to keep them out of the poor rolls, so too did they use the fines for these same actions to fund the city's poor.[19]

In classical conceptions of civil society, thinkers tied philanthropy and charity endeavors to civilizing efforts. It was, in Adam Ferguson's contention, the responsibility of those who led a "polished society" to support "the beggar, who depends upon charity." As the historian Jessica Choppin Roney has demonstrated in the context of eighteenth-century Philadelphia, the lack of a strong central government allowed urban dwellers to take responsibility for various civic-minded efforts, including poverty relief.[20] They were not alone. From New York City to Charleston magistrates used the tavern trade to provide relief to its poorest residents. Besides offering licenses to certain indigent urbanites, lawmakers included statutes through which their city's poor might find monetary aid from the fines leveled at those men and women who kept a tavern without license.[21]

Reflecting long-held notions of philanthropy, order, and masculine paternalism, colonial magistrates often targeted urban publicans as responsible for the "proper" management of colonial America's taverns. Leaders expected a tavern keeper to act, in the words of one New Englander, as "an Honest and a Watchful Centinel over the Peace, Safety, and Regularity of the City." These gatekeepers of civility should help gentlemen in their quest to shape a healthy and decorous empire.[22]

Officials especially concentrated on whom they would and would not grant a tavern license. New Englanders were perhaps the most proactive with such reforms, relying on those they deemed most "fit" to regulate taverns "for the Entertainment of Strangers and Travellers."[23] Pennsylvania followed suit in 1721, declaring that justices had the final say on who they approved "fit Persons to keep Taverns." Such tavern keepers, Pennsylvania magistrates noted, should be dedicated to "Maintaining of good Order." Connecticut also passed "several acts . . . for the due regulation of lycenced houses" beginning in 1716, stressing that only those who were considered "fit and suitable to keep an house or houses of public entertainment" should be considered. Yet New Englanders continued to outstrip all others in sheer effort. Not only were tavern keepers expected to serve only travelers and strangers, but by 1759 magistrates demanded that said "fit" publicans must expel any town dweller from his or her tavern by nine o'clock at night. "Singing, fiddling, piping, or any other Musick, dancing, or reveling" was also not to be accepted. Of course, law did not always translate into practice. As was so often the case, many tavern keepers ignored such statutes with little punishment.[24]

Ordinary women—widowed, married, or "feme sole"—had long run taverns.[25] But their efforts were not without struggle, for in classic conceptions of civility, even elitist women were deemed more likely to cave in to uncivil behavior than were their masculine counterparts. Their sexual, "animal nature" constantly lurked under the feminine surface, waiting to be brought to the fore by the revelries and temptations of public society.[26] Northeastern leaders were hesitant to provide licenses to women in the seventeenth and early eighteenth century, as they considered men the worthiest people to govern a civil society and its most important establishments. By the mid-eighteenth century, however, economic necessity prompted magistrates to allow women like Rachel Masters—an ordinary Bostonian who had been recently widowed and would have to rely on public welfare if she was not granted a tavern license—the opportunity to operate their own licensed taverns. Cases like Masters' represented an upward trend in widows operating taverns in New England.[27] Southern women, meanwhile, had long managed their own taverns. In the Chesapeake and Low Country, in fact, females controlled the day-to-day operations of many—if not most—taverns. Widows like Bowcock and Shields of Williamsburg often remarried as a means of financial increase, just as southern men would often purchase a tavern and then allow their wives to manage the establishment. As Sarah Hand Meacham has demonstrated, even those taverns that society perceived as being operated by men were often run by women.[28]

Female tavern keepers occupied a liminal space between servicing and challenging the patriarchal order.[29] The widowed owner of an ordinary Williamsburg tavern, Anne Pattison, served a variety of roles, ranging from brokering the sale of horses to lending cash on credit to assisting her bond laborers with chores such as cooking, gardening, washing dishes, laundering, shopping, and serving food and drinks.[30] In one sense, Pattison was a shrewd businesswoman enmeshed in local and global webs of commerce and trade. In another sense, however, she performed the more private role of many women by taking care of domestic duties around the tavern.[31] Licensed female tavern keepers thus gained footholds in male-dominated spheres of public consumption but generally did so under the guise that men were guiding these movements. Whether applying for a widower's tavern license or operating a tavern with their husband, women had to operate within well-worn tracks of male supremacy, even if the act was a ruse. In this way, women remained intertwined in prevailing notions of civil society, which were firmly directed at maintaining men's public status.

While leaders worried about who ran urban taverns and how they regulated what went on in them, they were especially wary of specific sorts of unfree people who might enter these spaces as patrons, gaining access to the drink and services that taverns promised. Once again, urban taverns surfaced as primary spaces through which elitist colonists might define their relationship with "others" in British America. Enslaved blacks, unsurprisingly, emerged as leaders' most feared potential tavern goers. Here Chesapeake and Low Country gentlemen took the lead, as they lived in constant dread of slave disorder or, heaven forbid, rebellion. Southern leaders existed in a society where, whether lounging on their plantations or walking through an urban street, they were almost constantly surrounded and outnumbered by enslaved peoples. Elitist whites believed they had to keep enslaved blacks in an inferior position if their society was to thrive. Thus while white colonists often sidestepped tavern regulation in the southern colonies, enslaved blacks, quite simply, did not (at least not without strict punishment).

When the Stono Rebellion unfolded in South Carolina in 1737, southern leaders' fears surrounding slave anarchy, disorder, and violence reached new heights. Their general paranoia was reflected in the 1740 South Carolina "Act for the better ordering and governing Negroes and other Slaves in this Province":

> If any Keeper of a *Tavern* or Punch-House, or Retailer of strong Liquors, shall give, sell, utter, or deliver to any Slave, any BEER, ALE, CYDER, WINE, RUM, BRANDY, or other SPIRITOUS LIQUOURS, or STRONG LIQUOUR whatsoever, without the Licence or Consent of the Owner, or such other Person having the Care or Government of such Slave; every Person so offending, shall forfeit the Sum of *five Pounds* Current Money for the first Offence, and for the second Offence *ten Pounds*; and shall be bound in a Recognizance in the Sum of *One Hundred Pounds* Current Money with one or more sufficient Sureties before any of the Justices of the Court of General Sessions not to offend in the like Kind and be of good Behaviour for one Year and for Want of such sufficient Sureties to be committed to Prison without Bail or Mainprize, for any Term not exceeding three Months.[32]

South Carolina leaders made themselves quite clear: enslaved peoples were not to have access to any alcoholic beverages whatsoever. Offenders would be punished with fees, public humiliation, and, eventually, imprisonment. Yet the 1740 act had limited success. In 1756, the Grand

Jurors of South Carolina complained that "the great numbers of taverns in *Charles*-Town" that sold liquor to blacks was "productive of many evils." A few years later, Charleston magistrates declared that the great number of licenses "for retailing spirituous liquors" had "debauched . . . the morals of our slaves." "Frequent thefts" and various other obstructions to the public good apparently ensued because of so many lewd, uncontrolled taverns.[33]

Such paranoia spread throughout the rest of the colonies.[34] In 1741, New York City's inhabitants came to believe that a poor white tavern keeper had hosted enslaved men and women who planned to burn the city to the ground. The city's magistrates ultimately burned thirteen blacks at the stake, hung seventeen blacks and four whites, and banished seventy more blacks (often to their ultimate death in the Caribbean island of Hispaniola).[35] Thereafter, other colonies took a harsher approach to the "good Regulation" and "suitable Management" of blacks. In 1751, for example, Philadelphia's magistrates banned blacks from carrying weapons, "meeting and accompanying together . . . in great Companies or Numbers," and "tippling or drinking in or near any House or Shop where strong Liquors are sold."[36]

Leaders expected enslaved peoples to enter the tavern only as servile workers. Surviving probate inventories and travel narratives attest to the importance of these peoples for the tavern trade and civil society at large. Yet, in white men's eyes, black servants and slaves were to respect their inferior social status. As Salinger contended, "The tavern supported gender, status, and race hierarchies within early American society, ultimately sustaining the privilege of well-born white males."[37] Only in transgressing these bounds—or in their sale—did enslaved and servile laborers merit distinction in white men's eyes.

As demonstrated by the New York City fiasco of 1741, white colonists remained paranoid about the possibility of a slave uprising. Yet slave resistance methods, such as running away, caused white men to recognize enslaved tavern workers in ways that they would not have done on an everyday basis. The owner of Charleston's Crown Inn, for instance, advertised that his "Negro named *John*, West-India born, aged about 40," had recently fled. The tavern keeper described John in detail, explaining that the runaway slave "had on when he went away a blue bays Jacket, cloth colour breeches or ticken strip'd." A Pennsylvania tavern keeper, similarly, lamented the escape of her male slave, Joe, in 1778. She described Joe: "He had on when he went away from said tavern, a brown coloured cloth coat, old leather breeches, felt had, and good shoes, he has a stooping awkward walk, his legs bending forward as if the calf grew on his shins, his foreteeth somewhat shattered, has a lump on his collar bone." As establishments that promised their "Gentlemen" customers "good Lodgings, and also Stabling and Pasture for their Horses," these taverns relied on the labor of slaves like John and Joe. Thus their owners went into far greater detail in describing the men's physical and psychological features than they probably ever had before. Similar descriptions accompanied tavern keepers' attempts to sell their valuable slaves. In civil society's eyes, these were people who merited distinction only as objects to be sold or as rebellious disturbers of societal order. If enslaved tavern workers remained in their deferential place, they were largely overlooked by white tavern goers.[38]

Colonial leaders also worried about Indians consuming too much alcohol in taverns. Native Americans commonly entered British American urban centers to trade and settle legal accounts. In many magistrates' minds, however, Indians should be kept away from cities and the myriad taverns they harbored because they simply could not handle the availability of strong liquor. Byrd noted in 1728, "Nothing has been so fatal to [Indians] as their ungovernable passion for rum," and in 1735 the *South Carolina Gazette* ran a poem memorializing different nations' favorite beverages:

The *Russ* loves Brandy, *Dutchman* beer
The *Indian* rum most mighty
The *Welch man* sweet metheglin quaffs
The *Irish* aquavitae
The *French* extol the *Orleans*-grape
The *Spaniard tipples* sherry
The *English* none of these escape
For they with all make merry.[39]

Fearing that access to hard liquor would lead already susceptible Native Americans to become even less controllable and create fissures in the ongoing balancing act of civil society, leaders instated laws forbidding Indians from tavern going.[40] Yet laws prohibiting Indians from purchasing liquor were, as the historian Peter Mancall noted, rather "short-lived, inconsistent, and ineffective."[41] Much to leaders' ire, sneaky tavern keepers and greedy merchants continued to sell liquor to Indians. One Bostonian begged for "some more effectual Provision . . . to restrain Tavern keepers . . . from supplying the Indians with Strong Liquors," arguing that while Indians were "as peaceable a people as any whatsoever" when "not heated with Liquor," drunkenness threw their ranks into "Feuds and Quarrels . . . that sometimes and indeed often, end[ed] in Murder." If kept out of the tavern space and away from liquor, British American and Native American leaders agreed, Indians, merchants, and British American civil society would enjoy a better future.[42]

Gentlemen's efforts to keep ordinary and unfree people out of taverns and away from liquor reveal the complicated and ever-evolving power relationships of British American civil society. Magistrates issued a variety of legal measures aimed at dissuading certain members of society from tavern going and the alcoholic beverages that such endeavors promised. Shrewd tavern keepers also relied on locked liquor cabinets and closed-off rooms to further dissuade servants and the lower sorts from imbibing strong liquors. Ultimately, they expected lower-class and unfree peoples to serve only as inferior workers in taverns, thus maintaining the tenuous order of civil society. As in civil society at large, elitist tavern goers demanded the labor of their social inferiors to enjoy their own tavern experiences while also doing everything in their power to keep those same people out of taverns and away from the drink and revelry that they offered. Their efforts, however, were only partially successful, for ordinary whites and blacks continued to convene in urban taverns throughout the colonies. And, as we will see, gentlemen often joined these "others" in their revels.

If a rake was to thrive, he needed a seedy network of drinking spaces. His requests were fulfilled by an even more controversial (and much more illegal) web of urban taverns: unlicensed, or "disorderly" and "bawdy," taverns. Within these spaces, fringe members of society ran their own taverns (often without a license), traded goods to people officially prohibited from buying them, convened (sometimes violently) away from the prying eyes of most leaders, and sold their bodies on their own terms. Ultimately, unlicensed taverns fueled an informal, "embedded" urban economy, which, in the words of the historian Ellen Hartigan-O'Connor, "maintained a space in the marketplace for those who were excluded—by reasons of status, race, gender, or credit—from buying in the formal economy." As linchpins of this underground world, unlicensed tavern keepers connected a diverse set of ordinary, unfree, and wealthy tavern goers through the exchange of myriad goods and services. But unlicensed taverns also represented yet another contradiction in British American societal order, for just as many leaders damned them as representative of the denigration of civil society, so too did many others (some of those same men, in fact) flock to these very spaces for their rakish respites.[43]

Despite rakes' fondness for unlicensed taverns, these illegal spaces came under harsh fire at midcentury. Leaders especially worried about ordinary colonists' and unfree peoples' actions in these relatively uncontrolled spaces. It was one thing for a man like Goelet and his companions to drop into an unlicensed tavern for an evening—such actions probably did more to establish control than to disintegrate it—but ordinary and unfree men and women running their own drinking spaces beyond the confines of societal order raised the hackles of colonial magistrates. Hence one Bostonian's equation of the "Multiplication of [disorderly] Taverns" with an "Excess of Riot and Debauchery" and another Philadelphian's assertion that the "enormous" increase in "Dram Shops [had led] to the great Corruption of Morals in the Populace."[44] One New Englander fell into outright indignation as he damned his country's propensity for disorder:

> There are also among us *Unlicensed Houses*, (*too many such!*) where our Young Sparks Drink and Game, and Revel for whole Nights together, and Perhaps *Every Night*. And such Vile Houses will be kept . . . [for] the Club of *Rakes*, truly so call'd. And these spend whole Nights in Drinking and Gaming, it is to be fear'd at their Fathers and Masters Expence. The quantitys of *Wine* and *Brandy-Punch* drank (or rather destroy'd) by these Clubs, is incredible. So that their practice is *an Excess of Riot* with an Emphasis.[45]

These spaces allegedly not only birthed but also encouraged disorderly behavior among their uncivil company.

Brandishing laws that punished ordinary colonists "*for keeping an Ale-House, without* License," urban magistrates tried to regulate unlicensed taverns—when they could. The midcentury records of New York City Royal Attorney General John Tabor Kempe are littered with accounts of unlicensed tavern keepers who were caught in their illegal deeds. In just one New York City court session in the early 1760s, magistrates charged eight separate citizens with "keeping a Disorderly house and Entertaining negroes" or "keeping a disorderly and Bawdy house." The New York City widow Catharine Carroe proved especially unruly. She came before the supreme court for "keeping an Infamous Disorderly house, at all hours of the Night People Quarreling and fighting." Not only had Carroe sold wine in her house without a license, but there were also "Evidences in [Carroe's tavern] of a Murder." Unlike the licensed

Williamsburg tavern keeper Anne Pattison, Carroe used her tavern trade to overtly shirk rather than confirm expectations of femininity and civility. Such illegal tavern actions occurred throughout the colonies. From Philadelphia to Charleston citizens kept "Dram-Shops" and "Bawdy Houses" that "retailed spirituous Liquors . . . and drew much of their subsistence from Dealings with Negroes" and other uncivil guests. Though magistrates sought to regulate these spaces, their sheer numbers and mutability made them impossible to quash. Combined with such a transient nature, "bawdy" houses' ability to offer patrons a potent mix of illegally traded goods, people, and ideas made them irresistible.[46]

The opportunity to consume beverages, goods, and services otherwise deemed beyond their station proved especially alluring to ordinary and unfree tavern goers. Unlicensed tavern keepers cultivated a rather healthy informal economy at midcentury. Primarily centered on the exchange of secondhand (often stolen) clothes and alcoholic beverages, this unregulated trade propped up disorderly houses and allowed poor and unfree peoples a heightened opportunity to consume goods their social superiors so often enjoyed. By the time an article of clothing or a bottle of liquor arrived in an unlicensed tavern, it had often trickled through a complex network of theft, enslavement, and elopement. The New York City tavern keeper Ann Brooks was fined fifty pounds and sentenced to three months in jail in 1749 after being "convicted of dealing with Negroes, and receiving stolen Goods from them." One midcentury Williamsburg resident similarly complained, "It is owing to this practice, of buying from the *negroes*, that *Williamsburg* abounds with little dram shops," while officials fined the midcentury New York City tavern keeper William Gillin for "Keeping a Most Infamous and Disorderly House" where he sold "Sundry goods Stolen." Numerous to the point of ubiquity and necessary for almost every facet of society, slaves and ordinary whites could use their status to pilfer goods. Having successfully committed a theft, a colonist could sell her loot on the secondhand market. With a steady flow of customers and a lack of legal control, there was no better place to do this than the unlicensed tavern.[47]

Though trade goods made unlicensed taverns desirable, their alcoholic options might have been their biggest draw for ordinary and unfree people. Living in a society that repeatedly attempted to stop them from consuming "spirituous liquors," many colonists were eager to skirt the rules through overt consumption and the altered mental state that it promised, not to mention the opportunity of temporary pain relief during a time when many ordinary people would have constantly dealt with the nagging pains of minor infections, toothaches, and bowel disorders.[48] Much of this alcohol consumption looked quite informal when compared to the imbibing that went on in licensed taverns. New York City magistrates, for instance, issued a 1741 act that attempted to stop "several Persons . . . not being Tavern-Keepers" from "dispos[ing] of Strong Liquors from their Cellars or Stores, under the Quantity of Five Gallons." The act mentioned that buyers often carried the illegally obtained alcohol off with them, only further alluding to the small-scale, unlicensed, ungoverned alcohol consumption that disorderly houses offered ordinary and unfree urbanites. With so much illicit "Rum, Brandy, Spirits [and] . . . other strong Liquors" exchanging hands in "Houses, Yards . . . Sheds [and] Shelters, Places or Woods near or adjacent to them," magistrates feared that the city might become one big disorderly house.[49]

The combination of alcohol, illegal trading, and uncivil patrons created an arena marked by rude verbal exchanges, including slander, swearing, violence, and behavior sometimes bordering on insanity. Ordinary colonists—often inebriated and angry—utilized the "Open and Publick" nature of disorderly taverns to air their grievances. In 1764, for instance, the baker Leonard Coons stumbled drunkenly out of a lower-class tavern in the West Ward of New York City, "being sick and distempered in his Body and ill with a purging and flux." Onlookers reported that Coons next "discharged his Odurs and Excrements into his Breeches Wickedly and Blasphemously in the presence and hearing of divers Liege Subjects of our said Lord the King worthy of Credit." As if he had not done enough already, Coons proceeded to hoist three pieces of cheese in his grimy hands, which he profanely declared signified the Father, the Son, and the Holy Ghost. Standing in a steaming, soiled pair of breeches and reeking of alcohol, Coons ended his diatribe by screaming out to the gathering crowd, "Christ . . . is a Sinner as well as Other Men. . . . May the Thunder Strike God if me he should punish!" Profane, filthy, and drunken, Coons represented the uncivil exchanges that self-professed gentlemen came to perceive as representative of all disorderly houses and their supposed uncivil patrons by the eighteenth century.[50]

But Coons was hardly the only offender. In 1759, a New York City tavern keeper engaged in a heated, vulgar debate with two of his customers. "Damn you, you Irish son of a Bitch," the New York City tavern keeper John Myers screamed at Patrick Coyne, all the while pointing to a window in his tavern: "I have fucked your Wife oftener than you have in that Room!" Myers continued to spit vitriol at Coyne, calling him a "Bloody Irish Papist Son of a Bitch" and swearing that he had "fucked [Coyne's] wife oftener than [Coyne] has." As an Irish immigrant living in Protestant-heavy, Catholic-wary New York City, Patrick Myers might expect occasional slurs regarding his assumed religion, but such public, slanderous words directed at his wife would not stand. Patrick and his wife, Elizabeth, soon thereafter took Myers to court for slander, and won. We do not know what happened between John Myers and Elizabeth Coyne in the days preceding this public standoff. Elizabeth steadfastly declared that she had always remained faithful to her husband, while Myers asked for the case to be dropped. Small spats that local people overheard but were not affected by, such clashes were some of the most well known features of disorderly houses, especially since newspapers throughout the colonies reported regularly on uncivil conflicts and word of mouth from bystanders spread even more rapidly. The Coynes, for instance, specifically complained that John Myers's tavern was directly in "the presence and Hearing" of their close neighbors, not to mention "divers other [civil] & faithfull" British subjects. Myers's attempt to "deprive . . . Elizabeth of her good Name and Fame" and to bring the Coynes "to the utmost Scandal, Contempt, and Infamy" consequently not only sullied this ordinary couple's reputation but also forced bystanders to witness the uncivil exchange.[51]

Beyond the temptation of material goods, drunkenness, and raucous behavior, prostitution also ran rampant in British American "bawdy" drinking establishments. As one of mankind's oldest professions, prostitution had been a concern in colonial cities from their founding. Bostonians seemed especially resistant (at least publicly) to the rise of brothels in their "city upon a hill": the Boston minister Cotton Mather attempted to rally a group of men to burn the city's brothels to the ground in the early eighteenth century, and two major brothel riots broke out in 1734 and 1737, resulting in the destruction of many of Boston's lewd spaces. As "Seats of Idleness [which] produce many Mischiefs to the overthrow of the Bodies, wasting of the Livelyhoods, and indangering the Souls of those who frequent them," houses of prostitution came under fire in every British American city by midcentury.[52]

Despite magistrates' various attempts to temper prostitution, this popular pastime flourished. The Bostonian Hannah Dilley admitted in May 1753 to permitting "Men, and other suspected Persons not of good Behaviour or Fame, to resort to her Husband's House [a felt maker], and carnally to lie with Whores, which they said Hannah then and there procured for them." And in 1761, Charlestonians were aghast to learn of a runaway slave named Quamino, "well known in town" and "intimate with abundance of black prostitutes, and rogueish fellows." A fugitive white servant woman named Catharine Fitzgerald, finally, was believed to "reside in some of the houses of ill fame in the suburbs" of New York City. Fitzgerald probably escaped to "the *Holy Ground*," which one visitor to New York City described as an area "contiguous within the consecrated liberties of St. Paul's [Church]" where "above 500 ladies of pleasure keep lodgings." Whether colonial leaders liked it or not, prostitution formed a "vital part of the sexual culture of the [midcentury British American] city." The "bawdy" profession was here to stay, and so were the "houses of ill fame" that harbored it.[53]

Hard liquor, fine consumables, raucous interactions, and flesh-for-sale made disorderly taverns loci of uncivil behavior. Importantly, however, ordinary and unfree peoples were hardly their only patrons. No matter certain gentlemen's condemnation, many elitist colonists continued to utilize the growing web of disorderly and bawdy houses for their lewd exploits. Unlicensed urban taverns were the perfect places for rakish behavior. Here a libertine gained easy access to all the excesses and pleasures he might want. Bedecked in the finest fashions and boasting a sword at his hip (which, as we will see, carried its own dangers), a rake asserted his status in a lower-class tavern the moment he stepped through the door.

Despite magistrates' repeated attempts to do away with these "Seats of Idleness and Debauchery," elitist colonists were well known to be among "Brothel-Houses'" most regular customers. In the popular Philadelphia broadside *Hilliad Magna: Being the Life and Adventures of Moll Placket-Hole* (1765), the fictional Philadelphia prostitute Moll Placket relied on wealthy customers for her "*Bawdy-House*" to thrive. "Having furnished herself with handsome Husseys," Moll-Placket soon "had much Custom, and the *Rich*, who were furnished by her in that Way, paid her so largely, that she herself became *Rich*, and bought a House and sundry Lots of Ground." Moll ran the most popular bawdy house in Philadelphia for "Gentlemen," in one case pursuing a "pretty Country Girl" through the market when one of her "Rich Customers" desired her company. Though Moll Placket-Hole's story is technically fictional, it was based on well-known societal maxims of the mid-eighteenth century. Gentlemen throughout the colonies did indeed rely on prostitution rings for rakish behavior, and these urban spaces did indeed thrive. The sex and drunkenness of bawdy houses not only allowed gentlemen rakes to assert their sexual and monetary power over those ordinary and unfree peoples whose illegal transactions sullied the reputation of British American civil society; they also offered otherwise civil men the opportunity to briefly don an uncivil guise with little to no repercussions. As the historian Clare Lyons noted regarding early modern English gentlemen rakes, such behavior was as much about "the will to outrage others" as it was "simply to enjoy excess." Because British America's urban streets, taverns, and brothels were even less regulated than their British counterparts, colonial rakes could "outrage others" through violence, sex, and destruction more than perhaps anywhere else in the British Empire.[54]

If a rake was not entangled with a prostitute or poor servant in a "bawdy" or "disorderly" house, he was probably gathered with his libertine colleagues in the tavern's great room (a generous description for these establishments). Yet, as hinted in Goelet's narrative, these elitist men most likely did not drink alone; rather, they tumbled into a space occupied by lower-class and unfree people. But they did not do so to win friends or seek common ground. Poor whites and black slaves, after all, represented the very bottom rungs of civil order. And while unlicensed taverns provided ordinary and unfree peoples the opportunity to consume goods and services usually denied them, the arrival of a rowdy group of gentlemen rakes soon reminded the "lower sorts" of their inferior status.

Elitist rakes notably relied on disorderly behavior to gain control of the tavern space. As one article from the 1767 *New-York Gazette* (reprinted from the *London Magazine*) explained, a true rake committed "every kind of tumult and disorder . . . [in] bawdy-houses . . . such as jumping about the rooms, putting out the candles, spilling the liquors, breaking the glasses, kicking the waiters, &c. &c." Rakish young gentlemen were well known for such actions by the eighteenth century. William Byrd II recorded in 1712, "Several of our young [Williamsburg] gentlemen were before Mr. Bland this morning for a riot committed at Su Allen's [tavern] . . . but came off with paying 10 shillings a piece." Among the "young gentlemen" who Byrd mentioned were five of the most powerful men in Virginia, including Ralph Wormeley III (future sheriff, customs collector, and vestryman of Christ Church, not to mention the son of one of the richest men in Virginia) and John Grymes (future member of the House of Burgesses for Middlesex and receiver general). Although we cannot know exactly what happened in Su Allen's tavern that night, we can gather a few key facts from the records. Byrd's note, "but came off with paying 10 shillings a piece," is important. These young gentlemen must have made quite a mess to pay ten shillings each (ten shillings was equal to about a week's wages for a worker or a craftsman).[55] One must imagine that if the young men were not such prominent members of society, they might have been briefly jailed or publicly shamed. It is also imperative to note that Susan "Su" Allen was charged only one year after this riot with "keeping a disorderly house." It is not a stretch to believe that these gentlemen knew that Allen's tavern offered more than just the pleasures of drink. It was the perfect stage for the rake.[56]

Gentlemen rakes often broadcast their disorderly intentions through the ultimate "attitude of defiance": violence. Elitist colonists had long ridiculed ordinary colonists' love of tavern fighting and boxing matches. Leaders in the port city of Perth Amboy, New Jersey, just across the bay from New York City, must have been disgusted when one sailor died after a boxing match at a local tavern in 1749. A show of bravery from one man had apparently led to resentment from another, which resulted in "a trial of skill at boxing" between the two. After the bloody match, the two men "drank friends" before "the person who boasted of his strength, died in a few minutes after." Ordinary southern tavern goers were even more prone to brawl, as social norms often demanded physical recourse if one felt dishonored. A visitor to the southern colonies remembered joining a crowd who gathered to watch two brawlers "Kicking, Scratching[,] . . . Biting[,] . . . Throttling, Gouging [the eyes], [and] Dismembering [the genitals]." This was hardly the type of behavior in which leaders expected allegedly cultured gentlemen to engage. But it did not stop many of them from doing so.[57]

Though elitist men occasionally came to blows with each other in genteel taverns and coffeehouses, rakes' brawls in disorderly and bawdy houses were more deliberate actions with specific intentions.[58] By engaging in organized and spontaneous brawls at disorderly taverns, rakes not only used one of ordinary colonists' favorite pastimes to assert their masculinity and social capital but also eschewed civil ideals of polite interaction. Often carrying a sword on their hip, a pistol at their breast, and an air of condescension, these raucous gentlemen were ready for a scrap.[59] And scrap they did. In an especially disturbing case from 1756, a group of men "detain'd one Thomas Watts, a young simple Man," at a Maryland tavern for three days of hell. They pushed and pulled the recently freed indentured servant about, punching and kicking him all the while. After beating poor Watts until he could no longer stand, let alone resist, the tormenters pushed him into the chimney corner, swept soot onto his face, threw water on him, and scalded his genitals with a firebrand, "which burnt him in a terrible Manner." Having heard the violence from outside, another patron finally gained access to the tavern and carried

Watts home to his mother, "where he died almost as soon as they could lay him in his Bed, his Body being all over Wounds, Bruises, and Burns." Although "the Magistrates were very industrious to find out the hellish Authors," the records suggest that the men who committed this horrible crime were never brought to justice. How, one wonders, were these men able to imprison and torture Watts in a tavern for "near three days" without anyone stopping them? (Only when Watts was already as good as dead did "one Man" take the poor boy to die at his mother's house.) Why did they want to do such a thing?[60]

The case of poor Thomas Watts was, thankfully, an extreme one. Most of the violence perpetrated by rakes resembled the riotous actions of those five Williamsburg gentlemen at Susan Allen's disorderly tavern. Tables turned, fists bared, and punch bowls rolling, such unruly conduct transformed the tavern space into an uncivil sphere of chaos but not of torture or death. And gentlemen rakes would have left as they entered—boisterous, condescending, and socially powerful. At least for self-professed elites, uncivil behavior did not ultimately make one uncivil.

British American popular media, in fact, celebrated gentlemen's rakish behavior. Following in the footsteps of their British compatriots, colonial printers created and reprinted a variety of works featuring the rake and the libertine.[61] As Lyons contended, "The young men of popular print culture of the 1760s were creating a masculine sexuality that expected a period of youthful sexual experimentation." The media "produced" the rake just as much as the rake created himself. In 1759, for instance, the Philadelphian Abraham Weatherwise reprinted a London poem called "Proper Ingredients to Make a Modern Beau" in his *Father Abraham's Almanack*. A playful take on the rake, the poem noted that a true libertine should demonstrate "the appearance of a grand estate; A clouded cane, a sword with silver hilt, a ring, a watch, a snuff-box double gilt; a gay, effeminate, embroider'd vest." In the popular London periodical turned four-volume set, *The Connoisseur* (originally published from 1754 to 1756), colonists followed the exploits of London rakes as they played "the most wild and extravagant pranks, that wantonness and debauchery can suggest." The editor of *The Connoisseur*, "Mr. Town," took a rather sarcastic tone in his tales of "men of the town." The Englishman followed these libertines as they went about "beating the rounds" (which usually entailed "taking a tour of the principal bawdy-houses," acting riotously, and committing "a rape on a modest woman"). *The Connoisseur* sold well in colonial cities by the 1760s. Whether certain colonists liked it or not, many otherwise "polite" men enjoyed reading about—and acting as—the rake.[62]

Despite its popularity and general acceptance throughout the British Atlantic world, rakish behavior garnered its fair share of criticism from elitist British Americans. Reflecting on his own place in society in 1755, a young John Adams declared, "Let others waste the bloom of Life, at the Card or billiard Table, among rakes and fools, and when their minds are sufficiently fretted with losses, and inflamed by Wine, ramble through the Streets, assaulting innocent People, breaking Windows or debauching young Girls." Adams continued to damn gentlemen's rakish actions, recounting a young girl who, being seduced by "a fine Gentleman with laced hat and waist coat, and a sword," was left nine months later "with [a bastard] Child [and] without a Friend upon Earth that will own her." Adams was hardly alone in his wariness of the gentleman rake: Benjamin Franklin addressed attempts at reforming "*Rakes* and *Beaus* . . . in their morals," and Dr. Alexander Hamilton lamented that "three young rakes" ruined his New York City tavern discussion when they "bounced in upon" his company and turned the conversation "from a grave to a wanton strain[,] . . . [for] there was nothing talked of but ladys and lovers, and a good deal of polite smutt." Having shared two toasts with the rakes, Hamilton and one compatriot "went home like two philosophers," while the rest of their company—swayed by smutty conversation and alcohol—went "whoreing" with the rakes in the city's many disorderly houses.[63]

By appropriating shocking modes of behavior, British American rakes brought the mutable nature of civil society full circle. Not only did elitist colonists attempt to keep ordinary and unfree people in taverns as servants rather than guests, but certain gentlemen also joined these allegedly uncivil tavern companies. Rakes and libertines utilized every possible opportunity for incivility in bawdy and disorderly houses: they fought, fornicated, and frolicked to an extreme degree and in doing so thumbed their noses at polite notions of civility. Like the eighteenth-century British American planters whom the historian Trevor Burnard recently investigated, British American urban rakes (most of whom also owned slaves and some of whom ran plantations) utilized extreme actions of violence to solve "the problem of discipline through the application of terror" over socially inferior colonists. Actual punishment of rakish behavior, after all, was seldom severe, and implementation of violent tactics had tangible, immediate effects on those targeted. Specifically, urban leaders wanted to keep lower-class and unfree people in a place of fear, inferiority, and deference. Gentlemen knew that they could act uncivilly without being considered permanently uncivil by their peers.[64]

Ultimately, the rakish behavior of gentlemen further demonstrates elitist colonists' muddled and contradictory efforts to direct a British American civil society. Just as they perceived the lower sorts as exhibiting a dangerous disregard for deference, so too did many self-professed gentlemen utilize those same sorts' taverns as spheres through which to assert their power. Although leaders repeatedly emphasized that the lines between civil and uncivil society were clear and hard, moreover, they crossed them whenever they deemed it necessary (or simply fun). Such actions fit within anxious urbanites' larger attempts to realize a British American civil society. They made up the rules as they went and expected those they deemed inferior to stay in their place. After 1765, however, these contradictions would come back to haunt elitist colonists in real ways.

5 / "They will begin to think their united power irresistible": The Stamp Act and the Crisis of Civil Society

By 1765, the Philadelphian William Bradford—like so many other owners of taverns and coffeehouses throughout British North America—had established the London Coffee House as a nucleus of his city's social, commercial, and ideological development. The courthouse, post office, academy, charity schools, theater, customhouse, and Mason's lodge all lay within a few blocks, as did religious centers like Christ Church, the Presbyterian church, and the Great Meeting-House of the Friends. Nearby businesses, meanwhile, brought customers to the coffeehouse's doors. Genteel patrons could read the newspaper, sip a beverage, or while away the day perusing books and chatting with fellow guests.[1] When the Stamp Act arrived on North America's shores in July 1765, however, the London Coffee House—and many other urban taverns and coffeehouses—were cast into a crisis of imperial policy and civil society. During the Stamp Act Crisis (August 1765–April 1766), taverns and coffeehouses emerged as spaces that revealed the contradictions of civil society more poignantly, and catastrophically, than ever before.

Though a well-established center of imperial belonging and civil sociability, the London Coffee House was transformed into the heart of opposition to the Stamp Act after August 1765 (Figure 5).[2] When Philadelphia's recently appointed stamp collector, John Hughes, refused to step down from his post in early September 1765, Bradford invited colonists to convene at his tavern, light bonfires, and shout threats at Hughes's nearby residence. Barricaded inside his home as angry colonists arrived from Bradford's tavern, Hughes wrote to his "old Friend"

Benjamin Franklin (who currently resided in England) on the night of September 16 that this letter "may be the last you will receive from [me], as the Spirit or Flame of Rebellion is got to a high Pitch amongst the North Americans. . . . [A] Sort of Frenzy or Madness has got such hold of the People of all Ranks, that I fancy . . . my Property, and perhaps my Life, may be lost in this Province." The night ended without bloodshed, but Hughes woke the next morning to a "violent disorder" that would confine him to his bed for the next three weeks.[3]

The arrival of the detested stamps and his official commission on October 4, 1765, only made matters worse for the frightened stamp collector. Bradford once again used word of mouth to organize a mob at his coffeehouse and joined his fellow resisters in beating muffled drums and ringing the state house bells. With the chief justice's genteel son, William Allen, "at their head animating and encouraging the lower class," the mob marched toward Hughes's house. When the alderman, Benjamin Shoemaker, confronted the throng and demanded who had ordered them to convene, they replied simply that "they had their orders from the [London] coffee-house" and threw him out of their way. Bradford and seven other prominent Philadelphians shuffled through the angry crowd that surrounded Hughes's home and convinced the bedridden man to resign. After stepping down, Hughes warned London that if British America's "mobbing gentry" continued to be allowed to act in such a way, "her empire in North America is at an end; for I dare say . . . they will begin to think their united power irresistible." By organizing their efforts within and around the urban coffeehouse, ordinary and elitist colonists had combined their forces to bring down the Philadelphia stamp master.[4]

The historian Peter Thompson has documented the centrality of Bradford's London Coffee House to the urbane development of Philadelphia, while other scholars have investigated how the Stamp Act affected tavern going in New York City and Boston.[5] So too have historians uncovered the festive culture that fueled resistance to the Stamp Act.[6] This chapter explores the connections between public politics and tavern going to demonstrate how taverns and coffeehouses became key stages on which ordinary and genteel colonists navigated the convoluted future of British American civil society during the Stamp Act Crisis. Specifically, investigating the Stamp Act Crisis through the lens of the tavern not only establishes the ongoing centrality of these public spaces for British American society building but also reveals how problematic the contradictions of civil society had become by 1765. On the one hand, leaders

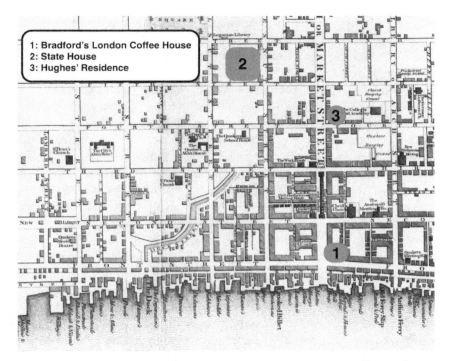

1: Bradford's London Coffee House
2: State House
3: Hughes' Residence

FIGURE 5. "Bradford's London Coffee House and the Stamp Act Riots of 1765." Created by author from Benjamin Easburn, *A Plan of the City of Philadelphia, the Capital of Pennsylvania, from an Actual Survey* (London: Andrew Drury, 1776). Retrieved from the Library of Congress, Washington, DC, December 19, 2016, https://www.loc.gov/item/gm71002155/.

had long publicly disdained class mixing in taverns and had done everything in their power to impose order on the urban landscape. Gentlemen especially relied on Old World traditions of spatial exclusivity, consumer power, and cosmopolitan identity formation to establish themselves as polite leaders of British North America.

Yet their theories of civil order were steadily overshadowed by messy, often contradictory, realities. Not only had class mixing in urban taverns become a popular and profitable pastime by midcentury, but supposedly genteel men joined their English colleagues by relying on the colonies' seediest urban taverns for their rakish pursuits. Whether gentlemen liked to admit it or not, they had helped to nurture a society defined by ambiguity and confusion where their perceived power diminished by the day in exchange for the rising influence of ordinary and unfree people. The long-smoldering inconsistencies of elitist colonists' civilizing mission provided the perfect tinder to set fire to the Stamp Act resistance—and keep it burning hot.

Colonists generally interpreted clashes over the Stamp Act as an ultimate test for the tenuous future of British American civil society rather than an event that marked a separation with the British Empire.[7] Yet, more than anything, this pivotal incident only further muddied the already murky waters of order and distinction in British North America's urban centers. Urbanites deemed fellow countrymen who supported the Stamp Act "Enemies to the Public Repose" and thus stripped them of the protections of civil society, even if they possessed considerable social capital. Colonists who resisted the Stamp Act (and deemed themselves "Friends of Liberty"), meanwhile, took advantage of the mutable nature of civility to negotiate their own identities. Steadily, one's political allegiance came to outstrip his social status in his locality.[8] In these ongoing acts of improvisation, moreover, elitist colonists often joined their social inferiors in coercive actions: certain gentlemen were willing to take their "rakish" behavior to new heights in opposing the Stamp Act but not without dangerous recourse. As had always been the case with British American civil society, new lines were drawn just as others were crossed.

Colonists thus convened in urban taverns to debate—and, in some cases, violently restructure—ever-changing notions of order and disorder, civility and incivility. Taverns' societal centrality, lenient regulatory measures, access to alcohol, and ability to offer multiple services to a diverse set of white men made them ideal spaces for such negotiations, which played out in three interrelated ways. First, self-professed gentlemen leaders utilized certain tavern and coffeehouses' existing communication networks to hurl threats at their foes while also attempting to bring order to ordinary colonists. Classic theories of civil societal order judged this tactic as the most genteel and logical. Yet, as has been well established, classical theories tended to disintegrate in the face of reality.

Second, and most commonly, ordinary and polite colonists capitalized on urban taverns' public preeminence to damage property in a riotous manner. Gentlemen once again donned the guise of the rake in order to act in ways otherwise deemed below their station, while ordinary colonists utilized their growing political power to establish their authority over stamp officials and governing bodies. In an ideal scenario, resistance efforts would have never extended beyond these tactics. By 1765, however, colonial society was far from ideal.

The third and most extreme tactic unfolded when groups consisting primarily of ordinary colonists united to commit acts of all-out violence on those they considered representative of injustice. Gentlemen rakes tended to drop out of these affairs, as they deemed such actions destructive to classical notions of the civilizing process and, perhaps even more important, damaging to the colonies' relationship with the empire. No matter gentlemen's detestation of many of these measures, they had to embrace the influence of ordinary colonists if they were to realize their shared goal: topple the Stamp Act and, in turn, guarantee a prosperous (if forever altered) future for British American civil society.

It is not as if tavern riots emerged out of nowhere in 1765. Riotous protest, in fact, had long affected the colonial tavern space as well as the British American urban landscape.[9] One source has estimated that 159 riots occurred in the colonies between 1740 and 1775, and at least nineteen people lost their lives to riots between 1700 and 1765. During the Stamp Act unrest, at least sixty riots broke out in twenty-five different locations.[10] Though colonial riots rarely ended in mortal injury, these frightful events were hardly tame. Usually involving anywhere from ten to one hundred men from varying social backgrounds, riots were violent affairs intended to punish specific offenders and effect immediate change.

While it would be easy to assume that leaders deemed riotous activity as the disorderly revels of uncivil colonists, self-professed gentlemen's comprehensions of riots, like their ideas surrounding civil society, proved complicated. Though colonial leaders generally dissuaded riotous proceedings (especially when they targeted elitist peoples), gentlemen sometimes took the helm of riots for personal or local motives. Riotous activity, after all, had been a mainstay of the British social system for hundreds of years: many English leaders saw popular protest as a sign of a functioning government and thus expected such activity to occasionally break out.[11] If riots resulted in minimum damage to person or property and remained under the control of gentlemen leaders, they were deemed rather natural and orderly, at least as riots went. When the wealthy Boston merchant John Rowe witnessed a husband and wife "set on the Gallows for Cruelly & Willfully endeavouring to starve their Child" in 1764, he supported the mob's decision to pelt the man with stones, contending that such extralegal punishment "was what he deserved."[12] Those rioters deemed orderly or justified regularly escaped strict punishment, as leaders considered their actions unfortunate but necessary checks on governmental power. Participants in Boston's bread riots (1713), New

Jersey's tenant riots (1745–54), and Boston's Knowles riots (1747) enjoyed protection because of public agreement with their cause, combined with a lack of official power to stop them. As would become clear in 1765 and 1766, right and wrong was often in the eye of the beholder when it came to riots.[13]

Only when riotous behavior extended beyond middling- and upper-class colonists' control did elitist colonists deem such actions as falling wholly into the realm of incivility. Of course, extending beyond the control of civil society was not the same as entirely excluding gentlemen. As they often did in their rakish tavern interactions, otherwise genteel colonists frequently joined ordinary and unfree people in their tumultuous, destructive, and sometimes violent behavior during the Stamp Act riots. Other gentlemen, meanwhile, deemed such incivility as dangerous revels of the lower sorts that needed to be snuffed out immediately. But it was not this easy. Though often damned by colonial magistrates, rioters frequently escaped punishment. Not only did colonial leaders lack sufficient policing measures to discipline the masses, but the fact that they were so often outnumbered by the lower sorts often made any such efforts futile. As with the contradictions of British American society that had arisen over the past fifty years, incivility continued to intertwine with civility during the turbulent period of 1765 to 1766.

"Civil" Resistance: Nonviolent Threats and Political Mobilization

Middling- and upper-class colonists attempted to direct the masses by establishing genteel urban taverns and coffeehouses (along with a handful of nearby, interconnected urban spaces and landmarks) as headquarters of nonviolent, orderly resistance to the Stamp Act. They penned coercive tracts, hosted grand dinners and majestic spectacles, organized their consumer power to oppose British statutes they considered oppressive, and communicated with fellow colonists throughout British North America. In doing so, elitist tavern goers hoped to direct an "orderly" sort of resistance that would allow them to maintain local power while also demonstrating their power and loyalty to the Crown.

Colonial politicians had long recognized the importance of the tavern space for acquiring and directing an audience. When Dr. Hamilton arrived at a New York tavern in 1744, he could hardly find a seat before "a band of town politicians in short jackets and trowsers" rushed to his table, "curious to know who them strangers were who had newly arrived in town." A little over a month later, Dr. Hamilton listened as "great crowds of the politicians of the town" read out the recently arrived news at a Newport tavern. Though mocked by Dr. Hamilton for their numerous "orthographicall blunders," the aspiring leaders nonetheless utilized the tavern space's public nature for their own political goals.[14] Whereas politicians' use of taverns for self-promotion generally amused Hamilton, they disgusted John Adams. The Boston lawyer lamented in 1760 that taverns had become "in many Places the Nurseries of our Legislators." Adams ridiculed certain politicians as nothing more than villains who secured "the Votes of a Taverner" and in turn used the allure of "Phlip [flip, a popular alcoholic beverage] and Rum" to acquire votes from the "Rabble." No matter Adams's damning criticisms, politicians exploited taverns' public nature to gain a mass following and, often, achieve a semblance of control over diverse peoples. Taverns, as Hamilton and Adams noted, offered leaders a central space where they could distribute their messages—and copious amounts of alcohol—widely and effectively. As resistance to the Stamp Act unfolded, colonial leaders relied on certain taverns to do the same thing.[15]

On October 31, 1765, a meeting took place at Burns Coffee House in New York City that permanently disrupted the colonies' long-standing and lucrative trade relationship with the British Empire. Having convened in the exclusive coffeehouse a day before the dreaded Stamp Act was to go into effect, at least two hundred New York City merchants decided to use the colonies' massive consumer power to get London's attention. The "Non-Importation Agreement" they drew up stipulated that New York's merchants, who were just as short on the silver specie that the Stamp Act required as their social inferiors, refused to import goods from England until the official repeal of the act. Colonists had long understood their position within the British Empire according to the vast quantities of goods they imported from Britain. Such imports gave them a real stake in the empire and, in turn, a sense of economic importance in the larger world. By using the language of consumerism, these coffeehouse merchants hoped to influence ordinary colonists and English policy makers alike without destruction, rioting, or bloodshed.[16]

It was no accident that New York City's merchants gathered in a coffeehouse to enact this shocking edict. Coffeehouses like Burns Coffee House (New York City), Bradford's London Coffee House (Philadelphia), the Crown Coffee House (Boston), and the Carolina Coffee House (Charleston), after all, had opened with the express purpose of offering polite customers the opportunity to make trade deals, organize committee and club meetings, and hold grand balls and dinners.[17] Customers simply utilized these services for their newly defiant measures. By temporarily refusing to import the very goods that made coffeehouses so desirable, merchants and publicans made their point loud and clear: they would not support trade and taxation beyond their control, especially when the trade demanded levels of silver beyond their reach and pocketbooks. The New York City merchants' actions had immediate implications in the colonies. Philadelphia's merchants adopted a similar agreement on November 7, with Boston following on December 1, 1765.[18]

After witnessing the success of the merchants at Burns Coffee House, New York City's Sons of Liberty established their permanent headquarters at the Merchant Coffee House (Figure 6). Boasting multiple rooms in its two levels and a balcony on the roof, the Merchant Coffee House on Wall Street attracted diverse customers from throughout the city and the British Empire, thus making it an ideal spot from which to operate their resistance. The prime location and myriad services offered by the Merchant Coffee House allowed the Sons to exchange letters with their brethren in Philadelphia and initiate relationships with many of the most notable colonial presses.[19]

Until the repeal of the Stamp Act, New York City's Sons of Liberty used the Merchant Coffee House to resist the Stamp Act with, in their words, "the utmost Decency."[20] Those colonists who represented the Stamp Act, however, hardly deemed the New York City Sons' acts as civil or decent. While hiding in his city's fort, Governor Cadwallader Colden received a coercive letter penned by New York City's Sons of Liberty on November 1, 1765. They hung the letter "up at the [Merchant] Coffee House all Day" so that the whole city would understand their mission before they delivered the missive to Colden in the evening. Having heard rumors that Colden planned to subdue the rebellious city by military force, New York's Sons warned him, "If you dare to Perpetrate any Such murderous Act . . . You'll die a Martyr to your own Villainy, & be Hang'd . . . upon a Sign-Post, as a Memento to all wicked Governors, and that every Man, that assists you, Shall be, surely, put To Death." While the Sons of Liberty almost surely never intended to kill Colden, the governor did not dismiss their letter, noting that "A Rebellious Mob" organized by elitist colonists in the Merchant Coffee House took control of New York City later that night. Frightened for his and his followers' safety, Colden spent November 2, 1765, planning the best means of barricading his fort: reinforced walls, embankments, "light artillery," "One hundred hand Grenades," and "A Howitzer to be mounted on each Curtin towards the Town."[21]

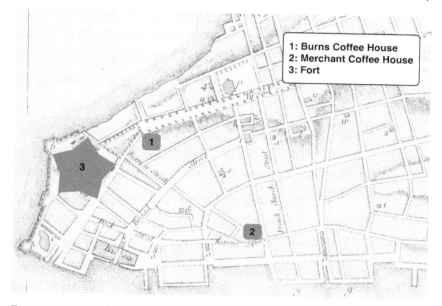

FIGURE 6. Detail from John Montrésor, *Plan de New-York et des environs* (Paris: Goerges-Louis Le Rouge, 1777). Retrieved from the New York Public Library Digital Collections, New York, NY, December 19, 2016, http://digitalcollections.nypl.org/items/510d47da-ee31-a3d9-e040-e00a18064a99.

Pointing to their civil intentions, New York's Sons of Liberty contended in another letter, posted in the Merchant Coffee House on November 5, 1765, that they "acted not as a Mob, but as Friends to Liberties."[22] Colonial leaders wanted to make sure that colonists followed through with their coercion—as long, that is, as the rioters were white, male, and under the general control of civil leaders. But this proved a tricky proposition, for while leaders relied largely on mass resistance to further their own cause at home, they also needed to represent themselves as loyal subjects in control of the colonies to their superiors in London. Hence New Yorkers' professions that they were "Friends to Liberties" days after they had threatened Governor Colden's life and wrested control of the city from him. Here, yet again, emerged the inconsistencies of civility: one might represent himself as genteel while acting quite the opposite. Such contradictions would afford elitist colonists valuable power, for a time.

Having established themselves at the Merchant Coffee House, New York City's leading resisters began to utilize the tavern for further meetings and communications with their colleagues throughout the colonies. When a ship's captain arrived in New York City's harbor in December 1765 with "a stampt let-pass" from England, he knew to immediately post this detested paper in the Merchant Coffee House. "Numbers with dejected countenances" immediately flocked to see the stamped paper. Something had to be done. Expecting that "Troops would be sent from England to enforce their Submission to the Stamp Act," the New York City Sons of Liberty soon sent agents to a New London, Connecticut, tavern to organize a military alliance between Connecticut and New York. As soon as the New York representatives arrived in the Connecticut tavern, they "sent for 6 or 7 Inhabitants of New London who were known to be most violent against the Stamp Act." New York's Sons of Liberty thus sought to extend their network of power by means of planned tavern interactions. These spaces had served New Yorkers well in the past, and resisters assumed taverns would continue to help them in the future. They also sent agents to Norwich, Connecticut, and Boston, Massachusetts, to muster allies.[23]

Growing more anxious by the day, colonists throughout the rest of North America rushed to transform taverns into their de facto headquarters for coercion and threats. Though the Annapolis Sons of Liberty professed their "Faith and true Allegiance to his Majesty King GEORGE the Third" at a local tavern, they also publicly threatened "every Stamp-Pimp, Informer, or Favourer of the [Stamp] Act" by constructing effigies and making loud toasts. "A concourse of [Williamsburg] gentlemen" intercepted the newly arrived chief distributor of stamps for Virginia, George Mercer, as he walked into town and ushered him to the local coffeehouse. "Declaring they would not depart" until Mercer resigned, the growing crowd coerced Mercer into promising "that neither he, nor any deputy for him, should put that law in execution." This declaration "gave such general satisfaction" that the town erupted into celebration almost immediately.[24]

Bostonian gentlemen echoed their brethren in Philadelphia and New York City by adopting a single tavern—the Royal Exchange Tavern—to threaten all who opposed their coercive measures. Having "stuck up" a paper at the popular Exchange Tavern in August 1765 detailing the efficacy of their leaders, the Boston rebels also stressed their willingness "to rise again on a like occasion." Boston's governor, Francis Bernard, lamented on August 18, 1765, "I am entirely at the mercy of the Mob; &

how merciless it is I have seen: I have no place of Safety to resort to, but this fort with a weak garrison." Barricaded inside Castle William and feeling more helpless by the day, Bernard could only exclaim, "It is well if this Spirit does not run thro' the continent."[25] It was, however, too late to stop this blaze.

Bostonians gathered once again at the Royal Exchange Tavern on November 5, 1765 to make a far grander show of order, liberty, and power. Though November 5 (Guy Fawkes Day, also known as Gunpowder Day or Pope's Day) had long been marked by violence, disorder, and lower-class revelry, on this day "the morning was all quietness" since the once-warring North and South Ends had "in a very orderly manner . . . engaged in a union" based on their shared distaste for the Stamp Act (and extensive bribes from elitist Bostonians, including John Hancock). Rather than fight each other in the city center with brickbats and clubs, the two sides "met in King-Street where the union was established in a very ceremonial manner." Once little more than a riotous shoemaker, Ebenezer MacIntosh now donned military garb and flashed a genteel "rattan cane" as he led the South End parade (complete with popes, devils, and other effigies signifying slavery and oppression) through the city to the Liberty Tree and on to the Royal Exchange Tavern for a "Union Feast." Boston's leaders—some of whom marched side by side with MacIntosh—provided the South End rabble-rouser with these polite accessories in the hope that it would subdue him. In this instance, it worked. After taking "their rooms and seats respectively," both the genteel and the ordinary tavern guests joined in a "grand supper," complete with "loyal healths" and "toasts proper to the occasion and present day." The *Boston Evening Post* noted that the North and South Enders "who had formerly been at variance were joining together with heart and hand in flowing bowls and bumping glasses; and were so united as even to eradicate from their memory all former enmity." Continuing the day's general decorum, "the whole closed at nine o'clock in good order."[26]

Here, then, was the pinnacle of societal order that elitist colonists wanted to display to the Crown. "Several Gentlemen" controlled the most disorderly of all Bostonians on what was traditionally the most riotous of days. They used a shared abhorrence for the Stamp Act, not to mention the promise of money, to unite these two sides and in the process maintained as much order "as could hardly be expected among a concourse of several thousand people." Although on past Pope's Days "the servants and negroes would disguise themselves and . . . engage each other with great violence," on this November 5 "not a club was seen among the whole, nor was any negro allowed to approach near the stage." The "Union Feast" at the Royal Exchange Tavern symbolized a civil decorum that transcended the street and parade. Men from both sides of town convened in one of Boston's most popular public spaces, among the most civilized company and equipage, to express not only their distaste for the Stamp Act but also their loyalty to the Crown and love of English liberty. According to the *Boston Gazette*, "This union . . . may be looked upon as perhaps the only happy effect arising from the stamp act." Boston's middling- and upper-class leaders liked to think that they had gotten that much closer to fully realizing a British American civil society.[27]

Bostonians' relative success was not without precedent, as Newport's elitist colonists also adopted a local tavern to threaten officials, organize public support, and profess the success of civil resistance. Like Boston's MacIntosh, an ordinary "Irish young Fellow" named John Webber lured the masses to a tavern with barrels of rum and wedges of cheese (provided by Newport's leaders, who hoped to direct the day's proceedings). After filling themselves with the complimentary victuals, the tavern goers set off on a parade, complete with the haltered, hanging effigies of three local gentlemen: Augustus Johnston (the Newport stamp distributor), Martin Howard Jr., and Dr. Thomas Moffat. Despite the relatively coercive nature of the day's events, the *Newport Mercury* reported that the early part of the day was generally "conducted with Moderation, and no Violence offered to the Persons or Property of any Man." "Moderation" is, of course, a subjective term. Three Loyalists whose hanging effigies were burned in front of the Town House by drunken rioters probably felt little comfort. Nor did the sign posted to the effigies warning, "That Person who shall Efface this Publick Mark of Resentment will be Deem'd an Enemy to liberty and Accordingly meet with Proper Chastisement," inspire very much comfort in many citizens of Newport. Nevertheless, in the minds of the gentlemen who directed the day's proceedings and the ordinary colonists who followed Webber, their resistance measures were a resounding success.[28]

When allegedly civil leaders were not directing genteel parades, they often led efforts to burn newly arrived stamps. Never one to miss out on a chance to organize against the Stamp Act, William Bradford recounted to New York City's Sons of Liberty on February 14, 1766, how he had turned his Philadelphia Coffee House into a stage for flames and festivity. After intercepting a parcel of stamped papers destined for Maryland, Bradford brought the "Infernal Stamps" back to his "very full Coffee House," where they were "consumed by fire amidst loud acclamations."

Bradford assured the New York Sons of Liberty, "You may depend that a watchful Eye shall be kept in this Province." Using his coffeehouse as his headquarters, Bradford remained more than ready to make "proper Use" of any more stamps that found their way into Philadelphia.[29]

Bradford was not alone. After burning "a stamped News-Paper" in a "stately Bonfire" on January 31, 1766, Marblehead's residents "retired to a Tavern, where many Toasts expressive of their Regard to the happy Constitution procur'd by their Ancestors, were drank." Earlier that month, a group of twenty men "calling each other Liberty boys and not by their proper names," forced themselves onto a ship in New York City's port and destroyed "five boxes" of stamps. The Milford, Connecticut, Sons of Liberty tried and "found guilty of Slavery and Imposition" a sheet of "detestable" stamped paper on January 24, 1766. The Sons tasked "A common Hangman" with executing the paper by flame later that evening. All watched as colonists from Philadelphia to Milford cheered on the flames of resistance.[30]

Having led the "lower sorts" in a variety of military and civil endeavors over the past half century, elitist men well realized the need for ordinary colonists in their resistance to the Stamp Act. A group of gentlemen supported lower-class leaders such as Ebenezer MacIntosh and John Webber in their exploits, even going so far as to dress up MacIntosh in military garb, commend ordinary whites on keeping blacks away from the stage, and praise Webber for the "moderation" of his effigy-carrying parade. In a rather interesting twist, elitist leaders realized that they must ally with the masses they had so struggled to control (and distance themselves from) if they were to gain any ground in this resistance. They also knew that there was no better place to order throngs of ordinary colonists than their own city taverns and coffeehouses. Affluent Newport citizens surely funded Webber's offerings of rum and cheese (though he was ultimately imprisoned), while upper-class Bostonians sat side by side with MacIntosh and his men at the Union Feast and leading members of Philadelphia society joined in the stamp burning at Bradford's Coffee House.[31] The wealthier and more powerful sector of the colonial resistance to the Stamp Act encouraged mobs of colonists to gather in taverns and intimidate their political foes, as long as they maintained a sense of "order," "moderation," and control. But these gentlemen played a dangerous game, for their actions only further jumbled the already convoluted societal order within which urbanites had existed over the past half decade. As 1765 wore on, it became clear that acts of nonviolent coercion were often the exception to the rule. These coercive acts of destruction, importantly, extended beyond genteel notions of civil resistance.

The Revels of the "Rabble": Disorderly Property Destruction Prevails

Although colonial leaders strove to organize their own coffeehouses and city taverns as centers of civil resistance to the Stamp Act, opposition measures frequently devolved into disorderly riots that resulted in demolished structures, ransacked houses, and frightened families. Self-appointed leaders held an illusory leash around the neck of "the many headed hydra."[32] This should not have come as a surprise. Elitist men, after all, had never really "controlled" ordinary colonists. Instead, they had retreated to their own taverns, theater boxes, and mansions over the past fifty years to distance themselves from those they considered of inferior social status. Or they had joined those they so often damned in a blur of rakish revelry. Ordinary colonists had their own complicated agendas, and they would take matters into their own hands when they saw fit. Such impulses, unfortunately, often culminated in riots and property damage.[33]

Where gentlemen usually preferred to capitalize on the public nature of preselected genteel taverns to commit more symbolic measures of resistance, ordinary colonists and their rakish colleagues often relied on taverns' more raucous character to incite destruction throughout colonial cities. Many taverns offered disgruntled colonists a well-known place to convene, copious amounts of alcohol, lax regulatory measures, and a socially diverse, ready-made group of fellow rioters. To many elitist colonists' ultimate frustration, such tavern riots lay beyond punishment measures. The lower sorts had too much public support and leaders too little power. Various urban taverns consequently served ordinary colonists' hardscrabble realities far more than gentlemen's pipe dreams of civil resistance.

Although Boston gentlemen liked to tout their "Pope Day" parade as indicative of the success of civil measures, such an event proved the exception to the rule, as confusion, property destruction, and disintegration of elitist-controlled resistance efforts defined 1765 and 1766. On August 14, a tavern club of supposedly civil Bostonians who called themselves the "Loyal Nine" attempted to control local resistance to the Stamp Act. After meeting in a local distillery on the night of August 13, they decided to decorate a nearby "Liberty Tree" with the effigy of the local stamp officer, Andrew Oliver. Surrounded by a number of residences and taverns, Boston's Liberty Tree became an informal nerve center of opposition over the next two weeks (see Figure 7, below). Unfortunately for the "Loyal Nine," their alleged control of the situation quickly fragmented.[34]

August 14 started off as a rather orderly day but rapidly descended into chaos. First "the Mob," as the governor of Massachusetts, Francis Bernard, described the Stamp Act rioters, displayed Oliver's effigy at the Liberty Tree during the afternoon. They then reconvened in local taverns to gain further public support and watch the tree through doors and windows. When Sheriff Greenleaf arrived later in the day to destroy the effigy, an angry mob, complete with around "50 Gentlemen Actors . . . disguised with trousers & Jackets on," ran him off.[35] These Boston "Gentlemen" were indeed "Actors." Like gentlemen rakes who convened in midcentury taverns, this group of fifty men traded their velveteen coats and powdered wigs for more uncivil identities—in this case wearing rough trousers and jackets—to signify their participation in riotous activity. Having helped to run off the sheriff, the "Gentlemen Actors" continued the day's riot by parading Oliver's drooping effigy in front of the Town House where Governor Bernard and his fellow officials sat for a council meeting. The "many thousands" of men "gave three huzza's by way of defiance & passed on." As if the sight of gentlemen "actors" and ordinary colonists marching side by side was not maddening enough for Barnard and his fellow magistrates, things were about to get worse.[36]

The throng proceeded deeper into Boston and steadily beyond the control of magistrates. After tearing down a building they believed would serve as the stamp office, the angry mob stoned Oliver's fine home. Apparently this is where the "Gentlemen Actors" had enough. Marching ceremoniously alongside their social inferiors remained within the blurry bounds of civility, but tearing down a fellow gentleman's mansion (even if they did not necessarily like him) was absolutely unheard of. According to Governor Bernard, the gentlemen rabble-rousers retreated to their civil abodes. Ordinary colonists had taken matters into their own hands. As Oliver rushed his wife and children out the back door and gathered friends to help him protect his home, the disorderly throng beheaded Oliver's effigy and burned it on Fort Hill within view of the city. Having stomped out the burning remains of Oliver's effigy, they returned to Oliver's home, tore down his garden fence, and broke through his back door "declaring they would kill him." Though Oliver eventually escaped with his life, "the Terrors of the first Night" in Boston had begun. Genteel resisters had lost any sort of control over their enraged compatriots.[37]

Even though Oliver publicly promised the next day that he would never act as stamp officer, Governor Bernard lamented that "the lower Part of the Mob were not so easily pacified." No matter the "Gentlemen Actors'" attempts to "prevent any further Mischief being done to

Mr. Oliver or his House," the mob threatened more violence on Oliver's person and property and demanded an audience with Governor Bernard. Barricaded within the city's fort, Bernard reflected, "This riot has exceeded all other known here, both in the Vehemence of Action & mischievousness of intention." Boston's people had defied Bernard's, elitist colonists', and the British monarchy's authority the previous day through a variety of violent acts ignited in and around taverns. Through these extreme actions Boston's rioters had made themselves clear: Bernard related on August 15, 1765, "The Stamp Act shall not be executed here; that a Man who offers a stamped Paper to sell, will be immediately killed; that all the power of Great Britain shall not oblige them to submit to the Stamp Act."[38]

Only twelve days later, ordinary colonists decided to flex their muscles once again, this time causing "destructions, demolitions, and ruins" that wreaked havoc on Boston's officials. After convening in the many taverns surrounding the Liberty Tree during the day, the "rage-intoxicated rabble"—now led by the shoemaker Ebenezer MacIntosh rather than "Gentlemen Actors"—proceeded to the Town House in the evening and lit a bonfire amid cries of "liberty & property." Their first target was the home of Charles Paxton, Marshal of the Court of Admiralty, surveyor of the port, and known supporter of the Stamp Act. On arriving, however, they found only the home's landlord since Paxton was but a tenant and had already "quitted the house with his best effects." The landlord convinced the "incensed & implacable Mob" to join him at a local tavern and share "a barrel of punch" rather than tear down his house. Since the throng was most likely stopping at different taverns throughout their revels, the landlord knew this was an effective strategy for redirecting their anger. The mob gladly accepted and convened at a nearby tavern where they no doubt gained more followers. Having well utilized their ad hoc tavern headquarters, the intoxicated crowd overflowed back into Boston's streets.[39]

By the end of the night, MacIntosh's mob had destroyed the homes and property of three officials: Registrar Deputy of the Admiralty William Story, Comptroller of Customs Benjamin Hallowell, and Lieutenant-Governor Thomas Hutchinson (Figure 7). Though all three men's homes were ransacked, Hutchinson's received the worst treatment. His haughty attitude, combined with attempts to stop the mob on August 14, had made him a prime target for the angry, drunken rioters. As the crowd "beset [Hutchinson's] house on all sides," Hutchinson only just escaped with his daughter in his arms. According to Bernard, after breaking into the house "with a most irresistible fury," the rabble "immediately look't about for [Hutchinson] to murder him." Finding that Hutchinson had escaped, "they went to work with a rage scarce to be exemplified by the most Savage people" as they broke windows and doors, stole property amounting to almost £1,000, burned priceless manuscripts and records, and ultimately razed the house to the ground. Ordinary Bostonians realized the long-developing destruction of genteel consumption distinction in one fell swoop, as they tore Hutchinson's markers of civility—his mansion, books, and china—to pieces.[40]

Many of Boston's leaders—including those who most publicly detested the Stamp Act—were appalled at the proceedings of August 26, 1765. Josiah Quincy Jr. deplored the actions of the "incensed populace" as "totally unjustifiable," and years later, the colonial supporter and noted minister Jonathan Mayhew condemned the "riotous and fellonious proceedings" of the Boston mob, "who had the effrontery to cloke their rapacious violences with the pretext of zeal for liberty." Fearing that "it was now becoming a War of plunder of general leveling," many of Boston's elitist citizens began to remove their valuables to the countryside. Bernard mustered a militia to patrol the streets and, on learning that the plebeian Ebenezer MacIntosh had led the attack on Hutchinson's home, imprisoned the South End shoemaker.[41]

Such elitist attempts to instate their visions of civil control, however, proved fruitless. No matter urban magistrates' disapproval of ordinary colonists' disorderly actions, much of Boston still supported them. When the townspeople learned that Bernard had appointed a leader to the local militia patrol, "a mob of 2 or 300" men surrounded the recently commissioned officer's house and "demanded his inlistments & that he would discharge the Men." The officer refused to do either, and the crowd promised that they would level his house in the future. MacIntosh, meanwhile, benefited from leaders' concerns about being named as rioters in the recent destruction. He could start providing names of his "employers" and destroy the reputations of many of the same men who purportedly detested the recent violence. Amid growing fears of further riots and promises that the customhouse would be pulled down unless MacIntosh was released from imprisonment, customs officers implored Sheriff Greenleaf to discharge MacIntosh, which he immediately carried out. When Hutchinson heard about MacIntosh's release, he could only chastise the sheriff and look fearfully to the future.[42]

Although Boston's tavern rioters received the most attention from contemporaries and historians, they were hardly singular in their

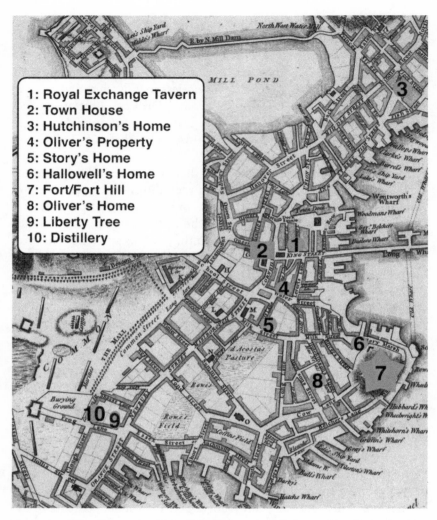

1: Royal Exchange Tavern
2: Town House
3: Hutchinson's Home
4: Oliver's Property
5: Story's Home
6: Hallowell's Home
7: Fort/Fort Hill
8: Oliver's Home
9: Liberty Tree
10: Distillery

FIGURE 7. "The Stamp Act Tumult in Boston, 1765." Created by the author from Sir Thomas Hyde Page and William Faden, *A plan of the town of Boston, with the intrenchments &c. of His Majestys forces in 1775: From the observations of Lieut. Page of His Majesty's Corps of Engineers; and from the plans of other gentlemen* (London; Engraved & printed for Wm. Faden, 1777). Retrieved from the Library of Congress, Washington, DC, December 19, 2016, https://www.loc.gov/item/gm71000620/.

destructive actions. Charleston's lower sorts took matters into their own hands on October 20 by hanging their stamp collector's effigy in front of "Mr. Dillon's [Tavern][,] . . . being the most central and Public part of the Town" (Figure 8). The leaders inscribed the gallows with the words "LIB-ERTY and STAMP-ACT" and watched from Dillon's Tavern as "a great concourse of people incessantly resorted to the place of exhibition." As night began to fall, the two-thousand-strong mob threw the effigies in a cart and paraded them through Charleston's principal streets until they arrived at the home of George Saxby, "the then supposed distributor of stamps." The mob proceeded to break the home's windows even though another man occupied the house. Luckily, the current resident allowed the angry mob to enter his home, or they would have surely "level[ed] it with the ground." After throwing the stamp "cage" out of the ravaged home, the mob buried a coffin inscribed with "American Liberty" while muffled bells from nearby St. Michael's Church rang in the background.[43]

By utilizing Dillon's Tavern for riotous, destructive proceedings, Charleston colonists effected change rather quickly. Caleb Lloyd, dis-tributor of stamps for South Carolina, watched from Charleston's Fort Johnson as the enraged mob tore through the town and attacked his home. Lloyd's decision had been made for him. He posted his resigna-tion and publicly resigned on October 21, 1765. When the Englishman George Saxby, inspector of stamps for North Carolina, South Carolina, and Bermuda, arrived in Charleston on October 28, 1765, a group of "upwards of seven thousand souls" surrounded him as he read his public resignation from aboard a small ship in Motte's Wharf. "The air rang with the musick of bells, drums, hautboys, violins, huzza's, [and] firing of cannon" as Saxby and Lloyd stepped from the boat and were led to Dillon's Tavern under a Union flag inscribed with "Liberty." The disorder began, and ended, in "the most central and Public part of the Town," Dillon's Tavern.[44]

This wave of disorder spilled from urban centers into smaller sur-rounding towns. Dartmouth, Massachusetts, tavern goers surrounded a merchant "with a Load of Butter and cheese in a Horse Cart, put up in an uncommon box" as he arrived at a local tavern. The mob broke open the merchant's mysterious package expecting to uncover stamped papers intended for the tavern keeper but found only butter and cheese. After the innkeeper allowed them to search his house for stamps, the colonists' "rage was mitigated, and after some Expostulation they dis-persed." When the governor of North Carolina attempted to convince the residents of Wilmington to "receive the stamps" with a "grand

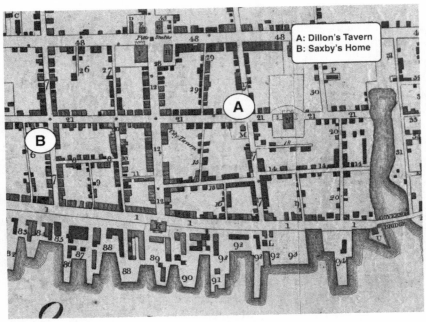

A: Dillon's Tavern
B: Saxby's Home

FIGURE 8. Edmund Petrie, Adam Tunno, and the Phoenix Fire-Company of London, *Ichnography of Charleston, South-Carolina: at the request of Adam Tunno, Esq., for the use of the Phœnix Fire-Company of London, taken from actual survey, 2d August 1788* (London: E. Petrie, 1790). Retrieved from the Library of Congress, Washington, DC, December 19, 2016, https://www.loc.gov/item/80692362/.

[tavern] entertainment," the mob replied with destruction. Having first pleaded with his subjects to help their imperial "Mother," then promised to "make a present of stamped licenses to the tavern keepers," and finally offered those present a whole roasted ox for a feast, Governor Tryon could only wait for their reply. And reply they did. A witness reported, "This diabolical proposal was answered with a general hiss, after which the roasted ox was hung upon the gallows." The observer noted that the ox's full carcass "probably hangs to this day" since "the very negroes disdained to taste the bait of slavery which was laid for their masters."[45]

Although elitist men attempted to control resistance to the Stamp Act through and from their own taverns, ordinary colonists had largely outstripped such measures by 1765. In cities throughout British North

America, mobs convened in an arbitrary network of taverns to wreak havoc on those they considered enemies to British liberties. The lower sorts capitalized on taverns' frequency, accessibility, plentiful amounts of alcohol, and lax regulations to facilitate their mission to level and ransack homes, hang and burn stamp officers in effigy, and set fire to stamped papers. When officials or gentlemen challenged such measures, they received disdain and snubs from their supposed social inferiors. The tavern space helped ordinary colonists to extend their voice well beyond the boundaries of elitist influence. As the mob gained steam, however, certain actions surpassed mere property damage.

Violent Terror

Where other measures of resistance to the Stamp Act had fallen within the boundaries of civil coercion without property damage, or had even extended beyond ideals of civility in property damage without physical violence, certain instances erupted into all-out destruction and terror. Stamp officers fled for their lives as colonists convened in taverns to plot "low level" brutal proceedings intended to effect immediate change through a potent combination of physical violence, spectacle, property destruction, and coercion.[46] Many elitist urbanites, of course, abhorred such tactics. John Adams considered such terror "a very atrocious Violation of the Peace and of dangerous Tendency and Consequence." Mass terror was the antithesis of the civil society that men like Adams hoped to cultivate. No matter, for much resistance to the Stamp Act in North America was wholly beyond civil control. Akin to their rakish behavior, otherwise civil men led and joined their social inferiors in disorderly activities. They did not flee as the "Gentlemen Actors" had done in Boston when things got out of hand; on the contrary, elitist and ordinary colonists alike joined together in terroristic, destructive, and uncivil behavior. They did so, interestingly, not to profess themselves enemies to the Crown (or even those fellow gentlemen they accosted) but, somewhat contradictorily, to assert their allegiance to the British Empire and, in turn, their hopes for a happy future for the British Empire in America. The lines between civility and incivility had always been muddled. More than ever before, certain colonists capitalized on the mutable nature of civility to effect immediate change.[47]

On September 18, 1765, five hundred angry colonists armed with staves accosted Connecticut's stamp master, James Ingersoll. They hanged him in effigy, slandered his character, and threatened to kill him and destroy his home. Determined to force Ingersoll's resignation from the office of stamp master, the mob escorted Ingersoll as their "prisoner" down the road to a local tavern. Here a crowded room waited to try Ingersoll for the crime of attempting to enforce the Stamp Act. Yet Ingersoll's captors had to move him out of the tavern's front room, for apparently the very sight of the stamp master "seemed to enrage the people." Though Ingersoll noted that the gentlemen who took him to a private second-floor room "behaved with Moderation and Civility," their fellow tavern goers did not exhibit such decorum. One of the mob's leaders stumbled up from the ground floor with furious colonists on his heels and warned Ingersoll that if he did not resign soon the people would overpower him. Exclaiming that he "did not think the Cause worth dying for," Ingersoll bounded down the tavern steps, struggled through the crowded great room, leaped onto a chair, and shouted his resignation speech. Though peaceful cheers, toasts, and further declarations marked the rest of that September day, they brought Ingersoll little comfort. Less than a month later, Ingersoll lamented to the London stamp commissioners that "the rage of the people is so great that it is almost dangerous to say a word in favour of a Submission to the Act. . . . [I]t is at present absolutely impossible for me to distribute any of the papers."[48]

Ingersoll had been the victim of terrorist tactics. Though the gentleman escaped physical violence and had briefly found protection with civil men who took him upstairs, his captors made it quite clear that they were not above violent measures. Having trapped Ingersoll in a tavern as their prisoner, surrounded him with an unruly mob of aggressive colonists, and forced him to shout his resignation amid cheers and half-empty glasses, these Connecticut tavern goers consciously transformed their local tavern into a center of violence and terror. No police force burst through the door to stop them. No rival colonists called for leniency. This tavern became a space of collective anger where five hundred colonists could convene to make their own futures. To drive home the power of their actions, Ingersoll's captors later paraded him in front of Hartford, Connecticut's assembly house and courthouse—centers of civil society—and then made Ingersoll read his resignation "within the Presence and Hearing of the Assembly." As anger over the Stamp Act blazed on, others would use their local taverns for even more devious purposes.[49]

Henry Van Schaack no doubt readied himself for confrontation when a noted Albany Son of Liberty, William Benson, requested on Saturday, January 4, 1766, that Van Schaack "step over to Thomas Williams's,

Innkeeper" since "a number of People were assembled there and wanted to speak to [him] immediately." Van Schaack had read accounts of how colonists in other cities often treated alleged stamp collectors: once you were named, Van Schaack knew, your property, reputation, and perhaps even life were in grave danger. A crowd of "between thirty and forty" greeted the accused in the tavern with three cheers meant, in Van Schaack's estimation "to intimidate me" (which it did). In an effort surely inspired by Jared Ingersoll's accosters in a Hartford tavern four months earlier, the Albany Sons of Liberty "surrounded" Van Shaack, informed him that rumors abounded of his request to fill the stamp office, and demanded that Van Schaack swear he "never had apply'd for that office and never would." Van Schaack promised that he had never applied for the dreaded position, but declared "That a Mob or any drunken set of men" had no right to make him swear "in that illegal way." Van Schaack accordingly pushed his way out of the tavern and fled home. His problems had only just begun.

The following day, January 5, Van Schaack discovered that the Sons of Liberty, angry at his impudence the night before, intended to "assemble to destroy me and my property" on January 6. He did what anyone would do at such a terrifying juncture and spent January 5 appealing to the local magistrates for aid. They were of little help and simply recommended that he give in to the Sons' demands and sign the declaration. Disgusted and terrified, Van Schaack spent the evening of January 6 "abroad" until he heard the angry mob (now numbering in the hundreds) leave Williams's Tavern and begin to crash through the streets toward his home. Apprehensive that the mob was about to "pull [his home] down and destroy [his] effects," Van Schaack sent one of his most trusted associates to the mayor's mansion to beg for last-minute aid. His friend, however, could not gain admittance. Finding "the door of justice shut up" against him, Van Schaack slunk off to the woods as the drunken, angry mob broke his windows, tore down his balcony, and ransacked his home. Using Williams's Tavern as their meeting place, the throng spent the rest of the night terrorizing the town in their search for Van Schaack. They threatened Van Schaack's known friends, forced others to declare their detestation of the Stamp Act, and finally dragged Van Schaack's burning sleigh through the city. Van Schaack, meanwhile, hid among the snowy trees and shivered, terrified of what further horrors the next day might bring.

When Van Schaack tramped back through the snow into Albany "early the next morning [January 7]," he found a "threatening paper" pinned to the door of his Dutch church. The paper, signed by the Sons of Liberty, demanded that Van Schaack meet them the next day at Williams's Tavern at ten in the morning "to prevent worse consequences." The Sons pinned another paper next to their threatening statement with a drawing of Van Schaack hanging from gallows, labeled, "Henry Van Schaack, the just fate of a traytor." When Van Schaack tore down the paper, the Sons posted another on the South Gate of the city's walls desiring all to convene at Williams's Tavern at five that afternoon in order to debate "the most unexampled insolence to the Cause of Liberty that ever appeared." This was the last straw for Van Schaack. Realizing that if he did not comply "it was more than probable that [he] should be ruined," Van Schaack tendered his public resignation on January 7. Having driven the "traytor" from their ranks, the Albany Sons sent a letter to the New York City Sons on January 15 requesting "your Commands on any matters that may require the Assistance of the Sons of Liberty residing in Albany."[50]

Ingersoll and Van Schaack—both elitist men—had been treated as if they were disorderly criminals because they represented the alleged evils of the Stamp Act. Resisters to the Stamp Act overpowered, imprisoned, and threatened the stamp officers. In Ingersoll's case, he had to scream out his resignation in fear of being beaten by a tavern mob and was then paraded in front of the governor and other colonial magistrates as a sign of the mob's power. Van Schaack, meanwhile, was chased through town, had to watch from the forest as his property was destroyed, and was publicly threatened multiple times. In both cases, colonists used premier structures of civil society—the assembly house, courthouse, and church—as spaces through which to assert their terroristic goals. In their minds, supporting the Stamp Act was countercurrent to the success of British American civil society and thus must be resisted by any means necessary.

While Ingersoll's and Van Schaack's experiences were perhaps the most publicized, exhilarating instances of terror that played out in taverns from 1765 to 1766, angry colonists throughout British North America enacted similar forms of punishment on plenty of other victims. In January 1766, New Haven colonists "openly assembled" and "forcibly took a seafaring man from a tavern who was convicted as a mercenary informer." As the mob dragged the traitor out of the tavern, a constable appeared to "suppress the riot, but his endeavors were fruitless." The unruly pack whipped the unfortunate informer out of the city with only the clothes on his back, promising that far deadlier punishments awaited him if he ever returned.[51] A few months earlier, a blackened-faced group of men viciously attacked the stamp officer, Martin Howard, as he left a Newport, Rhode Island, tavern.[52] Having barely escaped his assailants, Howard fled home with an angry mob in tow. The violent rabble tore Howard's home to the ground, looted it, and proceeded to other targets.[53]

Though those elitist colonists who disliked the Stamp Act often exploited taverns for resistance measures, other elitist men also utilized taverns' public nature to *deride*—and even violently accost—opposition to the Stamp Act. The New York City lawyer William Smith, for example, took matters into his own hands in January 1766 by using the center of the New York resistance movement, the Merchant Coffee House, as a stage on which to ridicule those who opposed the Stamp Act. Smith (anonymously) pinned a "Pasquinade" to the wall of the Merchant Coffee House and watched colonists "croud & huddle round" the "Carricature" titled "Mirror." With this poem, Smith attacked lawyers and merchants who so benefited from colonial resistance. Smith ended his "Pasquinade" with an extremely damning, dark turn:

Behold your strange disordered Throng
In vile procession march a long
Pity's your due ye Simple fools
Ye have not sense to see your Tools
Consider well the way you run
Break loose before your quite undone
Consult the mirror see it shews
Your Eggers on will turn your foes
The Fiend Rebellion holds you fast
You'll find when all the folly's past
The Time shall come when Friend I
Will point you out to swing by dozens.[54]

Smith turned the coffeehouse into a "mirror" rather than a microscope— a place for colonists to reflect on their coercive actions instead of planning more. Colonists had long utilized coffeehouses and city taverns as arenas for literary duels and polite belles lettres, and the Merchant Coffee House served Smith the same purpose. He chastised colonists for their "follies" and warned the "strange disordered Throng" that "Your Eggers on will [soon] turn your foes."[55] Smith's success, of course, was limited. The "Fiend Rebellion" did indeed hold so many colonists "fast."

Later in January, men employed by the governor of South Carolina beat a "Son of Liberty who had been engaged most part of the day in the wars of Bacchus" nearly to death when he attempted to "introduce himself into their company" at a Charleston tavern. The Sons of Liberty had, of course, spent the earlier part of the day accosting the governor at his estate. Reflecting on the attack on their fellow member, the Charleston Sons of Liberty lamented, "Our liberty here is very low." "Any opposition will now be fruitless," they despaired, "as those yet hearty in the cause of liberty are but few in number." Marked, violent resistance obviously affected the Sons as well.[56]

No matter occasional backlashes, colonists' violent actions continued to terrify stamp officers, governors, and British officials. The secretary of state for the American colonies, Henry Seymour Conway, anticipated in a December 1765 letter that "Time will produce a Recollection, which may lead these unhappy People back to a Sense of their Duty" and dissuade further "Acts of Outrage and Violence." Ingersoll, still reeling from "the Extraordinary instance of violence" he had endured in that tavern in September, wrote to the stamp commissioners in London to beg forgiveness and future aid. Governor Bernard cried that Boston was "in an actual state of Rebellion[;] . . . the People here at present are actually mad." He considered the Stamp Act "like some sudden Accident to a human body, which occasions its flinging out some latent disease, which if it had ben concealed much longer would have been past curing." Bernard hoped that the "State Doctors" had discovered the disease in time and would "apply proper remedies to it." Looking forward, both sides knew that something had to change, and fast. Colonists established taverns as their own personal headquarters of violence, coercion, and terror, while colonial officials continued to retreat to forts and country homes.[57]

Civility and Liberty Reign Supreme?

March 1766 brought less concentrated tavern coercion, violence, and terror as the Sons of Liberty planned mass demonstrations.[58] Little did colonists know that on March 19, 1766, Parliament repealed the detested Stamp Act. By early April mutterings of the repeal arrived in the colonies' taverns, and on May 16, 1766, Boston received official news from London that the act had indeed been repealed. Overjoyed Bostonians rang the town's bells, decorated their anchored ships, and adorned the Liberty Tree with flags. The *Newport Mercury* exclaimed on May 19 that "united Efforts of the Inhabitants of these Colonies, in Conjunction with their numerous Friends in Great-Britain, in the glorious Cause of LIBERTY, have at last terminated in a TOTAL REPEAL OF THE STAMP-ACT."[59]

The repeal of the Stamp Act brought a sense of elation to British North America, and colonists flocked to local taverns and coffeehouses to celebrate. New York City's Sons of Liberty spent May 26 in a civil procession. After listening to a patriotic sermon at Trinity Church, they repaired to "the Field of Liberty" amid cannon fire and festivity. The Sons, finally, collected "at their usual House of publick Resort"—the Merchant Coffee House—"where an elegant Entertainment was prepared, attended with a Band of Musick, and . . . a Number of loyal and constitutional Toasts." William Bradford, meanwhile, used his Philadelphia Coffee House as a center of civil celebration. Having read news of the appeal "aloud at [Bradford's] London Coffee House," a "multitude" of Philadelphians conducted the ship's captain who brought news of the repeal to the coffeehouse where they plopped a "Gold laced Hat" on his head and treated him to "A large Bowl of Punch, in which he drank Prosperity to America." The next day, Philadelphians illuminated the city's buildings and streets and devoted all their efforts to celebration. The *Pennsylvania Gazette* noted that although violence and disorder was "common on such occasions," the "universal Satisfaction of [Philadelphia's] Inhabitants" elicited a day without "any Riot or Mob." The Boston Sons turned all of Boston into a festival, complete with bells, bonfires, "a magnificent Pyramid, illuminated with 280 lamps" placed under the Liberty Tree, and, of course, copious amounts of liquor. In addition to the city's myriad taverns, Bostonians could visit private homes for libations since certain colonists, having adorned their homes with "Figures characteristic of Those to whom we bear the deepest Loyalty and Gratitude," opened their doors to visitors. Colonists from Charleston to Cambridge followed suit with fireworks, tavern toasts, and other public professions of imperial loyalty and pride. None of these celebrations was marked by disorder or aggression. The time for such overt incivility, colonists thought, was surely over.[60]

In many colonists' minds, their actions had been more than justified. They had simply fought to uphold the purity of British liberty and the success of their vision for the future of British American society. Their orderly and disorderly actions had helped cement the repeal. Sometimes ordinary colonists' goals aligned with those of elitist colonists, and sometimes they did not. As is so often the case, victory had a soothing effect on past evils and conflicts. Certain colonists even declared that property destruction had been a necessary evil. It was better to destroy a few buildings in the name of repealing the Stamp Act, after all, than to have *all* their property taken away by corrupt customs officers. Colonists believed that Parliament, aware of its mistakes, had repealed the Stamp Act and would act similarly in the future. Only bright skies lay in the colonies' ongoing relationships with the Mother Country. A letter published in the May 26, 1766, *Newport Mercury* declared, "Now [that] the detested Object of our Resentment is buried (never, I hope, to rise again) let us bury with it every animosity and cultivate Love and Friendship." The writer encouraged colonists to "especially endeavor to conciliate and secure the Esteem and Affection of our Parent State—On this our Happiness greatly depends." The Sons of Liberty began to dissolve once the repeal was announced, assuming civil society, now on the "right" track again, would "go on in its usual forms."[61]

Though Parliament repealed the Stamp Act, negotiations were far from over. Tavern-going colonists had spent the previous ten months refashioning traditional notions of imperial allegiance and civil society to resist taxation policies. Stamp officers had watched as colonists burned them in effigy, tore down their homes, stole their property, and threatened their safety. Royal governors, meanwhile, fled to the relative safety of their forts' walls as colonists convened in taverns and turned cities into virtual war zones. While many colonists were ready to move forward and forget the past, then, those men whose lives had been shaken to the core were not. Though Governor Bernard had been vocal in his opposition to the Stamp Act, he was even more passionate in his belief that colonists needed to be "taught that they have a superior." Many in London felt the same way, and would only tighten restrictions on the raucous British American colonies over the next nine years.[62] Thus, while colonists' ability to transform taverns into spaces of coercive, sometimes violent resistance to the Stamp Act had effected a repeal, such alterations were only temporary. In one short year, Parliament would issue the Townshend Revenue Act, throwing the colonies right back into a state of emergency. More than ever, anxious leaders had to confront ongoing questions of order and disorder but now in the context of an all-out imperial crisis and, eventually, a global war.

6 /   "As far from being settled as ever it was": The Revolutionary Transformation of Civil Society

Writing to a friend in October 1766, Massachusetts governor Francis Bernard could only reflect, "It seems to me America is as far from being settled as ever it was." The violence of the Stamp Act riots had solidified Bernard's insecurities regarding North America's order and allegiance. Many of Bernard's colonial compatriots, however, disagreed with the royalist governor's assessment. The celebrated gentleman John Adams reflected in 1766, "This Province is at present, in a State of Peace, order and Tranquility." John Dickinson (who eventually joined Adams as a founding father), meanwhile, contended, "My heart is *British*." Many colonists, in short, would have concurred with the author of a 1765 *London Magazine* article who declared that British Americans "possess as much virtue, humanity, civility, and let me add *loyalty to their Prince*, as is to be found among the like number in any part of the world." By 1766, colonists believed they had proved themselves loyal members of the British Empire, characterizing the "popular Clamor" engendered by the unpopular Stamp Act as an important stepping-stone to a successful British American civil society.[1]

Their supposed victory, however, was short lived, for the Stamp Act Crisis initiated a period of American history predicated on division and dissension more than collective progress. Despite leaders' frustrated efforts during the previous seven decades to negotiate their ideals of civil society in British North America, the shaky foundations of this facade would deteriorate over the next twenty years. While a considerable proportion of colonists remained tethered to previous notions of civility and liberty, refashioned conceptions of American societal order raged to the forefront of popular republican politics after 1773. Patriot committees of safety flourished in every colony and boasted at least seven thousand members by spring 1775. These extralegal committees wrestled for control of the masses through a carefully crafted set of goals intended to upend the status quo: they repackaged long-held ideals of British monarchy—especially liberty, order, and civility—to support rather than oppose nascent notions of American republicanism while also asserting that any who resisted their rebellious efforts would be punished.[2] Previous notions of social capital mattered less as colonists formed antimonarchical governing structures intended to bolster emerging nationalism and cull out those deemed enemies to the American cause.

The public stage of revolutionary contestation, as well as the ideological vision of America's future, steadily bifurcated from 1765 to 1783, first *among* urban taverns and eventually *between* urban and rural taverns. In the ten years preceding the opening shots of the American Revolution, urbanites commandeered taverns and coffeehouses according to localized political allegiance. Certain tavern keepers touted their establishments as centers of Patriot fervor, while others maintained their allegiance to the British Crown.[3] Ultimately, the American Revolution ushered in shifting forms of civil society. Hoping to maintain profits, tavern keepers transformed their spaces according to mercurial notions of political allegiance and the climate of war in which they existed. Such societal modifications proved both temporary and enduring, as American elites struggled to retain midcentury notions of civil society to unify—and retain power in—the early Republic.[4]

Colonial cities were transformed into divisive spheres of war, suffering, and occupation during the American Revolution. Urban taverns reflected such developments, primarily serving as militarized spaces and safe houses for citizens and soldiers as British and American forces occupied New York City, Boston, Philadelphia, Newport, and Charleston at different times between 1776 and 1783. During periods of occupation, soldiers and citizens convened in urban taverns in a struggle to uphold a semblance of civility. They utilized these central spaces for their more congenial prerevolutionary purposes such as balls, parties, and auctions. Unfortunately, with trade disrupted, urban environments ravaged, and populations in constant flux, British American cities and their taverns became defined by suffering more than civility after 1775.

American Patriots, meanwhile, steadily converted villages and their taverns into ad hoc, military-type spaces of control, policy making, and recruitment. Highlighting long-standing complications of class and power, tavern goers who held little social capital before the American Revolution emerged as leaders of organizations such as committees of safety and "anti-British" societies, enforcing their brand of justice by vetting and holding any dwellers who seemed likely to harbor allegiance to the Crown. One elitist Georgia Loyalist recalled that "everywhere the scum rose to the top" in committees of safety, and the historian T. H. Breen contended that "the insurgency thrust thousands of new men into positions of political responsibility."[5] Many colonial gentlemen who lent their support to the Patriot cause watched with stifled horror as committees of safety transformed midcentury notions of civility and order to fit their visions of an American republic. Although taverns continued to serve as central spaces through which colonists might realize a civil society, their societal goals had changed, at least in theory.[6]

To win the American Revolution, elitist men had to rethink their midcentury notions of civility, liberty, and order since Patriots had commandeered these royalist ideologies for their own rebellious purposes. As "the scum rose to the top" of republican committees of safety, elitist colonists also had to accept lower-class colonists' resistance to the deference that prerevolutionary leaders had worked so hard to realize.[7] Whether wealthy or impoverished, anyone who resisted the Patriot cause was branded a traitor to the American government and violently expelled from this American "civil" society.[8] The contradictions that elitist men had helped to cultivate in their frustrated efforts to realize a civil society in North America had finally come back to haunt them in real ways: the world that gentlemen such as Dr. Alexander Hamilton liked to think they inhabited—surfeit with genteel tavern clubs, societal order, and imperial allegiance—seemed more fictional than ever.

Internal Ruptures: Urban Taverns and the "Road to Revolution"

Tavern goers' success in forcing the repeal of the Stamp Act through a combination of civil resistance, coercion, and outright violence convinced many colonists of the necessity of such measures, even if they often highlighted the disorderly nature of their society. Having lamented in December 1765, "We have tried Prayers and Tears, and humble Begging and timid tame submission . . . and instead of Redress we have only increased our Burdens," John Adams reflected after the repeal of the

Stamp Act that the "Popular Compulsion, fear of Violence, of the Sons of Liberty &c." of the Stamp Act riots had "composed every wave of Popular Disorder into a smooth and peaceful Calm."[9] Though colonists' riotous actions occasionally extended beyond the bounds of civility, they had impelled change, and quickly. As British Parliament and King George III tested new taxation policies on the North American colonies after 1766, colonists replicated their anti-Stamp Act tactics, once again congregating in taverns to resist taxation and, they hoped, realize a more civil society.

Urban tavern goers gathered en masse to resist the Townshend Acts (1766-70), which taxed imported goods like paper, lead, paint, glass, and tea. In doing so, they repeatedly evoked their riotous activity during the Stamp Act, which they believed was a critical moment of British liberty and justice. On June 22, 1769, the Charleston native Christopher Gadsden reminded South Carolinians "of the noble spirit you were actuated with at the time of the Stamp-Act, which then enabled this province to do as essential service to the common cause, as any, without exception, in America." In Gadsden's mind, such resistance measures should retain an orderly character, which would signal larger efforts at civilization rather than a descent into savagery.[10] Eight months earlier, Gadsden had assembled Charlestonians who did not support the Townshend Acts at Dillon's Tavern before they set off on a grand parade to announce their dedication to nonimportation of British manufactured goods. With toasts, liberty trees, and assertions of imperial pride, the parade "drew up before the door" of Lieutenant Governor William Bull Jr.'s home and drank to the ninety-two Massachusetts legislators who had recently refused to accept the Townshend Act. Having made their point to the governor, Gadsden and his men returned to the long room of Dillon's Tavern "where 45 candles were placed on the table [in reference to the Englishman John Wilkes's number of protests to the English Crown], and 92 glasses were applied in resounding the voices of as many loyal and respectable toasts." Just as he had during the Stamp Act Crisis, the editor of the local newspaper was sure to note that Gadsden's proceedings were undertaken "in civil mirth and jollity;—without the least irregularity happening . . . such as must certainly reflect honour on the intention of their meeting, as well as to convince the world of their steady and fixed determination to join, upon all proper occasions, in support of the glorious cause of LIBERTY and their COUNTRY." As colonists rekindled nonimportation throughout North America by 1769, Gadsden could only remind South Carolinians that such efforts should revive "everything relative to the internal peace and welfare of the province." Here, in the minds of men like Gadsden, was the culmination of British American liberty and civility.[11]

While colonists in every major North American urban center defied the Townshend Acts, they especially looked to Boston as the center of resistance. Hence the editor of the Boston News-Letter's decision to publish a full list of tavern toasts on the anniversary of the repeal of the Stamp Act in 1769, which were thereafter reprinted in newspapers throughout colonial America. After congregating around Boston's popular Liberty Tree and piling into Dorchester's aptly named Liberty-Tree Tavern on August 14, 1769 (both had been hearts of resistance to the Stamp Act), New Englanders made clear to the empire their developing allegiances. While the king, queen, and royal family retained the top spot on colonists' toasting list, "America and her brave Sons of Liberty" earned the second toast in Boston. Dorchester's citizens, meanwhile, toasted "North America, and her fair Daughters of Liberty" in their second round. Both groups then raised numerous glasses celebrating different members of Parliament and other "Friends of America in Britain and those of Britain in America," as well as local factions such as the "Massachusetts Ninety-Two." Ideals of liberty and cosmopolitanism also made their way into the toasts, as New Englanders praised "Liberty without Licentiousness to all Mankind" while damning those "Traducers of America" whom colonists deemed enemies of civil society. Although Bostonians drank only fourteen toasts compared to Dorchester's booze-laden forty-five, both parties ended their toasts with exclamations of firmness, harkening back to the "14th of August [as the] Jubilee of Americans" and also encouraging "Strong Halters, Firm Blocks, and Sharp Axes, to all such as deserve either." As New Englanders made clear through their peaceful actions on August 14, 1769, they preferred civil to violent protest, but were more than willing to return to the disorderly conduct of the Stamp Act Crisis if necessary for the "Speedy Removal of all Task-Masters, and the Redress of All Grievances."[12]

Although leaders like Gadsden denounced violence as a resistance method that would "do infinitely more mischief than good" and the Boston News-Letter hoped to present an orderly, controlled populace, many resisters in other urban centers relied on physical coercion as their primary means of persuasion. Take Boston, for instance. Just because the Boston News-Letter depicted the city as a hive of order and civility did not mean that everyone living in the city felt that way. Ann Hulton, sister of a tax collector in Boston, watched in horror as drunken mobs took over the city in June 1768. Writing from the relative safety of Castle William in Boston's harbor, the Englishwoman exclaimed:

> The Mobs here are very different from those in O England where a few lights put into the Windows will pacify, or the interposition of a Magistrate restrain them, but here they act from principle & under Countenance, no person daring or willing to suppress their Outrages, or to punish the most notorious Offenders for any Crimes whatever, These Sons of Violence after attacking Houses, breaking Window, beating, Stoning & bruising several Gentlemen belonging to the Customs, the Collector mortally, & burning his boat, They consulted what was to be done next, & it was agree to retire for the night, All was ended with a Speech from one of the Leaders, concluding thus, "We will defend our Liberties & property, by the Strength of our Arm & the help of Our God, to your Tents O Israel."[13]

Here was a snapshot of Bostonians' resistance efforts that were in sharp contrast to the *Boston News-Letter*'s laudatory descriptions. In Hulton's telling, Boston was far more apt to violence than to peaceful toasts. The Sons of Liberty were better described as "Sons of Violence," with local magistrates and leaders too afraid to "punish the most notorious Offenders for any Crimes whatever." Cruelty and anarchy reigned supreme. Yet Hulton also noted another interesting aspect of the Boston mob's proceedings. Just as the *Boston News-Letter* included underhanded threats (i.e., the "Traducers of America" and "Speedy Removal of all Task-Masters, and the Redress of All Grievances") in its professions of liberty and justice, so too did these "Sons of Violence" lean on long-held ideologies of English constitutional liberty during their mad gathering. One of the leaders promised his followers, "We will defend our Liberties & property, by the Strength of our Arm & the help of Our God." Just as such professions of liberty, property, and Christianity had defined the midcentury colonies, so too would rebels utilize them to refashion their own form of that society.

Just because gentlemen penned their aspirations for civil protest did not mean that these highbrow measures actually worked.[14] Like their brethren in Boston, New York City's Sons of Liberty had erected a liberty pole in front of their own popular tavern, Bardin's Tavern, during the Stamp Act Crisis. And, like their Boston comrades, New York City's Sons of Liberty took on an increasingly violent character. By 1767, in fact, New York City's Sons of Liberty found themselves physically battling British troops for control of their liberty pole.[15]

The violence began on August 11, 1766, when British soldiers—appalled by New Yorkers' outright disdain for imperial policy—hacked the New York City liberty pole to pieces. For soldiers, the colonists' liberty pole was not a symbol of British allegiance and liberty, but representative of growing insurgence and disorder. They needed to nip this mania in the bud. Yet many colonists did not see it this way, and customers at Bardin's Tavern grew enraged when British soldiers sawed the "pine post" into logs. The British captain John Montresor reported that "2 or 3000 chiefly Sons of Liberty, headed by [Isaac] Sears . . . used the most scurrilous and abusive language against the officers and soldiers present who never seemed to resent it, till a volley of Brick Bats ensued and wounded some." Onlookers replaced tankards and punch bowls with bayonets, pistols, and swords as the soldiers attempted to regain order. Although August 11 ended without further bloodshed, on August 12 the Sons of Liberty swore that "they will have satisfaction of the Soldiers and that they will not permit them to beat their Retreat and Tattoo through the streets at their peril." The Sons had also not forgotten about the damaged relic of their success during the Stamp Act. As Montresor disgustedly noted, "The Sons of Liberty erected another high post in lieu of the other with 'George, Pitt and Liberty' and hoisted a large ensign thereon."[16]

New York City had descended into a brief period of anarchy because soldiers had cut down a pine pole next to a tavern. But the pole denoted more than just local unity. For instance, the Sons' decision to write "George, Pitt, and Liberty" on the pole was not taken lightly. For many colonists, these two men came to represent all that was good in the British Empire, in opposition to all that was bad: Parliament. In the 1760s, colonists still understood King George III as a noble, untainted representation of the English Constitution. He, more than anyone, might save them from Parliament! Colonists also linked William Pitt to their resistance efforts, especially after he rose in the Commons on January 14, 1766, and declared, "I rejoice that America has resisted [the Stamp Act]." In Pitt's eyes, America's opposition to the Stamp Act demonstrated their keen "defense of liberty, upon a general principle, upon a constitutional principle." This is exactly what colonists wanted to hear—hence their linkage of King George III and William Pitt with "liberty" on their liberty pole.[17] Even in acts that now seem quite rebellious and violent, colonists held firm in their convictions of British liberty and constitutional rights. Symbols like their liberty poles drove home such ideas, and British soldiers' attempts to stifle such measures would be met with the strictest resistance.

Many colonists understood the one-year anniversary of the repeal of the Stamp Act as a critical moment to celebrate the success of British liberty and their constitutional rights. In their minds, this was a day to celebrate "an affectionate regard for a People so firmly attach'd to that Constitution which is the Glory and Happiness of Englishmen, so Loyal to his Majesty, and resolutely determin'd to defend and support . . . Peace and good Order[,] . . . Liberty and Happiness." Where the Stamp Act "must have ruin'd the whole British Empire," colonists had effected its demise and, in turn, protected their civil liberties. On the night of March 18, 1767, New Yorkers hoped to celebrate the ascendancy of "Harmony" at Bardin's Tavern. Unfortunately, later that same night a group of soldiers once again cut down the liberty pole. Determined to render their beloved beacon of liberty impervious to British soldiers' malicious intent, New York City's Sons of Liberty gathered at Bardin's Tavern the next day and "erected another, more large and substantial [liberty pole], secured with Iron to a considerable height above Ground." The soldiers attempted to destroy the pole again that night, hacking at it with saws and shovels "without Effect." By Saturday night, March 21, the soldiers returned with a load of gunpowder, which they bored into the pole's base and ignited, "but this also fail'd."[18]

New York City's Sons of Liberty decided to take a militaristic approach to combat the "mischievous Spirits among the Soldiery," posting watchmen around the clock at Bardin's Tavern to guard their iron-clad liberty pole. Sunday night the watchmen ran off some sneaky soldiers, but at six o'clock on Monday evening, "a party of Soldiers march'd by the Post, and as they passed by Mr. Bardin's Tavern fir'd their Muskets, two of which were pointed at the House." The next morning a tavern goer was astonished to find shattered windows and a musket ball lodged in the building's timber. Such violence forced the governor and general of the magistrates of the city to intervene, which ended the confrontations, at least for a time.[19]

Imperial transformations only heightened tensions between New York City's residents and soldiery, as the Townshend Acts provided the Sons of Liberty with a renewed sense of mistreatment. Bardin's Tavern and the liberty pole, unsurprisingly, continued to serve as central spaces where New York's angry multitudes could convene to plan their disorderly frays and assert nonimportation. Where Gadsden was able to guide his "mechanics" in a relatively peaceful series of tavern-centered protests, the New York merchant Isaac Sears and his fellow Sons of Liberty had already established a tradition of violence and disorder in their resistance measures. New York City's residents had utilized uncivil protest measures in the past, and they had worked. As the Townshend Acts arrived on New York City's shores in 1767, these violent tactics would only find heightened support and efficacy.

Dubbing themselves the "United Sons of Liberty," a group of New Yorkers announced in a broadside on July 7, 1769, that they would congregate "on the first Monday Evening in every Month, at the House of Mr. De La Montagne." Yet this broadside declared more than the United Sons of Liberty's steadfast support of nonimportation measures, detestation for the recently initiated Quartering Act, or their need for "every Lover of constitutional Freedom" to join their fray. Importantly, the Sons asserted that they "have determined to drop all Party Distinction that may have originated from a Difference in Sentiments in other Matters" to resist the Townshend Acts. This New York tavern group was determined to return to the mind-set that had propelled them to victory during the Stamp Act Crisis. Although internal divisions had arisen among leaders of New York City's Sons of Liberty since the victory of 1766 (especially among middle-class revolutionaries, Isaac Sears, Alexander McDougall, and John Lamb), these men looked to the past and determined that "Supineness would prove as fatal to us, as a Disunion." They thus rallied together in De La Montagne's Tavern, perhaps clanking tankards over a tavern song that was spreading through the colonies at the time. Set to the popular British Navy song, "Heart and Oak," the colonial tavern ballad hearkened back to the Stamp Act Crisis with the verse, "The Tree their own Hands had to Liberty rear'd; They liv'd to behold growing strong and rever'd." According to the writer of this song, the liberty trees and poles established between 1765 and 1766 were not only signs of contemporary resistance but also remained markers of growing strength and a celebration of "Britannia's Glory." If not held in the greatest esteem, British American liberty and civility—along with the beloved liberty trees and poles—would wither under the desiccating oppression of Parliament's unjust taxation.[20]

Historians have well summarized the details of the "Battle of Golden Hill": after attempting yet again to destroy the liberty pole in front of De La Montagne's Tavern on January 13, 1770, British soldiers broke into the tavern, assaulted the waiter, destroyed lamps and bowls, and finally cut the liberty pole into pieces and piled it in front of the tavern door. This rash act ignited a two-day battle between soldiers and citizens, which, while not resulting in any deaths, created a schism between the two groups and ultimately forced the Sons of Liberty to relocate their liberty pole to a private field and purchase a neighboring tavern for their future efforts.[21] Despite the battle's relative popularity in historical studies, scholars have failed to integrate this conflict with larger ideologies of liberty and civility, nor have they connected New Yorkers' resistance efforts with the Stamp Act Crisis, as colonists would have.

By the time the actual violence of the Battle of Golden Hill took place on January 19, 1770, New Yorkers were firmly entrenched in the defiant mind-set that had impelled them during the Stamp Act Crisis. Supporters of the United Sons of Liberty described the liberty pole at De La Montagne's as

> a Pole, *sacred to Constitutional Liberty* . . . which had formerly been erected in Commemoration of the Repeal of the Stamp-Act, the Triumph of constitutional Liberty over the Attempts of arbitrary Power to destroy it; and as a Monument of Gratitude to his Majesty, and the British Parliament who repealed the Act, and to those Worthy Patriots, both in and out of Parliament, by whose Influence the repeal was obtain'd.[22]

In their minds, just as the liberty pole was inherently tied to their success at repealing the Stamp Act in 1766, so too was the maintenance of this pole imperative to the future success of British American civil society. Colonists' actions in 1765 and 1766 proved their "Gratitude to his Majesty" and their allegiance to the "constitutional Liberty" that symbolized civil society. In this vein, soldiers' attempts to cut down the pole—though seemingly only a trifle—were tantamount to Parliament's efforts to once again impose taxes on colonists.

Although a growing number of colonists looked to the Stamp Act Crisis as a high point of liberty and the endurance of British American civil society, many of their foes regarded this event as a low mark in the history of the British Empire in America when incivility reigned supreme. On January 19, 1770, the British Sixteenth Regiment stationed in New York City published a broadside defending their recent actions at the Battle of Golden Hill. In this broadside, the British soldiers used the same rhetoric of liberty and civility that the Sons of Liberty had so deftly employed over the past few years, contending that the New York Sons "may more properly be called real enemies to [civil] society." The soldiers attempted to represent the Sons of Liberty as "chagrined," raucous losers "as they pass thro' the streets, especially as these great heroes thought their freedom depended on a piece of wood." Ultimately, the soldiers scolded the Sons of Liberty for boasting "so mightily of your famous exploits, as you have heretofore done, (witness the late Stamp act)," for in their minds those rabble-rousers who once raised a pole in front of De La Montagne's Tavern were now "reduced to the low degree of having their place of general rendezvous, made [a Gallows Green]" and were little more than "murderers, robbers, traitors." The Stamp Act Crisis and the Battle of Golden Hill, in these soldiers' minds, were two sides of the same uncivil coin.[23]

Colonists ushered in the 1770s with bloodshed, uncivil behavior, and a growing reliance on taverns for these measures. Over the past three years, enraged Bostonians had regularly congregated at their Liberty Tree and in various taverns "to clear the Land of the Vermin [i.e., enforcers of the Townshend Acts] which had come to devour them," while colonists in other major cities like New York, Charleston, and Philadelphia joined the anti-Townshend fray in earnest. The Philadelphian John Dickinson argued that the Townshend Acts were "if possible, more dreadful than the Stamp Act," while Christopher Gadsden of South Carolina complained of the "momentous Crisis" that "riveted" colonists "in a Slavery beyond Redemption, and by far exceeding that of the Subjects of any absolute Monarch in Europe." Citizens of Newport, Rhode Island, concurred with Dickinson's allusions to slavery. After soldiers tore a copper plate commemorating the repeal of the Stamp Act from their beloved liberty tree in 1767, one resident exclaimed that "the same illiberal spirit, which then opposed every Exertion in Favour of Liberty [during the Stamp Act Crisis], was not effectually laid, and will never be satiated with anything short of *the enslaving America.*"[24]

Though these Sons of Liberty surely employed a heavy dose of hyperbole in their protestations, such assertions reveal changing conceptions of liberty, order, and civility, as well as how colonists understood their place in the empire. Dickinson bemoaned the thought that Englishmen saw colonists as little more than "ungrateful and undutiful" members of the empire. Gadsden concurred with Dickinson in his remarks that because colonists did not have a monarch "*at Home* with them," they "at this vast Distance shall have some Hundreds [of monarchs] least, if the late Measures are fixed upon us, and the Scriptures tell us no Man can serve Two Masters."[25] For a growing number of colonists, previous notions of civility and imperial allegiance seemed more distant—literally and metaphorically—than ever before.

Such violence, insecurity, and internal divisions affected rebellious and loyal colonists alike. Ann Hulton lamented in 1768, "From the inherent Republican, & leveling principles, here's no subordination in

the Society. Government is extirpated, & it is quite a state of Anarchy."
Royal governors joined British elites like Hulton in their disgust for colonists' violent efforts to upend the Townshend Acts. Governor William
Franklin of New Jersey told his father, Benjamin, in 1769 that he felt "all
the Nonsense about No. 45 is almost as much attended to in the Colonies as in England." A few months earlier, Benjamin Franklin (residing
in London and ever the British Loyalist) had complained to William, "I
am sorry to see in the American Papers that some People there are so
indiscreet as to distinguish themselves in applauding [Wilke's] No. 45,
which I suppose they do not know was a Paper in which their King was
personally affronted, whom I am sure they love and honour."[26]

Many colonists indeed latched on to the Englishman John Wilkes's
critiques of Parliament, especially the forty-fifth issue of his controversial *North Briton*, as indicative of their own struggles. The radical politician, after all, had lambasted Parliament, arguing that its ministers
"have sent the spirit of discord through the land, and I will prophecy,
that it will never be extinguished, but by the extinction of their power."
Yet what really got Wilkes in trouble were his thinly veiled attacks on
the monarchy. He lamented, "I wish as much as any man in the kingdom
to see the honour of the crown maintained in a manner truly becoming
Royalty. I lament to see it sunk even to prostitution." Furious at the publisher's wanton criticism, King George III had Wilkes imprisoned. Yet
Wilkes's words had been published, and their argument about Parliament's underhanded ability to corrupt the king especially resonated with
many North Americans. Radical-leaning colonists consequently gathered in taverns to celebrate Wilkes's efforts, sticking firmly to forty-five
in their number of toasts, bottles of wine, and other ceremonies. In the
eyes of loyal gentlemen like William and Benjamin Franklin, however,
such actions were in the same vein as colonists' violent reactions: they
were wasteful, uncivil, and disloyal revels of the masses.[27]

Parliament repealed the Townshend Acts in March 1770, thereby
tamping the flames of colonial dissent, at least for a time. Where Hulton
damned Boston for its rebellious character during the Townshend Acts,
she described reentering Boston in December 1770 in terms of overt
peace and civility: "We find the face of things exceedingly changed . . .
upon the appearance (or some steps toward Establishing) of these supports of Society [government or law], & protecting of Individuals. . . .
Peace & Order Takes place, & the past Scenes of confusion & disorder,
appears as a dream. We never thought ourselves more safe from the Sons

of Violence." For Hulton, it seemed as if the empire had managed to bring British American civil society back into relative stasis.[28]

Although colonists entered the 1770s unburdened by the Townshend Acts, all was not well. For one, Parliament insisted on retaining a tax on tea shipped to North America, which stung many colonists, wealthy and poor alike. Moreover, the previous five years of almost constant misbehavior had created a rather antagonistic relationship between colonists and Parliament. Watching anxiously while residing in London in January 1772, Benjamin Franklin exclaimed, "I see here no Disposition in Parliament to meddle farther in Colony Affairs for the present, either to lay more duties or to repeal any."[29] Franklin was largely right: Parliament would not issue any drastic taxes between 1770 and 1773, but, as would become so clear with their next round of sanctions in 1773, Parliament and King George III had hardly forgotten the colonies' insolence. Finally, the uncivil unrest that had marked British American urban centers over the past five years had both created and widened personal and political divisions among colonists. Colonists were forced to choose sides (often more than once) after 1773, when republican notions of civil society fully emerged in opposition to midcentury ideals of monarchical civility. Perhaps nowhere were these personal and political crises more apparent than in North Americans' tavern interactions. Division among urban taverns had already begun to rear its ugly head during the Townshend Acts. By the time the first shots of the American Revolution rang out at Lexington and Concord in April 1775, however, a combination of political factions and public impulses had rendered the British American urban social scene almost unrecognizable from midcentury fantasies.

Urban Taverns and the Transformation of Midcentury Civil Society

Colonial militiamen famously gathered at Lexington's Buckman Tavern to ready their assault on incoming British forces on April 19, 1775; yet urban colonists had already established a well-defined network of militant endeavors in urban taverns years before that fateful April day. It is no coincidence that a leading revolutionary, John Quincy Jr., titled his 1774 anti-British tract, *Observations on the Act of Parliament, Commonly Called the Boston Port-bill, with Thoughts on Civil Society and Standing Armies*.[30] Civil society remained a critical endeavor for colonists loyal and rebellious, and with Boston descending into relative anarchy after 1773 because of the Boston Massacre, the Boston Tea Party, and the resulting Coercive Acts of 1774 (not to mention a slew of tar and featherings), a growing number of colonists unified around their New England brethren in what they considered a shared endeavor to uphold—or, increasingly, reshape—British American civil society: "The Empire of Laws."[31] As these proto-republicans utilized urban taverns to assert their new brand of loyalty and patriotism on their localities, the question posed by the historian Kathleen D. McCarthy—"what distinguished civil society from civil disorder?"—seems more pertinent than perhaps ever before.[32]

A colonist who identified himself as "Junius Cato" in February 1773 especially embodied this societal flux. For Cato, Parliament and the Crown and their supporters were as "unconnected with us . . . as the inhabitants of the moon." Only by maintaining "measure[s] productive of every good and preventative of every evil in civil society" could North America's "noble friends of their country and of mankind" retain their societal hopes in the face of such "deceitful arts, the most successful weapons that can be used in the cause of tyranny." "The game is playing," Cato warned colonial resisters, "and your liberty and property are the stakes."[33] Celebrations like Boston's Union Feast on November 5, 1765, when the disorderly North and South Ends "in a very orderly manner . . . engaged in a union" under the watchful eye of loyal gentlemen in the Royal Exchange Tavern, became relics of a bygone era. As Cato's "game" unfolded in urban taverns after 1773, colonists who would never have been invited to the table at midcentury emerged as primary rule makers in this restructuring of "liberty and property."[34]

Colonists from Newport to Charleston took local governance into their own hands: they congregated in urban taverns, established extralegal committees, and enforced their controversial ideologies of North American liberty and civility on their surroundings. Although the First Continental Congress's 1774 boycott resolutions prompted colonists to form committees of safety (also called committees of inspection and correspondence) in virtually every town and village by 1775, the outbreak of the American Revolution in 1776 steadily scattered most of these committees into more rural settings. Philadelphia's committee of safety, for instance, retreated to nearby villages such as Lancaster in early July 1777 as British forces occupied their beloved city, and New York City's committee reconstituted its ranks in rural towns like Brookhaven in fall 1776. Often relying on well-known taverns as their central bases of operation, these committees, in the words of Breen, "literally enforced the Revolution" through a potent combination of public shame, political outrage, and mixed-class allegiance. Thus, although each committee of safety adjusted to local social and political conditions and was forced to retreat to rural environs, they all remained tethered to the same ultimate goals: restructure midcentury aspirations of civil society to fit their emerging notions of American republicanism.[35]

Rebels' understandings of republicanism remained firmly tethered to midcentury societal aspirations, even if they would have denied such an accusation. Hence their constant referral to the "Defence of our Rights and Liberties" in their transactions and hence their anxieties over "the precarious State of the Liberties of North America & . . . Several acts of the British parliament tending to the entire subversion of our natural and Charter rights." Though rebels hoped to distance themselves from the monarchy, their understanding of the "Rights" and "Liberties" that they repeatedly referred to in their justification of their extralegal rebellion originated in a world of monarchical allegiance. The king and Parliament were the problem, not the English Constitution and all the rights and liberties it promised. In this way, rebels' efforts to distance themselves from the monarchy also represented their struggles to gain a more intimate understanding of midcentury ideals such as civility, order, and liberty. Yet in such endeavors members of revolutionary committees of safety enjoyed a militant power that their midcentury forebears never fully harnessed. Where midcentury leaders struggled to maintain a legitimate and effective law enforcement entity that might promise the order they so desired, committee men could violently enforce their militant ideologies of societal order on their locality. Congress directed every colony to create committees "to superintend and direct all matters necessary for the security and defence of their respective colonies, in the recess of their assemblies and conventions." Here, in short, Congress declared committees of safety militant branches of power and (technically extralegal) law enforcement that should uphold republican ideals of civil society.[36]

Though committees relied on Congress for political legitimacy, they also tested changing ideologies of liberty and order in their locality. Having adopted the Merchant Coffee House as their center of operations in early 1775, Philadelphia's committee of safety spent the next two years fashioning its own form of local civil society (until, that is, British forces arrived in September 1777). Philadelphia's committee members, like their brethren throughout the colonies, especially concerned themselves with rooting out community members who held firm to monarchical and therefore traitorous forms of societal order. Thus, while committees originally formed as a means of enforcing the Continental Association's phased boycott of British imports in tandem with nonimportation efforts (boycotting began in December 1774), these tavern societies steadily adopted local issues and targets. The middling Philadelphia chemist recently appointed to the committee of safety, Christopher Marshall, noted that the printer Jabez Fitch "came by persuasion to the Coffee House" where the committee questioned him for publishing a controversial letter in a February issue of the *Pennsylvania Ledger*. Not only was this "extract of a Letter from Kent County on Delaware" laced with chastisements of the colonies' current political situation, but it also glorified monarchical society. In this author's opinion, the midcentury colonies were "blest with peace and plenty, under the happiest form of government in the world, every branch of business flourishing; men secured in their liberty and property; a trade open to foreign parts of the world; which occasioned a ready sale for our produce." British North America had once been the pinnacle of civility where men were "secured in their liberty and property," but now "violence of party and the appellations of Whig and Tory" had burned this societal Eden to the ground. "Who could think," the author concluded, "that a three-penny duty on tea could have occasioned all these difficulties, when only a refusal to purchase the article would have kept us free?" Fitch ultimately admitted to his coffeehouse jurors that a friend had sent him the piece, "upon which the people, with some reluctancy, let him go."[37] Fitch, however, would hardly be the last Philadelphian questioned and threatened for his societal allegiances.

Marshall noted dozens of committee-led trials that took place at the Merchant Coffee House over the next year. While most trials furthered the committee's efforts to uncover people or letters "inimical to the rights and liberties of America," the proceedings took on an increasingly militaristic—sometimes violent—character as the year wore on. William Bradford's willingness to use his London Coffee House as a center for oppositional measures over the past few years led to his appointment as captain of Philadelphia's militia, and by June 1775 he ordered sentries stationed at the Merchant Coffee House to survey the city's governor. Such coercive measures sent a clear message to the governor and his supporters: either accept evolving ideas of law, governance, and civil society or be forcefully expelled.[38]

About three months later, these underlying threats broke out into violence when revolutionaries called a local lawyer, Isaac Hunt, to the Merchant Coffee House, questioned him, and put him into a cart to be paraded through the city as punishment for speaking against Congress. The militia promised Hunt protection as they carted him "through the principal streets [and] acknowledged his misconduct in diverse places." So far, this seemed to at least generally meld with midcentury colonists' notions of orderly punishment. But colonial order had changed since then, and with committees of safety questioning colonists from the coffeehouse and a militia patrolling the streets, many colonists were on edge. The gentleman Dr. John Kearsley included himself in these anxiety-ridden ranks. Apparently, when the crowd stopped in front of Dr. Kearsley's house so that Hunt could make his declaration of misconduct to the city leader, "the Dr. threw open his window, [and] snapped a pistol twice amongst the crowd." Although a well-known and powerful member of Philadelphia society, the doctor's actions overshadowed his social capital in the changing political order. The mob captured Kearsley (slashing his hand with a bayonet in the scrum), escorted Hunt home, and threw the poor doctor into a cart in which they roughly pushed him back to the Merchant Coffee House. Ultimately, Bradford and his militia stopped the mob from tarring and feathering Kearsley but not from acting out their outrage, as they "broke [Kearsley's] windows and abused [his] house" after the coffeehouse trial. With a loyal militia, an enraged mob, terrified gentlemen, and a coffeehouse control center, Philadelphia's committee of safety was more than ready to effect militaristic control of its environs. It spent the rest of the year trying, terrorizing, jailing, and expelling those they deemed enemies to the American cause.[39]

In the abstract, prerevolutionary committees of safety tended to adopt midcentury colonists' ideas of liberty and order wholeheartedly. They believed that those members of society deemed disorderly—and thus unfit to enjoy the liberties of an American citizen—should be forced into compliance or violently expelled from that society. In many ways, such measures were nothing new. Midcentury leaders embraced *official* punishments that would maintain their vision of society in harmony and order. They even encouraged riotous activity if it remained under the umbrella of what they deemed civil order. The problem was that by 1775 extralegal committees of safety (often composed of ordinary men) had taken these measures into their own hands and had begun to use them *against* those very elitist men who had once employed them as a means of control. Suddenly, printers like Jabez Fitch, lawyers like Isaac Hunt, and doctors like John Kearsley took the place of villains and thieves. Where once they would have watched approvingly from their safe balconies as a lower-class counterfeiter was beaten through the streets, they now fired pistols from their balconies in an attempt to ward off angry mobs.

Beyond such militaristic efforts, the Philadelphia committee of safety utilized its power to reform notions of luxury and power among the populace. Grand balls held for visiting government officials, military leaders, and other prominent men had been a mainstay of midcentury British American civil society. Not only did these events provide local leaders with the opportunity to distinguish themselves to visiting figures as genteel, civil members of the British Empire, but they also demonstrated anxious gentlemen's status and power to lesser members of local society. Local gentlemen often held balls for influential visitors in their city's finest city tavern or coffeehouse. By November 1775, however, the First Continental Congress's recent actions forced Philadelphia's committee of safety to adjust long-held societal norms to fit the realities of the times.

Balls, a beacon of midcentury British American civil society, were not immune to the tumult of prerevolutionary America. In the wake of the "Intolerable Acts," the First Continental Congress penned its "Declaration of Resolves" in October 1774, which, by employing traditional ideologies of civility and liberty, contended that colonists held certain rights through "the immutable laws of nature [and] the principles of the English constitution." Committees of safety repeatedly utilized Congress's myriad "resolves" for their own purposes. On November 24, 1775, however, Philadelphia's committee members were faced with a difficult choice when they learned that George Washington's and John Hancock's wives would soon visit the city. Traditionally, the city's elitist colonists would have planned a grand ball in honor of Mrs. Washington and Mrs. Hancock without a second thought. They were, after all, the spouses of two of the most powerful revolutionary leaders in North America. But times had changed. According to Congress's resolves, committee members could only officially "assemble" in order to "consider of their grievances [and] petition the king." Congress deemed "all prosecutions, prohibitory proclamations, and commitments for the same . . . illegal." Thus, when word got out that members of the committee had instinctively planned a ball at Philadelphia's "City Tavern"—a frequent haunt of the First Continental Congress, which one member, John Adams, called "the most genteel [tavern] in America"—many residents declared the ball "contrary to the Eighth Resolve of Congress," since it would not be held for official purposes. Marshall recorded that he "heard some threats thrown out, that if the ball assembled this night . . . the [City] Tavern would cut but a poor figure to-morrow morning." Philadelphians would turn on the City Tavern for harboring an event that they considered illegal under Congress's rules.[40]

Ultimately, local leaders called off the ball at the City Tavern but not without drama and discord. Marshall spent the day of November 24 flitting about town—from Hancock's residence to that State House to Adams's residence to the Philosophical Hall—in a frenzied effort to avoid catastrophe. A "large and respectable" committee formed at the Philosophical Hall to deliberate "the propriety of this meeting or balls being held this evening in this city, at the [City] Tavern," which concluded with only one dissenting voice that this and all such meetings should be avoided "while these troublesome times continued." Gentlemen formed another committee to apologize to Mrs. Washington and Mrs. Hancock. Exhausted, Marshall spent the evening "pleasantly" with fellow rebels Samuel Adams and Colonel Dyer, "until Col. Harrison came to rebuke Samuel Adams for using his influence for the stopping of this entertainment, which he declared was legal, just and laudable." This November 24 evening ended much as the past few years had, with "many arguments . . . used by all present" to convince each other of their own correctness. The restructuring of civil society would not be an easy task.[41]

As Philadelphians utilized committees of safety to enforce and deliberate notions of civility, liberty, and law, colonists in other major urban centers also struggled to uphold their own committees of safety in their favorite coffeehouses and taverns and, in turn, shape the local landscape to their own means. William Edis, surveyor of the customs in Annapolis, Maryland, watched with disgust in May 1775 as "an infinite number of petty tyrannies [were] established, under the appellation of committees." Edis considered Annapolis's committee of safety nothing more than the revels of "a few despots" who "inflame the passions of the mob, and pronounce those to be enemies to the general good, who may presume any way to dissent from the creed they have thought proper to impose." In Edis's mind, these rabble-rousing "multitudes" had thrown out "the interests and happiness of the united British Empire"—in other words, monarchy—for an "arbitrary system" that favored "inflammatory addresses," "repeated misrepresentations," and "factious artifices." Yet for all of Edis's repugnance, he was powerless to stop the rise of the committee in Annapolis. Realizing that Annapolis's committee of safety had gained control of the city's taverns by November 1775, Edis declared that he "carefully avoid[ed] 'the busy haunts of men.'"[42]

Annapolis's committee was not the only extralegal urban congregation in Maryland, for a group of Baltimore men had formed an even more radical committee: the "Whig Club" of Grant's Tavern. The tavern club hunted down local "enemies to the Country" with vicious resolve. On December 4, 1776, the Whig Club demanded that the Loyalist-leaning sheriff of Baltimore County, Robert Christie Jr., leave the city lest his life be "sacrificed to an injured people." Christie attended Grant's Tavern that same night, where he was ordered to leave the city only hours later. The Whig Club also targeted previously untouchable Baltimore citizens like the wealthy merchant Melchior Keener, thereby demonstrating just how much ideologies of social capital had shifted over the past few years.[43] By June 1776, the Whig Club set its sights on the ultimate target, Governor Robert Eden. But Eden's luck held out, for he had garnered respect among Annapolis committee members, and they safely escorted him out of the colony in June 1776 rather than turn him over to the Whig Club, who wished to hold him ransom. Edis, unwilling to break his British "oath of allegiance," quickly followed suit and fled to the countryside. From Philadelphia to Baltimore to Annapolis, committee men had utilized a combination of tavern going, extralegal governance, and threats to, in the words of Edis, "assume the powers of all different branches of government."[44]

Rebellious urbanites utilized taverns and coffeehouses as their bases from which to enforce their own brand of civility and order. But such measures were easier planned than executed, for by the early 1770s many colonists shifted their allegiance by the day, hoping to capitalize on the unpredictable tides of political, economic, and social pressures in their never-ending quest for self-preservation.[45] The uptick in violence over the past few years only exacerbated leaders' difficulties, as did lingering feelings of reverence for the British monarchy. Even the radical Patriot wing of the Maryland Convention remarked in December 1775 that their countrymen remained "strongly attached to the English constitution" and that "to be free subjects of the king of Great-Britain . . . is to be the freest members of any civil society in the known world." Unfortunately, these Maryland Whigs no longer felt like "free subjects of the king of Great Britain" and hence believed that their once-great relationship with British civil society had to change.[46]

The Maryland Whigs' internal struggle over long-held notions of British liberty and civility point to another major obstacle for rebellious tavern committees: Loyalist opposition. Although Loyalists in Baltimore and Annapolis were rather powerless against the Whig Club and the committee of safety, at least one-third of the colonial population remained loyal to the British monarchy throughout the eighteenth century. Such numbers—combined with shifting allegiances, lingering reverence for royalty, and mistrust of the Patriot cause—compounded rebels' struggles to remake civil society after 1774.[47]

Although tavern committees prided themselves on rooting out and punishing local "Tories," their efforts were ultimately rooted in the fear that these Loyalists might unify to form veritable resistance measures. On April 29, 1775, when the Philadelphia committee questioned Jabez Fitch in the Merchant Coffee House for publishing a Loyalist letter, they were especially worried about the passage that asserted, "I believe, if the King's Standard were now erected, nine out of ten [colonists] would repair to it." While Marshall reassured himself in May 1775 that local Loyalists' "language is quite softened, and many of them have so far renounced their former sentiments . . . and are joined in the association," by July of the following year Marshall learned "of not less than four different clubs of Tories in this city, that meet frequently . . . at Widow Ball's, Lombard Street, one at the sign of the Pennsylvania Farmer, kept by Price, another at the Jones's beer house on the dock, and one at the sign of the King's Arms."[48]

Factious divisions affected every facet of tavern society by 1774. John Adams noted that Philadelphia's St. George Society, an elitist association established for English connection held in the Tun Tavern, had splintered that year. The members who considered themselves "staunch Americans" met at the City Tavern, while "staunch Britons" gathered at a tavern outside of town and "halfway men" convened at the Bunch of Grapes Tavern. With their compatriots in Annapolis maintaining a lingering allegiance to the idea of being "free subjects" of a monarchical-style civil society and colonists flip-flopping their loyalties by the day, radical tavern committees in the Middle Colonies had an uphill climb in front of them.[49]

So too did New York City's radical committee men, as powerful Loyalists like the printer James Rivington used his New-York Gazetteer to glorify allegiance to the British monarchy. On April 29, 1773, Rivington praised the "Sons of St. George" for their recent celebration at Hull's Tavern, where this "genteel Assembly with their presence; a royal Salute accompanied their gracious Sovereign's Health, and the Day and Evening passed with that friendly Gaiety, which has ever presided in these Anniversaries of the festal Albions." Though on the surface an innocent report of a tavern celebration, Rivington surely intended his glorification of King George III and these "festal Albions" to debase the rebellious committees' less than orderly tavern gatherings. Rivington laced his newspaper with reports on royal tavern celebrations over the next year, and included an especially damning poem in his January 19, 1775, edition, titled "The Case Stated on a Late Tavern Adventure: Or the humours of a noted Sedition Shop." The poem explicitly mocked the tavern committee man, claiming that he "deludes all the fools he can catch in his net . . . with *Sedition* and *Toddy* . . . at a well noted Tavern." At one point in the caustic poem, the author even went so far as to have a committee man's slave exclaim, "*Massa—you fool!*" for committing such treason. By November 1775, New York City's committee men had enough of the genteel Loyalist printer Rivington. Knowing that Rivington was about to reprint Joseph Galloway's Loyalist essay, *Candid Examination*, Isaac Sears and his committee men broke into Rivington's shop, destroyed his press, and played "Yankee Doodle" as they left the ruins. Rivington fled to London a few days later.[50]

As demonstrated by the Whig Club's efforts to capture Governor Eden and the New York City committee's destruction of Rivington's printing press, extralegal tavern groups took on a decidedly militaristic character after the battles of Lexington and Concord in April 1775. Chasing off Loyalists and governing local society according to murky notions of liberty and property was no longer enough. With British and Hessian soldiers en route to North America, tavern committees began to muster militias, gather weapons and ammunition, and punish local Tories with more violent tactics than ever before. They often did so with the express purpose of creating what they considered a more effective form of American civil society, which in many ways entailed Patriot leaders simply repackaging midcentury notions of British American civil society to fit their mercurial perceptions of republicanism. As British troops began to occupy North American cities and enforce their own governmental structures, however, these extralegal tavern committees fled to the countryside, where their deliberations took on an even more martial identity, forcing colonists to rethink how a civil society might operate.[51]

Geographical Divisions, Ideological Transitions

In early July 1777, Christopher Marshall and many of his Philadelphia committee men fled Philadelphia for the safety of the expanding but still relatively rural town of Lancaster. Only two months later, the Continental Congress followed suit, escaping Philadelphia before British troops took the city on September 26. Shortly after arriving in Lancaster, Marshall noted, "There has been for two weeks past in agitation by the friends of the States of America in [Lancaster], a plan in order to form a Society under the name of the Civil Society, in order to assist the present plan of government." This "Civil Society," Marshall explained, would continue the efforts of Philadelphia's committee of safety by calling on "each member . . . to take the Oath or Affirmation of Allegiance or leave the State." Most likely formed over a few drinks at William Ross's tavern (Philadelphia's radical refugees would hold a number of grand balls there over the next two years), this "Civil Society" was a far cry from the tavern club of the same name that Salem's merchants formed in February 1745 "for the Preservation of Friendship & Conversation."[52]

Rural committees of safety and organizations like Lancaster's Civil Society revealed Patriots' efforts to transform midcentury notions of civil society to support their militant forms of republicanism. This tavern club was not intended to encourage the charity, fellowship, and sociability of the Salem Civil Society. In fact, Lancaster's Civil Society forced local citizens—many of whom had lived in Lancaster long before the committee men arrived—to adjust to their ideals of patriotism and liberty or be violently evicted. Yet, even owing to such geographic, temporal, and political dissonance, Lancaster's Civil Society maintained the same core goals of its midcentury Salem namesake: utilize long-held ideologies of civil society to effect change—and quickly—in the surrounding populace. But these Patriot militants did so with more gusto than ever before, "examin[ing] all strangers passing through [Lancaster] respecting taking the test [of Patriot allegiance]." It was no coincidence that Lancaster's committee men chose the name "Civil Society" for their organization, nor should it come as a surprise that they, along with so many rural committees of safety throughout the colonies, continued to invoke terms like liberty and order in their professions of republicanism. Where midcentury colonists had worried about how competing empires and peoples might limit their own capacity to attain the culmination of civil society in America, Patriots now accosted those men deemed "dangerous to the Liberty's of America" and fretted over preventing "the dangers to which the colony is exposed by its internal enemies."[53] Such rural committees—and, by proxy, the Continental Congress—commandeered midcentury concepts of civility, liberty, and order according to emerging perceptions of republicanism. In doing so, they also restructured long-held forms of hierarchy and governance.

Urban centers and their taverns, meanwhile, groaned under the weight of wartime conditions. Just as republican tavern committees enforced their own brand of civil society on their rural surroundings, so too did the British Army and Loyalists living in occupied cities implement a variety of measures intended to ensure societal order and efficiency.[54] While American troops also occupied cities during the war, British military forces especially held sway over urban centers from New York City to Philadelphia to Newport to Charleston. Once nexuses of society building and hope, North American cities quickly descended into over-crowded, undersupplied, crime-ridden environs governed according to the rules of war. Amid such hardship, citizens and soldiers looked to urban taverns not so much as spaces where they could realize a mid-century-style civil society, but as places where they might briefly escape their lived reality, as balls, performances, and dinners continued to issue from public drinking spaces. Stepping outside the mirthful confines of the tavern, however, threw urban dwellers right back into an environ-ment defined by destruction, disorder, and danger. Taverns still mattered greatly to urbanites during the American Revolution. Their *reasons for mattering* had simply shifted.[55]

The Englishman Nicholas Cresswell experienced the fallout of this growing divide firsthand between 1774 and 1777. Having journeyed to North America at the age of twenty-four to seek his fortune as a planter, Cresswell found himself caught between past and present, loyalty and rebellion. Proud of his imperial identity, Cresswell had made the diffi-cult voyage to Virginia with the express purpose of benefiting from the booming economic sector that British North America promised. In his words, "I am sensible a person with a small fortune may live much better and make great improvements in America than he can possibly do in England." Yet shortly thereafter, the unfortunate young man found him-self trapped in Alexandria, Virginia, by the local committee of safety. Often coordinating its efforts around Richard Arell's popular tavern, the committee suspected that Cresswell was "a Tory (that is a Friend to the Country)," and as Cresswell explained, threatened him "with Tar and Feathers, Imprisonment and the D[evi]l knows what." The Alexandria committee had indeed taken on an increasingly militaristic identity after 1774, regularly drilling local militiamen, collecting funds to pur-chase weapons and ammunition, and seizing merchant ships. Cresswell became a target for their ire as the war broke out, and the committee forbade the young Loyalist from leaving the county on November 28, 1776, lest "they would confine me."[56]

Trapped and without hope of monetary improvement, Cresswell spent the next six months in a blur of drunkenness and anxiety. Rankled at his dissipation over the past few weeks, Cresswell exclaimed in December

1776, "A fine course of life truly, drunk every night, this is tampering with the Devil to it." Cresswell had thrown off his quest for wealth to cope with what he considered a hopeless situation. Though he did not enjoy the elitist identity that so often protected colonial rakes, the guise of the rake offered him an easy, albeit self-destructive and brief, escape from his present woes. No matter—Creswell and his fellow tavern rakes (they had dubbed themselves the "Blackeyed Club") only receded into social irrelevancy as they wasted weeks in blurs of drunkenness and debauchery. Cresswell needed a change of scene, and fast. Luckily, he snuck onto a merchant ship and escaped to New York City in May 1777.[57]

What Cresswell found in New York City was a far cry from boosters' professions of the city's grandeur. American and now British troops had transformed it into "a city of war" over the past year. Not only had flee-ing Americans burned one-third of the city to the ground in September 1776, but constant troop activity had also rendered the remaining urban environment almost unrecognizable.[58] Cresswell could only comment:

> If any author ever had an inclination to write a treatise upon stinks and ill smells, he never could meet with more subject matter than in New York, or anyone who had abilities and inclination to expose the various and unfeeling part of human nature or the various arts, ways and means, that are used to pick up a living in this world, I rec-ommend New York as a proper place to collect his characters. Most of the former inhabitants that possessed this once happy spot are utterly ruined and from opulence reduced to the greatest indigence.[59]

In Cresswell's contention, if New York City ever had been a center of economic prowess and civil expansion, that time had long passed. For Cresswell, the city represented a prime example of the downfall of Brit-ish American civil society. Much as he had during his confined condition in Alexandria, Cresswell spent the next two months relying on taverns to escape the "complication of stinks" of New York City's destructed envi-ronment. One night, the young Englishman joined soldiers of the Royal Navy and Army for a ball at the Hull Tavern, after which he saved a Phil-adelphia Loyalist who had been left in a ditch for dead after mistreating a prostitute. On another night, he joined Hessian and British troops to celebrate the anniversary of King George III's birthday.[60] These were not men hoping to craft a civil society; they were men hoping to temporarily retreat from the Revolution's gravitational tug.

Like Cresswell, the Scottish grenadier John Peebles attended a seem-ingly never-ending flurry of parties, balls, performances, club meetings, and other romps in several different British American urban taverns between 1776 and 1782. In many ways, he also took on the identity of the rake rather than the revolutionary soldier. On January 18, 1777, Peebles danced "in a long Room at the Crown Coffee House" in occupied Newport, Rhode Island, to celebrate the queen's birthday. About a month later, the Scotsman found himself in occupied New York City, where he "Call'd at the Coffee House" one night, and "Din'd ashore at the Tavern" with a party of officers who "broke up in good spirits" a few hours later. While stationed in Philadelphia from January to May 1778, Peebles frequented the city's most popular taverns: he "had an Elegant dinner & good claret" with a club of soldiers at the Indian King Tavern and noted that Congress's previous haunt, the City Tavern, had been "fitted up & open'd to receive comp'y. In the Style of Public Rooms, every Eveng. (except Sunday) & a Ball every Thursday, the Expense defray'd first by a subscription of two days pay from every officer of the British & half a guinea for ball tickets." The first thing Peebles did on entering Charleston, after rebel forces conceded their beloved port city on May 11, 1780, was dine "at a house of entertainment with ½ doz[en] of our Regt."[61]

Peebles spent the rest of his American campaign in burned-out New York City, attending balls, clubs, and parties at Roubalet's Tavern and Strachan's Tavern (which had been the Merchant Coffee House before the war). Revelries with the St. George's Society, celebrations of military victories, club meetings, and farewell congregations for his colleagues defined Peebles's alcohol-fueled tavern visits. After six grueling years of military service, however, Peebles gained permission to return to England, away from the cruel juxtaposition of brutal warfare and tavern bonhomie that characterized his and so many other soldiers' North American campaign. Taverns had helped the British soldier to endure the hell of war, but he was ready to leave.[62]

By July 1777, similarly, Cresswell decided that his only choice was to flee America. His dreams of using British America's booming civil society for economic gain had been wholly crushed. As the dispirited Englishman left America for good, he could only remark that America had been "turned Topsy Turvy, changed from an earthly paradise to a Hell upon terra firma." "These unhappy [Patriot] wretches," Cresswell continued, "have substituted tyranny, oppression and slavery for liberty and freedom." The bitter Loyalist especially blamed the downfall of British American society on Congress's "strict and tyranicall laws," which various extralegal committees "executed with the utmost rigour." In Cresswell's mind, such actions did not support Patriots' contentions of the links between republican liberty and rural virtue but rather destroyed preexisting advantages: "the congress under the fallacious pretence of nursing the tender plant, liberty, which was said to thrive so well in American soil, have actually torn it up by the very root." North American society, in Cresswell's contention, had thrived at midcentury under the watchful eye of Britons. As soon as Americans attempted to cultivate their own fields of civility, order, and liberty, their "tender plant" withered on the vine.[63]

Whether living in New York City, Boston, Philadelphia, Newport, or Charleston, those thousands of Loyalists who remained in or fled to occupied cities joined Cresswell in their nostalgic fantasies of the urban past and their dour representations of the present. Elizabeth Drinker, a Quaker Loyalist who stayed in Philadelphia as British and American forces occupied the city at different times during the war, watched with horror as her once-genteel city seemed to descend into madness and her Quaker ideals seemed overpowered by the militaristic structures of war. With Philadelphia's committee of safety harassing her merchant husband daily for his refusal to sign a document of allegiance, Drinker narrated the steady decline of British American civil society, and, by proxy, her notions of a Quaker colony, in Philadelphia between 1776 and 1783. In early March 1777, Drinker criticized the American committee of safety—"our present ruling Gentry"—for ordering "a Young Man by the Name of Molsworth . . . hang'd on the commons." She could only remark, "A City heretofore clear of such business." When British forces managed to take Philadelphia in September 1777, Drinker's life only became more complicated. Now without her husband, whom Congress had forced south as their prisoner, Drinker was impelled to lodge a soldier in her home. While the young officer spent his days much as Peebles did—attending taverns, balls, concerts, and plays as much as possible—Drinker found her once-peaceful life declining into a scene of disorder, anxiety, and confusion. When British soldiers held a grand parade and organized a ball in a local tavern to see General Howe off in May 1778, Drinker exclaimed, "How insensible do these people appear, while our Land is so greatly desolated, and Death and sore destruction has overtaken and impends so many."[64]

Drinker's misfortunes continued when American military forces reoccupied Philadelphia in June 1778. Drinker narrated the struggle of Loyalists living in a city of war, as American soldiers took their homes for lodgings and hospitals. She also, importantly, remarked on the internal divisions festering among American military leaders, noting in March

1779, "Our great men, or the Men in Power, are quarreling very much among themselves."[65] Drinker's professions of internal disorder proved true in early October 1779, when a group of radical republicans promised "to drive from the city all disaffected persons [Tories] and those who supported them." After congregating in a rural tavern, the angry colonists—many of whom were militiamen—marched into Philadelphia, seized four prominent Loyalists, and paraded them through the streets to another tavern, where they publicly humiliated them. But the militants were not done. They next made their way to James Wilson's house, which Wilson and his friends had barricaded for protection. A deadly gunfight broke out between Wilson's men and the lower-class mob, which the gentleman-led First City Troop of Light Horse eventually broke up. Seven months later, Drinker reported that "A Friend from the Country . . . in publick Testimony this morning at the Bank House, said among other things that Pennsylvania [once] the flower of America, was now a Den of thieves." From Charleston to Philadelphia to Boston to New York City, the ravages of war weakened midcentury ideals of urbane civility.[66]

Many rebels, of course, declared that cities had always been hives of luxury and vice and pointed to the various publications that painted American republicanism in a positive light in contrast to the tyranny of the British monarchy. Yet, in detaching themselves from the British monarchy, Patriots repeatedly called on midcentury ideologies of liberty, civility, and order to assert the glory of American republicanism. In 1779, for instance, Somerset, New Jersey's committee of safety deemed those monopolizing men who damaged their local specie through selfish trade "the bane of civil society." Three years earlier, a Boston tavern club echoed midcentury leaders' assertions of societal order to support the republican cause. Club members opined, "It is universally allowed that no Civil Society can long subsist, without a proper, a certain Degree of Government, which should be supported by wise and salutary laws; These, we too well perceive, if neglected or condemned, only serve to heighten Anarchy and Confusion." A pretended tavern conversation between two "countrymen" (Andrew and Benjamin) over America's independence printed in the Pennsylvania Evening Post, finally, centered on those same ideologies that midcentury elitist colonists so fretted: liberty, order, and civil society. At one point in the newspaper article, Benjamin assured Andrew that "the men we chose in our county [for the Constitutional Convention] were honest worthy members of civil society" who "had long approved themselves stanch friends to the liberties of the people." In another section of the conversation, Andrew hoped that "the peace and good order of the state at this juncture" might be upheld.[67] The ideologies themselves had not changed that much since midcentury. Their use, however, had.

Despite such effusions, many elitist republican leaders shuddered at just how many compromises they had made in order to muster support for the American Revolution. Reflecting on recent Philadelphia riots in 1779, the Patriot doctor Benjamin Rush lamented, "Poor Pennsylvania has become the most miserable spot under the surface of the globe." Rush continued his dirge for American civil society by damning Philadelphia's lower-class tavern Patriots: "They call it a democracy[;] . . . a mobocracy in my opinion would be more proper." The Bostonian John Adams joined Rush in his mistrust of such uncivil measures, penning various tracts after 1776 to combat what he termed "democratical" hysteria.[68] Just because America's founders hoped to expel the British monarchy from North America did not mean that they wanted to do away with the societal structures they had worked so hard to realize. As ordinary colonists utilized ideologies like civility, order, and liberty to assert their own democratic hopes for country's future, elitist founders hoped to use those same perceptions to craft a midcentury-style American republic. This negotiation would not be easy.

Self-professed gentlemen could no longer hide behind the brick and mortar of genteel taverns and coffeehouses after 1776. As had been clearly demonstrated over the past decade, such edifices of power and exclusivity could be torn down far easier than they could be constructed, as could the reputation, authority, and social capital of their customers. The tumult that accompanied the years immediately preceding the war, not to mention the occupation of various cities by British and American troops thereafter, only further fractured these already shaky societal norms. If republican leaders were to retain momentum moving forward, they would have to alter their midcentury dreams of a British American civil society—and many of the hierarchical mechanisms it entailed—to fit the democratic-leaning republic that continued to spawn from revolution.

American Loyalists, meanwhile, seemed to experience prejudice and pain wherever they lived. As one might imagine, those Loyalists unable or unwilling to escape their rural homes experienced the hard, often violent reality of America's republican transformation in more intimate ways than their urban counterparts. For men like the Washington, Connecticut, Loyalist Joel Stone, civil society seemed a thing of the past, as "an invincible frenzy appeared to pervade the minds of the country people and those very men who so recently had held one in the highest esteem became the most implacable enemies."[69] Like Cresswell, Stone was lucky enough to escape his local tavern committee, ultimately finding relative refuge in New York City. Many of Stone's and Cresswell's compatriots, however, did not enjoy such fortunes. From Pennsylvania to South Carolina, men like the aforementioned Henry Drinker—a Philadelphian "held . . . in the highest esteem" before the Revolution—were treated as "the most implacable enemies" of their local committee. Drinker was forced south as a prisoner of the American Congress, while the former Rhode Island justice, Nathaniel Gardiner, "was hurried along amidst the insulting acclamations of the rabble" en route to "a public house kept by Capt Stone, a notorious money-gitting rebel," where he was briefly imprisoned in 1780. Local and county committees captured, questioned, taxed, attacked, and sometimes even killed hundreds of other Loyalists between 1776 and 1783.[70] Like American civil society, then, rural taverns became different things to different people: signs of the end of civil society for some, beacons of hope for others. It was in these spaces that proto-republicans and British monarchists alike had to come to terms with the imperialist, cosmopolitan identities they had worked so hard to cultivate before the revolutionary period.[71]

Certain cosmopolitan hopefuls such as Dr. Alexander Hamilton and William Byrd II never lived to see the American Revolution and thus went to their graves content with the pipe dream of midcentury British American civil cosmopolitanism. Many other self-proclaimed "citizens of the world," however, faced the ultimate challenge to their cosmopolitan identity as they were forced to come to terms with how midcentury notions of cosmopolitanism might fit the emerging national divide between Great Britain and America. Once so intent on being viewed as civil members of the British Empire by their metropolitan peers, certain colonial gentlemen came to believe that—no matter how ardently they participated in the various threads of imperial thought and culture—the British metropole did not see them as equals but rather as provincial upstarts on the fringe of a global empire. Whether a "staunch American," a "staunch Briton," or a "halfway man," every cosmopolitan hopeful had to refashion his identity around a cosmopolitanism that existed more in symmetry with national patriotism than ever.[72] And while Loyalists might try to retain the inherently imperial nature of cosmopolitan thought, their Patriot brethren had to deliberate a cosmopolitan, republican patriotism: one theoretically divorced from the empire that had spawned their cosmopolitan dreams in the first place while in reality still economically and ideologically connected to British societal trajectories.

British American Loyalists saw themselves as "cosmopolitan Patriots" defined by rational, benevolent, and enlightened worldliness, in contrast to revolutionaries, who they understood as falling deeper into irrational patriotism every day. Take the Savannah, Georgia, Loyalist James Habersham, for example. A man described as a "Citizen of the World" by the historian Frank Lambert, Habersham constantly cultivated his cosmopolitan identity by participating in the elitist tavern club called the St. Andrew's Society, consuming genteel products from around the globe, reading myriad erudite publications, speaking Latin, wearing the most fashionable attire, and staying "so connected" with men throughout the British Empire. Even when Habersham disagreed with Parliament's conduct in the Stamp Act and his sons fomented rebellion against him and his fellow Loyalists at Machenry's Tavern, Habersham retained his belief in the British Empire as the savior of "the rights of mankind." He viewed the Sons of Liberty as anticosmopolitan, uncivil upstarts who took the "powers of Government out of its proper and legal channel, and invest[ed] it in a Mob," consequently subverting all "Law and Government" and exposing North America to "Violence and Rapine." Habersham may have lost the access to many of those cosmopolitan channels he had enjoyed before 1765 (especially the urban spaces that flourished before the war), but this did not break his resolve. Rather, Habersham—like many other Loyalists throughout North America—held fast to mid-century notions of civil cosmopolitanism despite danger to his person, property, and life.[73]

Revolutionaries, meanwhile, adjusted rural taverns to fit their emerging political and ideological environments. Thomas Paine's groundbreaking pamphlet *Common Sense* was crucial to this proto-republican, cosmopolitan, multiclass political movement that exploded throughout America after 1765. Published in 1776, Paine's pamphlet reached an unprecedented American readership as it covered taverns' tables and became a center point of public discussion. While staying in an Alexandria, Virginia, tavern in 1776, Cresswell exclaimed, "A pamphlet called 'Commonsense' makes a great noise. . . [Paine's] sentiments are adopted by a great number of people." By espousing the virtues of a civil society free from the class and consumer struggles supposedly inherent in British monarchy, Paine spoke perhaps more to the lower classes than anxious gentlemen, and it worked. Hence an ordinary Bostonian's 1778 published "Creed," in which he declared, "I believe, that I have a *right* to life, liberty, and property, regardless of God's will and dependent of the will of what is termed civil society." For this "Free-man of Boston," mid-century notions of civil society had been "instituted by some artful men, under the pretence of general good, but really to impose their own rigid notions of slavish honesty upon freeborn souls." He simply wanted to adjust these societal goals to actually achieve the "general good." Central to such efforts, in this "Free-man of Boston's" opinion, was the dissolution of "ridged notions" of hierarchy.[74]

Many elitist Patriots remained unimpressed with Paine's democratic declarations. Reflecting on the Revolution in 1793, John Adams called the "levelling spirit" that spread throughout revolutionary America "Paine's yellow fever." The New York gentleman Governeur Morris clung stubbornly to midcentury ideals of hierarchy, declaring openly, "There never was, and never will be a civilized Society without an Aristocracy." It should thus come as no surprise that Morris deemed Paine "a mere adventurer *from England*, without fortune, without family connexions, ignorant even of grammar" when the English upstart publicly criticized Morris's friend, Silas Deane, in 1778.[75] Just because Loyalists liked to represent Patriots as anticosmopolitan traitors did not mean that republicans understood their mission as such. If Paine were to muster even the slightest support of conservative republican leaders, he needed to *at least* speak their cosmopolitan language.

Amid his repeated celebrations of patriotism, liberty, and justice, the perceptive Paine laced *Common Sense* with a deliberate cry for cosmopolitanism, requesting that all "ye that love mankind . . . stand forth!" As "every spot of the world over" was "overrun with oppression," America should "receive the fugitive, and prepare in time an asylum for mankind." Paine thus repeatedly attempted to appeal to republican cosmopolitans' desire for worldly equality. In one revealing instance, the English writer declared that republican Americans might "begin the world over again." In a passage of his popular *American Crisis* (November 21, 1778), furthermore, Paine overtly positioned himself as a detached, cosmopolitan thinker, declaring, "My attachment is to all the world, and not to any particular part."[76] Ultimately, *Common Sense* and the *American Crisis* were tracts that played to Americans' visions of constructing a more worldly cosmopolitanism (i.e., "asylum for mankind") by serving as better protectors of liberty than the corrupted British monarchy. Whether Paine himself truly believed in Enlightenment ideologies of cosmopolitanism was not important; he knew what his customers wanted, and he knew how to give it to them.[77]

Republicans' tavern interactions, once again, reveal much. After 1775, Patriot tavern clubs and committees took on a publicly antimonarchical character, which, ironically, still rested on many midcentury tenets of civil society. A radical tavern keeper and Patriot named Timothy Bigelow used his Worcester, Massachusetts, tavern to spawn the "American Political Society," which vetted local Loyalists, mustered arms and troops for the militia, and sent correspondence to other committees of safety. In 1775, Worcester's citizens elected Bigelow as their delegate to the Provincial Congress.[78] Lancaster's citizens also formed the aforementioned Civil Society tavern club in 1777, while John Adams remarked after visiting a Baltimore tavern in 1777: "They have a Fashion in this Town of reversing the Picture of King G[eorge] 3d. . . . One of these Topsy Turvy Kings was hung up in the Room, where we supped, and under it were written these Lines":

Behold the Man who had it in his Power
To make a Kingdom tremble and adore
Intoxicate with Folly, See his Head
Plac'd where the meanest of his Subjects tread
Like Lucifer the giddy Tyrant fell
He lifts his Heel to Heaven but points his Head to Hell.[79]

Dr. Alexander Hamilton would have been aghast to see such overt damnation of the king, as his generation's aspirations to civility and order were inherently connected with allegiance to—if not obsession with—the royal family. Yet it is also important to note that these Patriots *still* used King George to symbolize their own societal visions.[80] Even in their supposed detestation of the monarchy, republicans remained enthralled with those tenets of royalist civil society that bolstered the midcentury colonies. Thus while revolutionary America would have seemed to Dr. Hamilton like an alien environment when compared to the fictional world he contrived in his 1747 *History of the Tuesday Club*, Hamilton's vision of Annapolis never actually existed. Extending this continuum of societal hope and creation, North American Patriots capitalized on mercurial midcentury ideologies like liberty, order, and civility to craft their (equally fictitious) vision of a republican America. In doing so, Patriots bridged the gap between monarchy and republicanism, whether they would have liked to admit it or not.

Between 1766 and 1783, certain colonists used taverns to exploit the contradictions and complications of their civilizing efforts. Patriots relied on these central spaces to resist what they considered unfair attacks on their personal liberties and property, and eventually to reconstitute what they understood as an operational and successful society. From occluding networks of consumer goods to harassing those loyal to the Crown to publishing republican tracts to supplying local militias, tavern committees led by men who would never have mustered political power twenty years earlier served as arbiters of this transformation of American civil society. British royalists, meanwhile, attempted to maintain America's midcentury makeup, relying on urban taverns as an escape from the world that seemed to be crumbling around them. The dreams of a British American civil society that multiple generations had struggled so frustratingly to realize had been ravaged and repackaged in only seventeen traumatic years. Contradiction reigned supreme over the midcentury gentlemen's orderly aspirations, and taverns remained central spaces through which colonists might effect—or reflect on—these transformations. Looking forward, many of America's elitist leaders hoped to restructure their midcentury societal objectives to fit and guide this radical new republic. It would not be an easy task.

Conclusion

In early August 1784, the Charleston Library Society's elitist members announced that they had recently approved a motion to burn Adam Ferguson's *An Essay on the History of Civil Society* in front of their official meeting place, McCrady's Tavern. Although gentlemen from Charleston to New York City had clung to aspirations of civil society since the mid-eighteenth century (and embraced Ferguson's volume with open arms), the American Revolution had forced colonists to rethink midcentury notions of civility, liberty, and imperial allegiance. In the Charleston Library Society's words, though Ferguson had "*pretended* a wonderful veneration" of civil society in his 1767 book, his 1778 appointment as secretary to Britain's Carlisle Peace Commission—an organization created "for the sole purpose of subjugating three millions of freemen"—had revealed his true character: "A Tool to the British Ministry . . . [who symbolized the] violation of the rights of human nature, in degradation of genius and learning, and in prostitution of the feelings and independence of a Gentleman." At least in the eyes of the Charleston Library Company, Ferguson's failure to adjust his own ideologies of civil society and liberty to the republican American cause necessitated destruction of his most celebrated publication.[1]

The Charleston Library Society's public book burning went beyond ceremony, as the members hoped to physically and publicly demonstrate their altered conceptions of allegiance, political action, and civility. The Revolution had considerably disrupted the Society's mission. Not only did occupation and warfare render fee collection and meetings almost impossible, but a fire on January 15, 1778, destroyed all but 185 of their volumes (not to mention half of Charleston). Ferguson's *Essay on the History of Civil Society* apparently survived the flames, and a Society member spent the rest of the war hauling the library's remaining volumes with him from place to place for safety. By 1784, however, Charleston's Library Society members met once again in McCrady's Tavern and, like their compatriots throughout the new American nation, hurried themselves in "unbecoming British." Yet the Society decided that its first public action after the war would not be a commemorative speech or a dedication of republican-minded books. In a demonstration of nationalism, these proto-republicans determined to burn one of the most cherished beacons of prerevolutionary societal order and imperial allegiance. In doing so, they declared their support (even if tenuous and surface) of republicanism.[2]

Beyond public revelry, the Society's book burning revealed the elitist members' attempts to maintain local power. Having endured a revolutionary period defined by social chaos and class leveling, Charleston's prewar leaders hoped to retain at least a semblance of midcentury notions of hierarchy and order. Yet, as had become so clear over the past twenty years, self-professed societal leaders like Dr. Hamilton could not gather in a tavern and parade through the streets to keep the "great Leviathan of Civil Society under proper discipline and order." Instead, "the common Rascallion herd of men" whom Hamilton's Tuesday Club hoped to keep in an inferior place had risen to the forefront of popular American politics.[3]

Thus Charleston's Library Society *had* to burn Ferguson's volume: not doing so might publicly implicate them as curmudgeons clinging stubbornly to prerevolutionary tenets of monarchy and strict hierarchy, which many Americans had come to consider the very opposite of American republicanism. With ordinary men writing to Charleston's *Gazette* with barbs against the city's once-powerful ruling class (the "Nabob Phalanx in the legislature . . . [with] a *settled plan of ruling by a few, with a rod of iron*"), the members of the Library Society well realized that they had to show public support for notions of republican equality, even if they privately feared such democratic leanings. For the present at least, elitist Americans had to bow to the whims of the masses. Hence their public destruction of Ferguson's volume, a once-esteemed model of civility and liberty that a member had taken great pains to protect during the Revolutionary War.[4]

Despite (or perhaps because of) the upheaval of the American Revolution, certain midcentury anxieties lingered well into the 1780s: leaders still worried about the lower classes' supposed lack of deference and order, preachers and magistrates still damned overconsumption of alcohol and the societal ruin it might engender, and elitist men still hoped to separate themselves from social inferiors in their public endeavors.[5] However, an undercurrent of transformation marked American tavern goers' interactions more than ever before. Where midcentury leaders tended to project their own insecurities regarding insubordination and societal disorder onto their tavern interactions, these spectral fears emerged as tangible issues after the American Revolution. Ordinary men *had* cultivated a smoldering disdain for authority during the tumult of the Revolution, which they managed to translate into real social and political power in the early republic. These upstart "Localists" steadily found a voice against their "Cosmopolitan" opponents.[6] Elitist urbanites had watched their midcentury aspirations of civility and order crumble under the weight of revolution. Suddenly the shadows of lower-class insubordination and disorder that leaders so feared became a reality with the violent emergence of republican America.

By the time a group of fifty-five elites locked themselves in the Philadelphia State House in 1787, they had endured what many considered an all-out attack on their core ideologies of civility. These gentlemen leaders accordingly sought to realize an "Anglo-American Republicanism" that remained firmly rooted in midcentury notions of civility and order rather than divided by what they deemed the parochial politics of a two-party system.[7] It is no coincidence that the Federalist James Madison worried in 1788 whether a failure to embrace a republic with "so many separate descriptions of citizens" might equal "the end of civil society," nor should it come as a surprise that Madison also believed "Stability in government [i.e., a strong central government] is essential to national character . . . as well as to that repose and confidence in the minds of the people, which are among the chief blessings of civil society."[8] Still firmly tethered to so many facets of the monarchical world in which they had been raised and educated, "Federalists" like Madison believed that the American Constitution should reanimate midcentury ideals of order and elitism. A strong central government was critical in this early republican renegotiation of civil society.[9]

But, once again, it was no longer 1747. While most ordinary Americans agreed with the founders' general ideals of law, commerce, and unity, these "other founders" had fashioned their own notions of how a civil society should operate over the past twenty-five years. Jefferson and his "Anti-Federalists" envisioned a different sort of American civil society, where mechanisms of elitist influence should wither under the rising tide of individualism and equality. For Jefferson, ordinary colonists should elect a "natural aristocracy" who were best suited to organize America's complicated workings. The "artificial aristocracy" of midcentury civil society—so "distinguished by the splendor and luxury of their establishments"—simply had no place in Jefferson's vision.[10] For Jefferson, gentlemen aristocrats like James Madison, John Adams, and Alexander Hamilton (future secretary of the treasury) were relics of a bygone era.[11]

Although the Federalists controlled the newspaper narrative regarding civil society's alleged progress, interactions on the ground demonstrated how Jefferson's alternate future resonated with ordinary Americans.[12] While touring America in the 1780s, the German Johan David Schoepf was surprised at how many white Americans had embraced nascent ideologies of equality. During one tavern stay, Schoepf exclaimed that "all sorts of company . . . Generals, Colonels, Captains, Senators, Assemblymen, Judges, Doctors, Clerks, and crowds of Gentlemen, of every weight and caliber and every hue of dress, sat all together about the fire, drinking, smoking, singing, and talking ribaldry." He later reflected, "America knows no nobility, rather hates the thought of such a thing, and refuses any respect demanded by those whose only claim is that of descent or birth."[13] Had Americans truly obtained a democratic world of equality and hope? In a word, no.

Despite Schoepf's professions of American equality in this tavern, he (and other foreigners and Federalists) well realized the inherent contradictions of Jefferson's egalitarian vision.[14] Though a man who touted equality, Jefferson embodied the pinnacle of an American aristocracy: he owned and meticulously controlled hundreds of slaves, lived in an elaborate mansion, and had a bank-breaking penchant for expensive luxury goods.[15] Such contradictory behavior trickled into every facet of civil society during the early Republican Era. While visiting Charleston, South Carolina, Schoepf learned of the Order of Cincinnati, a local tavern organization composed of "the generals and other officers (who have served three years) in a society of friends for keeping alive the memory of the Revolution and their own common friendship." One among hundreds of such clubs and societies that sprang up in taverns across America in the 1780s, the Order of Cincinnati seemed to Schoepf common at first glance. Yet he soon realized that the Order brought in new members according to aristocratic notions of male succession and titles. How, Schoepf wondered, could such notions of "inheritance and merit" exist in a nation "where no titles are allowed and the citizens are forbidden to receive titles from foreign states?" Had not those Patriot generals, officers, and soldiers fought to *destroy* these very tenets of monarchical society? How could "an institution such as this . . . be projected and go so long undenounced?"[16] Whether Federalist or Anti-Federalist—and whether they liked to admit it or not—Americans' long association with British monarchical notions of hierarchy and social order fundamentally marked their forward progress.[17]

From gentlemen versus ordinary colonists to Loyalists versus Patriots to Federalists versus Anti-Federalists, Americans' perceptions of, and anxieties over, oppositional forces defined eighteenth-century North American civil society. Yet these lines were blurry, capricious, and contradictory, ever shifting to satisfy their members' fears and aspirations for the future. Such ongoing negotiations, importantly, often played out within America's most popular public space, the urban tavern. Where elitist colonists hoped to direct an orderly, hierarchical society based on long-standing tenets of sociable prowess and deference, they proved key participants in a New World societal order based on hierarchical transformation, commercial egalitarianism, and internal contradiction.

After 1765, however, British American colonists faced radical societal and ideological transformations that would further challenge their previous ideologies of civility and liberty. During the Stamp Act Crisis (1765–66), urban colonists utilized taverns as headquarters of opposition. Self-professed leaders liked to believe that they could direct resistance measures through notions of civility and order. Yet such civil tactics fell to the wayside as tavern goers relied on more uncivil actions. Although many gentlemen damned this riotous, disorderly behavior as destructive to their larger societal mission, it ultimately worked, as Parliament repealed the Stamp Act after only a year. Unfortunately, Parliament continued its efforts at taxation in North America, and colonists continued to congregate in taverns to violently resist each policy. Between 1766 and 1776, urban tavern goers steadily divided themselves along shifting but important lines of patriotism and allegiance. Extralegal tavern committees proved vital in this transformation, as they violently created and enforced altered rules of societal order that fractured midcentury elitist colonists' jealous assertions of hierarchy and order. Briefly but importantly, republican notions of liberty and equality reigned supreme (at least for white, landowning men).

With the end of the American Revolution, Federalists hurried to reassemble a society that retained as many of the British American civil tenets as possible—namely, hierarchy and elitist control—in the absence of the monarchy and the Old World rule it promised. Leaders hoped that "Societies, like individuals, have their periods of sickness," and this sickness—the rising tide of democracy—might soon be healed.[18] The Constitutional Convention was consequently as much about re-creating midcentury notions of civil society and curbing radical partisanship as it was about creating a republican American form of that society.

The "great Leviathan of Civil Society" was never truly under the "proper discipline and order" of powerful men as Dr. Hamilton had hoped. On the contrary, this "frantic animal" had blossomed into a full-blown goliath by the American Revolution, and those gentlemen who had attempted to cage it had to shift their strategies for society building. Of course, elitist Americans continued their endeavors at hierarchy and order in the early Republic, but their efforts would be fraught with more resistance and oversight than ever before. North American revolutionaries had harnessed tenets of British American civility and liberty in their efforts to craft a republican American version of midcentury civil society. This continuous negotiation would prove violent, ambitious, and world changing.[19]

Notes

Introduction

1. Alexander Hamilton, *The History of the Ancient and Honorable Tuesday Club*, 2 vols., ed. Robert Micklus (Chapel Hill: University of North Carolina Press, 1990), 1:241–42, 220; 2:254, 354–55. For well-read colonists like Hamilton, a "leviathan" would have referred both to a monstrous sea creature and, in the tradition of Thomas Hobbes, the brutish, rude, and inferior organism of political society that must be controlled by well-read, elitist leaders. Thomas Hobbes, *Leviathan; or, the Matter, Form, and Power of a Common-Wealth Ecclesiastical and Civil* (London: Andrew Crooke, 1651), 87.

2. Hamilton, *Tuesday Club*, 2:480–81, 1:318; Robert Micklus, "'The History of the Tuesday Club': A Mock-Jeremiad of the Colonial South," *William and Mary Quarterly* 40:1 (January 1983): 42–61.

3. According to the *Oxford English Dictionary*, a tavern is "a public house or tap-room where wine was retailed; a dram shop." Yet the *Oxford English Dictionary* also equates "tavern" with "public house." Its definition of a public house is as follows: "a building whose principal business is the sale of alcoholic drinks to be consumed on the premises; a pub, a tavern," or "an inn or hostelry providing food and lodging for travellers or members of the public, and usually licensed for the sale of alcohol." Colonial Americans called taverns "inns," "public houses," "ordinaries," "alehouses," and "coffeehouses." Although inns, taverns, and alehouses held individual distinctions in England, British American taverns were a mix of the three and thus did not garner such distinctions. In order to avoid confusion, I refer to these spaces primarily as taverns and occasionally as coffeehouses, which denotes a slight variation on the traditional tavern.

4. Owen Stanwood argued, "The years between 1690 and 1765 marked a golden age for the British American empire, which expanded in power and riches and enjoyed broad support from the colonial republic." Owen Stanwood, "The Protestant Moment:

Antipopery, the Revolution of 1688–1689, and the Making of the Anglo-American Empire," *Journal of British Studies* 46:3 (July 2007): 481–508. The historians McCusker and Menard earlier exclaimed, "For European Americans in British North America and the British West Indies, the years just before the American Revolution were a 'golden age.'" John J. McCusker and Russell Menard, *The Economy of British North America, 1607–1789* (Chapel Hill: University of North Carolina Press, 1985), 51. For a reflection on the "golden age" paradigm applied to (and challenged) regarding women's roles in colonial America, see Richard Middleton and Anne Lombard, *Colonial America: A History to 1763*, 4th ed. (Malden, MA: Wiley-Blackwell, 2011), ch. 4.

5. The average age of the signers of the Declaration of Independence (1776) was forty-four. See Todd Andrlik, "Ages of Revolution: How Old Were They on July 4, 1776?," *Journal of the American Revolution*, accessed July 11, 2018, https://allthingsliberty.com.

6. As Teresa M. Bejan argued, "For thinkers then, as now, determining what civility required could be complicated. . . . [T]he prosecution of incivility was often difficult to distinguish from persecution—as paradigmatically 'uncivil' groups like the early Quakers, American Indians, and English Catholics soon discovered." Teresa M. Bejan, *Mere Civility: Disagreements and the Limits of Toleration* (Cambridge, MA: Harvard University Press, 2017), 6 (also see 61–76). So too did Edmund S. Morgan contend that British American colonists considered Native Americans and enslaved blacks "uncivil, unchristian, and, above all, unwhite." Edmund S. Morgan, *American Slavery, American Freedom: The Ordeal of Colonial Virginia* (New York: Norton, 1975), 329.

7. The Enlightenment thinker Jacob Vernet similarly supported state-centered, patrician-controlled politics as the most stable of all orders, arguing "human society could not exist without subordination." David Sorkin, *The Religious Enlightenment: Protestants, Jews, and Catholics from London to Vienna* (Princeton, NJ: Princeton University Press, 2008), 86 (quote), 71, 86–88. For urban development efforts in colonial America, see J. W. Reps, *The Making of Urban America: A History of City Planning in the United States* (Princeton, NJ: Princeton University Press, 1965); J. W. Reps, *Tidewater Towns: City Planning in Colonial Virginia and Maryland* (Charlottesville: University Press of Virginia, 1972); Elizabeth Milroy, *The Grid and the River: Philadelphia's Green Places, 1682–1876* (University Park: Pennsylvania State University Press, 2016).

8. The historian Jon Butler argued that "enormous social, economic, political, and cultural changes . . . created a distinctively modern and, ultimately, 'American' society in Britain's mainland colonies between 1680 and 1770." Where Butler attempted to define what was "modern" about colonial America (and, by proxy, America), this book seeks to understand how colonists at the time understood their attempts to realize a civil society. Jon Butler, *Becoming America: The Revolution before 1776* (Cambridge, MA: Harvard University Press, 2000), 2.

9. A vast literature exists on early modern ideologies of a civilizing mission. See, e.g., Norbert Elias, *The Civilizing Process: The History of Manners and State Formation and Civilization*, 2 vols., trans. Edmund Jephcott (Oxford: Blackwell, 1994–97); Anna Bryson, *From Courtesy to Civility: Changing Codes of Conduct in Early Modern England* (Oxford: Clarendon Press, 1998); Karen Ordahl Kupperman, ed., *America in European Consciousness, 1493–1750* (Chapel Hill: University of North Carolina Press,

1995); Michael Leroy Oberg, *Dominion and Civility: English Imperialism and Native America, 1585–1685* (Ithaca, NY: Cornell University Press, 1999); Andrew Fitzmaurice, "The Civic Solution to the Crisis of English Colonization, 1609–1625," *Historical Journal* 42:1 (March 1999): 25–51; Michael Leroy Oberg, "Between 'Savage Man' and 'Most Faithful Englishman': Manteo and the Early Anglo-Indian Exchange, 1584–1590," *Itinerario* 24:2 (July 2000): 146–69; Vaughn Scribner, "'The happy effects of these waters': Colonial American Mineral Spas and the British Civilizing Mission," *Early American Studies: An Interdisciplinary Journal* 14:3 (Summer 2016): 409–49; Keith Thomas, *In Pursuit of Civility: Manners and Civilization in Early Modern England* (Lebanon, NH: University Press of New England, 2018). For a contemporary account, see Adam Ferguson, *An Essay on the History of Civil Society*, 5th ed. (London: T. Cadell, 1767).

10. Alice Hanson Jones, "Wealth Estimates for the American Middle Colonies, 1774," *Economic Development and Cultural Change*, 18:4, pt. 2 (July 1970): 130; McCusker and Menard, *The Economy of British North America*, 51; Gary B. Nash, *The Urban Crucible: Social Change, Political Consciousness, and the Origins of the American Revolution* (Cambridge, MA: Harvard University Press, 1979), 161–262. For the Caribbean colonies' importance, see Russell R. Menard, "Plantation Empire: How Sugar and Tobacco Planters Built Their Industries and Raised an Empire," *Agricultural History* 81:3 (Summer 2007): 309–32; Matthew Parker, *The Sugar Barons: Family, Corruption, Empire, and War in the West Indies* (London: Bloomsbury, 2012).

11. Thomas Jones, *History of the New York during the Revolutionary War*, vol. 1, ed. Edward Floyd De Lancey (New York: New York Historical Society, 1879), 12 (Jones' emphasis); *New-York Mercury*, September 24, 1764.

12. *Pennsylvania Gazette*, August 31, 1758; Alan Taylor, *American Revolutions: A Continental History, 1750–1804* (New York: Norton, 2016), 20–23, 90–93; Bernard Bailyn, *The Ideological Origins of the American Revolution: Enlarged Edition* (Cambridge, MA: Harvard University Press, 1992), 55–93, 230–320.

13. *Britannica Academic*, s. v. "civil society," accessed December 14, 2015; Adam Seligman, *The Idea of Civil Society* (Princeton, NJ: Princeton University Press, 1995), 22, 25–26; Peter Borsay, *The English Urban Renaissance: Culture and Society in the Provincial Town, 1660–1770* (Oxford: Clarendon Press, 1991), ch. 10; John R. Ehrenberg, *Civil Society: The Critical History of an Idea* (New York: New York University Press, 1999); J. C. D. Clark, *English Society, 1660–1832: Religion, Ideology and Politics during the Ancien Regime*, 2nd ed. (Cambridge: Cambridge University Press, 2000), Introduction; Peter Burke, Brian Harrison, and Paul Slack, eds., Preface to *Civil Histories: Essays Presented to Sir Keith Thomas*, ed. Peter Burke, Brian Harrison, and Paul Slack (Oxford: Oxford University Press, 2000), v; Jonathan Barry, "Civility and Civic Culture in Early Modern England: The Meanings of Urban Freedom," in *Civil Histories*, 181–96; John Darwin, "Civility and Empire," in *Civil Histories*, 321–36; Jennifer Richards, ed., *Early Modern Civil Discourses* (New York: Palgrave Macmillan, 2003).

14. Steven M. DeLue, *Political Thinking, Political Theory, and Civil Society* (Boston: Allyn and Bacon, 1997); Chris W. Surprenant, "Liberty, Autonomy, and Kant's Civil Society," *History of Philosophy Quarterly* 27:1 (January 2010): 79–94; Jacqueline Anne Augustine, "Kant and the Moral Necessity of Civil Society" (PhD diss., University of Rochester, 1997).

15. Cesar Chesneau Du Marsais, "Philosopher," in *The Encyclopedia of Diderot & d'Alembert Collaborative Translation Project*, trans. Dena Goodman, University of

Michigan Library, Ann Arbor, 2002, accessed June 12, 2017 http://hdl.handle.net/2027/ spo.did2222.0000.001; originally published as "Philosophe," *Encyclopedie ou Dictionnaire raisonne des sciences, des arts et des métiers* (Paris, 1765), 12:509–511; Louis de Jacourt, *Natural Equality, Encyclopedia Project*, trans. Stephen J. Gendzier, accessed June 12, 2017, http://hdl.handle.net/2027/spo.did2222.0001.312; originally published as "Egalite naturelle," in *Encyclopedie ou Dictionnaire raisonne des sciences, des arts et des métiers* (Paris, 1755), 5:415; Denis Diderot (ascribed by Jacques Proust), "Political Authority [abridged]," *Encyclopedia Translation Project*, trans. Stephen J. Gendzier, accessed June 13, 2017, http://hdl.handle.net/2027/spo.did2222.0000.062; originally published as "Autorité politique [abridged]," in *Encyclopédie ou Dictionnaire raisonné des sciences, des arts et des métiers,*1:898–900 (Paris, 1751); Jean-Jacques Rousseau, *On the Social Contract; or Principles of Political Right* (1762), trans. G. D. H. Cole (London: J. M. Dent, 1913).

16. Marvin B. Becker, *The Emergence of Civil Society in the Eighteenth Century: A Privileged Moment in the History of England, Scotland, and France* (Bloomington: Indiana University Press, 1994); "Borghese Family Plaque" (created in the early seventeenth century, currently housed in the entrance of the Galleria Borghese, Rome, Italy). Gerhard Oestreich investigated ideas of early modern European social harmony in his *Neostoicism and the Early Modern State,* trans. David McLintock (Cambridge: Cambridge University Press, 1982). See also B. Ann Tlusty, *Bacchus and Civic Order: The Culture of Drink in Early Modern Germany* (Charlottesville: University Press of Virginia, 2001), 6–7. Gary B. Nash called American Patriots' rhetoric of "public virtue" and "public good"—inherently linked to ideologies of civil society—"catchwords [of] aristocratic politicians . . . [used] to cloak their own ambitions for aggrandizing wealth and power." Gary B. Nash, "Social Change and the Growth of Prerevolutionary Urban Radicalism," in *The American Revolution: Explorations in the History of American Radicalism*, ed. Alfred F. Young (DeKalb: Northern Illinois University Press, 1976), 27.

17. Per Sharon Salinger, this work employs the terms "class," "status," and "sort" interchangeably and often with a modifier (upper, middle, lower, lesser, middling, elitist) as a means to position colonists within an important (if admittedly muddled) colonial American hierarchy. This is not to argue that "class," as Karl Marx developed the term in the nineteenth century, existed as modern-day readers would understand it. Rather, I use the term as one among many to demonstrate differing levels of wealth, status, power, and identity in colonial America, which definitely existed at the time. See Sharon V. Salinger, *Taverns and Drinking in Early America* (Baltimore, MD: Johns Hopkins University Press, 2002), 247 n. 1, for her discussion on this same topic.

18. Jonathan Barry, Introduction to *The Middling Sort of People: Culture, Society and Politics in England, 1550–1800*, ed. Jonathan Barry and Christopher Brooks (New York: St. Martin's Press, 1994), 24. The current volume follows Emma Hart's description of a middling sort of urban colonists (specifically Charleston in her work): "Their presence gave urban white society in South Carolina a tripartite character. Their identity was not forged exclusively through struggle with a conflicting group of South Carolinians, but was instead wrought from their economic, cultural, and political responses to living in a flourishing urban environment. . . . When communities were forged across occupations, social structure ceased to be based mainly on profession. . . . Ultimately, it was such values that marked them out from elites and from plain folk." Emma Hart, *Building Charleston: Town and Society in the Eighteenth-Century British Atlantic*

World (Charlottesville: University of Virginia Press, 2009), 8–9. Historians of early modern England have also studied "sorts" of people extensively. See Keith Wrightson, "'Sorts of People' in Tudor and Stuart England," in Barry and Brooks, *The Middling Sort of People*, 28–52; Robert E. Brown, *Middle-Class Democracy and the Revolution in Massachusetts, 1691–1780* (Ithaca, NY: Cornell University Press, 1955); Lawrence E. Klein, "Politeness for Plebes: Consumption and Social Identity in Early Eighteenth-Century England," in *The Consumption of Culture, 1600–1800: Image, Object, Text*, ed. Ann Bermingham and John Brewer (London: Routledge, 1995), 362–82.

19. Steven C. Bullock, *Tea Sets and Tyranny: The Politics of Politeness in Early America* (Philadelphia: University of Pennsylvania Press, 2017) 1–8; John M. Dixon, *The Enlightenment of Cadwallader Colden: Empire, Science, and Intellectual Culture in British New York* (Ithaca, NY: Cornell University Press, 2016), 7; Tom Cutterham, *Gentlemen Revolutionaries: Power and Justice in the New American Republic* (Princeton, NJ: Princeton University Press, 2017), 1–2.

20. Many Scottish physicians were forced to immigrate to North America (especially the southern colonies) because of a lack of opportunities in England and Scotland, an excess of Scottish doctors, and a high demand for doctors in North America. Despite the supposedly high demand, achieving financial and social success as a physician in North America did not prove an easy task. They often relied on networking opportunities and side businesses to achieve these goals. See Peter McCandless, *Slavery, Disease, and Suffering in the Southern Lowcountry* (Cambridge: Cambridge University Press, 2011), 151–60. "Social capital"—defined by Putnam via Greene as "the organizations and connections that foster cooperation, trust, participation, the exchange of information, civil interaction, and coordinated activity in pursuit of social goals"—has emerged among political scientists and sociologists as a popular measurement of civil society and civic engagement. See Jack P. Greene, "Social and Cultural Capital in Colonial British America: A Case Study," in *Patterns of Social Capital: Stability and Change in Historical Perspective*, ed. Robert I. Rotberg (Cambridge: Cambridge University Press, 2001), 153, 153–71; Robert D. Putnam, "The Prosperous Community: Social Capital and Public Life," *American Prospect* 13:1 (Spring 1993): 35–42. As the historian Robert I. Rotberg asserted, "Societies work best, and always have worked best, where citizens trust their fellow citizens, work cooperatively with them for common goals, and thus share a civic culture. . . . In societies where distrust is prevalent and horizontal ties of mutual involvement are replaced by hierarchical politics, social capital is absent, and little civic engagement exists. . . . [S]ocial capital contributes to the making of civil society." Robert I. Rotberg, "Social Capital and Political Culture in Africa, America, Australasia, and Europe," in *Patterns of Social Capital*, 1. See also Richard Bushman, "American High-Style and Vernacular Cultures," in *Colonial British America: Essays in the New History of the Early Modern Era*, ed. Jack P. Greene and J. R. Pole (Baltimore, MD: Johns Hopkins University Press, 1984), 374; Jennifer Van Horn, "The Mask of Civility: Portraits of Colonial Women and the Transatlantic Masquerade," *American Art* 23:3 (Fall 2009): 8–35; Elizabeth Currid-Halkett, *The Sum of Small Things: A Theory of the Aspirational Class* (Princeton, NJ: Princeton University Press, 2017).

21. Samuel Johnson, quoted in Woodruff D. Smith, *Consumption and the Making of Respectability, 1600–1800* (London: Routledge, 2002), 179; Ronald Schultz, "A Class Society? The Nature of Inequality in Early America," in *Inequality in Early America*,

ed. Carla Gardina Pestana and Sharon Vineberg Salinger (Hanover, NH: University Press of New England, 1999), 203–21.

22. Gary B. Nash, *The Unknown American Revolution: The Unruly Birth of Democracy and the Struggle to Create America* (New York: Penguin Books, 2005), 318–19; Steven Rosswurm, *Arms, Country, and Class: The Philadelphia Militia and "Lower Sort" during the American Revolution, 1775–1783* (New Brunswick, NJ: Rutgers University Press, 1987); Billy G. Smith, *The "Lower Sort:" Philadelphia's Laboring People, 1750–1800* (Ithaca, NY: Cornell University Press, 1990); Keith Krawczynski, *Daily Life in the Colonial City* (Santa Barbara, CA: Greenwood Press, 2013), 257–94.

23. Michael Zuckerman, "Tocqueville, Turner, and Turds: Four Stories of Manners in Early America," *Journal of American History* 85:1 (June 1998): 24–27; Alexander Hamilton, *Gentleman's Progress: The Itinerarium of Dr. Alexander Hamilton, 1744*, ed. Carl Bridenbaugh (Chapel Hill: University of North Carolina Press, 1948), 25–26; Michael Zuckerman, "Authority in Early America: The Decay of Deference on the Provincial Periphery," *Early American Studies: An Interdisciplinary Journal* 1:2 (Fall 2003): 29. See also Michael Zuckerman, "Endangered Deference, Imperiled Patriarchy: Tales from the Marchlands," *Early American Studies: An Interdisciplinary Journal* 3:2 (Fall 2005): 232–52. Of course, such assertions are not without debate. In fact, a lively and heated exchange erupted between Zuckerman and Pole over issues of eighteenth-century deference. As J. R. Pole contended in 1999, "Professor Zuckerman's difficulty seems to stem from confusing deference with abject submissiveness." J. R. Pole, "A Target Respectfully Returns the Arrow," *Journal of American History* 86:3 (December 1999): 1449. For further debate on the topic of deference, see Michael Zuckerman, Aaron S. Fogleman, Kathleen M. Brown, John M. Murrin, and Robert A. Gross, "Deference or Defiance in Eighteenth-Century America? A Round Table," *Journal of American History* 85:1 (June 1998): 13–97. For the downfall of deference in colonial New York City particularly, see Joyce D. Goodfriend, *Who Should Rule at Home? Confronting the Elite in British New York City* (Ithaca, NY: Cornell University Press, 2017), ch. 7. The current work is concerned with what certain early American men *perceived* more than what actually occurred; there very well might have been a continuance of certain forms of deference, but many urbanites felt that it was not deferential enough. Hence their efforts to uphold ideals of civility.

24. Nancy Ruttenburg, *Democratic Personality: Popular Voice and the Trial of American Authorship* (Stanford, CA: Stanford University Press, 1998), 170 (quote); Harry S. Stout, *The Divine Dramatist: George Whitefield and the Rise of Modern Evangelicalism* (Grand Rapids, MI.: Eerdmans, 1991), 87–132; Odai Johnson and William J. Burling, *The Colonial American Stage, 1665–1774: A Documentary Calendar* (London: Associated University Presses, 2001), 76; *New England Weekly Journal*, December 4, 1739; David T. Morgan Jr., "George Whitefield and the Great Awakening in the Carolinas and Georgia, 1739–1740," *Georgia Historical Quarterly* 54:4 (Winter 1970): 532; Peter Charles Hoffer, *When Benjamin Franklin Met the Reverend Whitefield: Enlightenment, Revival, and the Power of the Printed Word* (Baltimore, MD: Johns Hopkins University Press, 2011); Frank Lambert, *"Pedlar in Divinity": George Whitefield and the Transatlantic Revivals, 1737–1770* (Princeton, NJ: Princeton University Press, 1994); Vaughn Scribner, "Transatlantic Actors: The Intertwining Stages of George Whitefield and Lewis Hallam Sr.," *Journal of Social History* 50:1 (Fall 2016): 1–27.

25. *Pennsylvania Gazette*, January 11, 1733. For midcentury colonial leaders' ideologies of the law and civil society, see William Pencack, Introduction to *Pennsylvania's Revolution*, ed. William Pencack (University Park: Pennsylvania State University Press, 2010), 10.

26. David Shields, *Civil Tongues and Polite Letters in British America* (Chapel Hill: University of North Carolina Press, 1997), xx; *Boston Evening-Post*, May 4, 1761. While a preponderance of works exist on notions of civil society in the early national period of America, few works tackle the colonial period. Happily, a recent uptick in scholarship on colonial civil society is apparent. Most recently, Jennifer Van Horn has investigated how Anglo-American colonists used their consumer identities to reflect on their own civility: Jennifer Van Horn, *The Power of Objects in Eighteenth-Century British America* (Chapel Hill: University of North Carolina Press, 2017), esp. 10–11 n.8 for Van Horn's understanding of civil society. See also John L. Brooke, *Columbia Rising: Civil Life on the Upper Hudson from the Revolution to the Age of Jackson* (Chapel Hill: University of North Carolina Press, 2010), 8–9; Van Horn, "The Mask of Civility," 8–35; Kathleen D. McCarthy, *American Creed: Philanthropy and the Rise of Civil Society, 1700–1865* (Chicago: University of Chicago Press, 2003), 1–29; Jessica Choppin Roney, *Governed by a Spirit of Opposition: The Origins of American Political Practice in Colonial Philadelphia* (Baltimore, MD: Johns Hopkins University Press, 2014), 187; Iain McDaniel, *Adam Ferguson in the Scottish Enlightenment: The Roman Past and Europe's Future* (Cambridge, MA: Harvard University Press, 2013), 6–7; Greene, "Social and Cultural Capital," in Rotberg, *Patterns of Social Capital*, 153–71.

27. Hamilton, *Tuesday Club*, 1:241. In Adam Ferguson's words, man was, "by nature, the member of a community" and should "forego his happiness and his freedom, where these interfere with the good of society." McDaniel, *Adam Ferguson in the Scottish Enlightenment*, 6; Seligman, *Civil Society*, 31; Becker, *The Emergence of Civil Society*, xx.

28. *Pennsylvania Gazette*, December 31, 1733. For fire as metaphor in early America, including ideologies of civil society, see Benjamin L. Carp, "Fire of Liberty: Firefighters, Urban Voluntary Culture, and the Revolutionary Movement," *William and Mary Quarterly* 58:4 (October 2001): 781–818. Tlusty took such an approach to German society, contending, "Society in the early modern German city, then, does not emerge as a simple two-part model of populace versus authority but as a complex collection of interest groups involved in a constant process of negotiation." Tlusty, *Bacchus and Civic Order*, 211. See also Beat Kümin, "Drinking and Public Space in Early Modern German Lands," *Contemporary Drug Problems* 32:1 (Spring 2005): 9–27.

29. "A Letter to a Friend in the Country, [25 September 1735]," *Founders Online*, National Archives, last modified October 5, 2016, http://founders.archives.gov [original source: Benjamin Franklin, *The Papers of Benjamin Franklin, Volume Two, January 1, 1735, through December 31, 1744*, ed. Leonard W. Labaree (New Haven, CT: Yale University Press, 1961), 65–88]; *Boston Evening-Post*, May 12, 1760; *Pennsylvania Gazette*, December 31, 1733; Hamilton, *Tuesday Club*, 1:241–42, 220; 2:254, 354–55.

30. For other investigations of how leaders sought to blend English traditions ("civic Republicanism") with American republicanism ("constitutional Republicanism") in their creation of an "Anglo-American Republicanism," see Derek McDougall, "Influences on Anglo-American Republicanism: The Contributions of Eric Nelson," *Australian Journal of Politics and History* 63:3 (September 2017): 457–565; Nathan

R. Perl-Rosenthal, "The 'Divine Right of Republics': Hebraic Republicanism and the Debate over Kingless Government in Revolutionary America," *William and Mary Quarterly* 66:3 (July 2009): 548–49. Republicanism remains murky and ill-defined. See Daniel T. Rodgers, "Republicanism: The Career of a Concept," *Journal of American History* 79:1 (June 1992): 11–38. The "unbecoming British" and "becoming America" line is a play on the titles of two books: Kariann Akemi Yokota, *Unbecoming British: How Revolutionary America Became a Postcolonial Nation* (Oxford: Oxford University Press, 2011) and Butler, *Becoming America*.

31. Richard Hofstadter, *America at 1750: A Social Portrait* (New York: Vintage Books, 1973), 4. A number of colonists and visitors compared the mid-eighteenth-century colonies' cities to England's "country towns." Hamilton, *Itinerarium*, 192–93; Andrew Burnaby, *Travels Through the Middle Settlements in North America in the Years 1759 and 1760* (Dublin: R. Marchbank, 1775), 169.

32. *Pennsylvania Gazette*, August 29, 1754; *Pennsylvania Gazette*, September 17, 1747; Linda Colley, *Britons: Forging the Nation, 1707–1837* (New Haven, CT: Yale University Press, 1992); Jack P. Greene, "Empire and Identity from the Glorious Revolution to the American Revolution," and Richard Dayton, "Knowledge and Empire," in *The Oxford History of the British Empire*, vol. 2: *The Eighteenth Century*, ed. P. J. Marshall (Oxford: Oxford University Press, 1998), 208–30, 231–52; Steven Sarson, *British America, 1500–1800: Creating Colonies, Imagining an Empire* (Oxford: Oxford University Press, 2005). A solid literature exists on the broader imperial connections that colonists enjoyed. See, e.g., Ian K. Steele, *The English Atlantic, 1675–1740: An Exploration of Communication and Community* (Oxford: Oxford University Press, 1986); Jack P. Greene, *Peripheries and Center: Constitutional Development in the Extended Polities of the British Empire and the United States, 1607–1788* (Athens: University of Georgia Press, 1987); David Hancock, *Citizens of the World: London Merchants and the Integration of the British Atlantic Community, 1735–1785* (Cambridge: Cambridge University Press, 1995); T. H. Breen, "Ideology and Nationalism on the Eve of the American Revolution: Revisions Once More in Need of Revising," *Journal of American History* 84:1 (June 1997): 13–39; Benedict Anderson, *Imagined Communities: Reflections on the Origin and Spread of Nationalism* (London: Verso, 2006).

33. Gary B. Nash, "The Social Development of Colonial America," in *Colonial British America*, 247. Such a method also follows Janet L. Abu-Lughod's decision to study cities in *Before European Hegemony*. Abu-Lughod contended that she wanted "to trace the connections among the highpoints of the archipelagos [cities]." Janet L. Abu-Lughod, *Before European Hegemony: The World System, A.D. 1250–1350* (Oxford: Oxford University Press, 1989), 14.

34. *New-York Mercury*, March 24, 1755; "Cadwallader Colden to Mrs. Colden, New York, Septr. 8, 1744," in Cadwallader Colden, *The Letters and Papers of Cadwallader Colden*, vol. 3: *1743–1747* (New York: New York Historical Society, 1919), 74. Boston, New York City, and Philadelphia harbored populations of between 13,000 and 16,000 by midcentury. While smaller cities farther south, like Annapolis and Charleston, each numbered fewer than 5,000 colonists by midcentury, they still fell in line with the same social and cultural changes occurring in cities to the north. Nash, *Urban Crucible*, 161, 179, 313. See also Carl Bridenbaugh, *Cities in the Wilderness: The First Century of Urban Life in America, 1625–1742* (Oxford: Oxford University Press, 1938). For ideas of the hopes and dangers of cities, see Arthur J. Weitzman, "Eighteenth Century

London: Urban Paradise or Fallen City?," *Journal of the History of Ideas* 36:3 (July–September 1975): 469–80. For how southern cities should be viewed as connected to rather than detached from northern urban development, see Hart, *Building Charleston*, 1–15; Paul Musselwhite, "Annapolis Aflame: Richard Clarke's Conspiracy and the Imperial Urban Vision in Maryland, 1704–8," *William and Mary Quarterly* 71:3 (July 2014): 361–62; Vaughn Scribner, "'Quite a genteel and extreamly commodious House': Southern Taverns, Anxious Elites, and the British American Quest for Social Differentiation," *Journal of Early American History* 5:1 (April 2015): 30–67. For those scholars who have pushed us to reconceive the city to countryside paradigm and, in turn, investigate the importance of "backcountry" operations for urban and imperial development, see Phyllis Whitman Hunter, *Purchasing Identity in the Atlantic World: Massachusetts Merchants, 1670–1780* (Ithaca, NY: Cornell University Press, 2001); Ann Smart Martin, *Buying into a World of Goods: Early Consumers in Backcountry Virginia* (Baltimore, MD: Johns Hopkins University Press, 2008); David J. Hancock, "The Triumphs of Mercury: Connection and Control in the Emerging Atlantic Economy," in *Soundings in Atlantic History: Latent Structures and Intellectual Currents, 1500–1830*, ed. Bernard Bailyn and Patricia Denault (Cambridge, MA: Harvard University Press, 2009), 112–40; Daniel B. Thorp, "Taverns and Tavern Culture on the Southern Colonial Frontier: Rowan County, North Carolina, 1753–1776," *Journal of Southern History* 62:4 (November 1996): 661–88; Daniel B. Thorp, "Doing Business in the Backcountry: Retail Trade in Colonial Rowan County, North Carolina," *William and Mary Quarterly* 48:3 (July 1991): 387–408.

35. David W. Conroy, *In Public Houses: Drink and the Revolution of Authority in Colonial Massachusetts* (Chapel Hill: University of North Carolina Press, 1995); Peter Thompson, *Rum Punch and Revolution: Tavern Going and Public Life in Eighteenth-Century Philadelphia* (Philadelphia: University of Pennsylvania Press, 1999), 9; Benjamin L. Carp, *Rebels Rising: Cities and the American Revolution* (Oxford: Oxford University Press, 2007), 63.

36. Shields, *Civil Tongues and Polite Letters*, xx, xix; Salinger, *Taverns and Drinking*, 5.

37. Henri Lefebvre, *The Production of Space* (Oxford: Blackwell, 1991), 92–94. For the geography of urban public space, see Peter G. Goheen, "Public Space and the Geography of the Modern City," *Progress in Human Geography* 22:4 (August 1998): 479–96. For space theory in early modern English taverns, see James R. Brown, "The Landscape of Drink: Inns, Taverns and Alehouses in Early Modern Southampton" (PhD diss., University of Warwick, 2007).

38. As Ruth Bloch noted, Habermas's "public sphere" has come "perilously close to dissolving into mush." Recognizing the relative devolution of this term, I utilize the "public sphere" less in terms of a Habermasian sphere of democratic development and more with the purpose of establishing a public place of contact, communication, and culture. Ruth H. Bloch, "Inside and Outside the Public Sphere," *William and Mary Quarterly* 62:1 (January 2005): 99; Jürgen Habermas, *The Structural Transformation of the Public Sphere: An Inquiry into a Category of Bourgeois Society* (Cambridge, MA: MIT Press, 1991), 1.

39. *Boston Gazette*, July 17, 1750; Kym S. Rice, *Early American Taverns: For the Entertainment of Friends and Strangers* (Chicago: Regnery Gateway, 1983), 31; Salinger, *Taverns and Drinking*, 185, also see 292 n. 10 for further discussion on numbers;

David Hancock and Michelle McDonald, ed., *Public Drinking in the Early Modern World: Voices from the Tavern, 1500–1800*, vol. 4: *America* (New York: Pickering and Chatto, 2011), 4:20; Serena R. Zabin, *Dangerous Economies: Status and Commerce in Imperial New York* (Philadelphia: University of Pennsylvania Press, 2009).

40. James Birket, *Some Cursory Remarks Made by James Birket in his Voyage to North America, 1750–1751* (New Haven, CT: Yale University Press, 1916), 22; Burnaby, *Travels*, 96–98, 135–36, 167–70; William Smith Jr., *The History of the Province of New-York: First Discovery to the Year 1732* (London: Thomas Wilcox, 1757), 189–94. For Williamsburg's number of taverns in the 1760s and 1770s, see the "eWilliamsburg" map at "Colonial Williamsburg," accessed October 3, 2012, http://research.history. org. For records indicating new taverns built in Annapolis, see James D. Kornwolf, *Architecture and Town Planning in Colonial North America*, vol. 2 (Baltimore, MD: Johns Hopkins University Press, 2002), 735. Kornwolf indicates that Middleton's Tavern was built in 1735, Reynolds Tavern in 1745 (although another historian has placed its construction in 1739), and Charles Carroll's tavern in 1750. For more on the taverns of Annapolis that were mentioned in the *Maryland Gazette*, see Walter B. Norris, *Annapolis: Its Colonial and Naval Story* (New York: Thomas Y. Crowell Co., 1925), 320, see also 858–59 for church numbers; William Mylne, *Travels in the Colonies in 1773–1775, Described in the Letters of William Mylne*, ed. Ted Ruddock (Athens: University of Georgia Press, 1993), 73.

41. For early modern British tavern culture, amenities, and developments, see Mark Hailwood, *Alehouses and Good Fellowship in Early Modern England* (Woodbridge: Boydell Press, 2014); Peter Clark, *The English Alehouse: A Social History 1200–1830* (New York: Longman, 1983). For an in-depth investigation of sport and leisure in colonial American taverns, see Nancy L. Struna, *People of Prowess: Sport, Leisure, and Labor in Early Anglo-America* (Urbana: University of Illinois Press, 1996), 143–64.

42. Zabin, *Dangerous Economies*, 55–100; Linda Sturtz, *Within Her Power: Propertied Women in Colonial Virginia* (London: Routledge, 2002), 90–150; Sarah Hand Meacham, *Every Home a Distillery: Alcohol, Gender, and Technology in the Colonial Chesapeake* (Baltimore, MD: Johns Hopkins University Press, 2009), ch. 4; Zabin, *Dangerous Economies*, ch. 3, 98–99; Hart, *Building Charleston*, ch. 4; Ellen Hartigan-O'Connor, *The Ties That Buy: Women and Commerce in Revolutionary America* (Philadelphia: University of Pennsylvania Press, 2009).

43. "Captain Thomas Walduck, Letter to John Searle, 1710," in Christine Sismondo, *America Walks into a Bar: A Spirited History of Taverns and Saloons, Speakeasies, and Grog Shops* (Oxford: Oxford University Press, 2011), 4 (quote); "Journal of a French Traveller in the Colonies, 1765, II," *American Historical Review* 27:1 (October 1921): 77. Realizing the massive amount of traffic that urban taverns brought in on a daily basis, nearby business owners often advertised their location in proximity to popular taverns rather than other public spaces. Dozens of neighboring businesses, including booksellers, tin makers, cloth merchants, watchmakers, and leather dressers promoted their establishments as located "next door," "opposite," or "near" New York City's oft-visited Merchant Coffee House in the 1750s and 1760s. *New-York Mercury*, September 10, 1759; *New-York Gazette*, November 13, 1758; *New-York Mercury*, April 8, 1754, November 15, 1762.

44. Thompson, *Rum Punch and Revolution*, 75–110; Salinger, *Taverns and Drinking*, 61–64.

45. For slave society versus society with slaves, see Allan Kulikoff, *Tobacco and Slaves: The Development of Southern Cultures in the Chesapeake, 1680–1800* (Chapel Hill: University of North Carolina Press, 1988).

46. See, e.g., Carp, *Rebels Rising*, which investigates the American Revolution through taverns, churches, waterfronts, homes, and court- or state houses.

47. T. H. Breen, "What Time Was the American Revolution? Reflections on a Familiar Narrative," in *Experiencing Empire: Power, People, and Revolution in Early America*, ed. Patrick Griffin (Charlottesville: University of Virginia Press, 2017), 234.

48. Eric Nelson argued that America's founders like Alexander Hamilton, John Adams, and James Wilson hoped to realize an American government *based on* a strong monarchy rather than resistant to it. Eric Nelson, *The Royalist Revolution: Monarchy and the American Founding* (Cambridge, MA: Harvard University Press, 2014). Various historians investigated how early national leaders hoped to quell partisan politics through public celebration and music. See Kirsten E. Wood, "'Join with Heart and Soul and Voice': Music, Harmony, and Politics in the Early American Republic," *American Historical Review* 119:4 (October 2014): 1083–1116; David Waldstreicher, *In the Midst of Perpetual Fetes: The Making of American Nationalism, 1776–1820* (Chapel Hill: University of North Carolina Press, 1997); Simon P. Newman, *Parades and Politics of the Street: Festive Culture in the Early American Republic* (Philadelphia: University of Pennsylvania Press, 1997); Lee Travers, *Celebrating the Fourth: Independence Day and the Rites of Nationalism in the Early Republic* (Amherst: University of Massachusetts Press, 1997).

Chapter 1

1. *Pennsylvania Gazette*, June 2, 1768. For the St. Andrew's Society meeting at the Bunch of Grapes, see *Pennsylvania Gazette*, June 2, 1768; February 21, 1771; March 28, 1771.

2. For contemporary examples of elitist preference of private taverns, see Cadwallader Colden, *Letters and Papers of Cadwallader Colden, Vol. V: 1755–1760* (New York: New York Historical Society, 1923), 181–82; John Adams, *Diary and Autobiography of John Adams*, Series 1, ed. L. H. Butterfield (Cambridge, MA: Harvard University Press, 1961), 1:172; Hamilton, *Itinerarium*, 125; Henry Melchior Muhlenberg, *The Journals of Henry Melchior Muhlenberg*, vol. 1, trans. Theodore G. Tappert and John W. Doberstein (Philadelphia: Muhlenberg Press, 1942), 278; See also Choppin Roney, *Governed by a Spirit of Opposition*, 59–103; Shields, *Civil Tongues and Polite Letters*, 55–98, 189–274.

3. Clark, *The English Alehouse*, 1; Thomas Brennan, "Taverns and the Public Sphere in the French Revolution," in *Alcohol: A Social and Cultural History*, ed. Mack P. Holt (Oxford: Berg, 2006), 107–20.

4. Van Horn, *Power of Objects*, 21. For colonists' fears of being transformed by supposedly "savage" peoples, see Susan Scott Parrish, *American Curiosity: Cultures of Natural History in the Colonial British Atlantic World* (Chapel Hill: University of North Carolina Press, 2006), 85–90. See also Bernard W. Sheehan, *Savagism and Civility: Indians and Englishmen in Colonial Virginia* (Cambridge: Cambridge University Press, 1980); Karen Kupperman, *The Jamestown Project* (Cambridge, MA: Harvard University Press, 2007), 161.

5. *Collections of the Massachusetts Historical Society, Volume V of the Third Series* (Boston: John H. Eastburn, 1836), 239–41. For British America's economic and demographic distinction, see Marc Egnal, *New World Economies: The Growth of the Thirteen Colonies and Early Canada* (Oxford: Oxford University Press, 1998), 1–24; Kenneth Morgan, *Slavery, Atlantic Trade, and the British Economy, 1660–1800* (Cambridge: Cambridge University Press, 2000), 61, 18–20; Lois Green Carr and Lorena S. Walsh, "The Standard of Living in the Colonial Chesapeake," *William and Mary Quarterly* 45:1 (January 1988): 135–59; Hofstadter, *America at 1750*, xi–60; Robert V. Wells, *The Population of the British Colonies in America before 1776: A Survey of Census Data* (Princeton, NJ: Princeton University Press, 1975), 259–296.

6. Birket, *Cursory Remarks*, 63–64, 69; Smith, *The History of the Province of New-York*, 187–88, 210 (emphasis Smith's); Lionel Chalmers, *An Account of the Weather and Diseases of South-Carolina*, 2 vols. (London: Edward and Charles Dilly, 1776), 1:35; Hart, *Building Charleston*, 47–48, 32–37, ch. 2; Bushman, *Refinement of America*, ch. 5.

7. Van Horn, *Power of Objects*, 9. See also Maya Jasanoff, "Collectors of Empire: Objects, Conquests, and Imperial Self-Fashioning," *Past & Present* 184:1 (August 2004): 109–36; J. G. A. Pocock, *Virtue, Commerce, and History: Essays on Political Thought and History, Chiefly in the Eighteenth Century* (Cambridge: Cambridge University Press, 1985), 108–9.

8. "Observations Concerning the Increase of Mankind, 1751," *Founders Online*, National Archives, last modified June 29, 2017, http://founders.archives.gov/documents/Franklin/01-04-02-0080 (original source: Franklin, *Papers*, 4:225–34).

9. Markman Ellis, *The Coffeehouse: A Cultural History* (London: Weidenfeld & Nicolson, 2004), 21; Sir Henry Blount, *A Voyage into the Levant* (London: By J.C. for William Crook, 1671), 20, 21, 54, 55, 138; William Biddulph, "A Letter Written from Allepo in Syria Comagena," in *Travels of Certaine Englishmen into Africa, Asia, Troy, Bythinia, Thracia, and to the Black Sea*, ed. Theophilus Lavender (London: Th. Haveland for W. Aspley, 1609), vi, 60, 66; George Sandys, *A Relation of a Journey Begun in An. Dom 1610* (London: W. Barrett, 1615), 66; Jordan Goodman, "Excitantia: Or, How Enlightenment Europe Took to Soft Drugs," in *Consuming Habits: Global and Historical Perspectives on How Cultures Define Drugs*, 2nd ed., ed. Jordan Goodman, Paul E. Lovejoy, and Andrew Sherratt (London: Routledge, 2007), 127; Anonymous, *"The Rules and Orders of the Coffee-House," A Brief Description of the Excellent Vertues of that Sober and Wholesome Drink, called coffee* (London: Paul Greenwood, 1674).

10. İlay Örs, "Coffeehouses, Cosmopolitanism, and Pluralizing Modernities in Istanbul," *Journal of Mediterranean Studies* 12:1 (2002): 119–45.

11. Alexander Pope, *The Rape of the Lock: Canto 3*, in *The Complete Poetical Works of Alexander Pope*, ed. Henry Walcott (Boston and New York: Houghton Mifflin & Co., 1903), 92–95.

12. M. P., *Character of Coffee and Coffee-Houses* (London: John Starkey, 1661), 1, 5–6.

13. Brian Cowen, *Social Life of Coffee: The Emergence of the British Coffeehouse* (New Haven, CT: Yale University Press, 2005), 89, 169–71; Thompson, *Rum Punch and Revolution*, 91; "The Rules and Orders of the Coffee-House"; M.P., *Character of Coffee and Coffee-Houses*, 1, 5–6; *Character of a Coffee-House with the Symptoms of a Town-Wit* (London: Jonathan Edwin, 1673), 3. For the rise and development of British

coffeehouses in England, see Cowen, *The Social Life of Coffee*; Ellis, *The Coffee House*; Markman Ellis, ed., *Eighteenth-Century Coffee-House Culture*, 4 vols. (London: Chatto and Pickering, 2006); Brian Cowan, "Publicity and Privacy in the History of the British Coffeehouse," *History Compass* 5:4 (June 2007): 1180–1213.

14. William Byrd II, *Another Secret Diary of William Byrd of Westover, 1739–1741: With Letters & Literary Exercises, 1696–1726*, ed. Maude H. Woodfin (Richmond: Dietz Press, 1942), xxiii; Hamilton, *Tuesday Club*, 1:xvi ("whin-bush Club" quote); Franklin, *Autobiography*, 44 ("Newton" quote); J. A. Leo Lemay, *The Life of Benjamin Franklin*, vol. 1: *Journalist, 1706–1730* (Philadelphia: University of Pennsylvania Press, 2006), 290.

15. The Exchange Coffee House opened in 1732, while the Merchant Coffee House came to be in 1737. Hamilton noted numerous visits to Todd's tavern during his 1744 peregrinations. He became quite fond of the "old Scotsman," Todd. See Hamilton, *Itinerarium*, 42–49, 79–80, 87–88, 176–84; *New-York Gazette*, June 21, 1762; *New-York Gazette Revived in the Weekly Post-Boy*, July 30, 1750; Carp, *Rebels Rising*, 65; *New-York Gazette*, April 4, 1763; Rice, *Early American Taverns*, 125–33. For "the old Coffee House," see *Pennsylvania Gazette*, June 5, 1735; Thompson, *Rum Punch and Revolution*, 90–94; Conroy, *In Public Houses*, 73–74, 89–96, 102, 135, 132, 119, 161, 233; Conroy, *In Public Houses*, 73–74, 89–96, 102, 135, 132, 119, 161, 233; Hart, *Building Charleston*, 109–10; Scribner, "'Quite a genteel and extreamly commodious House,'" 30–67.

16. Aytoun Ellis, *The Penny Universities: A History of the Coffee-Houses* (London: Secker & Warburg, 1956).

17. *Pennsylvania Gazette*, September 29, 1748; *New-York Gazette*, December 18, 1749.

18. Elihu Samuel Riley, *"The Ancient City": A History of Annapolis, in Maryland, 1649–1887* (Annapolis: Record Printing Office, 1887), 131; *Virginia Gazette*, April 18, 1745; July 25, 1751.

19. Shields, *Civil Tongues and Polite Letters*, 62; *South Carolina Gazette*, October 25, 1743; September 8, 1749; *New-York Gazette*, April 29, 1751; Julia Cherry Spruill, *Women's Life and Work in the Southern Colonies* (New York: Norton, 1972), 298 (quote); "Journal of a French Traveller, II," 741.

20. John Rowe, *Letters and Diary of John Rowe, Boston Merchant, 1759–1762, 1764–1779*, ed. Anne Rowe Cunningham (Boston: W. B. Clarke, 1903), 64, 88, 168; Francis Goelet, *The Voyages and Travels of Francis Goelet, 1746–1758*, ed. Kenneth Scott (London: Queen's College Press, 1970), October 2, 1750; [John Adams], "Proteus Echo no. 29 [On Politeness]," *New-England Weekly Journal*, October 23, 1727; Shields, *Civil Tongues and Polite Letters*, 99–140; Van Horn, "Mask of Civility," 9–35; Kenneth A. Lockridge, "Colonial Self-Fashioning: Paradoxes and Pathologies in the Construction of Genteel Identity in Eighteenth-Century America," in *Through a Glass Darkly: Reflections on Personal Identity in Early America*, ed. Ronald Hoffman, Mechal Sobel, and Fredrika J. Teute (Chapel Hill: University of North Carolina Press, 1997), 274–339.

21. Thompson, *Rum Punch and Revolution*, 106 (quote), 180, 146–50; Salinger, *Taverns and Drinking*, 196–7.

22. As Becker contended, "Eighteenth-century academies, provincial societies, and a host of intermediate institutions characteristic of civil society cast learning—economic, political, and scientific—into a polite mold." Becker, *Emergence of Civil Society*,

106. Although beyond the scope of this work, British American gentlemen also carved out other, less substantial polite spaces in cities. See William Black, "Journal of William Black, 1744 (continued)," *Pennsylvania Magazine of History and Biography* 1:4 (1877): 404–5; Naomi J. Stubbs, *Cultivating National Identity through Performance: American Pleasure Gardens and Entertainment* (New York: Palgrave Macmillan, 2013); Vaughn Scribner, "Cultivating 'Cities in the Wilderness': New York City's Commercial Pleasure Gardens and the British American Pursuit of Rural Urbanism," *Urban History* 45:2 (April 2018): 275–305; Scribner, "'The happy effects of these waters,'" 409–49.

23. Richard L. Bushman, *The Refinement of America: Persons, Houses, Cities* (New York: Vintage Books, 1992), ch. 4; Hamilton, *Itinerarium*, 51, 120.

24. Benjamin Franklin, *A Proposal for Promoting Useful Knowledge Among the British Plantations in America* (Philadelphia: Benjamin Franklin, 1743); Benjamin Franklin, *The Autobiography of Benjamin Franklin* (Boston: Houghton Mifflin & Company, 1906), 29–55; Choppin Roney, *Governed by a Spirit of Opposition*, 59–103.

25. "Directors of Library Company to John Penn," Philadelphia, August 3, 1741, 312, in "The Papers of Benjamin Franklin," Yale University, accessed February 25, 2012, http://www.yale.edu/franklinpapers/project.html; "A Short Account of the Library," in *A Catalogue of Books Belonging to the Library Company of Philadelphia* (Philadelphia: B. Franklin, 1741), 308.

26. "Library Company to John Penn," *Pennsylvania Gazette*, June 5, 1735; "A Short Account of the Library," in *Catalogue of Books*.

27. Ian K. Steele noted, "A bare majority of white adult male households and about one third of white adult female households were literate in colonial North America in 1660. . . . Adult male literacy in New England rose dramatically to 70 percent by 1710 and to 85 percent in 1760," but "elsewhere in English America there seems to have been no comparable transformation[;] . . . only a minority of the English-speaking adults in England or America could read and write well enough to do so regularly." Steele, *The English Atlantic*, 133–67, 266.

28. Gentlemen often kept extensive libraries in their estates. See Black, "Journal," 407; Kevin J. Hayes, ed., *The Library of William Byrd of Westover* (Madison, WI: Madison House, 1997); I. N. Phelps Stokes, *The Iconography of Manhattan Island, 1498–1909*, vol. 4 (New York: Robert H. Dodd, 1915), 512; Birket, *Cursory Remarks*, 67; *The Annual Report of the Library Company of Philadelphia for the Year 1964* (Philadelphia: Library Company of Philadelphia, 1964), 7; Smith, *History*, 195; *At the Instance of Benjamin Franklin: A Brief History of the Library Company of Philadelphia* (Philadelphia: Library Company of Philadelphia, 1995).

29. Peter Clark, *British Clubs and Societies, 1580–1800: The Origins of an Associational World* (Oxford: Oxford University Press, 2000), 37; *A Satyrical Description of Commencement. Calculated to the Meridian of Cambridge in New-England* (Boston: Heart and Crown, 1718); Jasper Danckaerts, *Journal of Jasper Danckaerts, 1679–1680*, ed. Bartlett Burleigh James and J. Franklin Jameson (New York: Charles Scribner's Sons, 1913), 267; "On the Need for an Academy," *Pennsylvania Gazette*, August 24, 1749.

30. "Constitutions of the Academy of Philadelphia," November 13, 1749, Franklin Papers, accessed January 21, 2018, http://franklinpapers.org.

31. "Constitutions of the Academy of Philadelphia," November 13, 1749, Franklin Papers, accessed January 21, 2018, http://franklinpapers.org; Edward P. Cheney,

History of the University of Pennsylvania, 1740–1940 (Philadelphia: University of Pennsylvania Press, 1940), 95; Krawczynksi, *Daily Life in the Colonial City*, 247, 251. Eventually, the College ousted Franklin and became riven by partisan and religious lines. See Choppin Roney, *Governed by a Spirit of Opposition*, 80–103, 112.

32. William Livingston, *The Independent Reflector, or Weekly Essays on Sundry Important Subjects More particularly adapted to the Province of New-York*, ed. Milton M. Klein (Cambridge, MA: Harvard University Press, 1963): "Number XVII: Remarks on our Intended College, Thursday, March 22, 1753," 171–77, 172 (quote); "Number XVIII: A Continuation of the Same Subject, Thursday, March 29, 1753," 178–83; "Number XIX: The Same Subject Continued, Thursday, April 1, 1753," 184–90; "Number XX: A Farther Prosecution of the Same Subject, Thursday, April 12, 1753," 191–98; "Number XXI: Remarks on the College Continued, Thursday, April 19, 1753," 199–206; "Number XXII: The Same Subject Continued and Concluded in, An Address to the Inhabitants of this Province, Thursday, April 26, 1753," 207–14.

33. Krawczynksi, *Daily Life in the Colonial City*, 251 (quote); Livingston, "Number XVII: Remarks on our Intended College," 171–77; *New-York Mercury*, June 4, 1753. For the growth of the college system in colonial America, see Beverly McAnear, "College Founding in the American Colonies, 1745–1775," *Mississippi Valley Historical Review* 42:1 (June 1955): 24–44; Lawrence Cremin, *American Education: The Colonial Experience, 1607–1783* (New York: Harper & Row, 1970); Meyer Reinhold, "The Quest for 'Useful Knowledge' in Eighteenth-Century America," *Proceedings of the American Philosophical Society* 119:1 (April 1975): 108–32; Krawczynksi, *Daily Life in the Colonial City*, 244–52.

34. For the Sea Captains Club meeting, see the *Pennsylvania Gazette*, June 30, 1768; Hunter, *Purchasing Identity*, 4 (quote); Adam Smith, *An Enquiry into the Wealth of Nations*, ed. Robert Reich (New York: Random House, 2000), 152; Thompson, *Rum Punch and Revolution*, 106–10. For merchant gentility, see Zara Anishanslin, *Portrait of a Woman in Silk: Hidden Histories of the British Atlantic World* (New Haven, CT: Yale University Press, 2016), 185–97.

35. "Probate Inventory of William Phillips, Innholder, Boston, 2 October, 1704, *Suffolk County Probate Inventories*, vol. 16, folios 50–1, Massachusetts State Archives, Boston, Massachusetts," and "Probate Inventory of George Emlen, Proprietor of the Three Tuns Tavern, 26 April, 1711, *Philadelphia Will Book C*, vol. 191 (B-F), ff. 235–53, Philadelphia City Archives," in Hancock and McDonald, *Public Drinking in the Early Modern World*, 4: 27–36, 45–50; "Emlen Inventory"; Spruill, *Women's Life and Work in the Southern Colonies*, 297 (quote); *New-York Journal*, January 28, 1768. For the Crown Coffee House, see Conroy, *In Public Houses*, 88–94.

36. Conroy, *In Public Houses*, 93–94; *New-York Mercury*, October 13, 1766; *General Advertiser*, March 9, 1749; David Hancock, *Oceans of Wine: Madeira and the Emergence of American Trade and Taste* (New Haven, CT: Yale University Press, 2009), 317. As British American gentlemen increasingly sought out "articles imported from opposite sides of the earth . . . as part of their daily diet," exclusive city taverns and coffeehouses became their stages upon which to act out their consumerist hopes and dreams. Although alcohol remained king in taverns and coffeehouses, coffee, tea, and chocolate gained popularity at midcentury as expensive, genteel, and worldly beverages. The fact that they contained caffeine did not hurt either. David Davies, *The case of labourers in husbandry* (London: G. G. and J. Robinson, 1795), 39. See also Bennett

Alan Weinberg and Bonnie K. Bealer, *The World of Caffeine: The Science and Culture of the World's Most Popular Drug* (London: Routledge, 2001), 58; Marcy Norton, "Tasting Empire: Chocolate and the European Internalization of Mesoamerican Aesthetics," *American Historical Review* 111:3 (June 2006): 660–91; Troy Bickham, "Eating the Empire: Intersections of Food, Cookery, and Imperialism in Eighteenth-Century Britain," *Past & Present* 198:1 (February 2008): 71–109.

37. Hancock, *Oceans of Wine*, 387 (quote).

38. Richard Owens, "Essays First Published in the *World*, 1753–1756," in *The Works of Richard Cambrige, Esq: Including Several Pieces Never Before Published*, ed. George Owen Cambridge (London: L. Hansard, 1803), No. 70, Thursday, May 2, 1754; David Cressy, *Coming Over: Migration and Communication between England and New England in the Seventeenth Century* (Cambridge: Cambridge University Press, 1987), chs. 9, 10.

39. *New-York Gazette*, June 21, 1762; *New-York Gazette Revived in the Weekly Post-Boy*, July 30, 1750. In the late eighteenth century, Philadelphia's City Tavern advertised the holdings of its "Subscription Room," where readers could find "all the daily papers published in Philadelphia, New-York, Boston, Baltimore &c. together with those of the principal commercial cities of Europe." The City Tavern's publican assured his patrons that such papers were to be "regularly filed and none permitted to be taken away on any account." Steele, *The English Atlantic*, 167; Hancock, *Oceans of Wine*, 270; Hancock and McDonald, *Public Drinking in the Early Modern World*, 4:390; Zachary Andrew Carmichael, "Fit Men: New England Tavern keepers, 1620–1720" (Master's thesis, Miami University, 2009).

40. Hamilton, *Itinerarium*, 166; "The Yearly Verses of the Printer's Lad, who Carrieth about the Pennsylvania Gazette," *Pennsylvania Gazette*, January 1, 1739.

41. Joseph Addison, *Spectator* No. 10, March 12, 1711; Richard Steele, *Spectator* No. 49, April 26, 1711. For more on such publications, see Lawrence E. Klein, *Shaftesbury and the Culture of Politeness: Moral Discourse and Cultural Politics in Early Eighteenth-Century England* (Cambridge: Cambridge University Press, 1994); Klein, "Politeness for Plebes," in *The Consumption of Culture*, 362–82; Lawrence E. Klein, "Property and Politeness in the Early Eighteenth-Century Whig Moralists: The Case of the *Spectator*," in *Early Modern Conceptions of Property*, ed. John Brewer and Susan Staves (London: Routledge, 1995), 221–31; John Fea, *The Way of Improvement Leads Home: Philip Vickers Fithian and the Rural Enlightenment in Early America* (Philadelphia: University of Pennsylvania Press, 2008), 89.

42. For the tavern packet system, see Steele, *The English Atlantic*, 113, 168–88; John Harrower, "Diary of John Harrower, 1773–1776," *American Historical Review* 6:1 (October 1900): 85–86, 101; William Gregory, "A Scotchman's Journey in New England in 1771," *New England Magazine* 12:3 (May 1895): 346.

43. Peter Kalm, *Peter Kalm's Travels in North America: The English Version of 1770*, ed. Adolph B. Benson (New York: Wilson-Erickson, 1937), 16; Hamilton, *Itinerarium*, 182; "Benjamin Franklin and John Foxcroft to Anthony Todd, 10 June 1763," *Founders Online*, National Archives, last modified March 30, 2017, http://founders.archives. gov (original source: Franklin, *Papers*, 10:276–84).

44. *Pennsylvania Gazette*, November 7, 1754; November 14, 1754; November 27, 1755; August 18, 1757; June 12, 1760; May 5, 1763; April 5, 1749; September 14, 1749; September 7, 1749; *New-York Post-Boy*, December 17, 1744, General Collections, NYHS.

According to the historian I. N. Phelps Stokes, "This tavern stood on the Cruger's wharf at the foot of So. William St. It was one of the resorts of privateers and a place of venue for 'prizes' captured." Stokes, *The Iconography of Manhattan Island*, 4:587.

45. *Virginia Gazette*, June 20, 1766; *Pennsylvania Gazette*, November 23, 1758; *New-York Gazette*, July 11, 1768.

46. *South Carolina Gazette*, June 5, 1749; William Bradford, *Books Just Imported from London* (Philadelphia: William Bradford, 1755); *Pennsylvania Gazette*, October 29, 1741; August 16, 1759. For London coffeehouse auctions, see Troy Bickham, *Savages within the Empire: Representations of American Indians in Eighteenth-Century Britain* (Oxford: Oxford University Press, 2005), 45–49.

47. "Journal of Alexander Macaulay," *William and Mary Quarterly* 11:3 (January 1903): 186–87; *Virginia Gazette*, March 28, 1745. Colonial American taverns have received little in-depth attention as centers of the slave trade. Sharon V. Salinger provided one paragraph in *Taverns and Drinking*, 57. David W. Conroy also gave slave sales little attention in Conroy, *In Public Houses*, 124.

48. Because no official slave auction houses existed in colonial America, these hyped events erupted from nearly every public and private space, including homes, ferries, warehouses, and churches. Their central location, wealthy clientele, and multifaceted consumer offerings positioned city taverns and coffeehouses as important slave sale points. *Pennsylvania Gazette*, December 2, 1736; September 1, 1763.

49. For more on how colonists understood certain slaves as fitting into different commodities groups, see Vaughn Scribner, "'A Genteel and Sensible Servant': The Commodification of African Slaves in Tidewater Virginia, 1700–1774," in *Order and Civility in the Early Modern Chesapeake*, ed. Debra Meyers and Melanie Perreault (Lanham, MD: Lexington Books, 2014), 175–94.

50. *Pennsylvania Gazette*, May 22, 1740; October 25, 1744.

51. *Virginia Gazette*, October 10, 1755; David Thompson, *British Museum Clocks* (London: British Museum Press, 2004), 104; Roy Porter, *English Society in the Eighteenth Century* (New York: Allen Lane, 1982), 243. See also *Boston Evening-Post*, September 2, 1751; *Virginia Gazette*, September 5, 1755.

52. *New-York Gazette*, July 4, 1749; *South Carolina Gazette*, June 25, 1753; August 15, 1768.

53. *Pennsylvania Gazette*, June 20, 1765.

54. *New-York Gazette or Weekly Post-Boy*, October 31, 1749; *Pennsylvania Gazette*, June 1, 1749; *New-York Gazette or Weekly Post-Boy*, November 28, 1748.

55. *Pennsylvania Gazette*, March 5, 1772; March 12, 1772.

Chapter 2

1. *New-York Weekly Journal*, February 13, 1748.

2. As the historian Richard Bushman contended, "So powerful was the ideal [of the cultivation of gentility and civility] that it became inextricably associated with human progress itself. The degree to which a person, or people, or a place had achieved gentility and urbanity was a measure of progress from barbarism to civilization." Bushman, "American High-Style and Vernacular Cultures," in *Colonial British America*, 358.

3. See also Benjamin L. Carp, "'Fix'd almost among Strangers': Charleston's Quaker Merchants and the Limits of Cosmopolitanism," *William and Mary Quarterly* 74:1

(January 2017): 77–108; Tao Zhijian, "Citizen of Whose World? Goldsmith's Oriental-ism," *Comparative Literature Studies* 33:1 (1996): 15–34; Nancy L. Rhoden, ed., *English Atlantics Revisited: Essays Honoring Professor Ian K. Steele* (London: McGill-Queen's University Press, 2007), vii; Vaughn Scribner, "Cosmopolitan Colonists: Gentlemen's Pursuit of Cosmopolitanism and Hierarchy in Colonial American Taverns," *Atlantic Studies: Global Currents* 10.4 (December 2013): 467–96.

4. Garrett Wallace Brown, *Grounding Cosmopolitanism: From Kant to the Idea of a Cosmopolitan Constitution* (Edinburgh: Edinburgh University Press, 2009), 5–6.

5. Constantin-Francois Volney, *Lectures on history, Delivered in the Normal School of Paris, by C.F. Volney, Author of the Ruins of Empires, Member of the National Insti-tute of France, &c. &c.* (London: Oriental Press, 1800), 116; Brown, *Grounding Cosmo-politanism*, 116, 4–5. Ancient religious texts like the Quran espoused certain notions of shared, cosmopolitan responsibility regardless of political or religious affiliation, suggesting "mankind is naught but a single nation," as did the Egyptian pharaoh Akh-naton. Ali, *Holy Quran*, 2:213. For the influence of Greek and Roman ideologies on the British Empire, see Anthony Pagden, *Lords of All the World: Ideologies of Empire in Spain, Britain and France, c. 1500–c. 1800* (New Haven, CT: Yale University Press, 1995).

6. Francis Bacon, *Essays Moral, Economical, and Political. By Francis Bacon, Baron of Verulam, and Viscount St. Albans* (London: J. Cundee, 1800), 55.

7. John Knox, *The American Crisis, by a Citizen of the World; Inscribed to Those Members of the Community, Vulgarly Named Patriots* (London: W. Flexney, 1777), 11–12.

8. *Boston Post Boy*, August 29, 1763.

9. M. Maty, ed., *Miscellaneous Works of the Late Philip Dormer Stanhope, Earl of Chesterfield*, 3 vols. (Dublin: W. Watson, 1777), 2:203. The Scotsman living in London (and frequent tavern goer), James Boswell, similarly exclaimed in 1762, "I consider mankind in general, and therefore cannot take a part in their quarrels when divided into particular states and nations." James Boswell, *Boswell's London Journal, 1762–1763*, ed. Frederick A. Pottle (New Haven, CT: Yale University Press, 1950), 77.

10. For an investigation of how cosmopolitanism defined the Enlightenment, see Anthony Pagden, *The Enlightenment and Why It Still Matters* (Oxford: Oxford Uni-versity Press, 2013), Introduction.

11. Roy Porter, *Enlightenment: Britain and the Creation of the Modern World* (New York: Allen Lane, 2000), 239.

12. *New-York Mercury*, December 11, 1752.

13. Englishmen in Great Britain faced the same problems. Writing in 1776, the English historian Edward Gibbon contended, "It is the duty of the patriot to prefer and promote the exclusive interest and glory of his native country . . . but a philosopher must be permitted to enlarge his views and to consider Europe as one great Republic whose various inhabitants have attained almost the same level of politeness and cul-tivation." Edward Gibbon, *The History of the Decline and Fall of the Roman Empire* (London: Strahan & Cadell, 1776), 4:163.

14. Boehm, "Cosmopolitanism," 4:458. As Boehm argued, "Cosmopolitanism as a mental attitude always manifests itself in the form of a compromise with nationalism." Schlereth also dealt with cosmopolitan's contradictions, in Thomas J. Schlereth, *The Cosmopolitan Ideal in Enlightenment Thought: Its Form and Function in the Ideas of*

Franklin, Hume, and Voltaire, 1694–1790 (Notre Dame, IN: University of Notre Dame Press, 1977).

15. Benjamin Franklin, *Memoirs of the Life and Writings of Benjamin Franklin*, vol. 2 (London: Henry Colburn, 1818), 285, 337; Hamilton, *Itinerarium*, 185–86; Choppin Roney, *Governed by a Spirit of Opposition*, 59–79.

16. Hamilton, *Itinerarium*, 185-86.

17. Alexander Mackraby, "Philadelphia Society before the Revolution: Extracts from the Letters of Alexander Mackraby to Sir Philip Francis," *Pennsylvania History of History and Biography* 11 (1887): 283; Black, "Journal," 405.

18. David Pietersz DeVries, *Voyages from Holland to America, 1632–1634*, trans. Henry C. Murphy (New York: New York Historical Society, 1853), 52.

19. William Hutton, *An History of Birmingham*, 3rd ed. (London: Thomas Pearson, 1795), 296–99; Rice, *Early American Taverns*, 79.

20. Hamilton, *Itinerarium*, 20–21,19, 26, 47–48.

21. Birket, *Cursory Remarks*, 10; Wells, *Population of the British Colonies*, 69–70.

22. Byrd, *Another Secret Diary*, 280; Byrd, *Secret Diary*, 331; Nicholas Cresswell, *The Journal of Nicholas Cresswell, 1774–1777* (London: Jonathan Cape, 1925), 209–10; Danckaerts, *Journal*, 67; Franklin, *Autobiography*, 23.

23. John Fontaine, *The Journal of John Fontaine: An Irish Huguenot Son in Spain and Virginia, 1710–1719*, ed. Edward Porter Alexander (Charlottesville: University of Virginia Press, 1972), 116–19.

24. Mackraby, "Philadelphia Society before the Revolution," 278–79, 286.

25. Danckaerts, *Journal*, 67.

26. Clark, *British Clubs and Societies*, 2.

27. "An Essay on Conversation," *American Weekly Mercury*, July 23, 1730.

28. Richard Steele, *Tatler* No. 46, 1709; Clark, *British Clubs and Societies*, 41. England—especially London—abounded with clubs. For an amusing contemporary list of these clubs in poem or song form, see Edward Ward, *A Compleat and Humourous Account of All the Remarkable Clubs and Societies in the Cities of London and Westminster* (London: J. Wren, 1667–1731).

29. Hamilton, *Tuesday Club*, xvi.

30. Hamilton, *Tuesday Club*, xvii.

31. Hamilton, *Itinerarium*, 43–45, 116, 133, 191, 21; *New-York Weekly Journal*, February 13, 1748; Krawczynski, *Daily Life in the Colonial City*, 443; John Blake, *Public Health in the Town of Boston, 1630–1822* (Cambridge, MA: President and Fellows of Harvard College, 1959), 45.

32. As the historian Christer Petley noted, gluttony and excess became important parts of elite society by the eighteenth century, especially among the planter class in the British Caribbean. As self-conscious gentlemen, colonists like Hamilton would have enjoyed fine foods but would have tried to avoid drinking or eating to excess. Christer Petley, "Gluttony, Excess, and the Fall of the Planter Class in the British Caribbean," *Atlantic Studies: Global Currents* 9:1 (January 2012): 85–106.

33. Hamilton, *Tuesday Club*, 21, 26.

34. "Toper" was a term commonly used in the colonial period to describe fellow drinkers (often those who were overly jolly in their libations) in a tavern setting. Hamilton noted, "I put my horses up att one Waghorn's att the Sign

of the Cart and Horse. There I fell in with a company of toapers." Hamilton, *Itinerarium*, 42.

35. Hamilton, *Itinerarium*, 41–43, 151–52.

36. Klein, *Shaftesbury and the Culture of Politeness*, 4.

37. "An Essay on Bumpers," *New-York Gazette or Weekly Post-Boy*, December 19, 1748. This author warned against the dangers of toasting and drunkenness in polite company. This "Essay" caused a backlash that lasted weeks. See "To the Author of the Essay on Bumpers," *New-York Gazette or Weekly Post-Boy*, December 26, 1748; "Hezekiah Broadrim," "To the Author of the Sayings . . . Concerning Bumpers," *New-York Weekly Journal*, January 2, 1748/49; Addison, *Spectator* No. 23, March 27, 2011. See also *Spectator* No. 504, October 8, 1712; No. 31, April 5, 1711; No. 19, March 22, 1711; Klein, "Property and Politeness," 221–31. For more on the opportunities and dangers of conversation, see James Forrester, *The Polite Philosopher; or, an Essay on that Art, which Makes a Man happy in Himself, and agreeable to Others* (London, reprinted in New York: J. Parker and W. Weyman, 1758); Dallett Hemphill, "Manners and Class in the Revolutionary Era: A Transatlantic Comparison," *William and Mary Quarterly* 63:2 (April 2006): 345–72.

38. Hamilton, *Itinerarium*, 144.

39. Adams, *Diary*, 1:348–49.

40. Hamilton, *Itinerarium*, 189–90, 144, 83–84; "Remarks on the Behaviour, of the Author of the Letter to the Author, of the late *Essay on Bumpers*, published in the *New-York Gazette*, Number 309," *New-York Weekly Journal*, January 9, 1748–49, No. 786.

41. Hamilton, *Itinerarium*, 85–87.

42. Hamilton, *Itinerarium*, 189–90.

43. For eighteenth-century English civil society, see Becker, *The Emergence of Civil Society*, 66–114; Thomas, *In Pursuit of Civility*, 1-10.

44. *Pennsylvania Gazette*, August 21, 1757; John Dunn, "The Contemporary Political Significance of John Locke's Conception of Civil Society," in *Civil Society: History and Possibilities*, ed. Sudipta Kaviraj and Sunil Khilnani (Cambridge: Cambridge University Press, 2001), 39–48; Colley, *Britons*, 11–54.

45. *Pennsylvania Gazette*, August 28, 1755; Hamilton, *Itinerarium*, 31; P. J. Marshall, "Presidential Address: Britain and the World in the Eighteenth Century: I, Reshaping the Empire," in *Transactions of the Royal Society*, 6h ser., vol. 8, ed. David Eastwood (Cambridge: Cambridge University Press, 1998), 18. See also Bejan, *Mere Civility*, 6; Maura Jane Farrelly, *Anti-Catholicism in America, 1620–1860* (Cambridge: Cambridge University Press, 2018), 1–103.

46. Clark, *British Clubs and Societies*, 302.

47. *Pennsylvania Gazette*, July 5, 1733; July 4, 1734.

48. John Price, *The Advantages of Unity Considered, in a Sermon Preach'd Before the Antient and Honourable Society of Free and Accepted Masons* (Bristol: Samuel Worrall, 1748), 22.

49. Margaret C. Jacob, *Radical Enlightenment: Pantheists, Freemasons, and Republicans* (London: George Allen & Unwin, 1981), 115.

50. Margaret C. Jacob, *Strangers Nowhere in the World: The Rise of Cosmopolitanism in Early Modern Europe* (Philadelphia: University of Pennsylvania Press, 2006), 97 (quote). Although by the 1730s the Freemasons had published their "secret" customs, many contemporaries still did not trust them. See, e.g., Hamilton, *Itinerarium*, 19;

Jessica Harland-Jacobs, "'Hands across the Sea': The Masonic Network, British Imperialism, and the North Atlantic World," *Geographical Review* 89:2 (April 1999): 237–53.

51. Clark, *British Clubs and Societies*, 302.

52. Emrys Jones, "Age of Societies," in *Welsh in London, 1500–2000*, ed. Emrys Jones (Cardiff: University of Wales Press, 2001), 54–87.

53. *Pennsylvania Gazette*, February 13, 1734; March 13, 1734; February 15, 1733; February 23, 1731; March 11, 1731.

54. *Pennsylvania Gazette*, February 13, 1750; August 23, 1750; May 17, 1750; November 15, 1750; August 22, 1751; May 23, 1751; November 16, 1752; August 23, 1753; May 17, 1753; May 24, 1759; November 20, 1760.

55. Niel Caplan, "Some Unpublished Letters of Benjamin Colman, 1717–25," *Massachusetts Historical Society Proceedings* 77:1 (1965): 137; "Andrew Elliot to his Brother, November 18, 1750," Andrew Elliot Letters, 1747–1777, NYHS.

56. Hamilton, *Itinerarium*, 49, 182, 118, 70, 133.

57. Fontaine, *Journal*, 114–16.

58. Anna Wells Rutledge, "A Cosmopolitan in Carolina," *William and Mary Quarterly* 6:4 (October 1949): 640.

59. Cresswell, *Journal*, 53, 175, 153, 233, 209–10, 137–39.

60. Cresswell, *Journal*, 205.

61. Cresswell, *Journal*, 235–36.

62. Elaine Breslaw, *Dr. Alexander Hamilton and Provincial America: Expanding the Orbit of Scottish Culture* (Baton Rouge: Louisiana State University Press, 2008), x.

63. Tony Claydon, *Europe and the Making of England, 1660–1760* (Cambridge: Cambridge University Press, 2007), 3–4; Anna Suranyi, *The Genius of the English Nation: Travel Writing and National Identity in Early Modern England* (Newark: University of Delaware Press, 2008), 17–18; Alison Games, *The Web of Empire: English Cosmopolitans in an Age of Expansion, 1560–1660* (Oxford: Oxford University Press, 2008); Colley, *Britons*.

64. See, e.g., Robert Gibson, *Best of Enemies: Anglo-French Relations since the Norman Conquest* (London: Sinclair-Stevenson, 1995).

65. Hamilton, *Itinerarium*, 106–8, 156.

66. Gerald Newman, *The Rise of English Nationalism: A Cultural History, 1740–1830* (New York: St. Martin's Press, 1987), 13; "Leopold Mozart to Lorenz Hagenauer, 28 May 1764, London," in *Mozart: A Life in Letters*, ed. Cliff Eisen, trans. Stewart Spencer (New York: Penguin Books, 2006), 35.

67. Rosamond Bayne-Powell, *Travellers in Eighteenth-Century England* (London: Benjamin Blom, 1951), 138–39; Adams, *Diary*, 1:14 (coxcomb quote).

68. For examples of negative depictions of the French by Englishmen, see Thomas Nugent, *The Ground Tour* (London: S. Birt, 1749), 118–19; Arthur Young, *Travels, During the Years 1787–1788 and 1789 Undertaken more Particularly with a View of Ascertaining the Cultivation, Wealth, Resources and National Prosperity, of the Kingdom of France* (London: George Bell and Sons, 1792), 197–99, 8.

69. Hamilton, *Itinerarium*, 116, 130. For colonial American bathing habits, see Kathleen Brown, *Foul Bodies: Cleanliness in Early America* (New Haven, CT: Yale University Press, 2009), 293–360; Scribner, "'The happy effects of these waters,'" 409–49.

70. Hamilton, *Itinerarium*, 139, 147.

71. Hamilton, *Itinerarium*, 73, 156, 58.

72. *Pennsylvania Gazette*, September 5, 1754; August 5, 1756; November 15, 1759; April 19, 1759. Imperialist toasts were hardly unique to the British American colonies. See also Martyn J. Powell, *The Politics of Consumption in Eighteenth-Century Ireland* (New York: Palgrave Macmillan, 2005), 25–28.

73. *Pennsylvania Gazette*, March 6, 1733/4.

74. *Pennsylvania Gazette*, November 15, 1759.

75. "Journal of a French Traveller, II" 75, 82.

76. Hamilton, *Itinerarium*, 73; Peter Kalm, "Peter Kalm, Scientist from Sweden (Excerpt from his journal, *En Resa til Norra America (1753–61),*" in *This Was America*, ed. Oscar Handlin (Cambridge, MA: Harvard University Press, 1949), 14, 33. The English elite Sir W. Batten disgustedly noted in the late seventeenth century, "I think The Devil Shits Dutchmen." Samuel Pepys, *The Diary of Samuel Pepys*, vol. 2, ed. Henry B. Wheatley (London: George Bell and Sons, 1893), entry for July 19, 1667. For more negative depictions of the Dutch by Englishmen, see William Temple, *Observations Upon the United Provinces of the Netherlands*, in *The Works of Sir William Temple, Bart.*, Complete in Four Volumes (London: F. C. and J. Rivington, 1814), 163–64 (Temple originally published this tract in 1673); John Smith, *England's Improvement Reviv[e]d* (London: Tho. Newcomb, 1673), 2; William De Britaine, *The Dutch Usurpation* (London: Jonathan Edwin, 1672), 14; *The Emblem of Ingratitude: A True Relation of the Unjust, Cruel and Barbarous Proceedings Against the English at Amboyna* (London: William Hope, 1672); Patrick Barclay, *The Universal Traveller; or, A Complete Account of the Most Remarkable Voyages and Travels* (London: Printed for J. Purser and T. Read, 1735), 303; Owen Felltham, *A Brief Character of the Low Countries* (London: Henry Seile, 1652), 5, 1–2.

77. James Delbourgo, *A Most Amazing Scene of Wonders: Electricity and Enlightenment in Early America* (Cambridge, MA: Harvard University Press, 2006), 143.

78. "From Benjamin Franklin to James Parker, 20 March 1751," *Founders Online*, National Archives, last modified November 26, 2017, http://founders.archives. gov (original source: Franklin, *Papers*, 4:117–121); *Pennsylvania Gazette*, October 9, 1729.

79. Addison, *Spectator* No. 49, April 26, 1711.

80. Forrester, *The Polite Philosopher*, 33–34.

Chapter 3

1. Hamilton, *Itinerarium*, 6–7; Hamilton, *Tuesday Club*, 1:241–42, 220; 2:254, 354–55. Thomas E. Brennan, David Hancock, and Michelle McDonald also argued that historians need to understand taverns primarily as businesses; see Thomas E. Brennan, David Hancock, and Michelle McDonald, eds., *Public Drinking in the Early Modern World: Voices from the Tavern, 1500–1800*, vol. 4 (London: Pickering & Chatto, 2011), xix–xx. In a review of Salinger's *Taverns and Drinking in Early America*, David Conroy noted, "In a broad cross-section of taverns distinctions of rank in manner and address among white males became blurred." David W. Conroy, "Review of *Taverns and Drinking in Early America*, by Sharon Salinger," *New England Quarterly* 76:4 (December 2003): 656.

2. Thompson, *Rum Punch and Revolution*, 16, 75; Conroy, *In Public Houses*, 2; Carp, *Rebels Rising*, 97. Hancock and McDonald, finally, argued, "Wealthy gentlemen

and legislators rubbed elbows with craftsmen and labourers" in British American taverns. Hancock and McDonald, *Public Drinking in the Early Modern World*, 4:275. In another publication, Hancock argued, "It is doubtful that drinking together eroded the orders of society . . . as recent scholars have suggested." Hancock, *Oceans of Wine*, 390.

3. *Newport Mercury*, August 24 to 31, 1767; *Boston Evening-Post*, July 11, 1757.

4. Charles Woodmason, *The Carolina Backcountry on the Eve of the Revolution: The Journal and Other Writings of Charles Woodmason, Anglican Itinerant*, ed. Richard J. Hooker (Chapel Hill: University of North Carolina Press, 1953), 7; Adams, *Diary*, 1:172.

5. *New-York Weekly Journal*, October 22, 1750.

6. Hamilton, *Itinerarium*, 18, 125; Muhlenberg, *Journals*, 278.

7. Excerpts from Thomas Cooper, *The Statutes at Large of South Carolina*, 5 vols. (Columbia, SC: A. S. Johnson, 1836–39), 3:581–85, 1741, no. 680, "An Additional Act to an Act entituled an Act for the Better Regulating Taverns and Punch Houses," in Hancock and McDonald, *Public Drinking in the Early Modern World*, 4:179; For regulation of the New England tavern space, see Conroy, *In Public Houses*, 1–156. For Philadelphia, see Thompson, *Rum Punch and Revolution*, 1–20.

8. Bridenbaugh, *Cities in the Wilderness*, 144–74; Nash, *Urban Crucible*, 1–53; Carp, *Rebels Rising*, 1–22.

9. Thompson, *Rum Punch and Revolution*, 16, 75; Hancock and McDonald, *Public Drinking in the Early Modern World*, 4:275. Nancy L. Struna similarly argued that social equality in colonial taverns "seems unlikely, especially given persistent rank, gender, and race divisions throughout the colonies." Struna, *People of Prowess*, 152.

10. Thompson's chapter is more about how *advertisements* often appealed to a wide audience than specific instances of cross-class interaction. Thompson, *Rum Punch and Revolution*, 79.

11. Jessica Kross, "'If you will not drink with me, you must fight with me': The Sociology of Drinking in the Middle Colonies," *Pennsylvania History* 64 (Winter 1997): 49; Laura Van Berkel, Christian S. Crandall, Scott Eidelman, and John C. Blanchar, "Hierarchy, Dominance, and Deliberation: Egalitarian Values Require Mental Effort," *Personality and Social Psychology Bulletin* 41:9 (September 2015): 1–16. See also Emily Zitek and Larissa Z. Tiedens, "The Fluency of Social Hierarchy: The Ease with Which Hierarchical Relationships Are Seen, Remembered, Learned, and Liked," *Journal of Personal and Social Psychology* 102:1 (January 2012): 98–115.

12. Kempe Papers, Box 11, Folder 2, NYHS; *New-York Gazette, or Weekly Post-Boy*; November 27, 1752. Theft was rather common in mixed-class taverns. See *Pennsylvania Gazette*, September 11, 1760; *South Carolina Gazette*, July 27, 1765.

13. *Boston Evening-Post*, July 11, 1757.

14. *South Carolina Gazette*, 15 July 1732; Hamilton, *Itinerarium*, 144; Forrester, *Polite Philosopher*, 29.

15. For itinerancy in colonial America and the dangers associated with these travelers, see Robert J. Gamble, "'For Lucre of Gain and in Contempt of the Laws': Itinerant Traders and the Politics of Mobility in the Eighteenth-Century Mid-Atlantic," *Early American Studies: An Interdisciplinary Journal* 13:4 (Fall 2015): 836–55; T. H. Breen and Timothy Hall, "Structuring Provincial Imagination: The Rhetoric and Experience

of Social Change in Eighteenth-Century New England," *American Historical Review* 103:5 (December 1998): 1411–39.

16. Hamilton, *Itinerarium*, 162–63, 79.

17. Hamilton, *Itinerarium*, 80; Marquis de Chastellux, *Travels in North America, in the Years 1780, 1781, and 1782* (New York: White, Gallaher, & White, 1827), 248–49. For clothing and identity, see Richard Godbeer, *Sexual Revolution in Early America* (Baltimore, MD: Johns Hopkins University Press, 2002), ch. 9.

18. Mary A. Stephenson, "Wetherburn's Tavern Historical Report, Block 9, Building 31," in *Colonial Williamsburg Foundation Library Research Report Series—1167* (Williamsburg, VA: Colonial Williamsburg Foundation Library, 1990); "Inventory of Estate of Henry Wetherburn, March 16, 1761," Colonial Williamsburg Digital Library, accessed March 1, 2018, http://research.history.org. For southern taverns in particular, see Patricia A. Gibbs, "Taverns in Tidewater Virginia, 1700–1744" (Master's thesis, The College of William and Mary, 1968); Heather Wainwright, "Inns and Outs: Anne Pattison's Tavern Account Book, 1744–1749" (Master's thesis, Armstrong Atlantic State University, 1998). Wetherburn's two-story tavern harbored twelve slaves, a twenty-five-square-foot "Great Room," and ten smaller rooms. Moreover, the tavern held extensive stores of alcohol, silver utensils, ceramic pottery, and furniture of various qualities. See also Lauren Elizabeth Gryctko, "Inviting the Principle Gentlemen of the City: Privacy, Exclusivity, and Food Complexity in Colonial Taverns" (Master's thesis, The College of William and Mary, 2015).

19. You can "tour" colonial Williamsburg's streets, taverns, and shops in 3D on the Colonial Williamsburg Foundation's website. See "Virtual Williamsburg 1776," Colonial Williamsburg Foundation, accessed June 3, 2017, http://research.history.org.

20. "Wetherburn's Tavern," Colonial Williamsburg Online, accessed January 1, 2018, http://www.history.org/.

21. Stobart, Hann, and Morgan called streets spaces of commerce "and important arenas for public consumption, where people could access goods, knowledge, and information." Jon Stobart, Andrew Hann, and Victoria Morgan, ed., *Spaces of Consumption: Leisure and Shopping in the English Town, c. 1680–1830* (London: Routledge, 2007), 86; Miles Ogborn, *Spaces of Modernity: London's Geographies, 1680–1780* (New York: Guilford Press, 1998); Stephenson, "Wetherburn's Tavern Historical Report, Block 9, Building 31."

22. Anders Greenspan, *Creating Colonial Williamsburg: The Restoration of Virginia's Eighteenth-Century Capital*, 2nd ed. (Chapel Hill: University of North Carolina Press, 2009), 2.

23. Trevor Burnard and Emma Hart, "Kingston, Jamaica, and Charleston, South Carolina: A New Look at Comparative Urbanization in Plantation Colonial British America," *Journal of Urban History* 39:2 (March 2013): 214–34; Musselwhite, "Annapolis Aflame," 361–400; Scribner, "'Quite a genteel and extreamly commodious House,'" 30–67.

24. "Wetherburn Inventory."

25. Jennifer L. Anderson, *Mahogany: The Costs of Luxury in Early America* (Cambridge, MA: Harvard University Press, 2012), 1–2; "Wetherburn Inventory."

26. *South Carolina Gazette*, November 9, 1767; "Probate Inventory of Benjamin Backhouse, proved 21–3 September 1767," *Charleston County Will Books*, vol. 10 (1765–69), 176–80. South Carolina Department of Archives and History, Columbia,

South Carolina," in Hancock and McDonald, *Public Drinking in the Early Modern World*, 4:246; *Boston Post-Boy*, January 9, 1770; "An inventory of the goods & chattels rights & credits which were of John Beekman dec'd at the time of his death. Signed by Rob: Benson and Wm. Cockcroft, Appraisers. Endorsed: "filed 28 Sep. 1774" 8 leaves Unbound," Archives and Manuscripts Division, Miscellaneous Manuscripts, Box 4, Folder 17, NYPL.

27. "Wetherburn Inventory," *Virginia Gazette*, September 12, 1766; *New-York Journal*, January 28, 1768; "Probate Inventory of Samuel Wethered, Proprietor of the Bunch of Grapes Tavern, Boston, 12 July 1759, Suffolk County Probate Inventories, vol. 54, ff. 447–52, Massachusetts State Archives, Boston, MA," in Hancock and McDonald, *Public Drinking in the Early Modern World*, 4:48.

28. Cowen, *Social Life of Coffee*, 6–15; "Wetherburn Inventory."

29. "Probate Inventory of Benjamin Backhouse, proved 21–23 September 1767," *Charleston County Will Books*, vol. 10 of 100 (1765–69), 176–80; "South Carolina Department of Archives and History, Columbia, South Carolina," in Hancock and McDonald, *Public Drinking in the Early Modern World*, 4:245–48; "Probate Inventory of Samuel Wethered, Proprietor of the Bunch of Grapes Tavern, Boston, 12 July 1759, Suffolk County Probate Inventories, vol. 54, ff. 447–52, Massachusetts State Archives, Boston, MA," in Hancock and McDonald, *Public Drinking in the Early Modern World*, 4:48; "Table 3.1: Inventory of the Goods and Chattels of John Reynolds, 1745," in Patricia G. Markert, Thomas W. Cuddy, and Mark P. Leone, *Site Report for Phase III Archaeological Investigations at Reynolds Tavern (18AP23), 4 Church Circle, Annapolis, Maryland. 1982–1984* (Annapolis: Archaeology in Annapolis, 2013), 25–26; Hancock, *Oceans of Wine*, 337.

30. In Peter Buckley's contention, the "transparency of roles and actions" that the seating structure of public spaces engendered ultimately encouraged a "ritual of mutuality" among their inhabitants. Peter Buckley, "To the Opera House: Culture and Society in New York City, 1820–1860" (PhD diss., SUNY Stony Brook, 1984), 123; Elizabeth Maddock Dillon, *New World Drama: The Performative Commons in the Atlantic World, 1649–1849* (Durham, NC: Duke University Press, 2014), 6.

31. For a reflection of Georgian church architecture, see Hamilton, *Itinerarium*, 45. Although not pursued at length in this work, elitist colonists also found their own conflict with which pew they were assigned in relation to their social competitors. For class competition within the church, see Susan Dwyer Amussen, *An Ordered Society: Gender and Class in Early Modern England* (Oxford: Basil Blackwell, 1988), 137–44. For pew order and hierarchy in the English church, see Kevin Dillow, "The Social and Ecclesiastical Significance of Church Seating Arrangements and Pew Disputes, 1500–1750" (DPhil. diss., University of Oxford, 1990); Robert Tittler, "Seats of Power: The Symbolism of Public Seating in the English Urban Community, c. 1560–1620," *Albion* 24:2 (Summer 1992): 205–23; Christopher Marsh, "Order and Place in England, 1580–1640: The View from the Pew," *Journal of British Studies* 44:1 (January 2005): 3–26; Alexander Robertson, "Account Book. Scotch Presbyterian Church, 1784–1798," Manuscript Collections, NYHS.

32. Hamilton, *Itinerarium*, 53. The Hallam Company recommended before their first showing of Shakespeare's *The Merchant of Venice* that "ladies" give him "timely Notice . . . for their Places in the Boxes, and on the Day of the Performance . . . send their Servants early to keep them, in Order to prevent Trouble and Disappointment."

Virginia Gazette, August 21, 1752. For elite attempts to stage themselves on the theater stage, see Lisa Freeman, *Character's Theater: Genre and Identity on the Eighteenth-Century English Stage* (Philadelphia: University of Pennsylvania Press, 2002), 3.

33. "Richard Peters to the Proprietaries," November 29, 1747, accessed January 30, 2012, http://franklinpapers.org, See also *Pennsylvania Gazette,* November 26, 1747.

34. *Virginia Gazette,* October 24, 1771; November 17, 1752; *Pennsylvania Gazette,* September 9, 1756.

35. "Wetherburn Inventory."

36. For colonial price regulation of alcoholic beverages, see Thompson, *Rum Punch and Revolution,* 64–71.

37. Bill Hillier and Julienne Hanson, *The Social Logic of Space* (Cambridge: Cambridge University Press, 1984), 143–75.

38. Richard Addison, *The Spectator,* No. 145, Thursday, August 16, 1711. This writer was not alone in his complaints of tavern noise. In 1645, Boston legislators tried to outlaw singing as the "younger sort" who convened "in places of publick entertainment, to corrupt one another by their uncivill & wanton carriages" engaged in the practice of "rudely singing & making a noyse, to the disturbances of the family & other guests." By 1711, legislators expanded the definition of noise violation to include "Fidling, Piping or any Musick, Dancing, or Revelling." Hancock and McDonald, *Public Drinking in the Early Modern World,* 4:403–4. Although Bostonians proved far stricter than their colonial counterparts, such restrictions spoke to elitist colonists' condemnation of plebeian tavern revelry and consequent noise-making.

39. "Wetherburn Inventory." For examples of other taverns with screens, see "Inventory of Estate of John Burdett, August 27, 1746," Colonial Williamsburg Digital Library; "Inventory of Estate of Bowcock, March 16, 1730," Colonial Williamsburg Digital Library; "An Inventory of the Estate of James Shields Deceased," Colonial Williamsburg Digital Library; "Inventory of Estate of Thomas Pattison, March 21, 1743"; "Probate Inventory of Benjamin Backhouse, proved 21–3 September 1767," in Hancock and McDonald, *Public Drinking in the Early Modern World,* 4:246.

40. Brown also noted this possibility in Brown, "The Landscape of Drink," 72.

41. Hamilton, *Itinerarium,* 95, 180.

42. Hamilton, *Itinerarium,* 79–80, 54–55. For a good description of how Philadelphians dressed in 1750, see Gottlieb Mittelberger, *Gottlieb Mittelberger's Journey to Pennsylvania in the Year 1750 and Return to Germany in the Year 1754,* ed. Carl Theo. Eben (Philadelphia: John Jos McVey, 1898), 116. For British American fashion, see Bushman, *Refinement of America,* 69–74; Linda Baumgarten, *What Clothes Reveal: The Language of Clothing in Colonial and Federal America* (New Haven, CT: Yale University Press, 2002); Kate Haulman, *The Politics of Fashion in Eighteenth Century America* (Chapel Hill: University of North Carolina Press, 2011).

43. Carl Bridenbaugh, *Early Americans* (Oxford: Oxford University Press, 1981), 121–49; Steven C. Bullock, "A Mumper among the Gentle: Tom Bell, Colonial Confidence Man," *William and Mary Quarterly* 55:2 (April 1998): 231–58; Jack Lynch, "Of Sharpers, Mumpers, and Fourberries: Some Early American Imposters and Rogues," *Colonial Williamsburg Journal* (Spring 2005), accessed March 1, 2018, http://www.history.org; Thompson, *Rum Punch and Revolution,* 121; *South Carolina Gazette,* February 11, 1745; *Virginia Gazette,* November 4, 1763; October 13, 1774; February 23, 1769; Jonathan Prude, "To Look upon the 'Lower Sort': Runaway Ads and the Appearance

of Unfree Laborers in America, 1750–1800," *Journal of American History* 78:1 (June 1991): 143–59.

44. The Scottish gentleman William Black was welcomed into Annapolis in 1744 "by several Gentlemen of Distinction of that Province" who whisked him away to "the first Tavern in Town" and provided him "a Bowl of Punch and a Glass of Wine," while in 1750 Francis Goelet noted that he spent many evenings in Boston taverns "with several gentlemen of [his] acquaintance." Though Nicholas Cresswell had a "confounded mad frolic" because of gallons of wine and liquor in a Virginia tavern, he was sure to note that he did so among a genteel group of "Messrs. Neilson Cavan, Booker, one Doctor, Mr. Nichols and Doctor McGinnis." William Black, "Journal of William Black, 1744," *Pennsylvania Magazine of History and Biography* 1:2 (1877): 124; Goelet, *Voyages and Travels*, October 5, 6, 8, 9, 10, 12, 15, 16, 1750; Creswell, *Journal*, 138–39.

45. T. H. Breen, "'Baubles of Britain': The American and Consumer Revolutions of the Eighteenth Century," *Past & Present* 119:1 (May 1988): 76, 78; T. H. Breen, "An Empire of Goods: The Anglicization of Colonial America, 1690–1776," *Journal of British Studies* 25:4 (October 1986): 467–99; Mittelberger, *Journey*, 50. For the significance of ceramics and equipage, see Sarah Richards, *Eighteenth-Century Ceramics: Products for a Civilised Society* (Manchester: Manchester University Press, 1999). Meacham argued that "tea remained an expensive luxury item until the second half of the eighteenth century, and coffee was unavailable to most colonists until the late eighteenth century." Meacham, *Every Home a Distillery*, 12.

46. Peter Thompson, "'The Friendly Glass': Drink and Gentility in Colonial Philadelphia," *Pennsylvania Magazine of History and Biography* 113:4 (October 1989): 549–73; Ellis, *The Coffee House*; Goodman, "Excitantia," 121; Anonymous, *A brief description*; Norton, "Tasting Empire," 671–72; Weinberg and Bealer, *The World of Caffeine*; Hancock, *Oceans of Wine*, Introduction.

47. Thompson, *Rum Punch and Revolution*, 99; Salinger, *Taverns and Drinking*, 239–40.

48. Goelet, *Voyages and Travels*, October 10, 1750; "Journal of Josiah Quincy Jr.," 47. See also Karen Harvey, "Ritual Encounters: Punch Parties and Masculinity in the Eighteenth Century," *Past & Present* 214:1 (February 2012): 165–203.

49. Conroy argued for alcohol's leveling effects in Conroy, *In Public Houses*, 48.

50. *South Carolina Gazette*, May 4, 1734; *Virginia Gazette*, November 2, 1739; *Boston Post-Boy*, October 31, 1763.

51. Betty Leviner, "Patrons and Rituals in an Eighteenth-Century Tavern," in *Common People and Their Material World: Free Men and Women in the Chesapeake, 1700–1830*, ed. David Harvey and Gregory Brown (Williamsburg, VA: Colonial Williamsburg Foundation, 1992), 95–113; Shields, *Civil Tongues and Polite Letters*, 143; Salinger, *Taverns and Drinking*, 67.

52. Although town houses increasingly graced cities, furthermore, the warmth of taverns' fires (in contrast to the drafty nature of a town house) attracted many judges to these central spaces' cozy rooms. See Martha J. McNamara, *From Tavern to Courthouse: Architecture and Ritual in American Law, 1658–1860* (Baltimore, MD: Johns Hopkins University Press, 2004), 21.

53. "Cornehill vs. Bayley," Kempe Papers, Box 3, Folder 1, NYHS.

54. Byrd, *Another Secret Diary, 1739–1741*, 75.

55. Salinger, *Taverns and Drinking*, 65–66; McNamara, *From Tavern to Courthouse*.

56. Salinger, *Taverns and Drinking*, 48 (quote).

57. Sir William Keith, *The Observator's Trip to America, in a Dialogue Between the Observator and his Country-man Roger* (Philadelphia: Andrew Bradford, 1726), 11–12, 17.

58. Salinger, *Taverns and Drinking*, 73. For an image of the "Red Lion Tavern," see Frank E. Wallis et. al., *The Georgian Period: A Series of Measured Drawings of Colonial Work*, Part Nine (Boston: American Architect and Building News Co., 1902), 23.

59. Adams, *Diary*, 1:172–73; John Kendall, *The Life of Thomas Story, Carefully Abridged: In Which the Principal Occurrences and the Most Interesting Remarks and Observations are Retained* (London: Isaac Thompson, 1786), 155–56; Woodmason, *Carolina Backcountry*, 96–97.

60. Hamilton, *Itinerarium*, 95; *Virginia Gazette*, May 9, 1745; *South Carolina Gazette*, March 8, 1739. For lower-class colonists' attire, see Baumgarten, *What Clothes Reveal*, 106–49; Krawcynski, *Daily Life in the Colonial City*, 389–90; Diana Dipaolo Loren, *The Archaeology of Clothing and Bodily Adornment in Colonial America* (Gainesville: University Press of Florida, 2010).

61. Hamilton, *Itinerarium*, 95; *Pennsylvania Chronicle*, September 28 to October 5, 1767; *New-York Gazette*, April 8, 1751; Juli Hedgepeth Williams, *The Significance of the Printed Word in Early America: Colonists' Thoughts on the Role of the Press* (Westport, CT: Greenwood Press, 1999), 8–9. For speech patterns, see Joseph M. Williams, *Origins of the English Language: A Social and Linguistic History* (New York: Free Press, 1975), 356–57; Peter Burke, "A Civil Tongue: Language and Politeness in Early Modern Europe," in *Civil Histories*, 31–48. One runaway Irish Catholic servant was described by her owner according to her language patterns: "Upon her tongue she wears a brogue; And was she man would be a rogue." The owner continued by describing her costume: "Old gown she wore was of calico, would cover her down to the toe; Her petticoat was linsey bright, Striped up and down with blue and white; Brown linen smock—and by your leaves, It had a pair of whiten'd sleeves." *Pennsylvania Gazette*, June 29, 1769.

62. *New-York Weekly Journal*, October 22, 1750; Scribner, "'The happy effects of these waters,'" 409–49, 436; Elizabeth Drinker, *The Diary of Elizabeth Drinker*, vol. 1, ed. Elaine Forman Crane (Boston: Northeastern University Press, 1991), 164; Brown, *Foul Bodies*, 133–36. It is important to think about what elitist colonists *at the time* would have considered as smelling foul—not what our current notions of smell might entail. See Mark M. Smith, "Producing Sense, Consuming Sense, Making Sense: Perils and Prospects for Sensory History," *Journal of Social History* 40:4 (Summer 2007): 841–58; Constance Classen, David Howes, and Anthony Synnott, *Aroma: The Cultural History of Smell* (London: Routledge, 1994).

63. For ideas of scent and identity in early modern England, see William Tullett, "The Macaroni's 'Ambrosial Essences': Perfume, Identity, and Public Space in Eighteenth-Century England," *Journal for Eighteenth-Century Studies* 38:2 (June 2015): 163–80, 168 ("artificial atmosphere" quote); Mark S. R. Jenner, "Civilization and Deodorization? Smell in Early Modern English Culture," in *Civil Histories*, 127–44. John Milligan of New York offered customers a "great variety of Perfumes" in 1757. By 1761, Edward Agar, "chemist, in Beaver-street, from London," moved to New York. He outdid poor Milligan, selling genteel customers "Perfumery, of all sorts, viz.: Hard and soft Pomatum; Hungary, Lavender, Honey, and Orange Flower water." *New-York*

Gazette, or Weekly Post-Boy, October 10, 1757; *New-York Gazette*, September 14, 1761. Philadelphia also had perfumers (see *Pennsylvania Journal*, November 24, 1763), as did Boston (*Boston Post-Boy*, August 27, 1764, *Boston Evening-Post*, January 10, 1774), Newport (*New-Hampshire Gazette*, September 18, 1772), and Williamsburg (*Virginia Gazette*, April 4, 1766).

64. *Boston Evening Post*, July 11, 1757; Hamilton, *Tuesday Club*, 2:355–56.

Chapter 4

1. Goelet, *Voyages and Travels*, October 1, 1750.

2. Helen Berry, "Rethinking Politeness in Eighteenth-Century England: Moll King's Coffee House and the Significance of 'Flash Talk': The Alexander Prize Lecture," *Transactions of the Royal Historical Society* 11:1 (2001): 67 (author's emphasis).

3. Sarah M. S. Pearsall, "'The Late Flagrant Instance of Depravity in My Family': The Story of an Anglo-Jamaican Cuckold," *William and Mary Quarterly* 60:3 (July 2003): 554. For scholars who have proposed strict borders (at least in early modern people's eyes) between civil and uncivil during the "civilizing process," see Elias, *Civilizing Process*; Van Horn, "Mask of Civility," 18; Bushman, "American High-Style and Vernacular Cultures," in *Colonial British America*, 358, 369, 374.

4. "Rake" is derived from the religious term "rakehell," while "Libertine" originally meant "freedman" in fourteenth-century English, which itself traced back to the Latin term "libertus," which ancient Romans equated with a slave who had been set free. By the early modern period, religious leaders especially linked the terms to a lack of morals. "rake, n.7." *OED Online*, Oxford University Press, March 2016, Web March 21, 2016; "libertine, n. and adj." *OED Online*, March 2016. Oxford University Press, http://www.oed.com.ezp-prod1.hul.harvard.edu/view/Entry/107892?redirectedFrom =libertine (accessed March 21, 2016); Bryson, *From Courtesy to Civility*, 244–45; L. C. Jones, *The Clubs of the Georgian Rakes* (New York: Columbia University Press, 1942); Thomas A. Foster, *Sex and the Eighteenth-Century Man: Massachusetts and the History of Sexuality in America* (Boston: Beacon Press, 2006), 66–72, 115, 177–78.

5. Goodfriend, *Who Should Rule at Home*, ch. 7.

6. *New-Hampshire Gazette*, September 2, 1763. As Peter McCandless noted, "Blaming disease [and, in turn, incivility and misbehavior] on imprudent or irregular habits was routine. This was especially true if the people in question were immigrants, black, or poor and lived in crowded and disreputable quarters." McCandless, *Slavery, Disease, and Suffering*, 197–98. See also Van Horn, "Mask of Civility," 18; Marcel Bax and Dániel Z. Kádár, "The Historical Understanding of Historical (Im)politeness," *Journal of Historical Pragmatics* 12:1–2 (2011): 1–24.

7. Bryson, *From Courtesy to Civility*, 85, 159, 243–61; Phil Withington, "'Tumbled into the dirt': Wit and Incivility in Early Modern England," *Journal of Historical Pragmatics* 12:1–2 (2011): 156–77; Bejan, *Mere Civility*, 6.

8. Elias, *Civilizing Process*; Ira Berlin, *Many Thousands Gone: The First Two Centuries of Slavery in North America* (Cambridge, MA: Harvard University Press, 1998), 58; Hart, *Building Charleston*, 4; *South-Carolina Gazette*, August 27, 1772.

9. Berry, "Rethinking Politeness," 65–81; Clare A. Lyons, *Sex among the Rabble: An Intimate History of Gender and Power in the Age of Revolution, Philadelphia, 1730–1830* (Chapel Hill: University of North Carolina Press, 2006). The idea of a "rival

geography" was created by Edward Said and has been used by historians like Stephanie Camp to think about how slaves in the early South crafted their own identities. See Edward Said, *Culture and Imperialism* (New York: Alfred A. Knopf, 1993), 7, 58; Stephanie Camp, *Closer to Freedom: Enslaved Women and Everyday Resistance in the Plantation South* (Chapel Hill: University of North Carolina Press, 2004), 7.

10. *Virginia Gazette*, April 11, 1751.

11. *Boston Evening Post*, June 26, 1738.

12. *Georgia Gazette*, December 29, 1763; Cresswell, *Journal*, 175–76; *At a Court, held at Punch-Hall, in the Colony of Bacchus, The Indictment and Tryal of Sir Richard Rum* (Boston: n.p., 1724). See also Kristen D. Burton, "Intoxication and Empire: Distilled Spirits and the Creation of Addiction in the Early Modern British Atlantic" (PhD diss., University of Texas at Arlington, 2015).

13. Louis B. Wright, ed., *The Prose Works of William Byrd of Westover: Narratives of a Colonial Virginian* (Cambridge, MA: Harvard University Press, 1966), 173, 374; *South Carolina Gazette*, March 31, 1733. Although "people of fortune" also drank rum, they (usually) imbibed "very good" imported alternatives and (allegedly) did so with more self-control. Birket, *Cursory Remarks*, 9–10.

14. For instance, in 1773, the British lieutenant Frederick Mackenzie entered New York City and noted, "Rum is so cheap (the New England rum being only 1/9a Gallon) that at present we find the utmost difficulty in keeping [soldiers] from drinking to excess. . . . [T]he best Jamaica Rum is sold for 3/6 a Gallon; and french brandy for 5/6—The price of Wines I don't know; but at the tavern we paid 2/11 a bottle for Madeira and 3/6 for Claret. . . . I buy 16 Gallons of very good small bear for 2/11. . . . Porter is 7d a bottle." Frederick Mackenzie, *A British Fusilier in Revolutionary Boston: Being the Diary of Lieutenant Frederick Mackenzie, Adjutant of the Royal Welch Fusiliers, January 5-April 30, 1775*, ed. Allen French (Cambridge, MA: Harvard University Press, 1926), 19.

15. John Josselyn (like many colonists) referred to rum as "that cursed liquor called Rum, Rum-bullion, or kill-Devil, which is stronger than spirit of Wine, and is drawn from the dross of Sugar and Sugar Canes." John Josselyn, *John Josselyn, A Colonial Traveler: A Critical Edition of Two Voyages to New England*, ed. Paul Lindholdt (Hanover, NH: University Press of New England, 1988), 99.

16. "Letter 'To the Publisher of the Boston Evening-Post,' *Boston Evening-Post*, June 26, 1738," in Hancock and McDonald, *Public Drinking in the Early Modern World*, 4:549; Benjamin Franklin constantly railed against the evils of drinking in his writings. Benjamin Franklin, *Writings* (New York: Library of America, 1987), 1188; *Pennsylvania Gazette*, July 12, 1753.

17. *Virginia Gazette*, April 8, 1737; The *Virginia Gazette* reported that a York, Virginia, woman so taken to drink that her neighbors had nicknamed her *"Drunken Frank"* passed out next to her fireplace. When the flames began to lick her clothes, Drunken Frank was too inebriated to stamp them out. Friends found her "lying in the Chimney Corner in her House, with her Cloaths burnt off her Back, and her Arms, Breast, and Body so miserably burnt." The *Virginia Gazette*'s editor hoped that "this dreadful Example may be a Means to deter others too much addicted to excessive Drinking, from pursuing that pernicious Practice." *Virginia Gazette*, October 27, 1738. New Englanders often reported on ordinary colonists who had drunk too much at their local tavern and ended up freezing to death on

their way home. See, e.g., *New England Weekly Journal*, March 5, 1733; January 24, 1732.

18. *Boston Evening Post*, July 11, 1757; Struna, *People of Prowess*, 156–63.

19. William Waller Hening, *The Statutes at Large; Being a Collection of All the Laws of Virginia, From the First Session of the Legislature, in the Year 1619*, vol. 5 (Richmond: R. & W. G. Bartow, 1819), 103; *Anno regni Georgii II Regis Magnae Britanniae, Franciae, & Hiberniae, quindecimo. At a sessions of General Assembly begun and holden at the city of New-York, the fifteenth day of September 1741, and continued to the twenty seventh day of November following, during which time the following acts were passed* . . . (New York: William Bradford, 1741), 37–38. For more complaints about and laws restricting gaming throughout the colonies, see *Virginia Gazette*, September 5, 1751; "An Act to prevent private Lotteries within this Colony, Pass'd the 25th of November, 1747," in *Documents of the Assembly of the State of New York, Ninety Seventh Session—1874*, vol. 4 (Albany: Weed, Parsons, and Company, 1874), 731–32.

20. Choppin Roney, *Governed by a Spirit of Opposition*, chs. 3, 5.

21. Ferguson, *An Essay on the History of Civil Society*, 309; Bruce R. Sievers, *Civil Society, Philanthropy, and the Fate of the Commons* (Medford, MA: Tufts University Press, 2010), 5; McCarthy, *American Creed*; Conroy, *In Public Houses*, ch. 3.

22. *Boston Evening Post*, July 11, 1757.

23. *Boston Evening Post*, June 26, 1738; Carmichael, "Fit Men."

24. "Pennsylvania Laws, Statutes, etc., 1762," in *The Charters and Acts of Assembly [Octavio Edition]*, vol. 2 (Philadelphia: Miller, 1762); Charles J. Hoadly, ed., *The Public Records of the Colony of Connecticut, from October 1706 to October 1716* (Hartford: Case, Lockwood and Brainard, 1870), 328, 562–63; Charles J. Hoadly, ed., *The Public Records of the Colony of Connecticut, from May 1757 to March 1762* (Hartford: Case, Lockwood and Brainard, 1880), 259; Conroy, *In Public Houses*, 57–98; Paton Yoder, "Tavern Regulation in Virginia: Rationale and Reality," *Virginia Magazine of History and Biography* 87:3 (July 1979): 259–78.

25. Conroy, *In Public Houses*, 128–38. For middling women helping their husbands run taverns or running taverns by themselves, see Hart, *Building Charleston*, 137–38. For women generally running taverns, even if they were thought to be run by men, see Meacham, *Every Home a Distillery*, 64–81. Karin Wulf demonstrated how free women who were not married (designated "femes sole") maintained considerable commercial power; see Karin Wulf, *Not All Wives: Women of Colonial Philadelphia* (Philadelphia: University of Pennsylvania Press, 2005).

26. Van Horn, "Mask of Civility," 27.

27. "Rachel Masters, Widow, Petition (July 21, 1767)," Miscellaneous Bound Manuscripts, MHS. See also Conroy, *In Public Houses*, 128–38.

28. For percentages of women afforded tavern licenses in eighteenth-century cities, see Salinger, *Taverns and Drinking*, 263; Meacham, *Every Home a Distillery*, 64–65.

29. As Conroy noted in the context of colonial New England, "In their efforts to overcome their disadvantages and manage their houses to greater profit, widows sometimes came close to challenging the boundaries of prescribed female roles." Conroy, *In Public Houses*, 134. Karin Wulf further complicated women's urban roles in her investigation of unmarried women: Wulf, *Not all Wives*. See also Sarah Hand Meacham, "Keeping the Trade: The Persistence of Tavernkeeping among Middling Women in Colonial Virginia," *Early American Studies: An Interdisciplinary Journal*

3:1 (Spring 2005): 140–63; Kirsten E. Wood, *Masterful Women: Slaveholding Widows from the American Revolution through the Civil War* (Chapel Hill: University of North Carolina Press, 2004), 83–102.

30. "Anne Pattison Account Book (1743/4, Jan. 7–1749, June 13)," Reel B72 Mss 5: 3PZ783: 1, VHS; Wainwright, "Inns and Outs." For persico, see William Byrd II, *The Secret Diary of William Byrd of Westover, 1709–1712*, ed. Louis B. Wright and Marion Tinling (Richmond, VA: Dietz Press, 1941), 403 n. 1.

31. Pattison was not the only female tavern keeper to leave a detailed account book. See also "Jane Cazneau Account Book (1767–1771)," MHS. By the mid-eighteenth century, magistrates in New England also allowed poor people and women to open taverns so they would not become wards of the state, e.g., "Joseph Coolidge Petition (July 9, 1765)," "Rachel Masters, Widow, Petition (July 21, 1767)," "Joseph Goldthwait, Chimney Sweep, Petition (August 12, 1767)," Miscellaneous Bound Manuscripts, MHS.

32. *South Carolina Gazette*, May 31, 1740.

33. *Pennsylvania Gazette*, March 5, 1751; *South Carolina Gazette*, May 1, 1756; January 23, 1770.

34. *Virginia Gazette*, April 8, 1737.

35. Peter Charles Hoffer, *The Great New York Conspiracy of 1741: Slavery, Crime, and Colonial Law* (Lawrence: University of Kansas Press, 2003), 100–130; Jill Lepore, *New York Burning: Liberty, Slavery, and Conspiracy in Eighteenth-Century Manhattan* (New York: Alfred A. Knopf, 2005); Kross, "Sociology of Drinking," 34, 38–40. New York magistrates especially restricted black tavern attendance after this event. See, e.g., Kempe Papers, Box 11, Folder 1, NYHS. "Mother O'Neal" was indicted "for keeping a disorderly House, & entertaining Negroes" in 1765.

36. *Pennsylvania Gazette*, March 5, 1751.

37. Salinger, *Taverns and Drinking*, 244.

38. *South-Carolina Gazette*, November 6, 1736; May 1, 1736; *Pennsylvania Packet*, January 28, 1778. Salinger noted that colonists often did not "see" Native Americans in their tavern interactions: "With very few exceptions, journal writers and diarists failed to mention Indians, not because they were absent but because Indians did not warrant discussion any more than did other parts of the landscape." I would argue that tavern goers did the same with black servants and slaves. As long as blacks acted out their servile role, they receded into the background. Salinger, *Taverns and Drinking*, 237.

39. Wright, *Prose Works of William Byrd*, 219; *South Carolina Gazette*, September 20, 1735.

40. Reflecting Virginia's laws, Maryland forbade licensed liquor purveyors to sell an Indian more than one gallon of wine, brandy, or spirits or five gallons of cider or perry "within the space of one day." Doing so would result in a fine of 5,000 pounds of tobacco. Georgia denied Indians entrance to taverns unless they "first produc[ed] their Owner or Overseers leave in writing for doing so," while in 1767 the commissioners of Pensacola, Florida, had put into effect an act "empowering the magistrates of Charlotte county occasionally to prohibit the selling of rum, or other strong liquors, to the Indians." Gallus Thomann, *Colonial Liquor Laws* (New York: United States Brewers' Association, 1887), 81; Kenneth Coleman and Milton Ready, eds., *The Colonial Records of the State of Georgia, 1732–1782*, vol. 18 (New York: AMS, 1970), 223; *Virginia Gazette*, August 13, 1767.

41. Peter Mancall, *Deadly Medicine: Indians and Alcohol in Early America* (Ithaca, NY: Cornell University Press, 1995), 107; *Virginia Gazette*, August 13, 1767.

42. "Letter 'Boston Evening-Post,'" in Hancock and McDonald, *Public Drinking in the Early Modern World*, 4:549–50. For Native Americans' attendance—or lack of attendance—in urban taverns, see Salinger, *Taverns and Drinking*, 237–39.

43. Zabin, *Dangerous Economies*, 39; Hartigan-O'Connor, *The Ties That Buy*, 129; Conroy, *In Public Houses*, 125–31.

44. "New York City Supreme Court vs. Leonard Coons, January 1765," New York State Supreme Court Collection, 1691–1891, NYHS; "To the Venerable Father Janus," *New-England Courant*, February 19 to February 26, 1726; *Providence Gazette*, May 5, 1765; Salinger, *Taverns and Drinking*, 227.

45. *New-England Courant*, February 19 to February 26, 1726.

46. *Conductor Generalis, or the Office, Duty and Authority of Justices of the Peace,* 2nd ed. (New York: J. Parker, 1749), 1; Kempe Papers, Box 10, Folder 10; Box 1, Folder 2; Box 1, Folder 4, NYHS; *South Carolina Gazette*, August 27, 1772; *The Charters and Acts of Assembly of the Province of Pennsylvania*, vol. 1 (Philadelphia: Peter Miller, 1762), 183–84.

47. Zabin, *Dangerous Economies*, ch. 3; *New-York Gazette*, November 16, 1749; *Pennsylvania Chronicle*, August 31 to September 7, 1767.

48. Sarah Hand Meacham investigated the medicinal attributes of alcohol: Meacham, *Every Home a Distillery*, ch. 1.

49. *Anno regni Georgii II Regis Magnae Britanniae, Franciae, & Hiberniae*, 14; *The Charters and Acts of Assembly of the Province of Pennsylvania, in Two Volumes*, vol. 1 (Philadelphia: Peter Miller, 1762), 306–8.

50. "Hayman Levy vs. Barak Hays, 1773," Kempe Papers, Box 5, Folder 1, NYHS.

51. "Patrick Coyne and Elizabeth Coyne vs. John Myers, 1759, Supreme Court of Judicature," Kempe Papers, Box 3, Folder 1, NYHS.

52. Jack Tager, *Boston Riots: Three Centuries of Social Violence* (Boston: Northeastern University Press, 2001), 15; *Hilliad Magna, Being the Life and Adventures of Moll Placket-Hole, With a Prefatory Dialogue, and Some Moral Reflections, on the Whole* (Philadelphia: Anthony Armbruster, 1765), 3. For prostitution in antebellum Philadelphia, New York City, and New Orleans, see Nancy F. Cott, ed., *History of Women in the United States: Historical Articles on Women's Lives and Activities*, vol. 9: *Prostitution* (Munich: K. G. Sauer, 1993), 1–75. For colonial New York City, see Zabin, *Dangerous Economies*, 48–64, 151. For Philadelphia, see Lyons, *Sex among the Rabble*, 61–107.

53. *Halifax Gazette*, May 19, 1753; *South Carolina Gazette*, November 14, 1761; *New-York Gazette*, July 24, 1775; Patrick M'Robert, *A Tour Through Part of the North Provinces of America: Being, A Series of Letters Wrote on the Spot, in the Years 1774, & 1775. To Which Are Annex'd, Tables, Shewing the Roads, the Value of Coins, Rates of Stages, &c.* (Philadelphia: Historical Society of Pennsylvania, 1935), 5; Lyons, *Sex among the Rabble*, 101.

54. *Hilliad Magna*, 5–7; Bryson, *From Courtesy to Civility*, 246. For prostitution and tavern going in British America, see Salinger, *Taverns and Drinking*, 112–30; Lyons, *Sex among the Rabble*, 103–14.

55. Conversions of Virginia pounds into pounds sterling came from John J. McCusker, *Money and Exchange in Europe and America, 1600–1775: A Handbook* (Chapel Hill: University of North Carolina Press, 1978). For the daily wages of

tradesmen and farmers, see Gloria L. Main, "Gender, Work, and Wages in Colonial New England," *William and Mary Quarterly* 51:1 (January 1994): 39–66 (Table III).

56. *New-York Gazette*, March 26, 1767; Byrd, *Secret Diary*, 517; Louise E. Gray, Evelyn Q. Ryland, and Bettie J. Simmons, *Historic Buildings in Middlesex County, Virginia, 1650–1775*, ed. Walter C. C. Johnson (Charlotte, NC: Delmar Printing Company, 1978), "Rosegill"; "The Wormeley Family (Continued)," *Virginia Magazine of History and Biography* 36:1 (January 1928): 98–101; John Melville Jennings, ed., "From the Society's Collections: The Lamentations of John Grymes in Four Letters Addressed to William Blathwayt," *Virginia Magazine of History and Biography* 58:3 (July 1950): 388; Harold B. Gill Jr., "Williamsburg and the Demimonde: Disorderly Houses, the Blue Bell, and Certain Hints of Harlotry," *Colonial Williamsburg Journal* (Autumn 2001), accessed March 3, 2018, http://www.history.org . For a comparison of what ten shillings might have been equal to in 1712 (in relation to the twenty-first century), see "March the 19th 1711/12, An Inventory of Mr. Thos. Whitbys decd. Estate of York County," Colonial Williamsburg Digital Library, accessed March 23, 2016, http://research.history.org.

57. Bryson, *From Courtesy to Civility*, 253; *Pennsylvania Gazette*, December 19, 1749; Rhys Isaac, *The Transformation of Virginia* (Chapel Hill: University of North Carolina Press, 1982), 95 (quote). Southerners were not alone in their vicious fighting habits. See, e.g., the *Pennsylvania Gazette*, November 17, 1763: "a certain Thomas Wilson, who sometimes goes under the Denomination of a Schoolmaster, near 'Squire Richison, in Lancaster County, did (on Thursday Night, the third of November instant, at the House of Robert Eitches, *Tavern keeper*, at Mill creek, in Lancaster County) violently, and without any Provocation, assault Isaac Leaman, of Lampeter, in said County; and in said Assault most inhumanly bit off Part of his Nose, and also greatly detrimented one of his Fingers, all by the Force of his Teeth, whereby the said Isaac Leaman is now visibly much abused."

58. See, e.g., Elizabeth Drinker, *Extracts from the Journal of Elizabeth Drinker, from 1759 to 1807, A.D.*, ed. Henry D. Biddle (Philadelphia: J. B. Lippincott, 1889), 16; *Boston News-Letter*, September 8, 1763.

59. The British American Loyalist Elizabeth Lichtenstein Johnston recalled her father's midcentury rakish behavior, noting, "Gentlemen in those days usually carried small swords in full dress. . . . [H]aving what our American friends would call 'a little difficulty' with the custodian of the night [in Philadelphia], he drew his sword on him. . . . [T]o those who remember the accounts of the exploits of the 'Mohawks' at night in the streets of London, as related in the pages of the *Spectator*, it will be known that such encounters were not uncommon in the reign of Queen Anne." Elizabeth Lichtenstein Johnston, *Recollections of a Georgia Loyalist*, ed. Rev. Arthur Wentworth Eaton (New York: M. F. Mansfield & Co., 1901), 26–27.

60. Susan Fitzmaurice, "Changes in the Meanings of *Politeness* in Eighteenth-Century England: Discourse Analysis and Historical Evidence," in *Historical (Im)Politeness*, ed. Jonathan Culpeper and Daniel Z. Kadar (Bern: Peter Lang, 2010), 108; *New-York Mercury*, February 25, 1754.

61. For more on the rake in popular British media, see James Grantham Turner, *Libertines and Radicals in Early Modern London: Sexuality, Politics and Literary Culture* (Cambridge: Cambridge University Press, 2002); Jessica Munns, "Theatrical

Culture 1: Politics and Theater," in *The Cambridge Companion to English Literature, 1650–1740*, ed. Steven N. Zwicker (Cambridge: Cambridge University Press, 1998), 91.

62. Lyons, *Sex among the Rabble*, 162, 138–39; "Proper Ingredients to Make a Modern Beau," in Abraham Weatherwise, *Father Abraham's Almanack for 1759* (Philadelphia: Abraham Weatherwise, 1759). The original poem was featured in *The London Magazine: And Monthly Chronologer of 1736* (London: C. Ackers, 1736), 154; *The Connoisseur*, vol. 2, 5th ed. (Oxford: R. Baldwin, 1767), 145. For booksellers' advertisements of *The Connoisseur*, see *Pennsylvania Gazette*, March 2, 1758; *New-York Gazette*, June 6, 1763; *Boston News-Letter*, September 8, 1763; *New-Hampshire Gazette*, November 11, 1763; *Georgia Gazette*, May 2, 1765.

63. Adams, *Diary*, 1:14; "Silence Dogood, No. 14," *New England Courant*, October 8, 1722; Hamilton, *Itinerarium*, 177. For more condemnation of rakes by genteel society, in this case, by Lord Chesterfield (Philip Dorm Stanhope), see "Letter CXXI, London, November 8, O.S. 1750," in *The Works of Lord Chesterfield, Including His Letters to His Son* (New York: Harper & Brothers, 1853), 360–61. See also Forrester, *The Polite Philosopher*, 22.

64. For rakish violence in the early modern British urban center, see Robert Shoemaker, "Male Honour and the Decline of Public Violence in Eighteenth-Century London," *Social History* 26:2 (May 2001): 190–208. Bryson contended that "the defining purpose of libertine manners [was] pleasure in producing a shock effect." She also argued that going on the rake was so enjoyable because "these activities are experienced by others, and perhaps the self, as shocking." Bryson, *From Courtesy to Civility*, 253–54. See also Trevor Burnard, *Planters, Merchants, and Slaves: Plantation Societies in British America, 1650–1820* (Chicago: University of Chicago Press, 2015), 27. The historian John Beattie also noted that "it was not unusual for [early modern British] men to think of using physical force to get their way." John Beattie, "Violence and Society in Early-Modern England," in *Perspectives in Criminal Law: Essays in Honour of John Ll. J. Edwards*, ed. A. N. Doob and E. L. Greenspan (Aurora, ON: Canada Law Book, 1985), 47.

Chapter 5

1. For the central location of Bradford's London Coffee House, see John William Wallace, *An Old Philadelphian, Colonel William Bradford* (Philadelphia: Sherman & Co., 1884), 51. Thomas Lawrence, upholsterer, declared in 1756 that his new shop was "almost opposite the London Coffee House," while the bookseller James Rivington announced in 1761 that he had opened shop "at the Corner of Market and Front Streets, and facing the London Coffee House." *Pennsylvania Gazette*, May 27, 1756; May 28, 1761.

2. Bradford had established himself among Philadelphia's most powerful citizens long before 1765. After apprenticing under his uncle, Andrew Bradford, William opened his own Philadelphia printing shop and began publishing the *Pennsylvania Journal* in 1742. When the Philadelphia Associators Indian War broke out in 1747, Bradford joined the fray and proved himself as a captain. By 1754, the publisher–army veteran opened the elitist, subscriber-controlled London Coffee House right next to his bookshop and printing house, on the bustling southwest corner of Front and High Streets. "Bradford Family Papers Finding

Aid," processed by Meghan Vacca (May 2006), 1–3, HSP; Thompson, *Rum Punch and Revolution*, 106–10.

3. "Extracts of Letters from Mr. Hughes, appointed Distributor of Stamps for Pensilvania, Philada. Sept. 8–17, 1765," in *The Papers of Benjamin Franklin (Online Edition)*, accessed May 14, 2013, http://franklinpapers.org; see also Choppin Roney, *Governed by a Spirit of Opposition*, 162–65; Thompson, *Rum Punch and Revolution*, 142. Boston's John Marston cultivated a similar establishment. See Conroy, *In Public Houses*, 263.

4. "Hughes' Letters," republished in *The Register of Pennsylvania, Vol. II, No. 16 Philadelphia, Nov. 1, 1828*, ed. Samuel Hazard (Philadelphia: W. F. Geddes, 1828), 244–50.

5. Thompson provided two pages of discussion to the Stamp Act Crisis and its immediate aftermath, with cursory reference to the London Coffee House: Thompson, *Rum Punch and Revolution*, 141–42. Conroy noted issues of order and disorder in the Stamp Act Crisis but only in the context of Boston: Conroy, *In Public Houses*, 262–69. Carp gave the Stamp Act Crisis seven pages but only investigated it in the context of New York City: Carp, *Rebels Rising*, 81–87. Bushman provided one page of investigation to the Stamp Act Crisis: Bushman, *Refinement of America*, 166. Salinger did not investigate the Stamp Act Crisis in *Taverns and Drinking*, nor did Shields in *Civil Tongues and Polite Letters*; Choppin Roney referenced Widow Smith's Philadelphia tavern but did not analyze its importance: Choppin Roney, *Governed by a Spirit of Opposition*, 162–65.

6. See, e.g., Waldstreicher, *Perpetual Fetes*, ch. 1; Pauline Maier, *From Resistance to Revolution: Colonial Radicals and the Development of American Opposition to Britain, 1765–1776* (New York: Alfred A. Knopf, 1972), ch. 3.

7. Edmund S. Morgan and Helen M. Morgan, *The Stamp Act Crisis: Prologue to Revolution* (Chapel Hill: University of North Carolina Press, 1953); Carl Bridenbaugh, *Cities in Revolt: Urban Life in America, 1743–1776* (Oxford: Oxford University Press, 1955); Maier, *From Resistance to Revolution*, 51; Robert Kumamoto, *The Historical Origins of Terrorism in America, 1644–1800* (London: Routledge, 2014); Andrew Jackson O'Shaughnessy, *An Empire Divided: The American Revolution and the British Caribbean* (Philadelphia: University of Pennsylvania Press, 2000). Zachary McLeod Hutchins recommended that historians "think of the transatlantic tax debates as a conclusion to the Seven Years' War instead of a prelude to the American War of Independence. . . . [R]ather than reading the Stamp Act as a catalyst spurring colonial unification and the adoption of an American identity eventually inseparable from allegiance to the United States, we might view the duty's passage as an event revealing the insufficiency of British national identity as a force ensuring social cohesion." Zachary McLeod Hutchins, Introduction to *Community without Consent: New Perspectives on the Stamp Act*, ed. Zachary McLeod Hutchins (Hanover, NH: Dartmouth University Press, 2016), xiv. So too did Choppin Roney note the colonial precedents for the Stamp Act Crisis: Choppin Roney, *Governed by a Spirit of Opposition*, 160–62.

8. *Newport Mercury*, August 24 to August 31, 1767.

9. A considerable literature exists on the character and evolution of early American mobs and riots. See, e.g., Arthur Meier Schlesinger, "Political Mobs and the American Revolution, 1765–1776," *Proceedings of the American Philosophical Society* 99:4 (August 1955): 244–50; Gordon Wood, "A Note on Mobs in the American Revolution,"

William and Mary Quarterly 23:4 (October 1966): 635–42; Jesse Lemisch, "Jack Tar in the Streets: Merchant Seamen in the Politics of Revolutionary America," *William and Mary Quarterly* 25:3 (July 1968): 371–407; Edward Countryman, "The Problem of the Early American Crowd," *Journal of American Studies* 7:1 (April 1973): 77–90; Nash, *Urban Crucible*; Thomas Slaughter, "Crowds in Eighteenth-Century America: Reflections and New Directions," *Pennsylvania Magazine of History and Biography* 115:1 (January 1991): 3–34; Tager, *Boston Riots*.

10. Charles Tilly, "Collective Action in England and America, 1765–1775," in *Tradition, Conflict, and Modernization: Perspectives on the American Revolution*, ed. Richard Brown and Don Fehrenbacher (London: Academic Press, 1977), 63; Paul A. Gilje, *Rioting in America* (Bloomington: Indiana University Press, 1999), 25, 38; Tager, *Boston Riots*, 13–16. For a survey of different reasons for colonial American riots, see Kumamoto, *The Historical Origins of Terrorism in America*, 21–36. Groups of rioters usually consisted of 50 to 100 members. Wilcomb Washburn, *The Governor and the Rebel: A History of Bacon's Rebellion in Virginia* (Chapel Hill: University of North Carolina Press, 1957), 57–60.

11. Maier, *From Resistance to Revolution*, 1.

12. Rowe, *Letters and Diary*, 65.

13. For the ongoing debate over "mobbish" riots, disorder, and elitist control, see Tager, *Boston Riots*, 1–15. "Rough music" was a common form of unofficial punishment in British America. Colonists used it to publicly punish offenders (e.g., a crowd of colonists publicly beating a man who had physically abused his wife). William Pencack, "Introduction: A Historical Perspective," in *Riot and Revelry*, 3–20; Gilje, *Rioting in America*, 12–34; Thomas Humphrey, "The Anatomy of a Crowd: Making Mobs in Early America," *Journal of Early American History* 5:1 (April 2015): 68–92.

14. Hamilton, *Itinerarium*, 91, 166.

15. Adams, *Diary*, 1:128–29.

16. *Pennsylvania Gazette*, November 28, 1765; Robert F. Oaks, "Philadelphia Merchants and the Origins of American Independence," *Proceedings of the American Philosophical Society* 121:6 (December 1977): 409; Maier, *From Resistance to Revolution*, 88; Arthur Meier Schlesinger, *The Colonial Merchants and the American Revolution, 1763–1776* (New York: Columbia University Press, 1918), 80; Breen, "Ideology and Nationalism on the Eve of the American Revolution," 17; Andrew David Edwards, "Grenville's Silver Hammer: The Problem of Money in the Stamp Act Crisis," *Journal of American History* 104:2 (September 2017): 337–62.

17. Thompson, *Rum Punch and Revolution*, 91–93; Carp, *Rebels Rising*, 84–85.

18. For examples of correspondence between the New York Sons of Liberty and Sons of Liberty in other colonial centers, see "Joseph Allicocke to John Lamb, New York 21 November 1765," "Albany SOL to Sons of Liberty in New York (Messr. Joseph Alicocke & Isaac Sears), Albany January 15ᵗʰ 1766," "Major Durkee to Isaac Sears and SOL (NY) Feb 10 1766," John Lamb Papers, Reel 1, 1762–Dec. 1779, NYHS.

19. See, e.g., "Joseph Allicocke to John Lamb, New York 21 November 1765," John Lamb Papers, Reel 1, 1762–Dec. 1779, NYHS. In this letter, Allicocke, a New York Son of Liberty, told John Lamb, another New York Son of Liberty, "I observe with much discontent, what you relate touching the disunion of the People of Philadelphia, as it must needs have a disagreeable tendency to things in General, but more particularly at this critical Conjuncture as it appears to be a preventative from obliging the Stamp Master

to resign as he ought to be made to do." Alexander Colden also wrote to Cadwallader in November that the Sons of Liberty (in New York) "have wrote to Phila: that if they do not make Hughes resign as fully as the other Distributors have done They will disown them & hold no longer Correspondence with them." Cadwallader Colden, *The Letters and Papers of Cadwallader Colden*, vol. 7: *1765–1775* (New York: New York Historical Society, 1923), 95. For more on newspapers, see Morgan, *Stamp Act Crisis*, 88–90.

20. *Boston Evening Post*, November 18, 1765; *South Carolina Gazette*, December 17, 1765.

21. Colden, *Letters and Papers*, 7:85–90.

22. Colden, *Letters and Papers*, 7:91.

23. *New-Hampshire Gazette*, December 27, 1765; Francis Bernard, *The Papers of Francis Bernard Governor of Colonial Massachusetts, 1760–1769, Volume II: 1764–65*, ed. Colin Nicolson (Boston: Colonial Society of Massachusetts, 2012), 69.

24. *Boston Evening Post*, December 30, 1765; *New York Mercury*, November 25, 1765; *South Carolina Gazette*, January 7, 1766.

25. Bernard, *Papers*, 2:308.

26. *Boston Evening-Post*, November 18, 1765; Bernard, *Papers*, 2:397–98. For the tradition of Guy Fawkes Day in colonial America, see Waldstreicher, *Perpetual Fetes*, 18–24; Brendan McConville, "Popes Day Revisited, 'Popular' Culture Reconsidered," *Explorations in Early American Culture* 4:1 (2000): 258–80; Brendan McConville, *The King's Three Faces: The Rise and Fall of Royal America, 1688–1776* (Chapel Hill: University of North Carolina Press, 2006), 1–3.

27. *Boston Evening-Post*, November 18, 1765. Similarly, "a number of sailors" met at Machenry's Tavern in Savannah, Georgia on November 5 to combine their celebration of Guy Fawkes Day with their animosity to the Stamp Act. After one sailor dressed up as a stamp master and let his drunken comrades parade him through the streets while they beat him with cudgels and he screamed, "*No stamps, No riot act, Gentlemen*," the whole party ended up at Machenry's Tavern where they hung the poor fellow "up for a little while . . . in the presence of a crowd of spectators." The young man surely had more than a few free drinks waiting for him as his fellow "tars" let him down from the scaffolding. No matter the threatening nature of the spectacle, however, the *Georgia Gazette* was sure to note, "In all the exhibitions here of this kind, private as well as publick property has remained unmolested, and no outrages have been committed." *Georgia Gazette*, November 11, 1765.

28. "William Almy to Elisha Story, August 29, 1765," *Proceedings of the Massachusetts Historical Society* 55:1 (October 1921 to June 1922): 235–37; *Newport Mercury*, September 2, 1765; Morgan, *Stamp Act Crisis*, 145–50.

29. "William Bradford to the New York Sons of Liberty Committee, February 15, 1766," Lamp Papers, NYHS.

30. *Boston News-Letter*, February 6, 1766; "Deposition of Robert Rodgers, Late a Mariner on Board the Brigantine Polly, January 11, 1765," Kempe Papers, Box 11, Folder 9, NYHS; *Pennsylvania Gazette*, February 20, 1766.

31. For Webber's ultimate fate (which involved trying to hang himself in prison), see the *Boston Post-Boy*, November 4, 1765.

32. Peter Linebaugh and Marcus Rediker, *The Many-Headed Hydra: Sailors, Slaves, Commoners, and the Hidden History of the Revolutionary Atlantic* (Boston: Beacon Press, 2000).

33. *Boston Evening-Post*, November 18, 1765; *South Carolina Gazette*, December 17, 1765.

34. "Old Highways—1660 to 1708, From the Town Records," in Edward H. Savage, *Boston Events: A Brief Mention and the Date of More than 5,000 Events that Transpired in Boston from 1630 to 1880* (Boston: Tolman & Withe, 1884), 179; *Boston Gazette*, July 17, 1750. John Adams complained in 1761, "If you ride over this whole Province you will find, that, altho Taverns are generally too numerous, they are not half so numerous in one County, in Proportion to the Numbers of People and the Necessity of Business and Travellers, as in [Boston]. In most Country Towns, in this County, you will find almost every other House, with a sign of Entertainment before it." Adams, *Diary*, 1:192. For an illustrative map of the location of licensed taverns in Boston in 1736, see Salinger, *Taverns and Drinking*, 193 (fig. 13).

35. Bernard, *Papers*, 2:302–5; Rowe, *Letters and Diary*, 88–89; "Thomas Hutchinson Recounts the Reaction to the Stamp Act in Boston (1765)," in *The History of the Colony and Province of Massachusetts-Bay*, vol. 3, ed. Lawrence Shaw Mayo (Cambridge, MA: Harvard University Press, 1936), 86–88.

36. Bernard, *Papers*, 2:302–5.

37. Bernard, *Papers*, 2:302–5; Rowe, *Letters and Diary*, 88–89; "Hutchinson Recounts the Reaction," in *The History of the Colony*, 3:86–90. Archibald Hinshelwood of Nova Scotia noted on August 18, 1765, "There is a violent spirit of opposition raised on the Continent against the execution of the Stamp Act, the mob in Boston have carried it very high against Mr. Oliver. . . . [T]hey have even proceeded to some violence, and burnt him in effigy &c." "Archibald Hinshelwood to Joshua Mauger, Halifax, Nova Scotia, August 19, 1765," Gilder Lehrman Institute of American History, accessed May 14, 2014, https://www.gilderlehrman.org.

38. Bernard, *Papers*, 2:303–4.

39. "Journal of Josiah Quincy Jr., August 26, 1765," *Proceedings of the Massachusetts Historical Society* 4 (1860): 47–48; Bernard, *Papers*, 2:323, 337–39.

40. "Journal of Josiah Quincy Jr.," 48; Bernard, *Papers*, 2:338; Morgan, *Stamp Act Crisis*, 126–27.

41. "Journal of Josiah Quincy Jr.," 47; Jonathan Mayhew, *The Snare Broken; A Thanksgiving Discourse, Preached at the Desire of the West Church in Boston, N.E. Friday May 23, 1766. Occasioned by the Repeal of the Stamp-Act* (Boston: R.&S. Draper, 1766); Bernard, *Papers*, 2:339.

42. Bernard, *Papers*, 2:352; Thomas Hutchinson, *The Diary and Letters of Thomas Hutchinson*, ed. Peter O. Hutchinson (Boston: Houghton Mifflin, 1884), 71.

43. *South Carolina Gazette*, October 31, 1765.

44. *South Carolina Gazette*, October 31, 1765. For more on Dillon's Tavern as a center of resistance, see Mary C. Ferrari, "Charity, Folly, and Politics: Charles Town's Social Clubs on the Eve of the Revolution," *South Carolina Historical Magazine* 112:1–2 (January–April 2011): 50–83.

45. *Boston Evening-Post*, December 30, 1765; March 10, 1766; March 3, 1766.

46. Kumamoto, *Historical Origins of Terrorism*, Introduction; Cindy C. Combs, *Terrorism in the Twenty-First Century* (Upper Saddle River, NJ: Pearson Press, 2012).

47. Adams, *Diary*, 2:260.

48. Franklin B. Dexter, ed., "A Selection from the Correspondence and Miscellaneous Papers of Jared Ingersoll," in *Papers of the New Haven Colony Historical Society*,

vol. 9 (New Haven, CT: Printed for the Society, 1918): 342–48, 354–55; *Boston News-Letter*, September 26, 1765.

49. Dexter, "Papers of Jared Ingersoll," 348.

50. "Deposition of Henry Van Schaack, January, 1766," Kempe Papers, Box 12, Folder 2, NYHS; *New-York Gazette*, January 27, 1766; *Pennsylvania Gazette*, January 30, 1766; Henry Cruger Van Schaack, *Memoirs of the Life of Henry Van Schaack* (Chicago: A. C. McClurg & Company, 1892), 12–14; Thomas J. Humphrey, "Crowd and Court: Rough Music and Popular Justice in Colonial New York," in *Riot and Revelry*, 110–18; "Albany Sons of Liberty to Sons of Liberty in New York (Messr. Joseph Alicocke & Isaac Sears), Albany January 15, 1766," Lamb Papers, NYHS.

51. *Boston Evening-Post*, March 3, 1766.

52. Accosting gentlemen as they stepped out of elitist taverns was a tried and tested practice among villains. The December 19, 1748, edition of the *New-York Gazette* declared, "It seems to be now become dangerous for the good People of the City, to be late out a Nights without being sufficiently strong or well armed" after two "Gentlemen" were "attacked and knock'd down, by several Persons unknown" when leaving the Cart and Horse Tavern one night. Nine years later, "a Gentleman returning from the Coffee-House, was attacked by two Ruffians in Nassau-Street [New York], and robbed of his Watch and what Money he had about him." *New-York Gazette*, December 19, 1748; March 7, 1757.

53. "William Almy to Elisha Story, August 29, 1765," 235–37; *Newport Mercury*, September 2, 1765; Morgan, *Stamp Act Crisis*, 145–50; *Newport Mercury*, September 2, 1765.

54. William Smith, "The Mirror—A Pasquinade Set up at the Coffee House to Explain a Carricature in January 1766," William Smith Papers, Box 2, Lot 203, NYPL.

55. For taverns as centers of literature and "polite letters," see Shields, *Civil Tongues and Polite Letters*, ch. 3.

56. *South Carolina Gazette*, January 21, 1766.

57. Colden, *Papers*, 7:97; Dexter, "Papers of Jared Ingersoll," 351, 397; Bernard, *Papers*, 2:325, 355, 433. Apparently watching one's own effigy, shop, and home burn before publicly resigning from the role of stamp officer was not proficient punishment for Andrew Oliver, as on December 18 Boston's Sons of Liberty demanded that Oliver "appear under Liberty Tree at 12 o'clock to make a[nother] public Resignation." The notice was veiled with threats. Having warned Oliver that "noncompliance" would "incur the displeasure of the true Sons of Liberty," the Bostonians continued, "Provided you comply with the above, You shall be treated with the greatest politeness and humanity—If not—" Oliver knew better than anyone that these angry colonists were not bluffing. He accordingly read his resignation—again—in front of a crowd of at least 2,000 the next day. Bernard, *Papers*, 2:436.

58. This preparation for mass demonstration can especially be seen in the correspondence between the New York Sons of Liberty and various other Sons. The Providence Sons promised on February 17 that they could "at two Hours Notice Bring 3000 Men under the Tree of Liberty who would go anywhere for ye preservation of ye Constitution & that there is above 40,000 in that Province & New Hampshire who are Determined to take up Arms for ye same Purpose if Necessary." New York replied on February 20 "that it is the Determined and fixed resolution of the Sons of Liberty here, not to be enslav'd by any power on Earth, without opposing force to force." On March

8, 1766, the Baltimore Town Sons of Liberty assured the New York Sons that "we will pursue every necessary method to oppose the Introduction of that, or any other oppressive Arbitrary, and illegal Measure, amongst them, or ourselves." "Extract of a Letter from Providence, February 17, 1766"; "New York Sons of Liberty to Connecticut Sons of Liberty, February 20, 1766"; "Letter from Baltimore Town Sons of Liberty to New York Sons of Liberty, March 8, 1766," all in Lamb Papers, NYHS.

59. Pauline Maier investigated how news of the repeal "was sent north along Sons of Liberty communications channels in two successive waves" during April. Maier, *From Resistance to Revolution*, n. 64, 109–10; *Newport Mercury*, May 19, 1766.

60. *Pennsylvania Gazette*, May 29, 1766; May 22, 1766; *Boston Gazette*, May 26, 1766.

61. *Newport Mercury*, May 26, 1766; *New-York Gazette*, November 14, 1765.

62. Bernard, *Papers*, 2:75.

Chapter 6

1. Bernard, *Papers*, 2:75; Adams, *Diary*, 1:324; Paul Leicester Ford, ed., "The Writings of John Dickinson, Vol. I: Political Writings, 1764–1774," in *Memoirs of the Historical Society of Pennsylvania* 14 (Philadelphia: M'Carty and Davis, 1895), 267; "From the London Magazine, for December, 1765." This piece was reprinted in America as "The claims of the Americans impartially represented," *Newport Mercury*, April 7 to April 14, 1766. In a broader sense, such professions allude to colonists' long-term efforts at crafting times of historical flux into instances that revealed the greatness of the British Empire. Like the usurpation of King James II during the "Glorious Revolution" of 1688–89, many colonists argued that overthrowing the Stamp Act of 1765–66 represented the supreme triumph of British liberty and, by proxy, civil society. McConville, *King's Three Faces*, ch. 3.

2. For the predominance and strategies of committees of safety throughout the colonies, see Christopher F. Minty, "'Of One Hart and One Mind': Local Institutions and Allegiance during the American Revolution," *Early American Studies: An Interdisciplinary Journal* 15:1 (Winter 2017): 106; T. H. Breen, *American Insurgents, American Patriots: The Revolution of the People* (New York: Hill and Wang, 2010), 185–206; John Shy, "The American Revolution: The Military Conflict Considered as a Revolutionary War," in *Essays on the American Revolution*, ed. James H. Hutson and Stephen G. Kurtz (Chapel Hill: University of North Carolina Press, 2014), 121–56.

3. Just as numerous historians have revealed how urban taverns proved vital in the "coming of the Revolution," so too have myriad scholars traced the narrative of colonists' transition from "resistance to revolution" between 1765 and 1776. The role of urban taverns *during* the Revolutionary War, however, has received comparatively scant attention, as has the importance of prerevolutionary impetuses in defining how colonists continued to rely on taverns in the throes of the American Revolution. Benjamin Carp explained this absence by arguing that cities (and, in turn, their public spaces like taverns) had "rendered themselves obsolete" by 1776, while Carl Bridenbaugh and Gary B. Nash ended their investigations of urban centers and the American Revolution in 1776, thereby negating the importance of cities during the revolution. Pauline Maier joined Bridenbaugh and Nash in closing her analysis in 1776. Maier also, importantly, interpreted taverns merely as accompanying spaces of revolutionary

fervor and only mentioned civil society in passing in her investigation of how "Real Whig" ideologies "helped create a logical thrust toward revolution and independence." Those historians who have specifically studied the "coming of the revolution" through the lens of the tavern space, finally, have also stopped their investigations in the year 1776, with the sole exception being Peter Thompson's analysis of Philadelphia's taverns during the American Revolution. Carp, *Rebels Rising*, 213; Bridenbaugh, *Cities in Revolt*; Nash, *The Urban Crucible*; Conroy, *In Public Houses*, ch. 6 (his epilogue skips to "after the Revolution"); Maier, *From Resistance to Revolution*, xx–xxi; Carp, *Rebels Rising*, ch. 5. Shields skips to the early national period, leapfrogging the American Revolution: Shields, *Civil Tongues and Polite Letters*, ch. 9.

4. Woods, "Join with Heart and Soul," 1083–1116.

5. Johnston, *Recollections of a Georgia Loyalist*, 45; Breen, *American Insurgents, American Patriots*, 197.

6. Allegiance was a tricky issue during the American Revolution, especially for colonists who felt swept up in the waves of war. As numerous scholars have demonstrated, colonists would often join whatever side guaranteed their personal safety or, simply, whichever side controlled their locality. For this reason, this chapter follows those most outspoken Republicans and Loyalists while maintaining an appreciation for the complicated and conflicting notions of identity, patriotism, and allegiance in revolutionary America. See Minty, "'Of One Hart and One Mind,'" 110, also n. 23; Judith L. Van Buskirk, *Generous Enemies: Patriots and Loyalists in Revolutionary New York* (Philadelphia: University of Pennsylvania Press, 2002); Travis Glasson, "The Intimacies of Occupation: Loyalties, Compromise, and Betrayal in Revolutionary-Era Newport," in *The American Revolution Reborn*, ed. Patrick Spero and Michael Zuckerman (Philadelphia: University of Pennsylvania Press, 2016), 29–47.

7. Johnston, *Recollections of a Georgia Loyalist*, 45.

8. See, e.g., Minty, "'Of One Hart and One Mind,'" 99–132. Edward Larkin has argued, "We have only begun to scratch the surface of loyalism and the ways Loyalists challenge our notions of the Revolution, American democracy, civil society, and the state." Edward Larkin, "Loyalism," in *The Oxford Handbook of the American Revolution*, ed. Edward G. Gray and Jane Kamensky (Oxford: Oxford University Press, 2013), 305.

9. Adams, *Diary*, 1:279, 305, 324.

10. Ever obsessed with the civilization vs. savagery dyad, Britons often equated civility with orderly riots and incivility (and savagery/barbarism) with disorderly, violent riots. See Thomas, *In Pursuit of Civility*, 94, 148.

11. Christopher Gadsden, *The Writings of Christopher Gadsden, 1746–1805*, ed. Richard Walsh (Columbia, SC: University of South Carolina Press, 1966), 80, 85; *Essex Gazette*, November 1 to November 8, 1768; Daniel J. McDonough, *Christopher Gadsden and Henry Laurens: The Parallel Lives of Two American Patriots* (Sellinsgrove, PA: Susquehanna University Press, 2000), 99–107.

12. *Boston News-Letter*, August 24, 1769.

13. "Letter IV, Castle William Boston Harbor, June 30, 1768," in Ann Hulton, *Letters of a Loyalist Lady* (Cambridge, MA: Harvard University Press, 1927), 11–12.

14. Gadsden, *Writings*, 81.

15. Often constructed in front of or nearby popular taverns, liberty poles and trees had become common sights in British American cities after 1765. See Arthur

M. Schlesinger, "Liberty Tree: A Genealogy," *New England Quarterly* 25:4 (December 1952): 435–58.

16. G. D. Scull, ed., "Montresor Journals," in *Collections of the New-York Historical Society*, vol. 14 (New York: New York Historical Society, 1881), 382–83.

17. McConville, *King's Three Faces*, 249–51; "William Pitt's Defense of the American Colonies," Colonial Williamsburg Foundation, accessed July 26, 2018, http://www.history.org.

18. *New-York Journal* (supplement), March 26, 1767; *Virginia Gazette*, April 16, 1767; Carp, *Rebels Rising*, 90–92.

19. *New-York Journal* (supplement), March 26, 1767; *Virginia Gazette*, April 16, 1767; Carp, *Rebels Rising*, 90–92.

20. Sons of Liberty, "New York, July 7, 1769: At this Alarming Crisis . . . " (New York, n.p., 1769). Early American Imprints, Series 1, Evans 11379; "A Song, To the Tune of Heart & Oak, &c," *Pennsylvania Journal*, July 7, 1768; Carp, *Rebels Rising*, 91.

21. *Virginia Gazette*, April 16, 1767. See also "The King Agt. William McDougal," in Kempe Papers, Box 2, Folder 1, 1770, NYHS; *New-York Journal*, March 1, 1770; *New-York Gazette or Weekly Post Boy*, February 5, 1770. For secondary sources detailing the Battle of Golden Hill, see Carp, *Rebels Rising*, 89–92; Isaac Q. Leake, *Memoir of the Life and Times of General John Lamb: An Officer of the Revolution* (Albany, NY: Joel Munsell, 1857), 50–65; Richard Archer, *As if an Enemy's Country: The British Occupation of Boston and the Origins of the Revolution* (Oxford: Oxford University Press, 2010), 175; Jessie Lemisch, *Jack Tar vs. John Bull: The Role of New York's Seamen in Precipitating the Revolution* (London: Routledge, 1997), 131–34; Kenneth A. Daigler, *Spies, Patriots, and Traitors: American Intelligence in the Revolutionary War* (Washington, DC: Georgetown University Press, 2014), 29, 250; Schlesinger, "Political Mobs and the American Revolution," 245–48.

22. *New-York Journal*, February 8, 1770.

23. *New-York Journal*, March 1, 1770.

24. *Pennsylvania Gazette*, September 28, 1769; "Letters from a Farmer in Pennsylvania, to the Inhabitants of the British Colonies, Letter VIII," *Pennsylvania Gazette*, January 21, 1768; *Newport Mercury*, August 24 to August 31, 1767. For further discussion of slavery and revolution, see Burnard, *Planters, Merchants, and Slaves*, 257.

25. *Pennsylvania Gazette*, September 28, 1769; "Letters from a Farmer in Pennsylvania, to the Inhabitants of the British Colonies, Letter VIII," *Pennsylvania Gazette*, January 21, 1768; Gadsden, *Writings*, 76.

26. Hulton, *Letters*, 12–13; "William Franklin to Benjamin Franklin, January 2, 1769," Franklinpapers.org, accessed March 5, 2017, http://franklinpapers.org; "Benjamin Franklin to William Franklin, October 5, 1768," Franklinpapers.org, accessed March 5, 2017, http://franklinpapers.org.

27. John Wilkes, *The North Briton, 45, Saturday, April 23, 1763*, Constitution Society, accessed July 27, 2018, http://www.constitution.org. For instances of tavern celebrations of Wilkes and the number 45, see Carp, *Rebels Rising*, 92, 252. For more on Benjamin Franklin's time in London—and his overtly Loyalist identity until he was forced to choose sides in 1775—see George Goodwin, *Benjamin Franklin in London: The British Life of America's Founding Father* (New Haven, CT: Yale University Press, 2016). See also Arthur Cash, *John Wilkes: The Scandalous Father of Civil Liberty* (New Haven, CT: Yale University Press, 2008), 96–120.

28. Hulton, *Letters*, 28.

29. "Benjamin Franklin to William Franklin, January 30, 1772," Franklinpapers. org, accessed March 5, 2017, http://franklinpapers.org.

30. Josiah Quincy Jr., *Observations on the Act of Parliament, Commonly Called the Boston Port-Bill; with Thoughts on Civil Society and Standing Armies* (Philadelphia: John Sparhawk, 1774).

31. *Norwich Packet*, December 2 to December 9, 1773; See also Breen, *Marketplace of Revolution*, 293–331; Benjamin L. Carp, *Defiance of the Patriots: The Boston Tea Party and the Making of America* (New Haven, CT: Yale University Press, 2010); Hulton, *Letters*, 60–75.

32. McCarthy, *American Creed*, 24.

33. *Massachusetts Spy*, February 4, 1773. For further discussion of civil society in 1773, see *Massachusetts Spy*, November 18, 1773; *Norwich Packet*, December 2 to December 9, 1773.

34. Breen, *Marketplace of Revolution*, 254–93; *Boston Evening-Post*, November 18, 1765.

35. Breen, *American Insurgents, American Patriots*, 162 (quote), 160–206; Minty, "'Of One Hart and One Mind,'" 99–132; Jerrilyn Greene Marston, *King and Congress: The Transfer of Political Legitimacy, 1774–1776* (Princeton, NJ: Princeton University Press, 1987), 116–29. Committees of safety were not unique to the American Revolution—in fact, colonists relied on them heavily in the "Glorious Revolution" of 1688. In 1689, for instance, New Yorkers and New Englanders formed extralegal committees of safety to combat Edmund Andros's vision of British American rule in New England. Richard S. Dunn, "The Glorious Revolution and America," in *The Oxford History of the British Empire*, vol. 1: *The Origins of Empire: British Overseas Enterprise to the Close of the Seventeenth Century*, ed. Nicholas Canny (Oxford: Oxford University Press, 1998), 445–66. See also "Letter of Samuel Prince, 1689," in *Narratives of the Insurrections, 1675–1690*, ed. Charles M. Andrews (New York: Charles Scribner's Sons, 1915), 186–90.

36. "In Committee at Johnstown, June 5, 1776," Tryon County New York Committee Records, 1775–1794, Box 2, Folder 6, NYHS; Carolyn D. Hertz, "The Committees of Correspondence, Inspection and Safety in Old Hampshire County, Massachusetts, during the American Revolution" (Master's thesis, University of Massachusetts Amherst, 1993), 39, 72. Hertz also argued that "committees provided the 'cement' that united towns within the Province, and colonies up and down the continent" (76). For the lack of effective law enforcement in the midcentury colonial city, see Krawczynski, *Daily Life in the Colonial City*, 257, 274–75.

37. Christopher Marshall, *Passages from the Diary of Christopher Marshall, Kept in Philadelphia and Lancaster During the American Revolution*, vol. 1: *1774–1777*, ed. William Duane (Philadelphia: Hazard & Mitchell, 1839–49), 24; *Pennsylvania Ledger*, No. 3, February 11, 1775.

38. Marshall, *Diary*, 51, 30–32; "Bradford Family Papers Finding Aid," HSP, 1–3.

39. Marshall, *Diary*, 51, 30–32, 45–47; Drinker, *Diary*, 211, 214.

40. "Declaration and Resolves of the First Continental Congress, October 14, 1774," The Avalon Project, Documents in Law, History and Diplomacy, accessed March 11, 2017, http://avalon.law.yale.edu; Adams, *Diary*, 2:114, 118; Marshall, *Diary*, 58–59.

41. Marshall, *Diary*, 58–59.

42. William Edis, *Letters from America, Historical and Descriptive, Comprising Occurrences from 1769 to 1777* (London: William Edis, 1792), 210, 212–13, 235.

43. "R. Christie, Jr. to Jenifer, December 10, 1776," Journal and Correspondence of the Maryland Council of Safety, Vol. 12, p. 517, Archives of Maryland Online, accessed March 12, 2017, http://msa.maryland.gov; Charles Steffen, *The Mechanics of Baltimore* (Chicago: University of Illinois Press, 1984), 60–70; Emily Huebner, "The Whig Club: Judge and Jury in Baltimore," Finding the Maryland 400: A Maryland State Archives Project, accessed March 12, 2017, https://msamaryland400.wordpress.com/.

44. Edis, *Letters*, 288, 228; Bernard C. Steiner, "Life and Administration of Robert Eden," *Johns Hopkins University Studies* 16:7–9 (1898), 133.

45. For the jumbled nature of "Patriot" and "Loyalist" identity in Revolutionary America, see Donald F. Johnson, "Ambiguous Allegiances: Urban Loyalties during the American Revolution," *Journal of American History* 104:3 (December 2017): 610–31; Keith Mason, "The American Loyalist Problem of Identity in the Revolutionary Atlantic World," in *The Loyal Atlantic: Remaking the British Atlantic in the Revolutionary Era*, ed. Jerry Bannister and Liam Riordian (Toronto: University of Toronto Press, 2012), 39–74; Dror Wahrman, "The English Problem of Identity in the American Revolution," *American Historical Review* 106:4 (October 2001): 1236–62.

46. *Proceedings of the Convention of the province of Maryland, held at the city of Annapolis, on Thursday the seventh of December, 1775* (Annapolis, MD: Frederick Green, 1775). See also Perl-Rosenthal, "The 'Divine Right of Republics," 548–49.

47. In an oft-cited 1815 letter, John Adams estimated that up to one-third of colonists remained "averse to the revolution." "From John Adams to James Lloyd, 28 January 1815, *Founders Online*, National Archives, last modified November 26, 2017, http:founders.archives.gov.

48. *Pennsylvania Ledger*, February 11, 1775; Marshall, *Diary*, 24, 26, 91.

49. Thompson, *Rum Punch and Revolution*, 162; *Proceedings of the Convention of the Province of Maryland*. Colonists damned Parliament long before the king in the lead-up to the American Revolution. See McConville, *King's Three Faces*, 281–312.

50. *Rivington's New-York Gazetteer*, April 29, 1773, January 19, 1775; Ruma Chopra, "Printer Hugh Gaine Crosses and Re-Crosses the Hudson," *New York History* 90:4 (Fall 2009): 275–76. For instances of royal tavern celebrations, see *Rivington's New-York Gazetteer*, June 3, 1773; August 19, 1773; September 16, 1773; December 9, 1773; January 13, 1774; February 3, 1774; March 10, 1774; April 14, 1774; May 5, 1774; May 12, 1774; June 9, 1774; July 14, 1774; August 18, 1774. Rivington also published "Bellisarius's" damning piece in the March 9, 1775, issue of his *Gazette*: "If every man had thought for himself and not been led by the nose by a Cooper or an Adams, all might have been happy; but these inconsiderate people have made themselves idols, viz. liberty Trees, News-Papers and Congresses, which by blindly worshipping, have so engrossed their minds, that they give not the least attention to their several occupations, but attend at taverns, where they talk politicks, get drunk, damn King, Ministers, and Taxes; and *vow* they will follow any measures proposed to them by their demagogues, however repugnant to religion, reason and common sense."

51. Catherine O'Donnell Kaplan, *Men of Letters in the Early Republic: Cultivating Forums of Citizenship* (Chapel Hill: University of North Carolina Press, 2008), 24.

52. Marshall, *Diary*, 137; Hunter, *Purchasing Identity*, 142 (Salem civil society quote).

53. Marshall, *Diary*, 137; Minty, "'Of One Hart and One Mind,'" 115, 119 (quotes).

54. As the historian Donald F. Johnson contended, "Military occupation marked urban life during the Revolutionary War from its earliest days until its close." Johnson, "Ambiguous Allegiances," 613.

55. Benjamin Carp argued that cities (and, in turn, their public spaces like taverns) had "rendered themselves obsolete" by 1776. See Carp, *Rebels Rising*, 213.

56. Cresswell, *Journal*, 1, 128, 172. George Washington frequented the Alexandria Committee in 1774. When he ran for the House of Burgesses in July 1774, he used Arell's tavern to gain votes. See "[July 1774]," *Founders Online*, National Archives, last modified March 30, 2017, http://founders.archives.gov (original source: *The Diaries of George Washington*, vol. 3, *1 January 1771–5 November 1781*, ed. Donald Jackson [Charlottesville: University Press of Virginia, 1978], 259–264).

57. Cresswell, *Journal*, 175.

58. "Garish Harsin to William Radclift, February 13, 1776," in Mercantile Library Association, *New York City During the American Revolution* (New York: Privately Printed for the Association, 1861), 87.

59. Cresswell, *Journal*, 244–45.

60. Cresswell, *Journal*, 244.

61. Ira D. Gruber, *John Peebles' American War: The Diary of a Scottish Grenadier, 1776–1782* (Mechanicsburg, PA: Stackpole Books for the Army Records Society, 1998), 81, 89, 160–61, 379, 442, 497–98. For tavern parties in occupied New York City, see Oscar Theodore Barck, *New York City during the War for Independence: With Special Reference to the Period of British Occupation* (New York: Columbia University Press, 1931), 170–87. For more on the Philadelphia soldier-funded tavern assembly, see Frederich Ernst von Muenchhausen, *At General Howe's Side, 1776–1778: The Diary of General William Howe's aide de camp, Captain Friederich von Muenchhausen*, trans. Ernst Kipping (Monmouth Beach, NJ: Philip Freneau Press, 1974), 47.

62. Gruber, *John Peebles' American* War, 81, 89, 160–61, 379, 442, 497–98.

63. Cresswell, *Journal*, 81, 89, 160–61, 379, 442, 497–98, 259–60. For the change from Merchant Coffee House to Strachan's Tavern, see M. Harrison Bayles, *Old Taverns of New York* (New York: Frank Allaben Genealogical Company, 1915), 293.

64. Drinker, *Diary*, 1:224, 306.

65. Drinker, *Diary*, 1:341.

66. Nash, *The Unknown American Revolution*, 318 ("drive from the city" quote); Drinker, *Diary*, I: 370; Thompson, *Rum Punch and Revolution*, 174–75.

67. *New-Jersey Gazette*, September 1, 1779; *Boston News-Letter*, January 22, 1776.

68. L. H. Butterfield, ed., *Letters of Benjamin Rush*, 2 vols. (Philadelphia: American Philosophical Society, 1951), 1:243–44; Eric Foner, *Tom Paine and Revolutionary America* (Oxford: Oxford University Press, 2005), xxvii–xxxv.

69. "Orb and Scepter: Joel Stone Determines 'Sooner to Perish in the General Calamity than Abet . . . the Enemies of the British Constitution," in *The Price of Loyalty: Tory Writings from the Revolutionary Era*, ed. Catherine S. Crary (New York: McGraw-Hill, 1973), 164.

70. The Drinker family experienced much turmoil during the American Revolution. See Drinker, *Diary*, 1:214–360; "'Let Him Starve and Be Damned!': Nathaniel Gardiner of Rhode Island Experiences Barbarities En Route to Jail in Falmouth," in *The Price of Loyalty*, 207 (see also 55–86, 201–39).

71. Birket, *Cursory Remarks*, 25. While this chapter explores the cosmopolitan identity as colonists would have understood it, other historians have utilized the term for their own means.

72. For "staunch American" and "staunch Briton," see "Letter from John Adams to Abigail Adams, April 23, 1776," Adams Family Papers: An Electronic Archive (Massachusetts Historical Society), http://www.masshist.org, accessed April 19, 2017.

73. *New-York Mercury*, December 11, 1752; Frank Lambert, *James Habersham: Loyalty, Politics, and Commerce in Colonial Georgia* (Athens: University of Georgia Press, 2005), 23, 130, 136, 168–69.

74. Foner, *Tom Paine*, xxvii–xxxv; Cresswell, *Journal*, 136; *Pennsylvania Ledger*, March 18, 1778.

75. Adams, *Diary*, 2:106; "Letter from John Adams to Abigail Adams, 22 December 1793," Adams Family Papers: An Electronic Archive (Massachusetts Historical Society), accessed April 19, 2017, http://www.masshist.org; Max Farrand, *Records of the Federal Convention* (New Haven, CT: Yale University Press, 1911) 1:545; Jared Sparks, ed., *The Life of Gouverneur Morris, with Selections from His Correspondence and Miscellaneous Papers*, 3 vols. (Boston: Gray & Bowen, 1832), 1:202.

76. Thomas Paine, *Common Sense* (New York: Eckler, 1918), 37, x, 57; John Keane, *Tom Paine: A Political Life* (New York: Grove Press, 1995), 229–32; Thomas Paine, *The American Crisis* (London, 1776–83), ch. 7. In 1782, Paine contended that the American Revolution had allowed America's citizens to understand the world in a cosmopolitan light: "We see with other eyes; we hear with other ears; and think with other thoughts, than those we formerly used. We can look back on our own prejudices, as if they had been the prejudices of other people." Thomas Paine, *A Letter Addressed to the Abbe Raynal, On the Affairs of North America; in which the mistakes in the Abbe's account of the Revolution of America are corrected and cleared up* (Rockville, MD: Manor, 2008), 54.

77. J. C. D. Clark, *Thomas Paine: Britain, America, and France in the Age of Enlightenment and Revolution* (Oxford: Oxford University Press, 2018).

78. Conroy, *In Public Houses*, 283–85.

79. Marshall, *Diary*, 137; Adams, *Diary*, 2:259.

80. For midcentury colonists' obsession with the idea of the king and the royal family and how that translated into a "monarchical culture," see McConville, *The King's Three Faces*, 119–36; Richard Bushman, *King and People in Provincial Massachusetts* (Chapel Hill: University of North Carolina Press, 1992), 1–54.

Conclusion

1. *South-Carolina Gazette*, August 10 to August 12, 1784. Earlier that year, the Charleston Library Society announced that its meetings would be held at McCrady's Tavern. *South-Carolina Gazette*, July 1 to July 3, 1784. The *Pennsylvania Packet* published the *Edinburgh Courant*'s disgusted reply to learning of the Society's burning of Ferguson's *Essay on the History of Civil Society*. See *Pennsylvania Packet*, February 24, 1785; Ferrari, "Charity, Folly, and Politics," 50–61.

2. *A Catalogue of the Books Belonging to the Charleston Library Society* (Charleston, SC: A .E. Miller, 1826), iii–vii; James Raven, *London Booksellers and American Customers: Transatlantic Literary Community and the Charleston Library Society,*

1748–1811 (Charleston: University of South Carolina Press, 2002), 1–227; Hart, *Building Charleston*, 78; Yokota, *Unbecoming British*.

3. Hamilton, *Tuesday Club*, 1:241–42, 220; 2:254, 354–55. The historian Jerome J. Nadelhaft argued, "As the war dragged to a close, South Carolina's prewar ruling class attempted to reassert its power and return to the 'normalcy' of governing in the old manner, with its own interest not only understandably paramount but virtually unchallenged. That 'vulgar' lower orders would soon begin to 'inveigh against generous and exalted souls' did not seem to disturb or even occur to the old governing elite." Jerome J. Nadelhaft, *The Disorders of War: The Revolution in South Carolina* (Orono: University of Maine at Orono Press, 1981), 88.

4. *Gazette of the State of South Carolina*, August 19, 1784. As the historian Jackson Turner Main contended, many of the Society's members would have fallen under the umbrella of the "Cosmopolitan" party (eventually the Federalist Party) in their search for deference and order and their ability to find support in urban port centers along the Atlantic seaboard. "Localists" (eventually Anti-Federalists and Jeffersonian Republicans) were generally composed of inland/frontier agrarian men. Jackson Turner Main, *Political Parties before the Constitution* (Chapel Hill: University of North Carolina Press, 1973), xx, 32, 113. See also Woody Holton, *Unruly Americans and the Making of the Constitution* (New York: Hill & Wang, 2007), 179–262; Nash, *The Unknown American Revolution*, 366–422; Richard Hofstadter, *The Idea of a Party System: The Rise of Legitimate Opposition in the United States, 1780–1840* (Berkeley: University of California Press, 1969); Michael Wallace, "Changing Concepts of Party in the United States: New York, 1815–1828," *American Historical Review* 74:2 (December 1968): 453–91.

5. Mark Edward Lender and James Kirby Martin, *Drinking in America: A History* (New York: Free Press, 1982), 36; Nathan O. Hatch, *The Democratization of American Christianity* (New Haven, CT: Yale University Press, 1989). Benjamin Rush, *An Enquiry into the Effects of Ardent Spirits on the Human Mind and Body* (Philadelphia: Benjamin & Thomas Kite, [1784] 1816). As the historian Sarah Hand Meacham has argued, elitist colonists became especially worried about alcohol in the late eighteenth century because tea and coffee finally became more affordable and accessible to the majority of society, making drinking alcohol appear a willful, and thus especially uncivil, decision. Meacham, *Every Home a Distillery*, 120. See also Joanna Cohen, *Luxurious Citizens: The Politics of Consumption in Nineteenth-Century America* (Philadelphia: University of Pennsylvania Press, 2017); Astrid Franke, "Drinking and Democracy in the Early Republic," in *Civilizing and Decivilizing Processes: Figurational Approaches to American Culture*, ed. Christa Buschendorf, Astrid Franke, and Johannes Voelz (Newcastle upon Tyne: Cambridge Scholars Publishing, 2011), 69–73. The Charleston lawyer Timothy Ford noted the supposed evils of such "vice & debauchery" while visiting Philadelphia in 1785. According to Ford, a local gentleman had recently fallen to the pleasures of the tavern: "He unfortunately made such acquaintances as led him to excesses which smothering the seeds of reason & morality soon let loose the reigns of his passions. . . . [I]n this degree of vice a person never stands long at the same point." Indeed, after secretly marrying a "harlot," the young man eventually "took a portion of arsenick & closed a life stained with every vice by a most tragical and exemplary death." Timothy Ford, "Diary of Timothy Ford, 1785–1786, with notes by

Joseph W. Barnell," *South Carolina Historical and Genealogical Magazine* 13:3 (July 1912): 137–38.

6. Main, *Political Parties*, 32, 113, 388.

7. Holton, *Unruly Americans*, 162–212; Charles Beard, *An Economic Interpretation of the Constitution of the United States* (Toronto: Collier Macmillan Canada, 1913). As Jonathan Gienapp argued, "the Constitution was the culmination of the Revolutionary struggle against Great Britain. . . . it has often seemed to neatly capture the ideals and the contradictions of the American Revolution itself." He further noted that "constitutional disputants were in limbo, caught between assumptions that had been ingrained under the British constitution and the new realities of American republicanism." Jonathan Gienapp, *The Second Creation: Fixing the American Constitution in the Founding Era* (Cambridge, MA: Harvard University Press, 2018), 2, 6.

8. James Madison, "The Federalist Number 51: The Structure of the Government Must Furnish the Proper Checks and Balances Between the Different Departments," *Independent Journal*, February 6, 1788; James Madison, "The Federalist Number 37: Concerning the Convention in Devising a Proper Form of Government," *Daily Advertiser*, January 11, 1788.

9. Nelson, *The Royalist Revolution*, 184–233.

10. Thomas Jefferson, *The Writings of Thomas Jefferson: Memoir, Correspondence, and Miscellanies from the Papers of Thomas Jefferson*, vol. 1, 2nd ed., ed. Thomas Jefferson Randolph (New York: Gray and Bowen, 1830), 30; Gordon S. Wood, "Thomas Jefferson, Equality, and the Creation of a Civil Society," *Fordham Law Review* 64:5 (1996): 2133–47.

11. Holton, *Unruly Americans*, 227–78; Paul A. Gilje, *The Road to Mobocracy: Popular Disorder in New York City, 1763–1834* (Chapel Hill: University of North Carolina Press, 1987), 1–40.

12. Jennifer R. Mercieca, *Founding Fictions* (Tuscaloosa: University of Alabama Press, 2010), 1–41, 83–119.

13. Johan David Schoepf, *Travels in the Confederation, 1783–1784*, trans. and ed. Alfred J. Morrison (Philadelphia: William J. Campbell, 1911), 64–65.

14. The *Massachusetts Gazette* published a piece by a "Foreign Spectator" in 1787. In the article, the spectator exclaimed, "The progress of civil society in America has been the most rapid ever known. In two centuries a large continent has been improved by two or three millions of people. . . . Philadelphia, equal to the larger and more elegant cities of Europe, is only an hundred years old." The spectator's celebrations, however, were not without criticism. He noted, "But this civilization is very unequal— An overgrown lad has seldom that symmetry of parts, on which beauty and strength so much depends—The civil fabric of America somewhat resembles the colossus in Nebuchadnezzar's dream, made up of heterogeneous parts: there is brittle clay in the parts that bear up the whole; and too much silver and gold for the simple though excellent metals of copper and iron." "An Essay on the Means of Promoting Federal Sentiments in the United States," *Massachusetts Gazette*, August 31, 1787.

15. Annette Gordon-Reed, *The Hemingses of Monticello: An American Family* (New York: Norton, 2008); Annette Gordon-Reed and Peter Onuf, *"Most Blessed of the Patriarchs": Thomas Jefferson and the Empire of the Imagination* (New York: Liveright, 2017).

16. Schoepf, *Travels in the Confederation*, 205–10. See also Cutterham, *Gentlemen Revolutionaries*, 9–36.

17. McConville, *King's Three Faces*, 306–16; Nelson, *Royalist Revolution*.

18. As a fictional Loyalist in Crèvecoeur's *Sketches of Eighteenth Century America* opined, "Societies, like individuals, have their periods of sickness. Bear this as you would a fever or cold." He continued, "Must I then see my native country conquered by low, illiterate, little tyrants? Must I see the dearest bonds of society torn asunder? All our hopes, our views, our peace, all we had been bred to look on as sacred and useful—must I look upon all these things as indifferent?" Many urban gentlemen would have agreed with such sentiments in their opinions regarding the rise of democracy in early America. St. John de Crèvecoeur, *Sketches of Eighteenth-Century America: More "Letters from an American Farmer,"* ed. Henri L. Bourdin, Ralph H. Gabriel, and Stanley T. Williams (New Haven, CT: Yale University Press, 1825), 279, 283.

19. Hamilton, *Tuesday Club*, 1:241–42, 220; 2:254, 354–55; Edmund S. Morgan, *Inventing the People: The Rise of Popular Sovereignty in England and America* (New York: Norton, 1988), 239–306.

Bibliography

Archives

Historical Society of Pennsylvania (HSP)

Bradford Family Papers

Massachusetts Historical Society (MHS)

Jane Cazneau Account Book (1767–71)
Miscellaneous Bound Manuscripts

New York Historical Society (NYHS)

Account Book, Scotch Presbyterian Church, 1784–98. Manuscript Collections
Andrew Elliot Letters, 1747–77
General Collections
John Lamb Papers
John Tabor Kempe Papers
New York State Supreme Court Collection, 1691–1891
Tryon County New York Committee Records, 1775–94

New York Public Library (NYPL)

Miscellaneous Manuscripts
William Smith Papers

Virginia Historical Society (VHS)

Anne Pattison Account Book (Jan. 7 1743/4–June 13, 1749)

Newspapers
American Weekly Mercury
Boston Evening-Post
Boston Gazette
Boston News-Letter
Boston Post-Boy
Daily Advertiser
Essex Gazette
Gazette of the State of South Carolina
Georgia Gazette
Halifax Gazette
Independent Journal
Massachusetts Gazette
Massachusetts Spy
New-England Courant
New-England Weekly Journal
New-Hampshire Gazette
Newport Mercury
New-York Gazette
New-York Gazette or Weekly Post-Boy
New-York Gazette Revived in the Weekly Post-Boy
New-York Journal
New-York Mercury
New-York Weekly Journal
Norwich Packet
Pennsylvania Chronicle
Pennsylvania Gazette
Pennsylvania Journal
Pennsylvania Ledger
Pennsylvania Packet
Providence Gazette
Rivington's New-York Gazetteer
South Carolina Gazette

Published Primary Sources
"An Act to prevent private Lotteries within this Colony, Pass'd the 25th of November, 1747." In *Documents of the Assembly of the State of New York, Ninety Seventh Session—1874*, vol. 4. Albany: Weed, Parsons, and Company, 1874.

Adams, John. *Diary and Autobiography of John Adams.* Series One. Edited by L. H. Butterfield. Cambridge, MA: Harvard University Press, 1961.

Addison, Joseph. *Spectator* No. 10, March 12, 1711.

Anno regni Georgii II Regis Magnae Britanniae, Franciae, & Hiberniae, quindecimo. At a sessions of General Assembly begun and holden at the city of New-York, the fifteenth day of September 1741, and continued to the twenty seventh day of November following, during which time the following acts were passed . . . New York: William Bradford, 1741.

Anonymous. "*The Rules and Orders of the Coffee-House,*" *A Brief Description of the Excellent Vertues of that Sober and Wholesome Drink, called coffee.* London: Paul Greenwood, 1674.

"Archibald Hinshelwood to Joshua Mauger, Halifax, Nova Scotia, August 19, 1765." Gilder Lehrman Institute of American History, accessed May 14, 2014, https://www.gilderlehrman.org.

At a Court, held at Punch-Hall, in the Colony of Bacchus, The Indictment and Tryal of Sir Richard Rum. Boston: n.p., 1724.

Bacon, Francis. *Essays Moral, Economical, and Political. By Francis Bacon, Baron of Verulam, and Viscount St. Albans.* London: J. Cundee, 1800.

Barclay, Patrick. *The Universal Traveller; or, A Complete Account of the Most Remarkable Voyages and Travels.* London: Printed for J. Purser and T. Read, 1735.

Bernard, Francis. *The Papers of Francis Bernard Governor of Colonial Massachusetts, 1760–1769,* vol. 2: *1764–65.* Edited by Colin Nicolson. Boston: Colonial Society of Massachusetts, 2012.

Biddulph, William. "A Letter Written from *Allepo* in *Syria Comagena.*" In *Travels of Certaine Englishmen into Africa, Asia, Troy, Bythinia, Thracia, and to the Black Sea.* Edited by Theophilus Lavender. London: Th. Haveland for W. Aspley, 1609.

Birket, James. *Some Cursory Remarks Made by James Birket in his Voyage to North America, 1750–1751.* New Haven, CT: Yale University Press, 1916.

Black, William. "Journal of William Black, 1744." *Pennsylvania Magazine of History and Biography* 1:2 (1877): 117–32.

———. "Journal of William Black, 1744 (continued)." *Pennsylvania Magazine of History and Biography* 1:4 (1877): 404–19.

Blount, Sir Henry. *A Voyage into the Levant.* London: By J.C. for William Crook, 1671.

Boswell, James. *Boswell's London Journal, 1762–1763.* Edited by Frederick A. Pottle. New Haven, CT: Yale University Press, 1950.

Bradford, William. *Books Just Imported from London.* Philadelphia: William Bradford, 1755.

Burnaby, Andrew. *Travels Through the Middle Settlements in North America in the Years 1759 and 1760.* Dublin: R. Marchbank, 1775.

Butterfield, L. H., ed. *Letters of Benjamin Rush*. 2 vols. Philadelphia: American Philosophical Society, 1951.

Byrd II, William. *The Secret Diary of William Byrd of Westover, 1709–1712*. Edited by Louis B. Wright and Marion Tinling. Richmond, VA: Dietz Press, 1941.

———. *Another Secret Diary of William Byrd of Westover, 1739–1741: With Letters & Literary Exercises, 1696–1726*. Edited by Maude H. Woodfin. Richmond: The Dietz Press, 1942.

Caplan, Niel. "Some Unpublished Letters of Benjamin Colman, 1717–25." *Massachusetts Historical Society Proceedings* 77:1 (1965): 137.

A Catalogue of the Books Belonging to the Charleston Library Society. Charleston: A. E. Miller, 1826.

Chalmers, Lionel. *An Account of the Weather and Diseases of South-Carolina*. 2 vols. London: Edward and Charles Dilly, 1776.

Character of a Coffee-House with the Symptoms of a Town-Wit. London: Jonathan Edwin, 1673.

The Charters and Acts of Assembly of the Province of Pennsylvania. 2 vols. Philadelphia: Peter Miller, 1762.

Colden, Cadwallader. *The Letters and Papers of Cadwallader Colden*, vol. 3: *1743–1747*. New York: New York Historical Society, 1919.

———. *The Letters and Papers of Cadwallader Colden*, vol. 5: *1755–1760*. New York: New York Historical Society, 1923.

———. *The Letters and Papers of Cadwallader Colden*, vol. 7: *1765–1775*. New York: New York Historical Society, 1923.

Coleman, Kenneth, and Milton Ready, eds. *The Colonial Records of the State of Georgia, 1732–1782*. Vol. 18. New York: AMS, 1970.

Collections of the Massachusetts Historical Society, Volume V of the Third Series. Boston: John H. Eastburn, 1836.

Conductor Generalis, or the Office, Duty and Authority of Justices of the Peace. 2nd ed. New York: J. Parker, 1749.

The Connoisseur. Vol. 2, 5th ed. Oxford: R. Baldwin, 1767.

Cresswell, Nicholas. *The Journal of Nicholas Cresswell, 1774–1777*. London: Jonathan Cape, 1925.

Danckaerts, Jasper. *Journal of Jasper Danckaerts, 1679–1680*. Edited by Bartlett Burleigh James and J. Franklin Jameson. New York: Charles Scribner's Sons, 1913.

Davies, David. *The Case of Labourers in Husbandry*. London: G. G. and J. Robinson, 1795.

De Britaine, William. *The Dutch Usurpation*. London: Jonathan Edwin, 1672.

De Chastellux, Marquis. *Travels in North America, in the Years 1780, 1781, and 1782*. New York: White, Gallaher, & White, 1827.

"Declaration and Resolves of the First Continental Congress, October 14,

1774." Avalon Project, Documents in Law, History and Diplomacy, accessed March 11, 2017, http://avalon.law.yale.edu.

De Crèvecoeur, St. John. *Sketches of Eighteenth-Century America: More "Letters from an American Farmer."* Edited by Henri L. Bourdin, Ralph H. Gabriel, and Stanley T. Williams. New Haven, CT: Yale University Press, 1825.

De Jacourt, Louis. Natural Equality, Encyclopedia Project. Translated by Stephen J. Gendzier, accessed June 12, 2017, http://hdl.handle.net.

DeVries, David Pietersz. *Voyages from Holland to America, 1632-1634.* Translated by Henry C. Murphy. New York: New York Historical Society, 1853.

Dexter, Franklin B., ed. "A Selection from the Correspondence and Miscellaneous Papers of Jared Ingersoll." In *Papers of the New Haven Colony Historical Society,* vol. 9, 201–472. New Haven, VT: Printed for the Society, 1918.

Drinker, Elizabeth. *The Diary of Elizabeth Drinker.* Vol. 1. Edited by Elaine Forman Crane. Boston: Northeastern University Press, 1991.

———. *Extracts from the Journal of Elizabeth Drinker, from 1759 to 1807, A.D.* Edited by Henry D. Biddle. Philadelphia: J. B. Lippincott Company, 1889.

Du Marsais, Cesar Chesneau. "Philosopher." In The Encyclopedia of Diderot & d'Alembert Collaborative Translation Project, translated by Dena Goodman. Ann Arbor: University of Michigan Library, 2002, accessed June 12, 2017, http://hdl.handle.net

Edis, William. *Letters from America, Historical and Descriptive, Comprising Occurrences from 1769 to 1777.* London: William Edis, 1792.

The Emblem of Ingratitude: A True Relation of the Unjust, Cruel and Barbarous Proceedings Against the English at Amboyna. London: William Hope, 1672.

Encyclopédie ou Dictionnaire raisonné des sciences, des arts et des métiers. Paris, 1751, 1755, 1765.

Felltham, Owen. *A Brief Character of the Low Countries.* London: Henry Seile, 1652.

Ferguson, Adam. *An Essay on the History of Civil Society.* 5th ed. London: T. Cadell, 1767.

Fontaine, John. *The Journal of John Fontaine: An Irish Huguenot Son in Spain and Virginia, 1710–1719.* Edited by Edward Porter Alexander. Charlottesville: University of Virginia Press, 1972.

Ford, Paul Leicester, ed. "The Writings of John Dickinson, Vol. I: Political Writings, 1764–1774." In *Memoirs of the Historical Society of Pennsylvania* 14, 1–508. Philadelphia: M'Carty and Davis, 1895.

Ford, Timothy. "Diary of Timothy Ford, 1785–1786, with notes by Joseph W. Barnell." *South Carolina Historical and Genealogical Magazine* 13:3 (July 1912): 132–47.

Forrester, James. *The Polite Philosopher; or, an Essay on that Art, which Makes a Man happy in Himself, and agreeable to Others.* London; repr. New York: J. Parker and W. Weyman, 1758.

Franklin, Benjamin. *The Autobiography of Benjamin Franklin*. Boston: Houghton Mifflin & Company, 1906.

———. *Memoirs of the Life and Writings of Benjamin Franklin*, Volume Two. London: Henry Colburn, 1818.

———. *The Papers of Benjamin Franklin, Volume Two, January 1, 1735, through December 31, 1744*. Edited by Leonard W. Labaree. New Haven, CT: Yale University Press, 1961.

———. *The Papers of Benjamin Franklin, Volume Four, July 1, 1750, through June 30, 1753*. Edited by Leonard W. Labaree. New Haven, CT: Yale University Press, 1961.

———. *The Papers of Benjamin Franklin, Volume Ten, January 1, 1762, through December 31, 1763*. Edited by Leonard W. Labaree. New Haven, CT: Yale University Press, 1959.

———. *A Proposal for Promoting Useful Knowledge among the British Plantations in America*. Philadelphia: Benjamin Franklin, 1743.

———. *Writings*. New York: Library of America, 1987.

Gadsden, Christopher. *The Writings of Christopher Gadsden, 1746–1805*. Edited by Richard Walsh. Columbia: University of South Carolina Press, 1966.

"Garish Harsin to William Radclift, February 13, 1776." In Mercantile Library Association, *New York City During the American Revolution*, 85–87. New York: Privately Printed for the Association, 1861.

Gibbon, Edward. *The History of the Decline and Fall of the Roman Empire*. London: Strahan & Cadell, 1776.

Goelet, Francis. *The Voyages and Travels of Francis Goelet, 1746–1758*. Edited by Kenneth Scott. London: Queen's College Press, 1970.

Gregory, William. "A Scotchman's Journey in New England in 1771." *New England Magazine* 12:3 (May 1895): 343–52.

Gruber, Ira D. *John Peebles' American War: The Diary of a Scottish Grenadier, 1776–1782*. Mechanicsburg, PA: Stackpole Books for the Army Records Society, 1998.

Hamilton, Alexander. *Gentleman's Progress: The Itinerarium of Dr. Alexander Hamilton, 1744*. Edited by Carl Bridenbaugh. Chapel Hill: University of North Carolina Press, 1948.

———. *The History of the Ancient and Honorable Tuesday Club*. 2 vols. Edited by Robert Micklus. Chapel Hill: University of North Carolina Press, 1990.

Harrower, John. "Diary of John Harrower, 1773–1776." *American Historical Review* 6:1 (October 1900): 65–107.

Hening, William Waller. *The Statutes at Large; Being a Collection of All the Laws of Virginia, From the First Session of the Legislature, in the Year 1619*. Vol. 5. Richmond: R. & W. G. Bartow, 1819.

Hilliad Magna, Being the Life and Adventures of Moll Placket-Hole, With a Prefatory Dialogue, and Some Moral Reflections, on the Whole. Philadelphia: Anthony Armbruster, 1765.

Hoadly, Charles J., ed. *The Public Records of the Colony of Connecticut, from October 1706 to October 1716*. Hartford: Case, Lockwood and Brainard, 1870.

———, ed. *The Public Records of the Colony of Connecticut, from May 1757 to March 1762*. Hartford: Case, Lockwood and Brainard, 1880.

Hobbes, Thomas. *Leviathan; or, the Matter, Form, and Power of a Common-Wealth Ecclesiastical and Civil*. London: Andrew Crooke, 1651.

Hulton, Ann. *Letters of a Loyalist Lady*. Cambridge, MA: Harvard University Press, 1927.

Hutchinson, Thomas. *The Diary and Letters of Thomas Hutchinson*. Edited by Peter O. Hutchinson. Boston: Houghton, Mifflin, 1884.

Hutton, William. *An History of Birmingham*. 3rd ed. London: Thomas Pearson, 1795.

"Inventory of Estate of Henry Wetherburn, March 16, 1761." Colonial Williamsburg Digital Library, accessed March 1, 2018, http://research.history.org.

Jefferson, Thomas. *The Writings of Thomas Jefferson: Memoir, Correspondence, and Miscellanies from the Papers of Thomas Jefferson*. 2nd ed. Vol. 1. Edited by Thomas Jefferson Randolph. New York: Gray and Bowen, 1830.

Jennings, John Melville, ed. "From the Society's Collections: The Lamentations of John Grymes in Four Letters Addressed to William Blathwayt." *Virginia Magazine of History and Biography* 58:3 (July 1950): 388–95.

Johnston, Elizabeth Lichtenstein. *Recollections of a Georgia Loyalist*. Edited by Rev. Arthur Wentworth Eaton. New York: M. F. Mansfield & Co., 1901.

Jones, Thomas. *History of the New York During the Revolutionary War*. Vol. 1. Edited by Edward Floyd De Lancey. New York: New York Historical Society, 1879.

Josselyn, John. *John Josselyn, a Colonial Traveler: A Critical Edition of Two Voyages to New England*. Edited by Paul Lindholdt. Hanover, NH: University Press of New England, 1988.

"Journal of Alexander Macaulay." *William and Mary Quarterly* 11:3 (January 1903): 180–91.

"Journal of a French Traveller in the Colonies, 1765, II." *American Historical Review* 27:1 (October 1921): 70–89.

"Journal of Josiah Quincy Jr., August 26, 1765." *Proceedings of the Massachusetts Historical Society* 4 (1860): 22–51.

Kalm, Peter. "Peter Kalm, Scientist from Sweden (Except from his journal, *En Resa til Norra America (1736–61)*." In *This Was America*, edited by Oscar Handlin, 14–33. Cambridge, MA: Harvard University Press, 1949.

———. *Peter Kalm's Travels in North America: The English Version of 1770*. Edited by Adolph B. Benson. New York: Wilson-Erickson, 1937.

Keith, Sir William. *The Observator's Trip to America, in a Dialogue Between the Observator and his Country-man Roger.* Philadelphia: Andrew Bradford, 1726.

Kendall, John. *The Life of Thomas Story, Carefully Abridged: In Which the Principal Occurrences and the Most Interesting Remarks and Observations are Retained.* London: Isaac Thompson, 1786.

Knox, John. *The American Crisis, by a Citizen of the World; Inscribed to Those Members of the Community, Vulgarly Named Patriots.* London: W. Flexney, 1777.

"Leopold Mozart to Lorenz Hagenauer, 28 May 1764, London." In *Mozart: A Life in Letters,* edited by Cliff Eisen, translated by Stewart Spencer, 3–39. New York: Penguin Books, 2006.

"'Let Him Starve and Be Damned!': Nathaniel Gardiner of Rhode Island Experiences Barbarities En Route to Jail in Falmouth." In *The Price of Loyalty: Tory Writings from the Revolutionary Era,* edited by Catherine S. Crary, 206–8. New York: McGraw-Hill, 1973.

"Letter of Samuel Prince, 1689." In *Narratives of the Insurrections, 1675–1690,* edited by Charles M. Andrews, 186–90. New York: Charles Scribner's Sons, 1915.

Livingston, William. *The Independent Reflector, or Weekly Essays on Sundry Important Subjects More particularly adapted to the Province of New-York.* Edited by Milton M. Klein. Cambridge, MA: Harvard University Press, 1963.

The London Magazine: And Monthly Chronologer of 1736. London: C. Ackers, 1736.

Mackraby, Alexander. "Philadelphia Society before the Revolution: Extracts from the Letters of Alexander Mackraby to Sir Philip Francis." *Pennsylvania History of History and Biography* 11 (1887); *Pennsylvania Magazine of History and Biography* 11 (1887): 267–87.

"March the 19th 1711/12, An Inventory of Mr. Thos. Whitbys decd. Estate of York County." Colonial Williamsburg Digital Library, accessed March 23, 2016

Marshall, Christopher. *Passages from the Diary of Christopher Marshall, Kept in Philadelphia and Lancaster During the American Revolution,* vol. 1: 1774–1777. Edited by William Duane. Philadelphia: Hazard & Mitchell, 1839–49.

Maty, M., ed. *Miscellaneous Works of the Late Philip Dormer Stanhope, Earl of Chesterfield.* 3 vols. Dublin: W. Watson, 1777.

Mayhew, Jonathan. *The Snare Broken; A Thanksgiving Discourse, Preached at the Desire of the West Church in Boston, N.E. Friday May 23, 1766. Occasioned by the Repeal of the Stamp-Act.* Boston: R. & S. Draper, 1766.

Mittelberger, Gottlieb. *Gottlieb Mittelberger's Journey to Pennsylvania in the Year 1750 and Return to Germany in the Year 1754.* Edited by Carl Theo. Eben. Philadelphia: John Jos McVey, 1898.

M.P. *Character of Coffee and Coffee-Houses.* London: John Starkey, 1661.

M'Robert, Patrick. *A Tour Through Part of the North Provinces of America: Being, A Series of Letters Wrote on the Spot, in the Years 1774, & 1775. To Which Are Annex'd, Tables, Shewing the Roads, the Value of Coins, Rates of Stages, &c.* Philadelphia: Historical Society of Pennsylvania, 1935.

Muhlenberg, Henry Melchior. *The Journals of Henry Melchior Muhlenberg.* Vol. 1. Translated by Theodore G. Tappert and John W. Doberstein. Philadelphia: Muhlenberg Press, 1942.

Mylne, William. *Travels in the Colonies in 1773–1775, Described in the Letters of William Mylne.* Edited by Ted Ruddock. Athens: University of Georgia Press, 1993.

Nugent, Thomas. *The Ground Tour.* London: S. Birt, 1749.

"Orb and Scepter: Joel Stone Determines 'Sooner to Perish in the General Calamity than Abet . . . the Enemies of the British Constitution." In *The Price of Loyalty: Tory Writings from the Revolutionary Era,* edited by Catherine S. Crary, 161–65. New York: McGraw-Hill, 1973.

Owens, Richard. "Essays First Published in the *World,* 1753–1756." In *The Works of Richard Cambrige, Esq: Including Several Pieces Never Before Published,* edited by George Owen Cambridge. London: L. Hansard, 1803.

Paine, Thomas. *The American Crisis,* Chapter VII. London, 1776–1783

———. *Common Sense.* New York: Eckler, 1918.

———. *A Letter Addressed to the Abbe Raynal, On the Affairs of North America; in which the mistakes in the Abbe's account of the Revolution of America are corrected and cleared up.* Rockville, MD: Manor, 2008.

"Pennsylvania Laws, Statutes, etc., 1762." In *The Charters and Acts of Assembly [Octavio Edition].* Vol. 2. Philadelphia: Miller, 1762.

Pepys, Samuel. *The Diary of Samuel Pepys.* Vol. 2. Edited by Henry B. Wheatley. London: George Bell and Sons, 1893.

The Political Register, and Impartial Review of New Books, For 1769. Volume the Fifth. London: Printed for Henry Beevor in Little-Britain, 1769.

Pope, Alexander. *The Rape of the Lock: Canto 3.* In *The Complete Poetical Works of Alexander Pope,* edited by Henry Walcott, 92–95. Boston: Houghton Mifflin & Co., 1903.

Price, John. *The Advantages of Unity Considered, in a Sermon Preach'd Before the Antient and Honourable Society of Free and Accepted Masons.* Bristol: Samuel Worrall, 1748.

Proceedings of the Convention of the province of Maryland, held at the city of Annapolis, on Thursday the seventh of December, 1775. Annapolis, MD: Frederick Green, 1775.

"Proper Ingredients to Make a Modern Beau." In Abraham Weatherwise, *Father Abraham's Almanack for 1759.* Philadelphia: Abraham Weatherwise, 1759.

Quincy, Josiah, Jr. *Observations on the Act of Parliament, Commonly Called the*

Boston Port-Bill; with Thoughts on Civil Society and Standing Armies. Philadelphia: John Sparhawk, 1774.

"R. Christie, Jr. to Jenifer, December 10, 1776." Journal and Correspondence of the Maryland Council of Safety, vol. 12, p. 517. Archives of Maryland Online, accessed March 12, 2017, http://msa.maryland.gov.

The Register of Pennsylvania, Vol. II, No. 16 Philadelphia, Nov. 1, 1828. Edited by Samuel Hazard. Philadelphia: W. F. Geddes, 1828.

Rousseau, Jean-Jacques. *On the Social Contract; or Principles of Political Right.* Translated by G. D. H. Cole. London: J. M. Dent, 1913.

Rowe, John. *Letters and Diary of John Rowe, Boston Merchant, 1759–1762, 1764–1779.* Edited by Anne Rowe Cunningham. Boston: W. B. Clarke, 1903.

Rush, Benjamin. *An Enquiry into the Effects of Ardent Spirits on the Human Mind and Body.* Philadelphia: Benjamin & Thomas Kite, 1816.

Sandys, George. *A Relation of a Journey Begun in An. Dom 1610.* London: W. Barrett, 1615.

A Satyrical Description of Commencement. Calculated to the Meridian of Cambridge in New-England. Boston: Heart and Crown, 1718.

Schoepf, Johan David. *Travels in the Confederation, 1783–1784.* Translated and edited by Alfred J. Morrison. Philadelphia: William J. Campbell, 1911.

Scull, G. D., ed. "Montresor Journals." In *Collections of the New-York Historical Society*, vol. 14, 1–420. New York: New York Historical Society, 1881.

"A Short Account of the Library." In *A Catalogue of Books Belonging to the Library Company of Philadelphia.* Philadelphia: B. Franklin, 1741.

Smith, Adam. *An Enquiry into the Wealth of Nations.* Edited by Robert Reich. New York: Random House, 2000.

Smith, John. *England's Improvement Reviv[e]d.* London: Tho. Newcomb, 1673.

Smith, William, Jr. *The History of the Province of New-York: First Discovery to the Year 1732.* London: Thomas Wilcox, 1757.

Sons of Liberty. "New York, July 7, 1769: At this Alarming Crisis . . . " New York: n.p., 1769. Early American Imprints, Series 1, Evans 11379.

Sparks, Jared, ed. *The Life of Gouverneur Morris, with Selections from His Correspondence and Miscellaneous Papers.* 3 vols. Boston: Gray & Bowen, 1832.

Steele, Richard. *Spectator* No. 49, April 26, 1711.

Temple, William. *Observations Upon the United Provinces of the Netherlands.* In *The Works of Sir William Temple, Bart.* Complete in 4 vols. London: F. C. and J. Rivington, 1814.

Thomann, Gallus. *Colonial Liquor Laws.* New York: United States Brewers' Association, 1887.

"Thomas Hutchinson Recounts the Reaction to the Stamp Act in Boston (1765)." In *The History of the Colony and Province of Massachusetts-Bay*, vol. 3, edited by Lawrence Shaw Mayo, 86–90. Cambridge, MA: Harvard University Press, 1936.

Van Schaack, Henry Cruger. *Memoirs of the Life of Henry Van Schaack*. Chicago: A. C. McClurg & Company, 1892.

Volney, Constantin-Francois. *Lectures on history, Delivered in the Normal School of Paris, by C.F. Volney, Author of the Ruins of Empires, Member of the National Institute of France, &c. &c.* London: Oriental Press, 1800.

Ward, Edward. *A Compleat and Humourous Account of All the Remarkable Clubs and Societies in the Cities of London and Westminster*. London: J. Wren, 1667–1731.

Wilkes, John. *The North Briton, 45, Saturday, April 23, 1763*. Constitution Society, accessed July 27, 2018, http://www.constitution.org.

"William Almy to Elisha Story, August 29, 1765." *Proceedings of the Massachusetts Historical Society* 55:1 (October 1921–June 1922): 235–37.

"William Pitt's Defense of the American Colonies." Colonial Williamsburg Foundation, accessed July 26, 2018, http://www.history.org.

Woodmason, Charles. *The Carolina Backcountry on the Eve of the Revolution: The Journal and Other Writings of Charles Woodmason, Anglican Itinerant*. Edited by Richard J. Hooker. Chapel Hill: University of North Carolina Press, 1953.

The Works of Lord Chesterfield, Including his Letters to His Son. New York: Harper & Brothers, 1853.

"The Wormeley Family (Continued)." *Virginia Magazine of History and Biography* 36:1 (January 1928): 98–101.

Young, Arthur. *Travels, During the Years 1787–1788 and 1789 Undertaken more Particularly with a View of Ascertaining the Cultivation, Wealth, Resources and National Prosperity, of the Kingdom of France*. London: George Bell and Sons, 1792.

Secondary Sources

Abu-Lughod, Janet L. *Before European Hegemony: The World System, A.D. 1250–1350*. Oxford: Oxford University Press, 1989.

Amussen, Susan Dwyer. *An Ordered Society: Gender and Class in Early Modern England*. Oxford: Basil Blackwell, 1988.

Anderson, Benedict. *Imagined Communities: Reflections on the Origin and Spread of Nationalism*. London: Verso, 2006.

Anderson, Jennifer L. *Mahogany: The Costs of Luxury in Early America*. Cambridge, MA: Harvard University Press, 2012.

Andrlik, Todd. "Ages of Revolution: How Old Were They on July 4, 1776?" *Journal of the American Revolution*, accessed July 11, 2018.

Anishanslin, Zara. *Portrait of a Woman in Silk: Hidden Histories of the British Atlantic World*. New Haven, CT: Yale University Press, 2016.

The Annual Report of the Library Company of Philadelphia for the Year 1964. Philadelphia: Library Company of Philadelphia, 1964.

Archer, Richard. *As if an Enemy's Country: The British Occupation of Boston and the Origins of the Revolution*. Oxford: Oxford University Press, 2010.

At the Instance of Benjamin Franklin: A Brief History of the Library Company of Philadelphia. Philadelphia: Library Company of Philadelphia, 1995.

Augustine, Jacqueline Anne. "Kant and the Moral Necessity of Civil Society." PhD dissertation, University of Rochester, 1997.

Bailyn, Bernard. *The Ideological Origins of the American Revolution: Enlarged Edition*. Cambridge, MA: Harvard University Press, 1992.

Barck, Oscar Theodore. *New York City during the War for Independence: With Special Reference to the Period of British Occupation*. New York: Columbia University Press, 1931.

Barry, Jonathan. "Civility and Civic Culture in Early Modern England: The Meanings of Urban Freedom." In *Civil Histories: Essays Presented to Sir Keith Thomas*, edited by Peter Burke, Brian Harrison, and Paul Slack, 181–96. Oxford: Oxford University Press, 2000.

———. Introduction to *The Middling Sort of People: Culture, Society and Politics in England, 1550–1800*, edited by Jonathan Barry and Christopher Brooks, 1–27. New York: St. Martin's Press, 1994.

Baumgarten, Linda. *What Clothes Reveal: The Language of Clothing in Colonial and Federal America*. New Haven, CT: Yale University Press, 2002.

Bax, Marcel and Dániel Z. Kádár. "The Historical Understanding of Historical (Im)politeness." *Journal of Historical Pragmatics* 12:1–2 (2011): 1–24.

Bayles, M. Harrison. *Old Taverns of New York*. New York: Frank Allaben Genealogical Company, 1915.

Bayne-Powell, Rosamond. *Travellers in Eighteenth-Century England*. London: Benjamin Blom, 1951.

Beard, Charles. *An Economic Interpretation of the Constitution of the United States*. Toronto: Collier Macmillan Canada, 1913.

Beattie, John. "Violence and Society in Early-Modern England." In *Perspectives in Criminal Law: Essays in Honour of John LI. J. Edwards*, edited by A. N. Doob and E. L. Greenspan, 36–60. Aurora, ON: Canada Law Book, 1985.

Becker, Marvin B. *The Emergence of Civil Society in the Eighteenth Century: A Privileged Moment in the History of England, Scotland, and France*. Bloomington: Indiana University Press, 1994.

Bejan, Teresa M. *Mere Civility: Disagreements and the Limits of Toleration*. Cambridge, MA: Harvard University Press, 2017.

Berlin, Ira. *Many Thousands Gone: The First Two Centuries of Slavery in North America*. Cambridge, MA: Harvard University Press, 1998.

Berry, Helen. "Rethinking Politeness in Eighteenth-Century England: Moll King's Coffee House and the Significance of 'Flash Talk': The Alexander Prize Lecture." *Transactions of the Royal Historical Society* 11:1 (2001): 65–81.

Bickham, Troy. "Eating the Empire: Intersections of Food, Cookery, and

Imperialism in Eighteenth-Century Britain." *Past & Present* 198:1 (February 2008): 71–109.

———. *Savages within the Empire: Representations of American Indians in Eighteenth-Century Britain.* Oxford: Oxford University Press, 2005.

Blake, John. *Public Health in the Town of Boston, 1630–1822.* Cambridge, MA: President and Fellows of Harvard College, 1959.

Bloch, Ruth H. "Inside and Outside the Public Sphere." *William and Mary Quarterly* 62:1 (January 2005): 99–106.

Borsay, Peter. *The English Urban Renaissance: Culture and Society in the Provincial Town, 1660–1770.* Oxford: Clarendon Press, 1991.

Breen, T. H. *American Insurgents, American Patriots: The Revolution of the People.* New York: Hill and Wang, 2010.

———. "'Baubles of Britain': The American and Consumer Revolutions of the Eighteenth Century." *Past & Present* 119:1 (May 1988): 73–104.

———. "An Empire of Goods: The Anglicization of Colonial America, 1690–1776." *Journal of British Studies* 25:4 (October 1986): 467–99.

———. "Ideology and Nationalism on the Eve of the American Revolution: Revisions Once More in Need of Revising." *Journal of American History* 84:1 (June 1997): 13–39.

———. "What Time Was the American Revolution? Reflections on a Familiar Narrative." In *Experiencing Empire: Power, People, and Revolution in Early America*, edited by Patrick Griffin, 233–46. Charlottesville: University of Virginia Press, 2017.

Breen, T. H., and Timothy Hall. "Structuring Provincial Imagination: The Rhetoric and Experience of Social Change in Eighteenth-Century New England." *American Historical Review* 103:5 (December 1998): 1411–39.

Brennan, Thomas. "Taverns and the Public Sphere in the French Revolution." In *Alcohol: A Social and Cultural History*, edited by Mack P. Holt, 107–20. Oxford: Berg, 2006.

Brennan, Thomas E., David Hancock, and Michelle McDonald, eds. *Public Drinking in the Early Modern World: Voices from the Tavern, 1500–1800*, vol. 4. London: Pickering & Chatto, 2011.

Breslaw, Elaine. *Dr. Alexander Hamilton and Provincial America: Expanding the Orbit of Scottish Culture.* Baton Rouge: Louisiana State University Press, 2008.

Bridenbaugh, Carl. *Cities in Revolt: Urban Life in America, 1743–1776.* Oxford: Oxford University Press, 1955.

———. *Cities in the Wilderness: The First Century of Urban Life in America, 1625–1742.* Oxford: Oxford University Press, 1938.

———. *Early Americans.* Oxford: Oxford University Press, 1981.

Brooke, John L. *Columbia Rising: Civil Life on the Upper Hudson from the Revolution to the Age of Jackson.* Chapel Hill: University of North Carolina Press, 2010.

Brown, Garrett Wallace. *Grounding Cosmopolitanism: From Kant to the Idea of a Cosmopolitan Constitution*. Edinburgh: Edinburgh University Press, 2009.

Brown, James R. "The Landscape of Drink: Inns, Taverns and Alehouses in Early Modern Southampton." PhD dissertation, University of Warwick, 2007.

Brown, Kathleen. *Foul Bodies: Cleanliness in Early America*. New Haven, CT: Yale University Press, 2009.

Brown, Robert E. *Middle-Class Democracy and the Revolution in Massachusetts, 1691–1780*. Ithaca, NY: Cornell University Press, 1955.

Bryson, Anna. *From Courtesy to Civility: Changing Codes of Conduct in Early Modern England*. Oxford: Clarendon Press, 1998.

Buckley, Peter. "To the Opera House: Culture and Society in New York City, 1820–1860." PhD dissertation, SUNY Stony Brook, 1984.

Bullock, Steven C. "A Mumper among the Gentle: Tom Bell, Colonial Confidence Man." *William and Mary Quarterly* 55:2 (April 1998): 231–58.

———. *Tea Sets and Tyranny: The Politics of Politeness in Early America*. Philadelphia: University of Pennsylvania Press, 2017.

Burke, Peter. "A Civil Tongue: Language and Politeness in Early Modern Europe." In *Civil Histories: Essays Presented to Sir Keith Thomas*, edited by Peter Burke, Brian Harrison, and Paul Slack, 31–48. Oxford: Oxford University Press, 2000.

Burke, Peter, Brian Harrison, and Paul Slack. Preface to *Civil Histories: Essays Presented to Sir Keith Thomas*, edited by Peter Burke, Brian Harrison, and Paul Slack, v–viii. Oxford: Oxford University Press, 2000.

Burnard, Trevor. *Planters, Merchants, and Slaves: Plantation Societies in British America, 1650–1820*. Chicago: University of Chicago Press, 2015.

Burnard, Trevor, and Emma Hart. "Kingston, Jamaica, and Charleston, South Carolina: A New Look at Comparative Urbanization in Plantation Colonial British America." *Journal of Urban History* 39:2 (March 2013): 214–34.

Burton, Kristen D. "Intoxication and Empire: Distilled Spirits and the Creation of Addiction in the Early Modern British Atlantic." PhD dissertation, University of Texas at Arlington, 2015.

Bushman, Richard. "American High-Style and Vernacular Cultures." In *Colonial British America: Essays in the New History of the Early Modern Era*, edited by Jack P. Greene and J. R. Pole, 345–83. Baltimore, MD: Johns Hopkins University Press, 1984.

———. *King and People in Provincial Massachusetts*. Chapel Hill: University of North Carolina Press, 1992.

———. *The Refinement of America: Persons, Houses, Cities*. New York: Vintage Books, 1992.

Butler, Jon. *Becoming America: The Revolution before 1776*. Cambridge, MA: Harvard University Press, 2000.

Camp, Stephanie. *Closer to Freedom: Enslaved Women and Everyday Resistance in the Plantation South.* Chapel Hill: University of North Carolina Press, 2004.

Carmichael, Zachary Andrew. "Fit Men: New England Tavern Keepers, 1620–1720." Master's thesis, Miami University, 2009.

Carp, Benjamin L. *Defiance of the Patriots: The Boston Tea Party and the Making of America.* New Haven, CT: Yale University Press, 2010.

———. "Fire of Liberty: Firefighters, Urban Voluntary Culture, and the Revolutionary Movement." *William and Mary Quarterly* 58:4 (October 2001): 781–818.

———. "'Fix'd almost among Strangers': Charleston's Quaker Merchants and the Limits of Cosmopolitanism." *William and Mary Quarterly* 74:1 (January 2017): 77–108.

———. *Rebels Rising: Cities and the American Revolution.* Oxford: Oxford University Press, 2007.

Carr, Lois Green, and Lorena S. Walsh. "The Standard of Living in the Colonial Chesapeake." *William and Mary Quarterly* 45:1 (January 1988): 135–59.

Cash, Arthur. *John Wilkes: The Scandalous Father of Civil Liberty.* New Haven, CT: Yale University Press, 2008.

Cheney, Edward P. *History of the University of Pennsylvania, 1740–1940.* Philadelphia: University of Pennsylvania Press, 1940.

Choppin Roney, Jessica. *Governed by a Spirit of Opposition: The Origins of American Political Practice in Colonial Philadelphia.* Baltimore, MD: Johns Hopkins University Press, 2014.

Chopra, Ruma. "Printer Hugh Gaine Crosses and Re-Crosses the Hudson." *New York History* 90:4 (Fall 2009): 275–76.

Clark, J. C. D. *English Society, 1660–1832: Religion, Ideology and Politics during the Ancien Regime.* 2nd ed. Cambridge: Cambridge University Press, 2000.

———. *Thomas Paine: Britain, America, and France in the Age of Enlightenment and Revolution.* Oxford: Oxford University Press, 2018.

Clark, Peter. *British Clubs and Societies, 1580–1800: The Origins of an Associational World.* Oxford: Oxford University Press, 2000.

———. *The English Alehouse: A Social History 1200–1830.* New York: Longman, 1983.

Classen, Constance, David Howes, and Anthony Synnott. *Aroma: The Cultural History of Smell.* London: Routledge, 1994.

Claydon, Tony. *Europe and the Making of England, 1660–1760.* Cambridge: Cambridge University Press, 2007.

Cohen, Joanna. *Luxurious Citizens: The Politics of Consumption in Nineteenth-Century America.* Philadelphia: University of Pennsylvania Press, 2017.

Colley, Linda. *Britons: Forging the Nation, 1707–1837.* New Haven, CT: Yale University Press, 1992.

Combs, Cindy C. *Terrorism in the Twenty-First Century.* Upper Saddle River, NJ: Pearson Press, 2012.

Conroy, David W. *In Public Houses: Drink and the Revolution of Authority in Colonial Massachusetts.* Chapel Hill: University of North Carolina Press, 1995.

———. Review of *Taverns and Drinking in Early America*, by Sharon Salinger. *New England Quarterly* 76:4 (December 2003): 654–57.

Cott, Nancy F., ed. *History of Women in the United States: Historical Articles on Women's Lives and Activities*, vol. 9: *Prostitution.* Munich: K. G. Sauer, 1993.

Countryman, Edward. "The Problem of the Early American Crowd." *Journal of American Studies* 7:1 (April 1973): 77–90.

Cowan, Brian. "Publicity and Privacy in the History of the British Coffee-house." *History Compass* 5:4 (June 2007): 1180–1213.

———. *Social Life of Coffee: The Emergence of the British Coffeehouse.* New Haven, CT: Yale University Press, 2005.

Cremin, Lawrence. *American Education: The Colonial Experience, 1607–1783.* New York: Harper & Row, 1970.

Cressy, David. *Coming Over: Migration and Communication between England and New England in the Seventeenth Century.* Cambridge: Cambridge University Press, 1987.

Currid-Halkett, Elizabeth. *The Sum of Small Things: A Theory of the Aspirational Class.* Princeton, NJ: Princeton University Press, 2017.

Cutterham, Tom. *Gentlemen Revolutionaries: Power and Justice in the New American Republic.* Princeton, NJ: Princeton University Press, 2017.

Daigler, Kenneth A. *Spies, Patriots, and Traitors: American Intelligence in the Revolutionary War.* Washington, DC: Georgetown University Press, 2014.

Darwin, John. "Civility and Empire." In *Civil Histories: Essays Presented to Sir Keith Thomas*, edited by Peter Burke, Brian Harrison, and Paul Slack, 321–36. Oxford: Oxford University Press, 2000.

Dayton, Richard. "Knowledge and Empire." In *The Oxford History of the British Empire*, vol. 2: *The Eighteenth Century*, edited by P. J. Marshall, 231–52. Oxford: Oxford University Press, 1998.

Delbourgo, James. *A Most Amazing Scene of Wonders: Electricity and Enlightenment in Early America.* Cambridge, MA: Harvard University Press, 2006.

DeLue, Steven M. *Political Thinking, Political Theory, and Civil Society.* Boston: Allyn and Bacon, 1997.

Dillon, Elizabeth Maddock. *New World Drama: The Performative Commons in the Atlantic World, 1649–1849.* Durham, NC: Duke University Press, 2014.

Dillow, Kevin. "The Social and Ecclesiastical Significance of Church Seating Arrangements and Pew Disputes, 1500–1750." DPhil. dissertation, University of Oxford, 1990.

Dixon, John M. *The Enlightenment of Cadwallader Colden: Empire, Science, and Intellectual Culture in British New York.* Ithaca, NY: Cornell University Press, 2016.

Dunn, John. "The Contemporary Political Significance of John Locke's Conception of Civil Society." In *Civil Society: History and Possibilities,* edited by Sudipta Kaviraj and Sunil Khilnani, 39–48. Cambridge: Cambridge University Press, 2001.

Dunn, Richard S. "The Glorious Revolution and America." In *The Oxford History of the British Empire,* vol. 1: *The Origins of Empire: British Overseas Enterprise to the Close of the Seventeenth Century,* edited by Nicholas Canny, 445–66. Oxford: Oxford University Press, 1998.

Edwards, Andrew David. "Grenville's Silver Hammer: The Problem of Money in the Stamp Act Crisis." *Journal of American History* 104:2 (September 2017): 337–62.

Egnal, Marc. *New World Economies: The Growth of the Thirteen Colonies and Early Canada.* Oxford: Oxford University Press, 1998.

Ehrenberg, John R. *Civil Society: The Critical History of an Idea.* New York: New York University Press, 1999.

Elias, Norbert. *The Civilizing Process: The History of Manners and State Formation and Civilization.* 2 vols. Translated by Edmund Jephcott. Oxford: Blackwell, 1994–97.

Ellis, Aytoun. *The Penny Universities: A History of the Coffee-Houses.* London: Secker & Warburg, 1956.

Ellis, Markman. *The Coffeehouse: A Cultural History.* London: Weidenfeld & Nicolson, 2004.

———, ed. *Eighteenth-Century Coffee-House Culture.* 4 vols. London: Chatto and Pickering, 2006.

Farrand, Max. *Records of the Federal Convention.* New Haven, CT: Yale University Press, 1911.

Farrelly, Maura Jane. *Anti-Catholicism in America, 1620–1860.* Cambridge: Cambridge University Press, 2018.

Fea, John. *The Way of Improvement Leads Home: Philip Vickers Fithian and the Rural Enlightenment in Early America.* Philadelphia: University of Pennsylvania Press, 2008.

Ferrari, Mary C. "Charity, Folly, and Politics: Charles Town's Social Clubs on the Eve of the Revolution." *South Carolina Historical Magazine* 112:1–2 (January–April 2011): 50–83.

Fitzmaurice, Andrew. "The Civic Solution to the Crisis of English Colonization, 1609–1625." *Historical Journal* 42:1 (March 1999): 25–51.

Fitzmaurice, Susan. "Changes in the Meanings of *Politeness* in Eighteenth-Century England: Discourse Analysis and Historical Evidence." In *Historical (Im)Politeness,* edited by Jonathan Culpeper and Daniel Z. Kadar, 87–116. Bern: Peter Lang, 2010.

Foner, Eric. *Tom Paine and Revolutionary America*. Oxford: Oxford University Press, 2005.

Foster, Thomas A. *Sex and the Eighteenth-Century Man: Massachusetts and the History of Sexuality in America*. Boston: Beacon Press, 2006.

Franke, Astrid. "Drinking and Democracy in the Early Republic." In *Civilizing and Decivilizing Processes: Figurational Approaches to American Culture*, edited by Christa Buschendorf, Astrid Franke and Johannes Voelz, 63–86. Newcastle upon Tyne: Cambridge Scholars Publishing, 2011.

Freeman, Lisa. *Character's Theater: Genre and Identity on the Eighteenth-Century English Stage*. Philadelphia: University of Pennsylvania Press, 2002.

Gamble, Robert J. "'For Lucre of Gain and in Contempt of the Laws': Itinerant Traders and the Politics of Mobility in the Eighteenth-Century Mid-Atlantic." *Early American Studies: An Interdisciplinary Journal* 13:4 (Fall 2015): 836–55.

Games, Alison. *The Web of Empire: English Cosmopolitans in an Age of Expansion, 1560–1660*. Oxford: Oxford University Press, 2008.

Gibbs, Patricia A. "Taverns in Tidewater Virginia, 1700–1744." Master's thesis, College of William and Mary, 1968.

Gibson, Robert. *Best of Enemies: Anglo-French Relations since the Norman Conquest*. London: Sinclair-Stevenson, 1995.

Gienapp, Jonathan. *The Second Creation: Fixing the American Constitution in the Founding Era*. Cambridge, MA: Harvard University Press, 2018.

Gilje, Paul A. *Rioting in America*. Bloomington: Indiana University Press, 1999.

———. *The Road to Mobocracy: Popular Disorder in New York City, 1763–1834*. Chapel Hill: University of North Carolina Press, 1987.

Gill, Harold B., Jr. "Williamsburg and the Demimonde: Disorderly Houses, the Blue Bell, and Certain Hints of Harlotry." *Colonial Williamsburg Journal* (Autumn 2001), accessed March 3, 2018, http://www.history.org.

Glasson, Travis. "The Intimacies of Occupation: Loyalties, Compromise, and Betrayal in Revolutionary-Era Newport." In *The American Revolution Reborn*, edited by Patrick Spero and Michael Zuckerman, 29–47. Philadelphia: University of Pennsylvania Press, 2016.

Godbeer, Richard. *Sexual Revolution in Early America*. Baltimore, MD: Johns Hopkins University Press, 2002.

Goheen, Peter G. "Public Space and the Geography of the Modern City." *Progress in Human Geography* 22:4 (August 1998): 479–96.

Goodfriend, Joyce D. *Who Should Rule at Home? Confronting the Elite in British New York City*. Ithaca, NY: Cornell University Press, 2017.

Goodman, Jordan. "Excitantia: Or, How Enlightenment Europe Took to Soft Drugs." In *Consuming Habits: Global and Historical Perspectives on How Cultures Define Drugs*, 2nd ed., edited by Jordan Goodman, Paul E. Lovejoy, and Andrew Sherratt, 126–47. London: Routledge, 2007.

Goodwin, George. *Benjamin Franklin in London: The British Life of America's Founding Father.* New Haven, CT: Yale University Press, 2016.

Gordon-Reed, Annette. *The Hemingses of Monticello: An American Family.* New York: Norton, 2008.

Gordon-Reed, Annette, and Peter Onuf. *"Most Blessed of the Patriarchs": Thomas Jefferson and the Empire of the Imagination.* New York: Liveright, 2017.

Graves, C. P. "Social Space in the English Medieval Parish Church." *Economy and Society* 18:3 (1989): 297–322.

Gray, Louise E., Evelyn Q. Ryland, and Bettie J. Simmons. *Historic Buildings in Middlesex County, Virginia, 1650–1775.* Edited by Walter C. C. Johnson. Charlotte, NC: Delmar Printing Company, 1978.

Greene, Jack P. "Empire and Identity from the Glorious Revolution to the American Revolution." In *The Oxford History of the British Empire*, vol. 2: *The Eighteenth Century*, edited by P. J. Marshall, 208–30. Oxford: Oxford University Press, 1998.

———. *Peripheries and Center: Constitutional Development in the Extended Polities of the British Empire and the United States, 1607–1788.* Athens: University of Georgia Press, 1987.

———. "Social and Cultural Capital in Colonial British America: A Case Study." In *Patterns of Social Capital: Stability and Change in Historical Perspective*, edited by Robert I. Rotberg, 153–71. Cambridge: Cambridge University Press, 2001.

Gryctko, Lauren Elizabeth. "Inviting the Principle Gentlemen of the City: Privacy, Exclusivity, and Food Complexity in Colonial Taverns." Master's thesis, College of William and Mary, 2015.

Habermas, Jürgen. *The Structural Transformation of the Public Sphere: An Inquiry into a Category of Bourgeois Society.* Cambridge, MA: MIT Press, 1991.

Hailwood, Mark. *Alehouses and Good Fellowship in Early Modern England.* Woodbridge: Boydell Press, 2014.

Hancock, David. *Citizens of the World: London Merchants and the Integration of the British Atlantic Community, 1735–1785.* Cambridge: Cambridge University Press, 1995.

———. *Oceans of Wine: Madeira and the Emergence of American Trade and Taste.* New Haven, CT: Yale University Press, 2009.

———. "The Triumphs of Mercury: Connection and Control in the Emerging Atlantic Economy." In *Soundings in Atlantic History: Latent Structures and Intellectual Currents, 1500–1830*, edited by Bernard Bailyn and Patricia Denault, 112–40. Cambridge, MA: Harvard University Press, 2009.

Hancock, David, and Michelle McDonald, eds. *Public Drinking in the Early Modern World: Voices from the Tavern, 1500–1800*, vol. 4: *America*. New York: Pickering and Chatto, 2011.

Harland-Jacobs, Jessica. "'Hands across the Sea': The Masonic Network, British Imperialism, and the North Atlantic World." *Geographical Review* 89:2 (April 1999): 237–53.

Hart, Emma. *Building Charleston: Town and Society in the Eighteenth-Century British Atlantic World.* Charlottesville: University of Virginia Press, 2009.

Hartigan-O'Connor, Ellen. *The Ties That Buy: Women and Commerce in Revolutionary America.* Philadelphia: University of Pennsylvania Press, 2009.

Harvey, Karen. "Ritual Encounters: Punch Parties and Masculinity in the Eighteenth Century." *Past & Present* 214:1 (February 2012): 165–203.

Hatch, Nathan O. *The Democratization of American Christianity.* New Haven, CT: Yale University Press, 1989.

Haulman, Kate. *The Politics of Fashion in Eighteenth Century America.* Chapel Hill: University of North Carolina Press, 2011.

Hayes, Kevin J., ed. *The Library of William Byrd of Westover.* Madison, WI: Madison House, 1997.

Hemphill, Dallett. "Manners and Class in the Revolutionary Era: A Transatlantic Comparison." *William and Mary Quarterly* 63:2 (April 2006): 345–72.

Hertz, Carolyn D. "The Committees of Correspondence, Inspection and Safety in Old Hampshire County, Massachusetts, during the American Revolution." Master's thesis, University of Massachusetts Amherst, 1993

Hillier, Bill, and Julienne Hanson. *The Social Logic of Space.* Cambridge: Cambridge University Press, 1984.

Hoffer, Peter Charles. *The Great New York Conspiracy of 1741: Slavery, Crime, and Colonial Law.* Lawrence: University of Kansas Press, 2003.

———. *When Benjamin Franklin Met the Reverend Whitefield: Enlightenment, Revival, and the Power of the Printed Word.* Baltimore, MD: Johns Hopkins University Press, 2011.

Hofstadter, Richard. *America at 1750: A Social Portrait.* New York: Vintage Books, 1973.

———. *The Idea of a Party System: The Rise of Legitimate Opposition in the United States, 1780–1840.* Berkeley: University of California Press, 1969.

Holton, Woody. *Unruly Americans and the Making of the Constitution.* New York: Hill & Wang, 2007.

Huebner, Emily. "The Whig Club: Judge and Jury in Baltimore." Finding the Maryland 400: A Maryland State Archives Project, accessed March 12, 2017, https://msamaryland400.wordpress.com.

Humphrey, Thomas. "The Anatomy of a Crowd: Making Mobs in Early America." *Journal of Early American History* 5:1 (April 2015): 68–92.

———. "Crowd and Court: Rough Music and Popular Justice in Colonial New York." In *Riot and Revelry in Early America,* edited by William Pencack, Matthew Dennis, and Simon P. Newman, 107–24. University Park: Pennsylvania State University, 2002.

Hunter, Phyllis Whitman. *Purchasing Identity in the Atlantic World: Massachusetts Merchants, 1670–1780.* Ithaca, NY: Cornell University Press, 2001.

Hutchins, Zachary McLeod. Introduction to *Community without Consent: New Perspectives on the Stamp Act,* edited by Zachary McLeod Hutchins, xi–xxii. Hanover, NH: Dartmouth University Press, 2016.

Isaac, Rhys. *The Transformation of Virginia.* Chapel Hill: University of North Carolina Press, 1982.

Jacob, Margaret C. *Radical Enlightenment: Pantheists, Freemasons and Republicans.* London: George Allen & Unwin, 1981.

———. *Strangers Nowhere in the World: The Rise of Cosmopolitanism in Early Modern Europe.* Philadelphia: University of Pennsylvania Press, 2006.

Jasanoff, Maya. "Collectors of Empire: Objects, Conquests, and Imperial Self-Fashioning." *Past & Present* 184:1 (August 2004): 109–36.

Jenner, Mark S. R. "Civilization and Deodorization? Smell in Early Modern English Culture." In *Civil Histories: Essays Presented to Sir Keith Thomas,* edited by Peter Burke, Brian Harrison, and Paul Slack, 127–44. Oxford: Oxford University Press, 2000.

Johnson, Donald F. "Ambiguous Allegiances: Urban Loyalties during the American Revolution." *Journal of American History* 104:3 (December 2017): 610–31.

Johnson, Odai, and William J. Burling. *The Colonial American Stage, 1665–1774: A Documentary Calendar.* London: Associated University Presses, 2001.

Jones, Alice Hanson. "Wealth Estimates for the American Middle Colonies, 1774," *Economic Development and Cultural Change* 18:4, Part 2 (July 1970): 1–172.

Jones, Emrys. "Age of Societies." In *Welsh in London, 1500–2000,* edited by Emrys Jones, 54–87. Cardiff: University of Wales Press, 2001.

Jones, L. C. *The Clubs of the Georgian Rakes.* New York: Columbia University Press, 1942.

Kaplan, Catherine O'Donnell. *Men of Letters in the Early Republic: Cultivating Forums of Citizenship.* Chapel Hill: University of North Carolina Press, 2008.

Keane, John. *Tom Paine: A Political Life.* New York: Grove Press, 1995.

Klein, Lawrence E. "Politeness for Plebes: Consumption and Social Identity in Early Eighteenth-Century England." In *The Consumption of Culture, 1600–1800: Image, Object, Text,* edited by Ann Bermingham and John Brewer, 362–82. London: Routledge, 1995.

———. "Property and Politeness in the Early Eighteenth-Century Whig Moralists: The Case of the *Spectator.*" In *Early Modern Conceptions of Property,* edited by John Brewer and Susan Staves, 221–31. London: Routledge, 1995.

———. *Shaftesbury and the Culture of Politeness: Moral Discourse and Cultural*

Politics in Early Eighteenth-Century England. Cambridge: Cambridge University Press, 1994.

Kornwolf, James D. *Architecture and Town Planning in Colonial North America*, vol. 2. Baltimore, MD: Johns Hopkins University Press, 2002.

Krawczynski, Keith. *Daily Life in the Colonial City*. Santa Barbara, CA: Greenwood Press, 2013.

Kross, Jessica. "'If you will not drink with me, you must fight with me': The Sociology of Drinking in the Middle Colonies." *Pennsylvania History* 64 (1997): 28–55.

Kulikoff, Allan. *Tobacco and Slaves: The Development of Southern Cultures in the Chesapeake, 1680–1800*. Chapel Hill: University of North Carolina Press, 1988.

Kumamoto, Robert. *The Historical Origins of Terrorism in America, 1644–1800*. London: Routledge, 2014.

Kümin, Beat. "Drinking and Public Space in Early Modern German Lands." *Contemporary Drug Problems* 32:1 (Spring 2005): 9–27.

Kupperman, Karen Ordahl, ed. *America in European Consciousness, 1493–1750*. Chapel Hill: University of North Carolina Press, 1995.

———. *The Jamestown Project*. Cambridge, MA: Harvard University Press, 2007.

Lambert, Frank. *James Habersham: Loyalty, Politics, and Commerce in Colonial Georgia*. Athens: University of Georgia Press, 2005.

———. *"Pedlar in Divinity": George Whitefield and the Transatlantic Revivals, 1737–1770*. Princeton, NJ: Princeton University Press, 1994.

Larkin, Edward. "Loyalism." In *The Oxford Handbook of the American Revolution*, edited by Edward G. Gray and Jane Kamensky, 291–310. Oxford: Oxford University Press, 2013.

Leake, Isaac Q. *Memoir of the Life and Times of General John Lamb: An Officer of the Revolution*. Albany, NY: Joel Munsell, 1857.

Lefebvre, Henri. *The Production of Space*. Oxford: Blackwell, 1991.

Lemay, J. A. Leo. *The Life of Benjamin Franklin*, vol. 1: *Journalist, 1706–1730*. Philadelphia: University of Pennsylvania Press, 2006.

Lemisch, Jesse. "Jack Tar in the Streets: Merchant Seamen in the Politics of Revolutionary America." *William and Mary Quarterly* 25:3 (July 1968): 371–407.

———. *Jack Tar vs. John Bull: The Role of New York's Seamen in Precipitating the Revolution*. London: Routledge, 1997.

Lender, Mark Edward, and James Kirby Martin. *Drinking in America: A History*. New York: Free Press, 1982.

Lepore, Jill. *New York Burning: Liberty, Slavery, and Conspiracy in Eighteenth-Century Manhattan*. New York: Alfred A. Knopf, 2005.

Leviner, Betty. "Patrons and Rituals in an Eighteenth-Century Tavern." In *Common People and Their Material World: Free Men and Women in the*

Chesapeake, 1700–1830, edited by David Harvey and Gregory Brown, 95–113. Williamsburg, VA: Colonial Williamsburg Foundation, 1992.

Linebaugh, Peter, and Marcus Rediker. *The Many-Headed Hydra: Sailors, Slaves, Commoners, and the Hidden History of the Revolutionary Atlantic.* Boston: Beacon Press, 2000.

Lockridge, Kenneth A. "Colonial Self-Fashioning: Paradoxes and Pathologies in the Construction of Genteel Identity in Eighteenth-Century America." In *Through a Glass Darkly: Reflections on Personal Identity in Early America,* edited by Ronald Hoffman, Mechal Sobel, and Fredrika J. Teute, 274–339. Chapel Hill: University of North Carolina Press, 1997).

Loren, Diana Dipaolo. *The Archaeology of Clothing and Bodily Adornment in Colonial America.* Gainesville: University Press of Florida, 2010.

Lynch, Jack. "Of Sharpers, Mumpers, and Fourberries: Some Early American Imposters and Rogues." *Colonial Williamsburg Journal* (Spring 2005), accessed March 1, 2018, http://www.history.org.

Lyons, Clare A. *Sex among the Rabble: An Intimate History of Gender and Power in the Age of Revolution, Philadelphia, 1730–1830.* Chapel Hill: University of North Carolina Press, 2006.

Maier, Pauline. *From Resistance to Revolution: Colonial Radicals and the Development of American Opposition to Britain, 1765–1776.* New York: Alfred A. Knopf, 1972.

Main, Gloria L. "Gender, Work, and Wages in Colonial New England." *William and Mary Quarterly* 51:1 (January 1994): 39–66.

Main, Jackson Turner. *Political Parties before the Constitution.* Chapel Hill: University of North Carolina Press, 1973.

Mancall, Peter. *Deadly Medicine: Indians and Alcohol in Early America.* Ithaca, NY: Cornell University Press, 1995.

Markert, Patricia G., Thomas W. Cuddy, and Mark P. Leone. *Site Report for Phase III Archaeological Investigations at Reynolds Tavern (18AP23), 4 Church Circle, Annapolis, Maryland. 1982–1984.* Annapolis, MD: Archaeology in Annapolis, 2013.

Marsh, Christopher. "Order and Place in England, 1580–1640: The View from the Pew." *Journal of British Studies* 44:1 (January 2005): 3–26.

Marshall, P. J. "Presidential Address: Britain and the World in the Eighteenth Century: I, Reshaping the Empire." In *Transactions of the Royal Society,* 6th ser., vol. 8, edited by David Eastwood, 1–18. Cambridge: Cambridge University Press, 1998.

Marston, Jerrilyn Greene. *King and Congress: The Transfer of Political Legitimacy, 1774–1776.* Princeton, NJ: Princeton University Press, 1987.

Martin, Ann Smart. *Buying into a World of Goods: Early Consumers in Back-country Virginia.* Baltimore, MD: Johns Hopkins University Press, 2008.

Mason, Keith. "The American Loyalist Problem of Identity in the Revolutionary Atlantic World." In *The Loyal Atlantic: Remaking the British Atlantic in the Revolutionary Era*, edited by Jerry Bannister and Liam Riordian, 39–74. Toronto: University of Toronto Press, 2012.

McAnear, Beverly. "College Founding in the American Colonies, 1745–1775." *Mississippi Valley Historical Review* 42:1 (June 1955): 24–44.

McCandless, Peter. *Slavery, Disease, and Suffering in the Southern Lowcountry.* Cambridge: Cambridge University Press, 2011.

McCarthy, Kathleen D. *American Creed: Philanthropy and the Rise of Civil Society, 1700–1865.* Chicago: University of Chicago Press, 2003.

McConville, Brendan. *The King's Three Faces: The Rise and Fall of Royal America, 1688–1776.* Chapel Hill: University of North Carolina Press, 2006.

———. "Popes Day Revisited, 'Popular' Culture Reconsidered." *Explorations in Early American Culture* 4:1 (2000): 258–80.

McCusker, John J. *Money and Exchange in Europe and America, 1600–1775: A Handbook.* Chapel Hill: University of North Carolina Press, 1978.

McCusker, John J., and Russell Menard. *The Economy of British North America, 1607–1789.* Chapel Hill: University of North Carolina Press, 1985.

McDaniel, Iain. *Adam Ferguson in the Scottish Enlightenment: The Roman Past and Europe's Future.* Cambridge, MA: Harvard University Press, 2013.

McDonough, Daniel J. *Christopher Gadsden and Henry Laurens: The Parallel Lives of Two American Patriots.* Sellinsgrove, PA: Susquehanna University Press, 2000.

McDougall, Derek. "Influences on Anglo-American Republicanism: The Contributions of Eric Nelson." *Australian Journal of Politics and History* 63:3 (September 2017): 457–565.

McNamara, Martha J. *From Tavern to Courthouse: Architecture and Ritual in American Law, 1658–1860.* Baltimore, MD: Johns Hopkins University Press, 2004.

Meacham, Sarah Hand. *Every Home a Distillery: Alcohol, Gender, and Technology in the Colonial Chesapeake.* Baltimore, MD: Johns Hopkins University Press, 2009.

———. "Keeping the Trade: The Persistence of Tavernkeeping among Middling Women in Colonial Virginia." *Early American Studies: An Interdisciplinary Journal* 3:1 (Spring 2005): 140–63.

Menard, Russell R. "Plantation Empire: How Sugar and Tobacco Planters Built Their Industries and Raised an Empire." *Agricultural History* 81:3 (Summer 2007): 309–32.

Mercieca, Jennifer R. *Founding Fictions.* Tuscaloosa: University of Alabama Press, 2010.

Micklus, Robert. "'The History of the Tuesday Club': A Mock-Jeremiad of the Colonial South." *William and Mary Quarterly* 40:1 (January 1983): 42–61.

Middleton, Richard, and Anne Lombard. *Colonial America: A History to 1763.* 4th ed. Malden, MA: Wiley-Blackwell, 2011.

Milroy, Elizabeth. *The Grid and the River: Philadelphia's Green Places, 1682–1876.* University Park: Pennsylvania State University Press, 2016.

Minty, Christopher F. "'Of One Hart and One Mind': Local Institutions and Allegiance during the American Revolution." *Early American Studies: An Interdisciplinary Journal* 15:1 (Winter 2017): 99–132.

Morgan, David T., Jr. "George Whitefield and the Great Awakening in the Carolinas and Georgia, 1739–1740." *Georgia Historical Quarterly* 54:4 (Winter 1970): 517–39.

Morgan, Edmund S. *American Slavery, American Freedom: The Ordeal of Colonial Virginia.* New York: Norton, 1975.

———. *Inventing the People: The Rise of Popular Sovereignty in England and America.* New York: Norton, 1988.

Morgan, Edmund S., and Helen M. Morgan. *The Stamp Act Crisis: Prologue to Revolution.* Chapel Hill: University of North Carolina Press, 1953.

Morgan, Kenneth. *Slavery, Atlantic Trade, and the British Economy, 1660–1800.* Cambridge: Cambridge University Press, 2000.

Munns, Jessica. "Theatrical Culture 1: Politics and Theater." In *The Cambridge Companion to English Literature, 1650–1740,* edited by Steven N. Zwicker, 82–103. Cambridge: Cambridge University Press, 1998.

Musselwhite, Paul. "Annapolis Aflame: Richard Clarke's Conspiracy and the Imperial Urban Vision in Maryland, 1704–8." *William and Mary Quarterly* 71:3 (July 2014): 361–400.

Nadelhaft, Jerome J. *The Disorders of War: The Revolution in South Carolina.* Orono: University of Maine at Orono Press, 1981.

Nash, Gary B. "Social Change and the Growth of Prerevolutionary Urban Radicalism." In *The American Revolution: Explorations in the History of American Radicalism,* edited by Alfred F. Young, 3–37. DeKalb: Northern Illinois University Press, 1976.

———. "The Social Development of Colonial America." In *Colonial British America: Essays in the New History of the Early Modern Era,* edited by Jack P. Greene and J. R. Pole, 233–61. Baltimore, MD: Johns Hopkins University Press, 1984.

———. *The Unknown American Revolution: The Unruly Birth of Democracy and the Struggle to Create America.* New York: Penguin Books, 2005.

———. *The Urban Crucible: Social Change, Political Consciousness, and the Origins of the American Revolution.* Cambridge, MA: Harvard University Press, 1979.

Nelson, Eric. *The Royalist Revolution: Monarchy and the American Founding.* Cambridge, MA: Harvard University Press, 2014.

Newman, Gerald. *The Rise of English Nationalism: A Cultural History, 1740–1830.* New York: St. Martin's Press, 1987.

Newman, Simon P. *Parades and Politics of the Street: Festive Culture in the*

Early American Republic. Philadelphia: University of Pennsylvania Press, 1997.

Norris, Walter B. *Annapolis: Its Colonial and Naval Story*. New York: Thomas Y. Crowell Co., 1925.

Norton, Marcy. "Tasting Empire: Chocolate and the European Internalization of Mesoamerican Aesthetics." *American Historical Review* 111:3 (June 2006): 660–91.

Oaks, Robert F. "Philadelphia Merchants and the Origins of American Independence." *Proceedings of the American Philosophical* Society 121:6 (December 1977): 407–36.

Oberg, Michael Leroy. "Between 'Savage Man' and 'Most Faithful Englishman': Manteo and the Early Anglo-Indian Exchange, 1584–1590." *Itinerario* 24:2 (July 2000): 146–69.

———. *Dominion and Civility: English Imperialism and Native America, 1585–1685*. Ithaca, NY: Cornell University Press, 1999.

Oestreich, Gerhard. *Neostoicism and the Early Modern State*. Translated by David McLintock. Cambridge: Cambridge University Press, 1982.

Ogborn, Miles. *Spaces of Modernity: London's Geographies, 1680–1780*. New York: Guilford Press, 1998.

Örs, İlay. "Coffeehouses, Cosmopolitanism, and Pluralizing Modernities in Istanbul." *Journal of Mediterranean Studies* 12:1 (2002): 119–45.

O'Shaughnessy, Andrew Jackson. *An Empire Divided: The American Revolution and the British Caribbean*. Philadelphia: University of Pennsylvania Press, 2000.

Pagden, Anthony. *The Enlightenment and Why It Still Matters*. Oxford: Oxford University Press, 2013.

———. *Lords of All the World: Ideologies of Empire in Spain, Britain and France, c. 1500–c. 1800*. New Haven, CT: Yale University Press, 1995.

Parker, Matthew. *The Sugar Barons: Family, Corruption, Empire, and War in the West Indies*. London: Bloomsbury, 2012.

Parrish, Susan Scott. *American Curiosity: Cultures of Natural History in the Colonial British Atlantic World*. Chapel Hill: University of North Carolina Press, 2006.

Pearsall, Sarah M. S. "'The Late Flagrant Instance of Depravity in My Family': The Story of an Anglo-Jamaican Cuckold." *William and Mary Quarterly* 60:3 (July 2003): 550–82.

Pencack, William. "Introduction: A Historical Perspective." In *Riot and Revelry in Early America,* edited by William Pencack, Matthew Dennis, and Simon P. Newman, 3–20. University Park: Pennsylvania State University Press, 2002.

———. Introduction to *Pennsylvania's Revolution*, edited by William Pencack, 1–6. University Park: Pennsylvania State University Press, 2010.

Perl-Rosenthal, Nathan R. "The 'Divine Right of Republics': Hebraic Republicanism and the Debate over Kingless Government in Revolutionary America." *William and Mary Quarterly* 66:3 (July 2009): 548–49.

Petley, Christer. "Gluttony, Excess, and the Fall of the Planter Class in the British Caribbean." *Atlantic Studies: Global Currents* 9:1 (January 2012): 85–106.

Pocock, J. G. A. *Virtue, Commerce, and History: Essays on Political Thought and History, Chiefly in the Eighteenth Century*. Cambridge: Cambridge University Press, 1985.

Pole, J. R. "A Target Respectfully Returns the Arrow." *Journal of American History* 86:3 (December 1999): 1449–50.

Porter, Roy. *English Society in the Eighteenth Century*. New York: Allen Lane, 1982.

———. *Enlightenment: Britain and the Creation of the Modern World*. New York: Allen Lane, 2000.

Powell, Martyn J. *The Politics of Consumption in Eighteenth-Century Ireland*. New York: Palgrave Macmillan, 2005.

Prude, Jonathan. "To Look upon the 'Lower Sort': Runaway Ads and the Appearance of Unfree Laborers in America, 1750–1800." *Journal of American History* 78:1 (June 1991): 143–59.

Putnam, Robert D. "The Prosperous Community: Social Capital and Public Life." *American Prospect* 13:1 (Spring 1993): 35–42.

Raven, James. *London Booksellers and American Customers: Transatlantic Literary Community and the Charleston Library Society, 1748–1811*. Charleston: University of South Carolina Press, 2002.

Reinhold, Meyer. "The Quest for 'Useful Knowledge' in Eighteenth-Century America." *Proceedings of the American Philosophical Society* 119:1 (April 1975): 108–32.

Reps, J. W. *The Making of Urban America: A History of City Planning in the United States*. Princeton, NJ: Princeton University Press, 1965.

———. *Tidewater Towns: City Planning in Colonial Virginia and Maryland*. Charlottesville: University Press of Virginia, 1972.

Rhoden, Nancy L., ed. *English Atlantics Revisited: Essays Honoring Professor Ian K. Steele*. London: McGill-Queen's University Press, 2007.

Rice, Kym S. *Early American Taverns: For the Entertainment of Friends and Strangers*. Chicago: Regnery Gateway, 1983.

Richards, Jennifer, ed. *Early Modern Civil Discourses*. New York: Palgrave Macmillan, 2003.

Richards, Sarah. *Eighteenth-Century Ceramics: Products for a Civilised Society*. Manchester: Manchester University Press, 1999.

Riley, Elihu Samuel. *"The Ancient City": A History of Annapolis, in Maryland, 1649–1887*. Annapolis: Record Printing Office, 1887.

Rodgers, Daniel T. "Republicanism: The Career of a Concept." *Journal of American History* 79:1 (June 1992): 11–38.

Rosswurm, Steven. *Arms, Country, and Class: The Philadelphia Militia and "Lower Sort" during the American Revolution, 1775–1783*. New Brunswick, NJ: Rutgers University Press, 1987.

Rotberg, Robert I. "Social Capital and Political Culture in Africa, America, Australasia, and Europe." In *Patterns of Social Capital: Stability and Change in Historical Perspective*, edited by Robert I. Rotberg, 1–18. Cambridge: Cambridge University Press, 2001.

Rutledge, Anna Wells. "A Cosmopolitan in Carolina." *William and Mary Quarterly* 6:4 (October 1949): 637–43.

Ruttenburg, Nancy. *Democratic Personality: Popular Voice and the Trial of American Authorship*. Stanford, CA: Stanford University Press, 1998.

Said, Edward. *Culture and Imperialism*. New York: Alfred A. Knopf, 1993.

Salinger, Sharon V. *Taverns and Drinking in Early America*. Baltimore, MD: Johns Hopkins University Press, 2002.

Sarson, Steven. *British America, 1500–1800: Creating Colonies, Imagining an Empire*. Oxford: Oxford University Press, 2005.

Savage, Edward H. *Boston Events: A Brief Mention and the Date of More than 5,000 Events That Transpired in Boston from 1630 to 1880*. Boston: Tolman & Withe, 1884.

Schlereth, Thomas J. *The Cosmopolitan Ideal in Enlightenment Thought: Its Form and Function in the Ideas of Franklin, Hume, and Voltaire, 1694–1790*. Notre Dame, IN: University of Notre Dame Press, 1977.

Schlesinger, Arthur Meier. *The Colonial Merchants and the American Revolution, 1763–1776*. New York: Columbia University Press, 1918.

———. "Liberty Tree: A Genealogy." *New England Quarterly* 25:4 (December 1952): 435–58.

———. "Political Mobs and the American Revolution, 1765–1776." *Proceedings of the American Philosophical Society* 99:4 (August 1955): 244–50.

Schultz, Ronald. "A Class Society? The Nature of Inequality in Early America." In *Inequality in Early America*, edited by Carla Gardina Pestana and Sharon Vineberg Salinger, 203–21. Hanover, NH: University Press of New England, 1999.

Scribner, Vaughn. "Cosmopolitan Colonists: Gentlemen's Pursuit of Cosmopolitanism and Hierarchy in Colonial American Taverns." *Atlantic Studies: Global Currents* 10:4 (December 2013): 467–96.

———. "Cultivating 'Cities in the Wilderness': New York City's Commercial Pleasure Gardens and the British American Pursuit of Rural Urbanism." *Urban History* 45:2 (April 2018): 275-305.

———. "'A Genteel and Sensible Servant': The Commodification of African Slaves in Tidewater Virginia, 1700–1774." In *Order and Civility in the Early Modern Chesapeake*, edited by Debra Meyers and Melanie Perreault, 175–94. Lanham, MD: Lexington Books, 2014.

———. "'The happy effects of these waters': Colonial American Mineral Spas and the British Civilizing Mission." *Early American Studies: An Interdisciplinary Journal* 14:3 (Summer 2016): 409–49.

———. "'Quite a genteel and extreamly commodious House': Southern Taverns, Anxious Elites, and the British American Quest for Social Differentiation." *Journal of Early American History* 5:1 (April 2015): 30–67.

———. "Transatlantic Actors: The Intertwining Stages of George Whitefield and Lewis Hallam Sr." *Journal of Social History* 50:1 (Fall 2016): 1–27.

Seligman, Adam. *The Idea of Civil Society*. Princeton, NJ: Princeton University Press, 1995.

Sheehan, Bernard W. *Savagism and Civility: Indians and Englishmen in Colonial Virginia*. Cambridge: Cambridge University Press, 1980.

Shields, David. *Civil Tongues and Polite Letters in British America*. Chapel Hill: University of North Carolina Press, 1997.

Shoemaker, Robert. "Male Honour and the Decline of Public Violence in Eighteenth-Century London." *Social History* 26:2 (May 2001): 190–208.

Shy, John. "The American Revolution: The Military Conflict Considered as a Revolutionary War." In *Essays on the American Revolution*, edited by James H. Hutson and Stephen G. Kurtz, 121–56. Chapel Hill: University of North Carolina Press, 2014.

Sievers, Bruce R. *Civil Society, Philanthropy, and the Fate of the Commons*. Medford, MA: Tufts University Press, 2010.

Sismondo, Christine. *America Walks into a Bar: A Spirited History of Taverns and Saloons, Speakeasies, and Grog Shops*. Oxford: Oxford University Press, 2011.

Slaughter, Thomas. "Crowds in Eighteenth-Century America: Reflections and New Directions." *Pennsylvania Magazine of History and Biography* 115:1 (January 1991): 3–34.

Smith, Billy G. *The "Lower Sort:" Philadelphia's Laboring People, 1750–1800*. Ithaca, NY: Cornell University Press, 1990.

Smith, Mark M. "Producing Sense, Consuming Sense, Making Sense: Perils and Prospects for Sensory History." *Journal of Social History* 40:4 (Summer 2007): 841–58.

Smith, Woodruff D. *Consumption and the Making of Respectability, 1600–1800*. London: Routledge, 2002.

Sorkin, David. *The Religious Enlightenment: Protestants, Jews, and Catholics from London to Vienna*. Princeton, NJ: Princeton University Press, 2008.

Spruill, Julia Cherry. *Women's Life and Work in the Southern Colonies*. New York: Norton, 1972.

Stanwood, Owen. "The Protestant Moment: Antipopery, the Revolution of 1688–1689, and the Making of the Anglo-American Empire," *Journal of British Studies* 46:3 (July 2007): 481–508.

Steele, Ian K. *The English Atlantic, 1675–1740: An Exploration of Communication and Community*. Oxford: Oxford University Press, 1986.

Steffen, Charles. *The Mechanics of Baltimore*. Chicago: University of Illinois Press, 1984.

Steiner, Bernard C. "Life and Administration of Robert Eden." In *Johns Hopkins University Studies* 16:7–9. Baltimore, MD: Johns Hopkins University Press, 1898.

Stephenson, Mary A. "Wetherburn's Tavern Historical Report, Block 9, Building 31." In *Colonial Williamsburg Foundation Library Research Report Series—1167*. Williamsburg, VA: Colonial Williamsburg Foundation Library, 1990.

Stobart, Jon, Andrew Hann, and Victoria Morgan, eds. *Spaces of Consumption: Leisure and Shopping in the English Town, c. 1680–1830*. London: Routledge, 2007.

Stokes, I. N. Phelps. *The Iconography of Manhattan Island, 1498–1909*. Vol. 4 New York: Robert H. Dodd, 1915.

Stout, Harry S. *The Divine Dramatist: George Whitefield and the Rise of Modern Evangelicalism*. Grand Rapids, MI: Eerdmans, 1991.

Struna, Nancy L. *People of Prowess: Sport, Leisure, and Labor in Early Anglo-America*. Urbana: University of Illinois Press, 1996.

Stubbs, Naomi J. *Cultivating National Identity through Performance: American Pleasure Gardens and Entertainment*. New York: Palgrave Macmillan, 2013.

Sturtz, Linda. *Within Her Power: Propertied Women in Colonial Virginia*. London: Routledge, 2002.

Suranyi, Anna. *The Genius of the English Nation: Travel Writing and National Identity in Early Modern England*. Newark: University of Delaware Press, 2008.

Surprenant, Chris W. "Liberty, Autonomy, and Kant's Civil Society." *History of Philosophy Quarterly* 27:1 (January 2010): 79–94.

Tager, Jack. *Boston Riots: Three Centuries of Social Violence*. Boston: Northeastern University Press, 2001.

Taylor, Alan. *American Revolutions: A Continental History, 1750–1804*. New York: Norton, 2016.

Thomas, Keith. *In Pursuit of Civility: Manners and Civilization in Early Modern England*. Lebanon, NH: University Press of New England, 2018.

Thompson, David. *British Museum Clocks*. London: British Museum Press, 2004.

Thompson, Peter. "'The Friendly Glass': Drink and Gentility in Colonial Philadelphia." *Pennsylvania Magazine of History and Biography* 113:4 (October 1989): 549–73.

———. *Rum Punch and Revolution: Tavern Going and Public Life in Eighteenth-Century Philadelphia*. Philadelphia: University of Pennsylvania Press, 1999.

Thorp, Daniel B. "Doing Business in the Backcountry: Retail Trade in Colonial

Rowan County, North Carolina." *William and Mary Quarterly* 48:3 (July 1991): 387–408.

———. "Taverns and Tavern Culture on the Southern Colonial Frontier: Rowan County, North Carolina, 1753–1776." *Journal of Southern History* 62:4 (November 1996): 661–88.

Tilly, Charles. "Collective Action in England and America, 1765–1775." In *Tradition, Conflict, and Modernization: Perspectives on the American Revolution*, edited by Richard Brown and Don Fehrenbacher, 45–72. London: Academic Press, 1977.

Tittler, Robert. "Seats of Power: The Symbolism of Public Seating in the English Urban Community, c. 1560–1620." *Albion* 24:2 (Summer 1992): 205–23.

Tlusty, B. Ann. *Bacchus and Civic Order: The Culture of Drink in Early Modern Germany.* Charlottesville: University Press of Virginia, 2001.

Travers, Lee. *Celebrating the Fourth: Independence Day and the Rites of Nationalism in the Early Republic.* Amherst: University of Massachusetts Press, 1997.

Tullett, William. "The Macaroni's 'Ambrosial Essences': Perfume, Identity, and Public Space in Eighteenth-Century England." *Journal for Eighteenth-Century Studies* 38:2 (June 2015): 163–80.

Turner, James Grantham. *Libertines and Radicals in Early Modern London: Sexuality, Politics and Literary Culture.* Cambridge: Cambridge University Press, 2002.

Van Berkel, Laura, Christian S. Crandall, Scott Eidelman, and John C. Blanchar. "Hierarchy, Dominance, and Deliberation: Egalitarian Values Require Mental Effort." *Personality and Social Psychology Bulletin* 41:9 (September 2015): 1–16.

Van Buskirk, Judith L. *Generous Enemies: Patriots and Loyalists in Revolutionary New York.* Philadelphia: University of Pennsylvania Press, 2002.

Van Horn, Jennifer. "The Mask of Civility: Portraits of Colonial Women and the Transatlantic Masquerade." *American Art* 23:3 (Fall 2009): 8–35.

———. *The Power of Objects in Eighteenth-Century British America.* Chapel Hill: University of North Carolina Press, 2017.

"Virtual Williamsburg 1776." Colonial Williamsburg Foundation, accessed June 3, 2017, http://research.history.org .

Wahrman, Dror. "The English Problem of Identity in the American Revolution." *American Historical Review* 106:4 (October 2001): 1236–62.

Wainwright, Heather. "Inns and Outs: Anne Pattison's Tavern Account Book, 1744–1749." Master's thesis, Armstrong Atlantic State University, 1998.

Waldstreicher, David. *In the Midst of Perpetual Fetes: The Making of American Nationalism, 1776–1820.* Chapel Hill: University of North Carolina Press, 1997.

Wallace, John William. *An Old Philadelphian, Colonel William Bradford.* Philadelphia: Sherman & Co., 1884.

Wallace, Michael. "Changing Conceptions of Party in the United States: New York, 1815–1828." *American Historical Review* 74:2 (December 1968): 453–91.

Wallis, Frank E., et. al. *The Georgian Period: A Series of Measured Drawings of Colonial Work*. Part 9. Boston: American Architect and Building News Co., 1902.

Washburn, Wilcomb. *The Governor and the Rebel: A History of Bacon's Rebellion in Virginia*. Chapel Hill: University of North Carolina Press, 1957.

Weinberg, Bennett Alan, and Bonnie K. Bealer. *The World of Caffeine: The Science and Culture of the World's Most Popular Drug*. London: Routledge, 2001.

Weitzman, Arthur J. "Eighteenth Century London: Urban Paradise or Fallen City?" *Journal of the History of Ideas* 36:3 (July–September 1975): 469–80.

Wells, Robert V. *The Population of the British Colonies in America before 1776: A Survey of Census Data*. Princeton, NJ: Princeton University Press, 1975.

"Wetherburn's Tavern." Colonial Williamsburg Online, accessed January 1, 2018, http://www.history.org.

Williams, Joseph M. *Origins of the English Language: A Social and Linguistic History*. New York: Free Press, 1975.

Williams, Juli Hedgepeth. *The Significance of the Printed Word in Early America: Colonists' Thoughts on the Role of the Press*. Westport, CT: Greenwood Press, 1999.

Wood, Gordon S. "A Note on Mobs in the American Revolution." *William and Mary Quarterly* 23:4 (October 1966): 635–42.

———. "Thomas Jefferson, Equality, and the Creation of a Civil Society." *Fordham Law Review* 64:5 (1996): 2133–47.

Wood, Kirsten E. "'Join with Heart and Soul and Voice': Music, Harmony, and Politics in the Early American Republic." *American Historical Review* 119:4 (October 2014): 1083–1116.

———. *Masterful Women: Slaveholding Widows from the American Revolution through the Civil War*. Chapel Hill: University of North Carolina Press, 2004.

Wrightson, Keith. "'Sorts of People' in Tudor and Stuart England." In *The Middling Sort of People: Culture, Society and Politics in England, 1550–1800*, edited by Jonathan Barry and Christopher Brooks, 28–52. New York: St. Martin's Press, 1994.

Wulf, Karin. *Not All Wives: Women of Colonial Philadelphia*. Philadelphia: University of Pennsylvania Press, 2005.

Yoder, Paton. "Tavern Regulation in Virginia: Rationale and Reality." *Virginia Magazine of History and Biography* 87:3 (July 1979): 259–78.

Yokota, Kariann Akemi. *Unbecoming British: How Revolutionary America Became a Postcolonial Nation*. Oxford: Oxford University Press, 2011.

Zabin, Serena R. *Dangerous Economies: Status and Commerce in Imperial New York.* Philadelphia: University of Pennsylvania Press, 2009.

Zhijian, Tao. "Citizen of Whose World? Goldsmith's Orientalism." *Comparative Literature Studies* 33:1 (1996): 15–34.

Zitek, Emily, and Larissa Z. Tiedens. "The Fluency of Social Hierarchy: The Ease with Which Hierarchical Relationships Are Seen, Remembered, Learned, and Liked." *Journal of Personal and Social Psychology* 102:1 (January 2012): 98–115.

Zuckerman, Michael. "Authority in Early America: The Decay of Deference on the Provincial Periphery." *Early American Studies: An Interdisciplinary Journal* 1:2 (Fall 2003): 1–29.

———. "Endangered Deference, Imperiled Patriarchy: Tales from the Marchlands." *Early American Studies: An Interdisciplinary Journal* 3:2 (Fall 2005): 232–52.

———. "Tocqueville, Turner, and Turds: Four Stories of Manners in Early America." *Journal of American History* 85:1 (June 1998): 13–42.

Zuckerman, Michael, Aaron S. Fogleman, Kathleen M. Brown, John M. Murrin, and Robert A. Gross. "Deference or Defiance in Eighteenth-Century America? A Round Table." *Journal of American History* 85:1 (June 1998): 13–97.

Index